Environmental and Sustainability Education Policy

This timely collection surveys and critiques studies of environmental and sustainability education (ESE) policy since the mid-1990s. The volume draws on a wide range of policy studies and syntheses to provide readers with insights into the international genealogy and priorities of ESE policy. Editors and contributors call for renewed attention to the possibilities for future directions in light of previously published work and innovations in scholarship. They also offer critical commentary on the evolution of research trends, approaches and findings.

Including a wide range of examples of ESE policy and policy research, the book draws on studies of educational initiatives and legislation, policy making processes and rhetoric, ideological orthodoxy and critique, curriculum making and educational theory, globalisation and neoliberalism, climate change and environmental worldviews, and much more.

In addition, introductory commentary from the editors traces how ESE researchers have dealt with key trends, complexities and issues in the policy-practice-research nexus both conceptually and empirically. Throughout the collection, contributions illustrate how researchers might reimagine and reinvigorate policy research on ESE, including how working with other fields and diverse perspectives, ideas and expertise will aid the cross-fertilisation of a complex terrain of ideas, policy and practice.

This book is based on a special issue of *Environmental Education Research*.

Katrien Van Poeck is a Postdoctoral Researcher at Ghent University's Centre for Sustainable Development. She conducts and supervises research projects on experiential learning in the context of urban sustainability transitions and on sustainability in higher education, and coordinates the international research networks SEDwise ('Sustainability Education – Teaching and learning in the face of wicked socio-ecological problems') and 'Public pedagogy and sustainability challenges'. Empirically and theoretically examining education's role in building a more sustainable world, she aims to contribute to progressing scholarship on the relation between educative and political spaces.

Jonas A. Lysgaard is Associate Professor in the Danish School of Education at Aarhus University, Denmark. He conducts research on environmental and sustainability education that draws on theoretical perspectives inspired by Lacanian psychoanalysis and contemporary perspectives on materiality. His recent studies include work on educational ideals and philosophies of education, nature and realism as these apply to climate change, sustainable schools initiatives and health promotion.

Alan Reid is Associate Professor in the Faculty of Education at Monash University, Australia. He is the editor of the research journal, *Environmental Education Research*. He conducts a range of studies focused on teachers' thinking and practice in environmental and sustainability education, and associated traditions, capacities and issues in theory, research and practice. He is particularly interested in the history and possible future of the field.

Environmental and Sustainability Education Policy

International Trends, Priorities and Challenges

Edited by
**Katrien Van Poeck, Jonas A. Lysgaard
and Alan Reid**

LONDON AND NEW YORK

First published 2018
by Routledge

2 Park Square, Milton Park, Abingdon, Oxfordshire OX14 4RN
52 Vanderbilt Avenue, New York, NY 10017

Routledge is an imprint of the Taylor & Francis Group, an informa business

First issued in paperback 2019

British Library Cataloguing in Publication Data
A catalogue record for this book is available from the British Library

ISBN 13: 978-1-138-30174-0 (hbk)
ISBN 13: 978-0-367-89144-2 (pbk)

Typeset in Times New Roman
by RefineCatch Limited, Bungay, Suffolk

Publisher's Note
The publisher accepts responsibility for any inconsistencies that may have
arisen during the conversion of this book from journal articles to book chapters,
namely the possible inclusion of journal terminology.

Disclaimer
Every effort has been made to contact copyright holders for their permission to
reprint material in this book. The publishers would be grateful to hear from any
copyright holder who is not here acknowledged and will undertake to rectify
any errors or omissions in future editions of this book.

Contents

Citation Information

The chapters following the Preface were originally published in the journal *Environmental Education Research*. When citing this material, please use the original page numbering for each article, as follows:

Editorial Introduction

The roots and routes of environmental and sustainability education policy research
Katrien Van Poeck and Jonas A. Lysgaard
Environmental Education Research, volume 22, issue 3 (2016), pp. 305–318

Chapter 1

The roots and routes of environmental and sustainability education policy research – an introduction to a virtual special issue
Jonas A. Lysgaard, Alan Reid and Katrien Van Poeck
Environmental Education Research, volume 22, issue 3 (2016), pp. 319–332

Chapter 2

A Case Study of Dilemmas and Tensions: the writing and consultation process involved in developing a national guideline document for environmental education
Barry Law and Robyn Baker
Environmental Education Research, volume 3, issue 2 (1997), pp. 225–232

Chapter 3

Science: an unreliable friend to environmental education?
Martin Ashley
Environmental Education Research, volume 6, issue 3 (2000), pp. 269–280

Chapter 4

On the need to repoliticise environmental and sustainability education: rethinking the postpolitical consensus
Louise Sund and Johan Öhman
Environmental Education Research, volume 20, issue 5 (2000), pp. 639–659

Chapter 5

Education policy mobility: reimagining sustainability in neoliberal times
Marcia McKenzie, Andrew Bieler and Rebecca McNeil
Environmental Education Research, volume 21, issue 3 (2015), pp. 319–337

Chapter 6
The Quest for Holism in Education for Sustainable Development
Andrew Stables and William Scott
Environmental Education Research, volume 8, issue 1 (2002), pp. 53–60

Chapter 7
Tensions and transitions in policy discourse: recontextualizing a decontextualized EE/ESD debate
Robert B. Stevenson
Environmental Education Research, volume 12, issues 3–4 (2006), pp. 277–290

Chapter 8
Unsettling orthodoxies: education for the environment/for sustainability
Jo-Anne Ferreira
Environmental Education Research, volume 15, issue 5 (2009), pp. 607–620

Chapter 9
Education for sustainable development (ESD): the turn away from 'environment' in environmental education?
Helen Kopnina
Environmental Education Research, volume 18, issue 5 (2012), pp. 699–717

Chapter 10
Environmental Literacy: functional, cultural, critical. The case of the SCAA guidelines
Andrew Stables
Environmental Education Research, volume 4, issue 2 (1998), pp. 155–164

Chapter 11
Education for Sustainable Development, governmentality and Learning to Last
John Blewitt
Environmental Education Research, volume 11, issue 2 (2005), pp. 173–185

Chapter 12
The action competence approach and the 'new' discourses of education for sustainable development, competence and quality criteria
Finn Mogensen and Karsten Schnack
Environmental Education Research, volume 16, issue 1 (2010), pp. 59–74

Chapter 13
Pluralism in practice – experiences from Swedish evaluation, school development and research
Karin Rudsberg and Johan Öhman
Environmental Education Research, volume 16, issue 1 (2010), pp. 95–111

Chapter 14
Environmental education policy research – challenges and ways research might cope with them
Jeppe Læssøe, Noah Weeth Feinstein and Nicole Blum
Environmental Education Research, volume 19, issue 2 (2013), pp. 231–242

Chapter 15

Taking stock of the UN Decade of education for sustainable development: the policy-making process in Flanders
Katrien Van Poeck, Joke Vandenabeele and Hans Bruyninckx
Environmental Education Research, volume 20, issue 5 (2014), pp. 695–717

Chapter 16

Globalisation and education for sustainable development: exploring the global in motion
Stefan L. Bengtsson and Leif O. Östman
Environmental Education Research, volume 22, issue 1 (2016), pp. 1–20

Chapter 17

Environmental and sustainability education policy research: a systematic review of methodological and thematic trends
Kathleen Aikens, Marcia McKenzie and Philip Vaughter
Environmental Education Research, volume 22, issue 3 (2016), pp. 333–359

For any permission-related enquiries please visit:
http://www.tandfonline.com/page/help/permissions

Notes on Contributors

Kathleen Aikens is a PhD candidate in the Department of Educational Foundations and Researcher with the Sustainability and Education Policy Network at the University of Saskatchewan, Canada.

Martin Ashley is Emeritus Professor of Education at Edge Hill University, UK.

Robyn Baker is the Chair of the New Zealand Commission for UNESCO, and was previously Director of the New Zealand Council for Education Research.

Stefan L. Bengtsson is project coordinator at SWEDESD – Swedish International Centre of Education for Sustainable Development, Uppsala University, Sweden.

Andrew Bieler is a Research Associate with the Ontario Centre for Workforce Innovation, Canada.

John Blewitt is Director of the MSc Social Responsibility and Sustainability at Aston University, UK.

Nicole Blum is a Senior Lecturer in the Development Education Research Centre, UCL Institute of Education, UK.

Hans Bruyninckx is Executive Director of the European Environment Agency, Copenhagen, Denmark.

Noah Weeth Feinstein is Associate Professor of Curriculum and Instruction at the University of Wisconsin–Madison, USA.

Jo-Anne Ferreira is Director of Teaching and Learning at Southern Cross University, Gold Coast, Australia.

Helen Kopnina is a Researcher and Assistant Professor of Environmental Anthropology at The Hague University of Applied Science and Leiden University, The Netherlands.

Jeppe Læssøe is a Professor in the Danish School of Education, Copenhagen, Denmark.

Barry Law was previously a Lecturer in Education at the University of Canterbury, New Zealand, and is now Managing Director of The Sustainability Company.

Jonas A. Lysgaard is Associate Professor in the Danish School of Education at Aarhus University, Denmark.

Marcia McKenzie is Professor in the Department of Educational Foundations and Director of the Sustainability Education Research Institute, University of Saskatchewan, Canada.

Rebecca McNeil holds a Master's Degree in Environmental Studies from Dalhousie University, Canada, and is a communications strategist for the environmental sector in Vancouver, Canada.

Finn Mogensen is Associate Professor at University College West, Esbjerg, Denmark.

Johan Öhman is Professor of Education at Örebro University, Sweden.

Leif O. Östman is Professor of Curriculum Studies at Uppsala University, Sweden.

Alan Reid is Associate Professor in the Faculty of Education at Monash University, Australia, and the editor of the research journal, *Environmental Education Research.*

Karin Rudsberg is Senior Lecturer at Örebro University, Sweden.

Karsten Schnack is Professor Emeritus in Education in the Danish School of Education, Copenhagen, Denmark.

William Scott is Emeritus Professor of Education at the University of Bath, UK.

Andrew Stables is Senior Researcher at the International Semiotics Institute, Kaunas University of Technology, Lithuania.

Robert B. Stevenson is Adjunct Professor in the Cairns Institute and College of Arts, Society and Education, James Cook University, Australia.

Louise Sund is a Postdoctoral Fellow in the Division of Education at Mälardalen University, Sweden.

Joke Vandenabeele is a Lecturer in the Faculty of Psychology and Educational Sciences at KU Leuven, Belgium.

Katrien Van Poeck is a Postdoctoral Researcher at the Centre for Sustainable Development, Ghent University, Belgium.

Philip Vaughter is a Research Fellow with the Education for Sustainable Development Programme at the United Nations University Institute for the Advanced Study of Sustainability.

Preface

Alan Reid, Katrien Van Poeck and Jonas A. Lysgaard

We developed this research collection on environmental and sustainability education policy for two principal reasons. First, to bring together a range of historic to fresh insights into trends, priorities and challenges in such policies, focused on their development and implementation, impact and critique. And second, to ensure that those insights – arising as they do from a range of interests and theoretical concerns – are shown to emerge from studies that provide both a real-world grounding and empirical heft for readers. With this in mind from the very outset, we hope the collection offers some sense of the provenance of this work and its outcomes, while its form helps readers assess the strengths and limitations of key claims and arguments about policy and its research in this field.

In order to achieve these goals, the collection draws on over two decades of international studies previously published and discussed in the international research journal, *Environmental Education Research*. We are members of the editorial board for this journal, and developed a first version of this collection as a Virtual Special Issue in 2015. As with the research the journal continues to publish, we trust this 'second edition' shows there is, on the one hand, a healthy array of approaches to policy analysis, critique and commentary from around the world, while on the other, evidence of continued debate and development of some significance in the ways such studies may be both focused and prosecuted since the Virtual Special Issue.

Thus we also hope that this updated collection contributes to ongoing work in environmental education and its research, in two main ways:

- through illustrating the insights that can be derived from investigating how environmental and sustainability education policies are understood and studied; and,
- exploring key lines of possibility for where such work might go next, particularly in ways that might make a real difference to both policy and policy research.

We set out these expectations at the outset of this publication because environmental and sustainability education are dynamic and contested spaces for policy and policy development. Partly, this is because it is so contingent on the outcomes of how a variety of parties with diverse interests and powers wrestle with the ways in which education, environment and sustainability may come together (or not) in education/ environment/ sustainability policymaking. But also, there is the key recognition that the broader context for any policy study is wide ranging and complex, not just in terms of the fields of policy and policy studies in general, but also a study's particular substantive foci, the contexts and drivers for a policy development, and the degree to which it receives support, contestation and critique.

Thus for us, preparing a collection that advocates, illustrates or promotes largely one approach to analysis or critique, or that claims a tight set of overarching theoretical or empirical significance as insights, is neither sufficient nor representative of the international and evolving work of this field, no matter how powerful or convincing those insights might actually be. In fact, as the studies reproduced here show, they do run the gamut of working with (as well as rejecting) certain positivist to post-positivist underpinnings and frameworks for this work. While as a further dimension of their diversity, they embrace single cases for their units of analysis through to arguing for more meta-level reviews, if not more theoretically-rich and sophisticated work than that which may have been simply inconceivable or unachievable in previous times and contexts.

So amid this diversity, we'd observe that the reader shouldn't expect 'one preferred way' to doing policy studies in this field. Rather they should be able to detect some key 'family resemblances' across the multiplicities of theoretical and methodological orientation, focus and approach.

As a scan of the table of contents and the abstracts for the contributions will show, studies range widely in the ways they define and identify policy in formal and informal environmental and sustainability education, as well as how their authors work with outsider and insider accounts of the public and private faces of various policy types in different countries, contexts and levels of education. But in this, some key resemblances appear to emerge no matter what the particular study of a policy is, including in terms of its development, reception and evaluation.

Why do we raise these points? It is not simply to state the obvious: that there is commonality because they all had to meet the aims and scope, and publishing criteria for the journal. Rather, it is to suggest something more is afoot: at their heart, the authors of each study included here are concerned with addressing a particular aspect of the complex and shifting priorities and intersections of policy work in relation to education, environment and sustainability, at local, national and/or global levels. Thus, for us, some of the most pertinent resemblances between the studies can be detected in relation to how scholarly work is (or isn't) able to draw critical attention to specific *causal factors* shaping the development and fates of particular manifestations of policy and policy work.

On this, a particular interest to us is the quality and extent of their analysis of the role of *micro to macro institutions and their effects*, *the framing of political options and choices*, *the role of particular powers and networks*, and discerning whether *factors largely relate to the socioeconomic – or include aspects of the socioecological.* Thus there is another associated resemblance that readers might detect, arising from considerations of how the authors of these studies try to account for particular policy *sources and resources*, including how these are mobilised or frustrated. On some occasions, it may be primarily understood in terms of their key *ideas and ideologies*, but more often than not, it also requires analysis of the 'architectures' and 'architects' of *policy consensus and/or dispute*, if not their own positions in relation to each aspect.

As we discuss later in the collection, such initial, largely sensitising considerations for understanding some of the shared aspects of the studies can also raise a key question for reviewing and evaluating any policy study in this field, particularly in relation to any associated value(s) for the authors and readers of such work. In essence, they invite us to consider what can be reasonably and fairly attributed to the scope, objects and outcomes of each study, initially in isolation but also through comparison with other studies and the wider literature. It is important as a 'quality check' for understandable reasons: on what grounds should we assess a study's possible and actual contributions to this field, and/or that of policy studies more broadly? In other words, right from the start of this collection, we invite readers to consider how these authors establish and evaluate the *merits, effects* and *interactions* of particular policies in and across particular contexts, settings and situations, for insiders to this field, but also for outsiders trying to understand and appreciate what is going on here.

This invitation also helps us pinpoint another of our broader hopes for readers working with and across the studies in this collection: that these inquiries readily confirm that the fields of environmental education, and more recently, sustainability education, are ripe for deepening and broadening ongoing policy research. Another interest to us as the collection's editors is whether it can advance the ways in which scholars and researchers can both illustrate and question the relevance and valance of the aforementioned factors, as well as help probe and problematize their interconnections and interactions in these particular policy settings and contexts, if not in relation to other domains and spheres more broadly?

To illustrate why we think these matters are important to any 'disinterested' as much as 'interested' reader of the collection, we briefly revisit the outcomes of the late 1960s and the founding of many modern-day environmental education movements in the West. The touchstone to many (admittedly diverse) environmental education movements around the world is the production and preservation of ecologically safe and socially just spaces. Since those formative times and with those kinds of shared values in mind as a backdrop to what the fields of environmental and sustainability education are trying to achieve, we can highlight the following. Most democratic nations (be they in industrialising, industrialised or post-industrial contexts) have been expected to consider whether an explicit policy (such as a curriculum statement or law) that already commits schools to providing and evaluating some form of high quality, defensible education for its citizens, must do so largely in terms of a rationale that is primarily indexed to economic concerns, and thus economic policy.

Over the last 50 years, environmentalists and environmental educators, amongst others, have consistently argued that such a framing (especially its horizons and imperatives) is insufficient. There is a strong case for education policy to reflect other critical concerns, priorities and possibilities for education, including (but not limited to) those of their own. These concerns, of course, create some degree of tension with the aforementioned horizons for education, narrowly and broadly conceived, but if education is not simply an end in itself in most policy scenarios, debate needs to continue, amongst policymakers and citizens, as to what education is for.

For many environmentalists and environmental educators, a coherent and necessary response to growing local to international awareness of environmental pollution, including threats to traditional and modern livelihoods by unchecked industrialisation, requires governments (amongst others) to ensure that the provisions of education policy tackle topics and themes that might be grouped under a general category as follows: 'environmental issues'. On the one hand, this is to ensure education policy is not solely captured or circumscribed by economic considerations (important though these are for the industrial-related framings mentioned above). Rather, it is to ensure that education addresses the environmental dimensions to livelihoods and living together, which more often than not, will lead politicians, policy makers and citizens to address the vexed matter of whether and how teaching and learning address environmental issues that affect local communities and those further away, e.g. in relation to the negative affects of industrial processes, fuelled as these often are by a consumerist and consumptionist ideology prevalent in many Western nations.

To elaborate, since the times of the UN's Stockholm Conference on the human environment in 1972, at one level it is fair to say that education policies geared to promoting what amounts to a relatively crude 'education *about* the environment' have tended to remain largely uncontroversial in political circles. Associated policies for school geography, science, and so forth have typically dealt with key concepts and processes related to various dimensions and aspects of the environment, such as through ensuring or promoting a focus on certain aspects of natural history, physical and human geography, environmental systems and 'cultural studies' (e.g. on worldviews and traditions in human-environment relations). Nevertheless, as this collection shows, in 'fitting' such a (limited) form of environmental education into the curriculum, whether it is through a subject-specific, cross-curricular or infusional model, as some of the earliest studies and insights show that policy may actually provoke 'turf wars' about which subjects or approaches in schools should be expected to take ownership and responsibility for providing and shaping content and pedagogy, not just whether such a policy is needed or adequate in the first place. Accordingly, critical questions must continue to be asked as to whether teaching and learning about, say, economic activities should be nudged or pushed towards developing critical understandings of their effects – negative *and* positive – on historical and contemporary aspects of biodiversity, habitat, land use, natural resources, settlement patterns, atmospheric and oceanic processes, and so forth. But this isn't the only possibility.

Changing tack slightly can show why. Consider asking whether and how a policy for environmental or sustainability education also embraces what might be seen as a more full-blooded 'education *in* the environment'. The term is usually taken to imply education as not taking place largely indoors, such as in a school building. More often than not, it also suggests going beyond the schoolgrounds too. But if education is to take place in a range of environments, do we find ourselves on uneven and shifting terrain, so to speak, when we reflect on which environments formal education tends to happen in, as well as could happen in, that furthers the likelihood of worthwhile educational and environmental outcomes, for example? By raising this we offer a brief nod to those treating education *outside the classroom* as not just a common-sensical policy of providing excursions or fieldtrips (or limiting it to this, i.e. having an out-of-doors rather than an indoor classroom), but to raise something else. We can ask whether education policy thinking and practice pays close (enough) attention to the richer experiential possibilities and dimensions to education that may be afforded by regular and progressive educational activities in a wider range of familiar and unfamiliar (i.e. contrasting) environments. Such a 'quaking' of the educational terrain can prove particularly tricky in policy terms for at least two reasons: if educators and educationalists are tempted to fall back on school subject areas in classrooms as the principal and most legitimate landscape for education policy and its analysis, but also if key limiting factors on why *not* to pursue this are invoked, such as 'risk analysis', 'financial costs', 'teacher preparedness', amenability to 'high stakes testing', and so on.

Yet as some also argue in these pages, this is often only the start of such debates. Another nudge to the framing can push things further, by asking whether a worthwhile environmental or sustainability education policy actually takes another step by guaranteeing the provision of a robust 'education *for* the environment' in the lives of teachers and learners. Why is this seen to be important? Because it can raise critical questions about not just what is the scope and remit of anyone's experience of education – institutionally-based as well as in other contexts – but also what would count as the purpose of a worthwhile, credible and actionable education policy in this regard, and more generally. As some of the studies reproduced here try to show (alongside the wide-ranging literature review of policies that rounds out the collection), the political stakes will often ramp up very quickly with 'education *for* the environment' for both the advocates and opponents of policies framed with this end in view. This is because it typically promotes critical thinking, action-taking and an engaged citizenry through an environmental and/or sustainability education beyond the four walls of a school, and thus it can be highly demanding of those who are expected to enact or receive it, including in relation to its policy justifications, modes and resourcing.

But rather than risk the prospect of repeating in/out or for/against binaries (if not conceptual hair splitting and curricular cul-de-sacs on these matters), we might briefly recall the power of another recent framing embedded in another policy slogan: 'No jobs on a dead planet!' For us, the energy as much as the rhetorical form serves as a caution when probing the aforementioned concerns about policy for environmental and sustainability education. In this instance, we read this as arguing we should never meekly accept the pitting of economic and environmental policies against each other, including in attempts to establish deliberate boundaries when there are clear spillovers between them. As case studies and (urban?) fieldwork in a critical secondary school geography will often show, teachers and learners value chances to investigate the socioeconomic *and* socioecological dimensions to places and their dynamics, as part of an education about/in/for the environment. What is at stake then, is whether there are ideologies and frameworks for educational policy that support this?

Such a question is timely because as 2016's *Global Education Monitoring Report* from UNESCO reminds us, we live in an era of internationally agreed Sustainable Development Goals (SDGs). Education, economic and environmental policymakers around the world, as much as citizens of each and every nation, are urgently invited to consider a crucial set of priorities that these goals and their associated targets raise for life and livelihoods on this planet, by 2030.

The priorities for education, most notably centred on SDG4 ('quality education'), help focus attention on how often – and how well – those teaching and learning in these times are enabled or constrained by pre-existing policy to address all 17 goals. Most significantly for this collection, they can even raise whether education policies foster the critical examination of why addressing environmental issues in and through education won't automatically lead to equivalent sustainability outcomes. As expressed in the language of the monitoring report, these can concern, on the one hand, using education to balance the various needs of 'planet, prosperity, and people', and on the other, those of 'peace, place, and partnerships'.

Illustrating the possible interplay and complexity of all these Ps in education policy – including in relation to the priorities and provisions for environmental and sustainability education – is relatively simple, as much as it raises difficult questions. We might consider whether teachers and learners at various levels of an educational system consider why land, particularly in relation to land use and access to land, have proven to be such political flashpoints in and across private and public spheres over time, including in legal spheres (in an example well-known to recent mainstream and social media, consider the expansion of fossil fuel pipeline networks in times of climate change anxiety and contested contemporary and historic land rights). Drawing this out further, noting there is much that could be said about the ethics and dilemmas of existing and intersecting policies, policy interventions and policymaking, we may also inquire as to whether education policy addresses such matters too, e.g. in bringing together critical considerations of economy, environment and society about land under the umbrella of an 'education for sustainable development'? Doing so might well require a recognition and analysis of the values and attitudes, histories and traditions, and challenges and conflicts in, for example, land use (here, nearby and further away in time and space), aspects of which are often implicated in matters of historic and constitutional privileges to land, and 'changes' thereof. Sometimes these are expressed in education as scoped by policies and frameworks regarding access to safe dwelling, water and other resources, or about continuities and disruptions to the possibility of traditional and sustainable livelihood patterns, or the support (required/available) to others in times of the threat and experience of war, natural disasters, land disputes, and so on. Pushing this further though, another angle here may be to query how well educationalists, educators and education researchers recognise the scope and substance of responsibilities in the past, present and future for, or to, said land – be that for their own activities and flourishing, but also those of other communities, generations, inhabitants and systems of this earth. Put sharply, what does it mean in and for education policy circles to promote an education that encourages all 'to learn to live' here or there, including through times of change and the challenges recognised in the multiple SDGs – eradicating poverty, protecting the planet, and ensuring all people enjoy peace and prosperity – as its strapline puts it?

Crystallising this into a sharper question for environmental and sustainability education policy can also fold these comments back to a challenge that was recently raised by UNESCO, in its ongoing efforts to twin 'education for sustainable development' with 'education for global citizenship'. At the 'UNESCO Week for Peace and Sustainable Development: The Role of Education', Ottawa (Canada), 6–10 March 2017, a recurring and reflexive theme was an invitation to participants to engage the following: given what we know about policymaking (including its origins, implementation and impacts), *why should countries and their governance systems commit to articulating the opportunities and obligations of citizens to learn what is required in addressing sustainable development challenges of a range of scales, forms and (un)certainties?*

Clearly, policy studies are well placed to unpack whether this complex question is adequately taken on (if not taken up) in terms of the policies that might encourage – or discourage – this. For UNESCO, a key priority is considering how, when or who should be involved in both monitoring and evaluating the value(s) and impact(s) of associated policies. But as an offshoot to the brief example above concerning land, we might actually need to ask if there is a robust and compelling case that studies of educational policy in this space might require a 'due diligence' of sorts to the historic commitments of the fields of environmental and sustainability education, including how these have fared? In other words, how might policies at the UN level acknowledge diverse historic concerns and 'policy fates' in environmental education about, for example, addressing causes and consequences of environmental pollution in air, water and land, to more recent interests in reframing this, particularly in terms of priorities related to social and ecological justice, and sustainable lifestyles?

For some readers of this collection, it will actually be very clear that concerns about pollution, justice and lifestyle, like those for all the Ps above, can be argued to be deeply implicated in each other, and thus require a broader range of policy concerns than those of a high-quality education alone. But also, there is the recognition that a critical orientation towards a 'history of the present oriented to the future' opens up the possibility that this is actually an ongoing matter for inquiry, not solely one of acknowledging or addressing past dues. This is because questions of pollution, justice and lifestyle have become the bread and butter, so to speak, of much contemporary 'climate change education' worthy of the name, and not just environmental or sustainability education (see Part 1). Consequently, it is with a critical awareness of such markers of convergences and evolutions in discourses and terminologies, also reflected in the weighting of particular naming conventions and classifications for thought and practice nationally and internationally, that we find this collection offers some keen insights into their policy dimensions, including their continuities and disruptions at the level of macro policy, such as in the work of UNESCO (see Part 2).

In fact, a key feature of the collection is the commitment of many of the scholars repre-sented here to refuse these debates lingering too long in the cloisters of academia. Instead they (like us) want there to be a very real world dimension to investigating these often transboundary, transdisciplinary and pressing concerns. At its most pressing, this chal-lenges an inwardly focused orientation of policy research and researchers (e.g. developing theory primarily for the sake of theory, theorists or theoreticians) to broaden their vision: recognising their roles, responses and responsibilities to the contexts, horizons and tumults of this field. On the one hand, for example, we should ask, how could policy researchers as much as policy makers be more outwardly focused, responding to the challenge of the SDGs? While on the other, and perhaps most significantly for the research field too, how could their projects and studies anticipate and inform as much as react to or deconstruct what happens when the wider policy climate changes too?

To crystallise this out further, consider contemporary federal-level events in early 2017 in the USA, and their various echoes in events and responses around the world. How will intersecting as well as distinct communities of research, policy and practice address the fact that what was once apparently self-evident as an area for education policy and policy development – enshrined as it was in various National Acts for environmental education – is now increasingly imperilled as a wholesale policy commitment and priority? What is to be made of the apparent attempts to excise root-and-branch all related forms of policy, in ways that include its legislative underpinnings, history of commitments, institutions and agencies, and facts, including when "America First" is indeed part of the overarching policy rhetoric? Will researchers soon be writing what amount to obituaries of federal environmental education policy in the US? Will they be active participants in other counter or developmental actions to ensure environmental and sustainability education continues to exist credibly before and well beyond 2030 (whether that be 'marching for science' or other forms of everyday and strategic politics)? Or can it ever be sanctioned that an actual measure of the 'success' of policy in this regard in such troubling times is actually ironic to some extent: environmental and sustainability education would no longer be needed as currently conceived if their work is successful, and significant progress is made on fulfilling the SDGs by 2030?

Since the earliest days of environmental education, actively engaging and examining such tricky questions regarding the quality, value and 'expiry dates' of government-level policy, policymaking and policy critique, has been a mainstay of policy studies in this field (see Part 3). Indeed, for some researchers more broadly – if not for scholar activists in particular – it is as fundamental to this field as it is to their vision and justification of their work, on a number of grounds. First, there can be the usual matter of speaking truth to power, such as in questioning whether governments and other lead bodies of various stripes and powers are able to demonstrate as much as develop their obligations to, for example, long-established or international declarations and commitments on these matters. But also, to enrich, through education and research, what is understood and practiced locally to internationally as the culturally, ideologically or politically grounded under-standings of policy. Why? Because we have to recognise that policy will often frame how living well is understood, supported and achieved *in particular places and in the company of others on a shared planet*, including through distinct, and ongoing policies (including policy developments and reforms) focused on education, environment and sustainability.

So another critical edge may well be detected, that helps deflate the irony noted above (at least for a moment). For some in this field, policies about education, environment and sustainability can be argued to fail at the level of first principles if they only perpetuate anthropocentric perspectives, especially with regard to claims to the potentials and achievements of humanity in managing or stewarding life on this planet. Putting hubris aside for one moment, it is argued that this is because they don't usually give adequate room to considerations of the 'ecocentric' or 'biocentric', if not the role of the wider community of life, inanimate forces, or 'posthuman' considerations in influencing contemporary understandings of priorities in and for environmental and sustainability education. So to loop back to the legislative ambitions, horizons and commitments of policy, if environmental or sustainability education is to be compulsory for all human citizens of liberal and/or progressive democracies, a key question is not just what kind should it be, but how should it be framed and developed in and as a particular form of contemporary and future-oriented policy in these challenging times? (However, perhaps it is again somewhat ironical to raise this, but do government policy makers really do or want 'ecocentric' or 'posthuman' policy in this regard?)

As we hope the studies in this collection and the journal continue to show, close behind any particular attempt to either 'shift' or 'trouble' common-place assumptions about policy and policymaking in this field might well be a parallel set of concerns, that may provoke further deliberation and debate too. Typical of these, as hinted above, is the not inconsiderable matter of how environmental and/or sustainability education should be supported as well as judged as 'adequate' or 'successful' in policy, environmental and educational terms, over the short term as well as longer ones (even to the seventh generation?). Given this is a research collection, a key question then is how mindful are such considerations of what leading, seminal and emerging research practices, evidence bases, theoretical perspectives and practice development might have to say on this too, or simply can't say at this point in time (Part 4)? While what is clear to us in preparing this collection now is, how significant should it be for researchers to work with theoreticians and/or real-world practitioners to touch on associated questions of policy normativities and values, and the grounds for advancing their particular inquiries and debates, as well as recognising its limits? To begin to move towards some concluding comments, we would suggest the collection shows we are arguably entering a new phase in both the types of studies and orientations to study possible, and those taking place, that has actually lead to another Special Issue of this journal, focused on the Policy-Research relationship in environmental and sustainability education.

We suggest this possibility of a 'new phase' at this point rather than catalogue new theoretical orientations or perspectives, primarily because for policy matters in this field – its theories, practices, priorities and critique – there has to be increasing recognition that many environmental and sustainability education researchers, scholars, students and practitioners are always-already implicated in establishing and developing its principles, processes and outcomes of deliberation, argumentation, interpretation and analysis of a policy. Put differently, it implies a need for closer attention to reflexivity, because the work of said researchers, scholars, students and practitioners can also be that of policy actors, consultants, advisors, evaluators, testers, pilots, champions, embedded critics, and so forth.

Using the vocabulary found in some recent policy studies, it can translate into recognising the significance of some of this work as that of policy 'entrepreneurs' (and even possibly policy 'dopes' or 'dupes'), and thus the real possibility of a blurring of policy roles, positioning, and priorities of the categories mentioned above, intentionally or otherwise. Additionally, some contemporary studies of groups and individuals in these fields of inquiry are beginning to invoke the 'more-than-human' constituencies and forces within communities of policy action and practice as part of such reflexivity. As studies in some of the most recent special issues of *Environmental Education Research* show, there is increasing interest in re-examining the priorities of policy given shifting understandings of the realms of subjects, objects and relationalities in, for example, 'who' 'experiences' and 'contributes' to policy, but also to ask critical questions about the 'champions' (or 'opponents' or 'resisters' or 'silent parties' or 'silenced') of a particular policy when, for example, a 'new materialist' perspective is invoked. Thus, some of the most recent and provocative policy work has begun to probe whether (environmental) education policy is something that must always be treated largely as a matter for human experts and/or citizens to decide.

Another way of acknowledging that aspects of policy work must also reflect on and critique its focus, scope, priority and evaluation, is to engage the significance of attempts to reposition these times as those of what is now increasingly referred to as the 'Anthropocene' (or even the 'Capitalocene' or 'Chthulucene' to use, for example, Donna Haraway's alternative epochal sequestration). Acknowledging that to some extent, environmental and sustainability education policies must address, for example the 'art(s) of living on a damaged planet' can be to give space to deeper considerations of the worlds of the 'more-than-human' and 'post-human' in policy circles. So again, as we hope this collection (and the journal from which it draws) can show, such themes may provide both succour and challenge for a plenitude of vibrant questions for policy studies in environmental and sustainability education, including for particular policy cycles, ecosystems, possibilities and realities, if not the softer to harder horizons for policy development in these sectors.

Last but not least, we want to return to the fact that many contributors to this collection often argue their work has direct implications for praxis. These include on such matters as:

- to what degree *trust* might/can/should be placed in those working for an education ministry or organisation in taking a particular line in curriculum guidance on matters environmental or sustainable;
- how to respond to unexamined or prevailing *power relationships* in what happens (or doesn't) within the formal, informal and non-formal education systems in relation to education, environment and sustainability;
- whether a largely 'laissez-faire' attitude to policy is sufficient as a default or even a safe starting point for scholarship, or is increasingly proven *naïve* when addressing environmental challenges in a (neo)liberal education context; as well as
- probing how people (including scholars and researchers, not just policy makers or policy users) may engage information and reasoning *selectively* to persuade others about the merits of an argument for and/or against a certain policy (including any alternatives imagined in that space) – i.e. the need to attend to the *discourses* and *rhetoric* of the advocates and critics of policy in a wider range of settings – including those of researchers.

Not everyone sees these, nor is there an expectation that they should be obliged to. Perhaps then, it is actually a matter of raising some of our own reflexivities too, if not to signal those of any all-too-human shortcomings for a collection. The root of most of the limitations in this particular publication spring from the fact that it started life as a Virtual Special Issue from one journal only, with papers initially selected by the editors, and not, as might be expected of other special issues, in response to an invitation or open call. Other ways of checking the 'rudeness of health' of this collection include: first, not foregoing the responsibility to independently assess and debate the quality, scope and value of the research and studies that underpin the claims made herein (even if a study has already been 'peer reviewed'). Second, remembering to recognise that studies of environmental and sustainability education policy take place in a variety of settings, and are not always made public or written up for an English-speaking academic audience, let alone intended for such audiences alone, or appeared in time for this collection. Third, as we argue in the associated editorial comments and introduction to the collection that appeared in the journal, responding to the fact that the cross-fertilisation of ideas, perspectives and approaches from policy work more broadly (including, for example, critical policy studies) is, as yet, relatively underdeveloped. Fourth, noting that tensions between localist through to internationalist considerations are increasingly to the fore politically, perhaps with us you might wonder whether the horizon of 'new times' will also find this field capable and ready to produce a plethora of new and engaged studies across the spectrum of established approaches, as well as prompt innovative and ingenious forms that disrupt the insider-outsider binary? While finally, as introduced earlier, on the one hand, will we continue to ask how environmental and sustainability (education) policies can respond to overarching and far-reaching frameworks like the Sustainable Development Goals until 2030 (and more immediately, the Global Action Programme on Education for Sustainable Development), and on the other, consider further what are the proximal to distal effects of such matters of public concern as climate change on 'people, planet, and prosperity', as much as the various manifestations of various lurches to the Right politically and economically on 'peace, place, and partnerships' . . .?

Wrapping up our Preface, we end with a brief note of appreciation. First, we thank our publishers for their enthusiasm about the project, and all the contributors to this collection for their commitment to advancing studies of environmental and sustainability education policy. We also appreciate the feedback and steers of many colleagues at various conferences, seminars, workshops and network events, where we have road tested the ideas and reflections offered about this collection, most notably at research events in Porto, Budapest, Dublin, Gothenburg, Ghent, Uppsala, Washington DC and Copenhagen. Without our critical friends (including each other!), this collection would be much poorer in conception, imagination and execution. Of course, all errors and slips in judgement remain our own; while we can but look forward to receiving responses and critiques from the readers of this collection that help develop studies and the praxis of policy for environmental and sustainability education.

Editorial introduction

Katrien Van Poeck and Jonas A. Lysgaard

Environmental Education Research has developed a Virtual Special Issue (VSI) (http://explore.tandfonline.com/content/ed/ceer-vsi) focusing on studies of environmental and sustainability education (ESE) policy. The VSI draws on key examples of research on this topic published in the Journal from the past two decades, for three reasons. First, to provide readers with a series of snapshots into the genealogy of ESE policy research in this field. Second, to encourage renewed attention to previously published work. And third, to offer commentary on the evolution of research trends, approaches and findings.

Introduction

Although until recently it has been labelled an 'emerging field' of scholarship, environmental and sustainability education (ESE) research has experienced a significant growth in its scholarly literature over the past few decades (Wright and Pullen 2007; Scott 2009). Not only has there been an increase in the number of research articles on ESE, but also growth in the scholarly journals in which they are published and in the variety of academic authors writing about ESE. Arguably, these are all signs of a healthy and vibrant research field. But in order to fully exploit its potential, and to determine and discuss new directions and priorities for future research, a strong sense of the field's history and directions remains of utmost importance.

As early career researchers with an explicit wish to contribute to this field for the next 30–40 years, we were keen to accept an invitation to compose a first 'virtual special issue' (VSI) for *Environmental Education Research* focused on ESE policy research. Unlike a regular special issue, the aim of such a collection is not that of gathering new articles with a common focus, but rather exploring the body of ESE policy research literature published in the journal and bringing this together as a well-considered selection on the Journal's website.

Identifying key arguments, perspectives and approaches in the existing ESE policy research literature as well as connections with related fields of scholarship, through this stock-taking project we have sought to detect novel insights that might inspire future ESE policy and policy research. We were encouraged, however, to not stop there. With this VSI, our ambition has been to view such a collection of articles as a warm invitation for further research and debate to all interested researchers and fields, however close or distant neighbours they might be. While a good research field needs its own sense of history, it also needs friends and allies that will fill the future with intriguing and demanding collaborations, clashes, ruptures and perhaps even nuptials.

In 2006, Alan Reid and William Scott pre-figured some of these considerations in their comments on a collection of papers for a special issue, 'Researching education and the environment: retrospect and prospect', to mark the first 10 years of the journal. They argued that it is important to consider not just the 'roots' of the field but also the 'routes' into, across and out of this field (Reid and Scott 2006, 574). With this VSI we strive to rise to, and revisit, their challenge.

First, we aim to contribute to the collective development of a critical historical con-sciousness of the patterns and tensions in the field and how these are working. Next, we want the VSI to reveal and discuss some of the 'routes' affecting ESE policy research by addressing its relations with other academic fields, as well as the connections between research, policy-making and practice. And finally, throughout our discussions and reflections, to focus particular attention on the role and position of researchers within the tensions that characterise the roots and routes of ESE policy research.

The roots of ESE policy research

We started our explorations of the ESE policy research literature for this VSI by sur-facing and discussing our assumptions about the field, and then scrutinising them in light of a reading of all the back issues of *Environmental Education Research*, in order to identify research articles addressing key aspects of ESE policy. A screening of article titles and abstracts allowed us to quickly identify key arguments, perspec-tives, patterns and tensions characterising this 'transect' of the history of ESE policy research and, subsequently, to develop a shortlist of papers to be considered for this VSI collection.

Each of the articles we ended up including address at least one of the key topics we elaborate below. By bringing them together in a VSI, highlighting shared as well as diverging arguments and perspectives and connecting discussions in early work to ideas and arguments developed in recent articles, we trust the VSI will offer read-ers a genealogy of the field. Obviously, it can't pretend to be a neutral or objective representation of the field's history, but rather reflects the way in which ESE policy research articles in the journal have spoken to two emerging researchers against the backdrop of lively debates in contemporary ESE scholarship, as well as the theoreti-cal inquiries and discussions in which we are engaged.

With this collection then, we hope to foster renewed interest in formerly pub-lished work as well as in longer-lasting and evolving discussions in the field of ESE policy research. This, we hope, might inspire other researchers to supplement or question our reflections presented below, while suggestions for further research we have already developed in accompanying introductions to the VSI. After all, devel-oping a sense of history of a scholarly field cannot be left to individual or a few researchers. Rather, drawing lessons from earlier research should be a collective endeavour and responsibility to which this VSI modestly aims to contribute.

Through our explorations, wider consultations, various iterations, and 'editorial feedback', we have settled on the following key topics as foci for our selection for the VSI:

- the sensitive and contentious character of ESE and, thus, ESE policy;
- the purpose and focus of ESE and how this is or should be reflected in policy-making as well as in the naming of the field;
- the focus on providing solutions;
- the role and position of ESE (policy) researchers.

A contentious and politically sensitive field of scholarship

In revisiting all the past volumes of the journal, one of the first things we noticed was that even within its first few issues, scholars regularly claim that ESE policy research is anything but a neutral field of scholarship and that it inevitably involves controversy and political sensitivity.

For example, in their article about the development of a National Guideline for environmental education in New Zealand, Law and Baker (1997) highlight the dilemmas and tensions involved in this process as well as the sensitive and contentious nature of environmental education within a wider political environment. Their study emphasises the importance and difficulties of involving and acknowledging multiple viewpoints (e.g. Maori perspectives) in consultation and policy-making processes, and they go on to describe a key tension between passion for a particular policy and its political acceptability, if not expediency.

To date, this has remained a topic of keen interest in ESE policy research, as illustrated by McKenzie, Bieler, and McNeil's (2015) article in one of the journal's more recent issues. McKenzie and colleagues highlight the politics involved in the production and implementation of ESE policy and its productive and/or restraining effects on how sustainability is being conceived and mobilised in and through educational policy. ESE policy research should not be reduced to a quasi-neutral tool for enabling rational or technical decision-making, they argue. Rather, concerned with the twinning of sustainability with priorities of economic neo-liberalisation in education, researchers should address the fact that every policy serves some particular interest more than others. So rather than offering yet more findings, advice or simple solutions as to 'best' policy, the research community – including its champions and communicators – should also address the complex underlying factors that influence which policies may be developed, emulated, passed on, or passed over.

Returning to Law and Baker, they connect the political sensitivity of such ESE policy research to bureaucratic procedures and formal processes of government policies, but do so without explicitly relating the controversies involved to the specific character of the subject matter, that is, the complex, uncertain and contested nature of environmental and sustainability issues. Interesting insights and perspectives on the latter have later been developed by other scholars however, operating in another time and context. The societal and policy context surrounding ESE research in, for instance, Sweden and Denmark (Læssøe and Öhman 2010) differs considerably from the environmental education policy in New Zealand of the 1990s, and that too might also be considered a test-case for the neo-liberalist approaches to ESE recently criticised in a Special Issue of this Journal (Hursh, Henderson, and Greenwood 2015).

As democracy is a deeply rooted value in these Northern European societies, the strong commitment to researching democratically-oriented forms of ESE and for investigating how norms and values are constituted and selected in ESE practices is perhaps not surprising. Sund and Öhman (2014), for example, theorise the philosophical problems involved in embracing universal values and ethical ideals in ESE. Viewing universal values and ideals as essential aspects of political life, they argue for repoliticising ESE by unmasking its political dimension, dealing seriously with plurality and conflicts, seeing beyond the relativist-objectivist divide and using passion as a moving force.

Whereas Sund and Öhman question a universal *ethical* foundation for dealing with environmental and sustainability issues, Ashley (2000) problematizes an absolute conception of *scientific* 'truth' in this respect. In his article about the uneasy relationship between science and environmental education, he discusses the powerful yet provisional nature of scientific truth. He points to the limits of science as a 'model of rightness' that can tell us what to do and thus, offer us 'an escape' from the responsibility for those of our actions that have detrimental environmental consequences. Hence, he argues for curriculum policies that acknowledge a 'science of uncertainty' and a 'science with limits'. Preparation for adult life in a risk society, he stresses, requires general scientific literacy, scientific action competence, and an education in the philosophy, values clarification and citizenship skills needed to responsibly participate in a society of reflexive modernity. Returning to McKenzie, Bieler, and McNeil (2015), a key question here is not just the mobility of policy, but the epistemic and ontological aspects to notions of those policies and pedagogies that make or inhibit their mobility. For example, in a globalised discourse of education for sustainable development (ESD), can an umbrella organisation for Regional Centres of Expertise avoid necessary questions of how situated knowledges and practices can and can't be disseminated, transferred or modified?

The on-going struggle of pinning down the ESE field – or even of taming it – and finally understanding what it is about is certainly a glorious struggle. It will go on, and so should it, as the field moves under its own momentum and that brought about by others. A formless shapeshifter it is not, but from the very early discussions to the contemporary debates about the contentious and political nature of the field, ESE has endured as a wonderful battlefield of different political, ethical and moral interests and perspectives. Surely, one of the greater, yet frustrating, traits of the field?

What's in a name? The purpose and focus of ESE and how this is or should be reflected in policy-making

Another regularly re-occurring subject of discussion is how the field of research on education in relation to environmental and sustainability issues should be named. Underlying this semantic debate is a discursive struggle between 'competing paradigms' (Aikens, McKenzie, and Vaughter forthcoming), and hence diverging perspectives on the role and purpose of ESE. Two vital topics of disagreement that emerge within this discussion are: environmental education (EE) versus education for the environment (EfE) – a discussion about the *purpose* of education; and environmental education versus ESD – a discussion centred on the field's *subject matter and focus*.

In 2002, for example, Stables and Scott argued that the still emerging link between sustainable development and education should be approached cautiously and with a strong sense of the contested nature of the term 'sustainable development'. This is linked with a sharp critique of tendencies towards holistic understandings of concepts such as the environment, nature and sustainability within the field of ESE. The two emphasise that our field has been, and can be, severely harmed if we do not approach policy documents and policy-making with a strong pluralistic perspective and a continued focus on 'reflexive critiques of the human–nature relationship'. This does not 'guarantee the saving of the planet from ecological destruction', they admit, but then, 'nothing does'.

Stevenson (2006) looks back on some of the earlier discussions of ESD and what the concept offers the field, in the way of positive outlooks and inclusion of social and economic perspectives. But he also argues that the concept never escapes the fuzziness and ambiguity that is both a blessing and a hindrance for its impact on the policy–practice relationship in ESE. By quoting Stables and Scott (2002), Stevenson, among other things, warns us against the continued danger of a 'gap between policy sloganizing and policy implementation [that] is very great', and against using sustainable development as a 'salvation narrative'. This, he discerns, is a road towards an un-reflexive discourse brimming with unquestioned 'experts', centralised global institutions, and other top–down approaches to educational reform (cf. Huckle and Wals 2015). Yet, educators do not need to adopt a reified vision of 'what ESD should be'. The road ahead, he argued in 2006, should remain that where policy is informed by practitioners and practice in diverse cultural contexts, and engaged in a continuous and reflexive reconceptualization of the discourse of the field.

At this point, we can turn to Ferreira (2009) for further instruction. She presents a meta-analysis and critique of these debates on how we should name and understand our field and how this should be reflected in dealings with policy and practice. She shows how education *for* the environment or *for* sustainability has become an orthodoxy, and how different positions of researchers affect what is possible to think and do in ESE. Yet, she is not satisfied with orthodoxies in any guise, and in her barely contained critique of some of the main characters in the debate surrounding the naming of the ESE field and its various constituents and constituencies, she presents a refreshing argument for always questioning 'that which is' both within and outside of a field, and being especially aware of the constant lure of adapting to an orthodoxy. This analysis still rings true, and remains central, especially when dealing with policy perspectives internal and external to the field.

Thus after a decade of meta-reflections and critical perspectives on what constitutes the field of EE/EfE/ESD, Kopnina (2012) kicks the doors in with a heavy critique of the whole field, arguing that we are lost in squabbles over names, policy perspectives and undue pluralism. With a brave return to an explicitly ecocentric position, Kopnina takes a firm stand regarding the purpose of ESE: as environmental problems are severe, education should help their resolution. She argues that the field should put less emphasis on internal discussions about names (EE/ESD) and sub-names (sustainable development education, learning for sustainability, education for sustainability, etc.), and instead insists on a radical turn away from neo-liberally and anthropocentrically-biased education.

It is most likely that discussions of what the research field should be called, how it should be bounded, and policed, for that matter, will continue, spurred on by both internal development and the ebbs and flows of policy agendas nationally and internationally. Taking into account the diverging arguments of both Ferreira and Kopnina, it does however, seem more important than ever not to accept orthodoxies nor even heterodoxies, and at the same time have the courage to argue that this field must address the important questions of our time, whether or not we agree on what those are.

ESE as a problem solver? Solution-oriented research, policy and practice

Closely linked with debates around the name of the research field are discussions on how far we can go in instrumentalising both education and educational research and use it directly as a means to finding solutions to the complex and often dizzying challenges that we face. Policymakers and practitioners' demands to do so are well represented down the years of the journal. Clearly there is a great focus on delivering hard evidence, but also practically applicable approaches in order to more or less directly help policymakers and practitioners in creating solutions. Aikens, McKenzie, and Vaughter (forthcoming) extensive policy research literature review shows how 'sustainability imperatives' such as environmental and socio-cultural degradation have been identified by many ESE policy researchers as important 'policy drivers', that is, as factors that have largely contributed to the development of ESE policy.

A decade ago, Blewitt (2005) commented directly on how a national policy-driven ESD initiative finds itself at the crossroads of a managerial focus on predetermined outcomes and a more heuristic emphasis on how to question the underlying logics of the structures that surround learning today. Dogmatic insistence on pre-specified learning outcomes in terms of observable behaviour change or 'competences', he argued, will usually result in mere indoctrination and impedes the emergence of valuable, transformative learning that needs 'critical and reflective space and time'. This tension pops up again and again in different issues of the journal, and remains a conundrum within the field. How to deal with challenges through a system that represents and mimics these challenges to an extreme extent?

Rudsberg and Öhman (2010) put their trust in pluralist approaches as effective tools against technical proclivities in education tending towards behaviour modification. Through their study they show how it is actually possible to nurture pluralistic meaning making processes. While this might be a sign of a long overdue move away from rather simplistic hopes that implementation of an educational strategy will result in predetermined outcomes, they do themselves warn that pluralism is also a norm. A norm that scorns indoctrination, but still a norm that must be discussed, critiqued and not develop into one of the orthodoxies that Ferreira warns us against. Ferreira herself actually contributes to this discussion by explicitly questioning the open-endedness that is often associated with pluralistic education, wondering how education can be 'anything other than the achievement of some particular end'. All education is purposive and seeks to govern our conduct, she argues, but in so being, there is a huge difference in forming and shaping particular types of persons, e.g. critical thinkers willing and able to shape the future, versus people that are trained for 'correct' behaviour and steered, however gently, towards a particular vision.

This same tension is interestingly addressed by Mogensen and Schnack (2010) who critically reflect on how the notion of 'action competence' has increasingly been challenged over time by 'new', managerial interests in competences and quality criteria. They argue for resisting individualising and managerial tendencies and emphasise that action competence should remain an 'educational ideal' strongly connected with a concern for democracy, critical reflection, and enlightened and qualified action. One might wonder, however, whether the term 'competences' has not been co-opted too, and included in 'new', managerial orthodoxies too firmly by now, to prevent other understandings of this notion. In this respect, it was invigorating for us to read Stables (1998) paper about environmental literacy in an early volume of the Journal against the backdrop of this contemporary discussion that concerns us strongly. The distinction he makes between 'functional', 'cultural' and 'critical environmental literacy' creates a space for discussions about the role and purpose of education – a space that is often closed-down in debates focusing on 'competences'. Furthermore, his analysis of the UK national curriculum guidelines strikingly reveals how it is precisely the objective of fostering critical environmental literacy that threatens to be pushed into the background within policy-making processes.

The insistence on research as a machine that produces evidence-based solutions to complex issues, is not something that will disappear, but something that clearly needs a thorough going over from time to time in order for the field – and we as individual researchers – to be able to defend ourselves, the field and research institutions from too simplistic policy-driven demands for magic bullets if not ammunition, that will rid humanity/nations/societies of pressing problems.

The routes of ESE policy research

At the crossroads of research, policy-making and practice: the role and position of ESE policy researchers

Through the above-elaborated focus on offering solutions, ESE policymakers, practitioners and researchers seem to be caught up in a similar tension. Educators and policymakers are increasingly urged to deploy ESE in the pursuit of solving environmental and sustainability problems, and researchers experience a growing pressure to come up with evidence-based solutions and usable instructions for the former to do so, in the most efficient and effective ways. As shown above, several scholars argue for moving ESE policy and practice beyond the prevailing focus on pre-specified outcomes and competences in the pursuit of solving unsustainability. What does this mean, then, for ESE policy *research*? Aligning ourselves with the critique of ESE as a problem-solver, we believe that our research field must create time and space for more reflexive retrospection rather than for monitoring and evaluating pre-defined indicators.

Addressing research gaps that emerged from their literature review on ESE policy, Aikens, McKenzie, and Vaughter (forthcoming) make a case for increased attention for developments in critical policy research. These include a rejection of positivist frameworks that assume policy (research) to be a neutral process of problem identification and solution. Instead of trying to objectively determine 'what works,' critical ESE policy researchers should approach policy-making as a complex process in which multiple actors intervene and influence what counts as policy problems, what solutions are available, and how the latter are 'championed, borne, resisted or subverted in practice'. Acknowledging the tensions this may bring about, they argue that critical ESE policy research must include engagement with policy development and solutions and with generative political action.

Læssøe, Feinstein, and Blum (2013), too, thoughtfully address these issues in relation to the role and position of ESE policy researchers. Showing an appreciation of researchers' reservations towards cooperating with policy institutions and getting involved in the construction of often narrow policy agendas, they call on ESE researchers to be neither exclusively critically detached, nor naively involved. They make out a case for what Biesta (2009) calls a 'documentary role' of policy research, with interactive researchers that act as 'critical friends' and who document what is actually going on in different contexts and on different levels. Stables (1998) analysis of the SCAA guidelines and Blewitt's (2005) study of the 'Learning to last' initiative are examples of such documentary research. Recently, Van Poeck, Vandenabeele, and Bruyninckx (2014) analysed and documented how the UN Decade of ESD has been interpreted and transformed into national policy-making and how the latter influenced ESD practice in Flanders, Belgium. They each argue how the national policy-making process is inextricably intertwined with broader developments in environmental and educational policy, while in the case of Flanders, that give shape to a post-ecologist and post-political policy regime.

Although the latter affects what is possible and acceptable within Flemish ESD policy, Van Poeck and her colleagues conclude that it does not completely determine policy and practice. Just like the case described by Blewitt, the documenting of a policy process reveals emerging discrepancies by showing that what happens at particular instances during this process sometimes opens up a space for resistance against the bounds of dominant policy regimes.

In their article about different conceptual logics for globalisation in relation to ESD policy, Bengtsson and Östman (2015) also articulate a possible political role for ESE policy researchers. Drawing on an empirical analysis of Vietnamese and Thai ESD policy-making, they show how deterministic and universalising research approaches risk eliminating any 'theoretical space for politics'. Instead of focusing on the questions of what ESD ultimately is or should be, they argue, a contingent approach to ESE policy research can draw attention to the much more interesting question of what ESD can become though particular practices in particular spaces (cf. McKenzie, Bieler, and McNeil's (2015) arguments for a 'policy mobility' perspective). Doing so, they emphasise, can open up a space for interference, contestation and counter-hegemonic articulations, and foster spaces, even 'windows of opportunity' (Hardt and Negri 2000), for influencing policy-makers.

As such, ESE policy research aimed at documenting contingent practices might indeed, as Læssøe, Feinstein, and Blum (2013) argue, have the potential to incite more democratic and less top–down approaches to policy-making. Yet, this kind of research, we think, also highlights particular ethical and deontological questions that are important to collectively reflect upon as a field. Making spaces for resistance visible, after all, simultaneously renders them vulnerable to be tamed or co-opted by hegemonic discourses and regimes. As Hardt and Negri (2000) argue, all concepts potentially lose their critical and emancipating power over time as they get co-opted and included into the dominant discourse. Taking this into account thus seems to be a responsibility one cannot escape when engaged in documentary research. It should, therefore, not be aimed at closing discussions but rather at opening up, again and again, an interactive space for critical reflection and dialogue between policy-makers, researchers and practitioners.

At the crossroads of academic fields: routes into and out of ESE policy research

While arguing for considering both the roots and routes of the ESE research field, Reid and Scott (2006) also raised the question of whether this field is largely characterised by relations with other fields that function primarily as 'outside in' in terms of orientation and flows of concepts, interests, frameworks and findings, rather than 'inside out'. Reflecting on the articles we considered for this collection, we would say that, indeed, ESE policy research benefits from contributions of different academic fields but all the same it is obvious that our field also has something to offer to other, related fields.

As to the routes 'outside-in', several ESE policy analyses (e.g. Mogensen and Schnack 2010; Rudsberg and Öhman 2010; Van Poeck, Vandenabeele, and Bruyn-inckx 2014) clearly draw on theories and insights of *educational research and philosophy of education* to foster critical reflection on instrumental tendencies in ESE (policy). Also the field of *science studies* offers valuable insights that are addressed in the articles of, for instance, Stables (1998) and Ashley (2000). Acknowledging too that science cannot offer a monological 'truth' that allows escape from the responsibility to have to make choices, highlights the importance of moving beyond instrumental approaches in ESE practice, policy and research. Furthermore, Stables (1998) and Stables and Scott (2002) show the potential of connecting ESE research with *language and literary theory*. As we have already argued, the notion of 'literacy' might allow for a more nuanced conceptualisation of the (desired) outcomes of education than a focus on 'competences'. While as Sund and Öhman (2014) demonstrate, the fields of *political science and democracy theory* also affords interesting ways to deal with the inherent political character of sustainability issues.

Regarding the routes 'inside-out', we believe that by bringing all the aforementioned (and other) insights and perspectives together in a focus on both education and sustainability, ESE policy research clearly has some potential to challenge and inspire other related fields. For instance, the specificity of ESE and particularly the deep concerns about the far-reaching implications of sustainability challenges highlights the importance of 'engaged research' and, in so being, can put relevant ethical and deontological issues on the agenda of (*educational*) *policy research* (e.g. Stevenson 2006; Læssøe, Feinstein, and Blum 2013). Relatedly, the concerns about the consequences of sustainability problems and the undeniable materiality of the latter can challenge certain ideas and perspectives in *philosophy of education, (social) constructivism* and *critical theory* by revealing the need to move beyond an exclusive focus on discourse and language and to seriously take the material context of sustainability debates into account. Connecting this again with the 'outside in'-route from science studies to ESE research, we also believe that the growing interest in the '(post-) Anthropocene', the 'more-than-human' or 'more-than-social' also will spur interest in the emerging perspectives on how we engage with aspects of objects and subjects that exceeds the boundaries of language. Arguably many a scholar within this field has grown up with theories rooted in the linguistic turn and their associated important focus on power in language, deconstruction of the same, and the possibility of understanding the world through analysis of discourses. Recently new trends have emerged, and discussions about *material, topographical* or *mobility* 'turns' are surfacing across very different disciplines and fields. Among the theories that claim to be part of new 'turns' we find 'Speculative realism' (see, for example, Lysgaard and Fjeldsted 2015) that insist on a refreshing focus on objects and the Real that exist outside of language and how this continues to influence the social beyond the discourse.

Another perspective is McKenzie, Bieler, and McNeil's (2015) argument for the importance, within the social sciences, of focusing on 'the immense scale of movement of object, people, and ideas across the globe'. This is in order to 'explain the complex relationship between mobilities, moorings (…), spatial scales, and practices of place making, in order to describe how social worlds, like sustainability policy-making, are in part "made in and through movement"'. These, and other related perspectives (e.g. variants on Actor Network Theory, the new materialisms, etc.), claim to offer new tools that go beyond the strictly discursive and might be able to offer relevant and inspiring ideas, concepts, frameworks and findings to ESE policy research as well as the broader field of *educational research*. It is tempting to think that the field of ESE, because of the special nature of its areas of research, has the possibility, to be at the tip of the 'theory-developing spear' within educational research. And thus, some of these new exciting turns might find their foothold first in ESE, become translated into educational settings and then passed on to neighbouring fields.

Furthermore, the work done in ESE policy research – drawing on insights from educational and political theory – to criticise instrumental tendencies by conceptualising the *political* nature of sustainability issues (e.g. Rudsberg and Öhman 2010; Sund and Öhman 2014; Van Poeck, Vandenabeele, and Bruyninckx 2014) shows a certain overlap and shared concerns with particular perspectives in *sustainability science* and *transition studies* that also question instrumental, managerial and mechanistic approaches to sustainability transitions (e.g. Paredis 2013; Devolder and Block 2015). As such, these research fields can be considered complementary and bear potential for mutual synergies.

Operating in a field with fuzzy borders offers great scope for taking in the best of neighbouring fields (however far they might understand themselves to be from us), but also offers great possibility for cross-fertilisation from all of 'us' to all of 'them' (if one believes the purpose of such demarcations). As this collection of illustrative papers shows, the research presented over the years in *Environmental Education Research* represents a dense and thoughtful body of scholarship that not only stimulates a dynamic and fast-moving field, but also is more than grown enough to influence fields next to us (and perhaps even 'above' and 'under' us). Working with the specific links between education, environment, sustainability and policy has produced insights that remain too good not to revisit, and too good not to share. As such the articles in this VSI do not form a canon of what every good ESE researcher should at least know about ESE and policy, but offers everyone a potential vantage point to further push the field from the outside in, to the inside out.

Advancing a research field, we believe, requires more than improving the current scientific state-of-the-art by merely building further on (and, thus, reinforcing) existing theories and findings or by applying the latter to overlooked areas. As Alvesson and Sandberg (2014) argue, generating really interesting novel ideas and potentially influential path-breaking thinking demands that the basic assumptions underlying existing literature are examined, unpacked and challenged. Therefore, new research

> needs to attract attention from other researchers and practitioners, to lead to enthusiasm, to generate 'aha' and 'wow' moments, to trigger responses such as 'I have not thought about this before' or 'perhaps I should rethink this theme', and possibly to act as an effective tool for animating dialogue and reflexivity among practitioners. (24)

Similar considerations both guided the making of this VSI and constitute our hope as to what its publication might enable. Looking back at the laborious yet educative work of exploring all the volumes of the journal in view of the selection of articles, the papers that attracted our attention were not those that presented incremental, all too cautious, irrelevant and/or somewhat predictable or self-evident findings, but those that introduced distinctive voices in the field, that revealed and questioned taken for granted assumptions, and that stimulated transdisciplinarity and perspective-shifting.

Ferreira's (2009) remarkable article about 'orthodoxies' in our field, for instance, or Bengtsson and Östman's (2015) paper that interestingly points out how the logics of correspondence and determination that are omnipresent in ESE research influence (or constrain) researchers' observations and conclusions and how the exploration of alternative logics, can open-up new entry points for discussion of ESE policy. Alvesson and Sandberg (2014) emphasise that creating interesting and influential research contributions requires precisely such an open-ended, critical inquiry into prevailing assumptions instead of incrementally identifying and filling knowledge gaps in the available literature.

We want to add that, in our view, it also demands *collective* inquiry and reflection. With this VSI collection and editorial, we modestly aim to contribute to this endeavour by calling for renewed attention to various articles that, in themselves, reveal and challenge orthodoxies in ESE (policy) research, but also by exploring and unpacking some of the internal debates characterising the roots of our field, shed light on interesting routes into/across/out of neighbouring disciplines, policy and practice, and thus bear the potential to bring about 'path-(up)setting' (Alvesson and Sandberg 2014, 35) transdisciplinary dialogue.

Some concluding thoughts on 'researchers' and 'experts'

Many of the abovementioned researchers criticised an absolutist understandings of 'truth' as a foundation for addressing sustainability issues in *education*. We believe that the same criticism – and, thus, the impossibility to deduce from reality ('out there') a pure and monolithical truth that can be translated in undisputable, evidence-based guidelines on how to act – also goes for ESE (policy) *research*. Nevertheless, with this critique of a decidedly (and hence inadequate for these times) Modern approach to research, neither do we want to fall into a postmodern trap that renders some of the abovementioned concerns about the far-reaching consequences of sustainability problems simply relativistic, and thus irrelevant within a myriad of different, equally valued opinions and points of view.

What can we learn from the roots and routes of the field to move beyond a dichotomist distinction between modern and postmodern standpoints, and to further develop much-needed 'other-than-modern' (Garrison, Östman, and Håkansson 2015) approaches to ESE policy research? Taking into account the issues, insights and concerns raised above, an important prerequisite for this seems to be to preserve a space for ESE policy researchers to make 'documentaries' instead of taming and containing their work by the increasing pressure to offer 'evidence'. In line with this, we want to make out a case for letting ESE researchers be *researchers* instead of forcing them to take up the role of an *expert* since, as Bruno Latour (2010, 166 – our translation) argues, an expert-position reinforces the problematic Modern demarcation between science and politics:

> Basically, the expert (no matter how sympathetic and modest he might be) always reinforces the impossible Demarcation, attempting as he does to conceal from the public the kitchen of science in the making and to protect scientists from the interests and passions of the public. And the worst is that the cover of expertise is just sufficiently solid to allow politicians to hide behind expert's advices so that they do not have to decide by themselves and for themselves.

A journal such as *Environmental Education Research* can and does contribute to this challenge by creating time and space to report and reflect on the un-pure process of doing research ('the making of' – e.g. Blewitt 2005), to explore the 'roots' of the field as well as the 'routes' into, across and out of this field – crossing boundaries between academic fields and between research, policy and practice. Some of the initial questions that occupied us in preparing this VSI, were 'What has been investigated so far in ESE policy research?', 'What is lacking?' and 'Which approaches are overrepresented?'. Taking into account the above, we can now rephrase these questions. Is the field of ESE policy research characterised by a sound share of 'interesting', path-breaking research, or are incremental, irrelevant contributions over-represented? And are ESE policy researchers – by the context in which they operate – governed to act as researchers or as experts?

Reflecting on this in the light of our exploration of the volumes of this journal, we had to conclude that for us – two early career researchers who have written and reviewed for *Environmental Education Research* but are besides this not involved in the editorial process – asking these questions seems more interesting than answering them. We must remember that a Journal 'is not the field' and these are questions that should always be at the forefront of discussions within any field, including the journals that service it. We can gauge the health and vibrancy of our field by how well we all engage with such questions and remain critical of our own work, its impact, and how it adds to the field and its further progress. Therefore, we want to end this editorial by staging our questions as an invitation for a collective inquiry and (self-) reflection in ESE (policy) research.

We believe that the questions offer plenty of food for thought for authors, reviewers as well as the editorial board and office. Researchers and authors can reflect on their willingness to challenge their own taken-for-granted set of beliefs and to abandon (or interrupt) their preferred positions and frameworks in favour of exploring new perspectives and alternative assumptions. And what does this mean in terms of researcher identity, professional norms and career options? Reviewers can consider how to balance concerns for encouraging novel and interdisciplinary research contributions on the one hand, and demonstrated familiarity with and attentiveness to ESE research's heritage on the other. Or how to weigh methodological rigour – an important but never sufficient criterion for interesting findings – and less measurable or 'objectified' qualities such as imagination or the potential to unsettle orthodoxies?

The editorial board and office, with their broad view of the 'kitchen' of ESE research literature in the making, have a vital role in creating space for critically examining the roots of the field, for encouraging the exploration of new routes and for enabling dialogue – publicly, on the pages of the journal, or behind the scenes through refereeing communications – between a variety of positions, perspectives and academic fields.

We should all ask ourselves what we find in the 'kitchen' of any field and its journals. What tools of the trade are most used? Are there too many or too few chefs around? Any favourite spices that create the flavour this kitchen is renowned (or infamous) for? What dishes are served mostly? And does the audience like what they are served?

We are grateful for the chance to put this VSI together and hope that it can contribute to a better understanding of the inner workings of this particular slice of the field that *Environmental Education Research* represents, including its past, present and towards a bright(er) future.

Acknowledgement

The authors owe many thanks to Alan Reid for the inspiring discussions during the making of this VSI, as well as the valuable feedback on an earlier version of this editorial.

Disclosure statement

No potential conflict of interest was reported by the authors.

References

Aikens, K., McKenzie, M., and Vaughter, P. (2016). "Environmental and Sustainability Education Policy Research: A Review of Geographic and Thematic Trendsover Time." *Environmental Education Research*, 22 (3), 333–359.

Alvesson, M., and J. Sandberg. 2014. "Problematization Meets Mystery Creation: Generating New Ideas and Findings through Assumption Challenging Research." In *Critical Management Research: Reflections from the Field*, edited by E. Jeanes and T. Huzzard, 23–41. London: Sage.

Ashley, M. 2000. "Science: An Unreliable Friend to Environmental Education?" *Environmental Education Research* 6 (3): 269–280.

Bengtsson, S., and L. Östman. 2015. "Globalisation and Education for Sustainable Development: Exploring the Global in Motion." *Environmental Education Research*, Online First. doi:10.1080/13504622.2014.989960.

Biesta, G. 2009. *Educational Research, Democracy and TLRP. Methodological Development, Future Challenges*. London: TLRP.

Blewitt, J. 2005. "Education for Sustainable Development, Governmentality and Learning to Last." *Environmental Education Research* 11 (2): 173–185.

Devolder, S., and T. Block. 2015. "Transition Thinking Incorporated: Towards a New Discussion Framework on Sustainable Urban Projects." *Sustainability* 7 (3): 3269–3289.

Ferreira, J. 2009. "Unsettling Orthodoxies: Education for the Environment/for Sustainability." *Environmental Education Research* 15 (5): 607–620.

Garrison, J., L. Östman, and M. Håkansson. 2015. "The Creative Use of Companion Values in Environmental Education and Education for Sustainable Development: Exploring the Educative Moment." *Environmental Education Research* 21 (2): 183–204.

Hardt, M., and A. Negri. 2000. *Empire*. Cambridge: Harvard University Press.

Huckle, J., and A. E. J. Wals. 2015. "The UN Decade of Education for Sustainable Development: Business as Usual in the End." *Environmental Education Research* 21 (3): 491–505.

Hursh, D., J. Henderson, and D. Greenwood. 2015. "Editorial – Special Issue: Environmental Education in a Neoliberal Climate." *Environmental Education Research* 21 (3): 299–318.

Kopnina, H. 2012. "Education for Sustainable Development (ESD): The Turn Away from 'Environment' in Environmental Education?" *Environmental Education Research* 18 (5): 699–717.

Læssøe, J., N. Feinstein, and N. Blum. 2013. "Environmental Education Policy Research – Challenges and Ways Research Might Cope with Them." *Environmental Education Research* 19 (2): 231–242.

Læssøe, J., and J. Öhman. 2010. "Learning as Democratic Action and Communication: Framing Danish and Swedish Environmental and Sustainability Education." *Environmental Education Research* 16 (1): 1–7.

Latour, B. 2010. *Cogitamus: Six lettres sur les humanités scientifiques* [Cogitamus: Six letters on scientific humanities]. Paris: La Découverte.

Law, B., and R. Baker. 1997. "A Case Study of Dilemmas and Tensions: The Writing and Consultation Process Involved in Developing a National Guideline Document for Environmental Education." *Environmental Education Research* 3 (2): 225–232.

Lysgaard, J. A., and K. L. Fjeldsted. 2015. "Education between Discourse and Matter." In *Nature in Education*, edited by P. Kemp. LIT Verlag Dr. Wilhelm Hopf. http://pure.au.dk/portal/en/publications/id(1f0b49f0-9605-484d-a55f-6a4f38ed7b32).html

McKenzie, M., A. Bieler, and R. McNeil. 2015. "Education Policy Mobility: Reimagining Sustainability in Neoliberal times." *Environmental Education Research* 21 (3): 319–337.

Mogensen, F., and K. Schnack. 2010. "The Action Competence Approach and the 'New' Discourses of Education for Sustainable Development, Competence and Quality Criteria." *Environmental Education Research* 16 (1): 59–74.

Paredis, E. 2013. "A Winding Road. Transition Management, Policy Change and the Search for Sustainable Development." PhD diss., Ghent University, Ghent.

Reid, A., and W. Scott. 2006. "Researching Education and the Environment: Retrospect and Prospect." *Environmental Education Research* 12 (3–4): 571–587.

Rudsberg, K., and J. Öhman. 2010. "Pluralism in Practice – Experiences from Swedish Evaluation, School Development and Research." *Environmental Education Research* 16 (1): 95–111.

Scott, W. 2009. "Environmental Education Research: 30 Years on from Tbilisi." *Environmental Education Research* 15 (2): 155–164.

Stables, A. 1998. "Environmental Literacy: Functional, Cultural, Critical. The Case of the SCAA Guidelines." *Environmental Education Research* 4 (2): 155–164.

Stables, A., and W. Scott. 2002. "The Quest for Holism in Education for Sustainable Development." *Environmental Education Research* 8 (1): 53–60.

Stevenson, R. B. 2006. "Tensions and Transitions in Policy Discourse: Recontextualizing a Decontextualized EE/ESD Debate." *Environmental Education Research* 12 (3–4): 277–290.

Sund, J., and J. Öhman. 2014. "On the Need to Repoliticise Environmental and Sustainability Education: Rethinking the Postpolitical Consensus." *Environmental Education Research* 20 (5): 639–659.

Van Poeck, K., J. Vandenabeele, and H. Bruyninckx. 2014. "Taking Stock of the UN Decade of Education for Sustainable Development: The Policy-making Process in Flanders." *Environmental Education Research* 20 (5): 695–717.

Wright, T., and S. Pullen. 2007. "Examining the Literature: A Bibliometric Study of ESD Journal Articles in the Education Resources Information Centre Database." *Journal of Education for Sustainable Development* 1 (3): 77–90.

The roots and routes of environmental and sustainability education policy research

Jonas A. Lysgaard, Alan Reid and Katrien Van Poeck

This article introduces the themes of a virtual special issue (VSI) of *Environmental Education Research* (http://explore.tandfonline.com/content/ed/ceer-vsi) focused on policy research in environmental and sustainability education (ESE). The broad purpose behind preparing the VSI was to consider the challenges involved in linking particular concepts of environment and sustainability with key themes in educational policy, and how this remains a heavily contested practice. Examples drawn from two decades of studies published in the journal show how these might be illustrated, addressed, problematized and possibly transcended. The introduction traces how ESE researchers have dealt with key trends, complexities and issues in the policy-practice-research nexus both conceptually and empirically. It also illustrates how researchers within the field might reimagine and reinvigorate policy research on ESE, and how working with researchers from other fields who offer different perspectives, ideas and expertise might aid the cross-fertilisation of a complex terrain of ideas, policy and practice. In so doing, we hope the accompanying VSI inspires renewed interest into the (at times, fickle) relationship between ESE, and the dual worlds of possibility and tension that take place both within, and surrounding, their fields of policy and research.

Why a VSI about environmental and sustainability education policy research?

Linking particular concepts of environment and sustainability with key themes in educational policy remains a heavily contested practice. Whether it is carried out in relation to curriculum and pedagogy in schools or the public realm (Reid 2015), education on its own appears to create more than enough debate (Ozga 2007), while adding environmental perspectives and then the troublesome idea of sustainability (as with the Sustainable Development Goals), has made for neither clear waters nor smooth sailing, particularly in policy circles.

Practitioners, policy actors and researchers working with and across diverse levels of decision-making, of course, continue to face various shifts and combinations of intention, practice and claims as to what counts as 'useful knowledge'. Are they each to show awareness of research findings, for example? Or that they 'accept' them? Work out how they are locally applicable? Or expect that they are something they can act on, adopt or adhere to, for example? Keeping up, let alone knowing what to expect is on the horizon in policy, research and practice remains a perennial challenge (Nutley, Walter, and Davies 2007). So we might wonder, is there a way out of this, or even beyond, for all concerned? Must practitioners, policymakers and researchers, for example, remain locked in battle on these topics – be that through offensives, rear-guard actions, guerrilla tactics, and so on (Lingard 2013) – particularly given such a dynamic terrain for, and populace working in, environmental and sustainability education (ESE) policy, practice and their research?

The broad purpose behind this virtual special issue (VSI) is to press these concerns well beyond any sense of existential angst let alone rhetorical flourish. Our aim in preparing it has been to consider how such challenges might be illustrated, addressed, problematized and possibly transcended, by considering examples drawn from the last two decades of ESE policy research found within *Environmental Education Research*.

First, the contributions to the VSI illustrate how researchers have understood and dealt with policy issues in relation to the field, both conceptually and empirically. These illustrate a range of possible stances of researchers to influencing public policy, such as those described by Nutley, Walter, and Davies (2007, 11–12), as the *consensual*, *contentious*, and *paradigm-challenging*. An important (and of course, debated) argument within ESE research illustrates these distinctions well. It concerns whether the systemic and holistic demands associated with key environment and sustainability systems concepts can, do or should (not) comprise an isolated field of concern, particularly when it comes to education, or is some other form, configuration or relation to the wider world required, if not avoided to address these matters well?

In practical terms, such as in schools, this translates to questions such as: should ESE be hidden in corners of existing curricula, if not dusted down for special events or celebrations, for example, an Environment Day or Sustainability Festival, particularly so that it only ever amounts to the 'greenwashing' of education? Or, it is argued, mustn't ESE become (if not remain) core throughout curricula in general – and an education more generously conceived – so that the 'grand challenges' of the world can actually be addressed by society and by those wider social movements seeking to shape the focus and sense of what education is, and what it means to be educated in these times (Sund and Öhman 2014)?

Second, and relatedly, any claims to bold and vital ideas hitched to associated priorities in policy-making and practice cannot be dealt with, or researched, solely from inside one field alone. This is because any complex social problem always demands that those wider deliberative frames that create and position the notion of a field are engaged too, particularly if communities of research, policy and practice are to be able to pursue, test and refine the importance of the arguments advanced therein (Saunders 2007). With such a perspective, the *environmental* and *sustainability* and *education*, as well as their core concepts and contentions, can be seen to be not significantly different in importance to those of other fields made familiar through a shared labelling as 'adjectival educations'. Here, education as a public good, and thus as a way of wanting something for others – for example, health, justice, welfare, opportunity – demands explicit public policy and justification. It simply can't rely on 'policy fiat' or 'policy borrowing' to have traction. Equally, in recognising that processes of contextualisation, decontextualisation and recontextualisation are at work here too, to differing degrees, Lingard (2013, 118), relaying the words of Orland (2009, 115), notes:

> we can also see that research is and perhaps can only ever be one contributing factor for shaping education policy. … 'Even the most compelling and relevant research findings may fail to penetrate the policymaking process and, where research influences are manifest, their contributions are likely to be both indirect and incremental'.

What is at stake, it would appear, in such contexts and spheres for policy-making and its practice implications, is how to shape, govern, direct, and critique activities and actions in a contested space for education, be that for ESE or other matters of concern. This is because such spaces are always (to a certain extent) limited, contingent and fragile, particularly because of being subjected to various political forces at play in the '(eco)culture wars' of education – that is, understood as referring to the eco*nomic* and eco*logical* (Connolly 2013). Thus compelling critiques of the status quo about education, environment and sustainability also demand engagement with neighbouring, and often more powerful fields and demands on what should constitute educational priorities, and education itself (e.g. subjects, disciplines, fields of experience, and so forth). And in this, most crucially, a rich and critical research field is argued to be needed, to help develop, sustain, challenge and innovate it (see McKenzie, Bieler, and McNeil 2015). Why? Because it is simply naïve to believe that ESE research is to be used in a simple, linear and direct application, such that specific findings get channelled to a specific policy or practice, particularly when each component can act in parallel and interact dynamically, depending on the context and history of policy/innovation to hand.

So third, by way of a VSI, we use its contributions, introductions and editorial to trace how ESE researchers have actually dealt with trends, complexities and issues in the policy-practice-research nexus through specific examples drawn from the back catalogue and forthcoming contributions of the journal (e.g. Aikens, McKenzie, and Vaughter, forthcoming). There is a classic distinction to be recognised here in such papers: between research *of*/*for* policy (Gordon, Lewis, and Young 1977), and thus between the ends-in-view that contrast *enlightenment* with *engineering*.

While some have argued these are a continuum or can be combined, such as in the work of 'policy entrepreneurs' (see Kingdon (1984) and Ball and Exley (2010) – on how individuals might advocate certain policy ideas or proposals and play a key role in bringing research to policy-making by championing a set of findings that support their position), we note there has been little traction with such notions in this research field until recently, looking as it does, to innovate what it researches, theoretically and empirically.

However, a strong case can be advanced that during the UN Decade of ESD, Professors Arjen Wals, John Fien, Chuck Hopkins and Daniella Tilbury, each dallied with such entrepreneurial roles and opportunities in their own ways. As a topic ripe for further inquiry then, we will return to this in the editorial (http://dx.doi.org/10.1080/13504622.2015.1108393) when raising questions about the changing roles, responsibilities and careers of researchers, scholars, academics and 'policy workers' in this field. But before then, as Weiss (1999) has noted, interests, ideology, information, and institutions work as the key factors in shaping public policy and the use of research within this process. The policy actors here may include academics and researchers (as 'policy entrepreneurs' – as with the aforementioned professors in education), and from other fields. With the UN Decade, for example, information about the 'state of the earth' had been previously used to shape interests and ideologies about development at UN conferences in Stockholm, Rio and Johannesburg. It also appears in their agendas aimed at policy makers, with these being designed to change the practices and cultures of institutions, including those of education. Key policy mechanisms here included, Chapter 36 of Agenda 21, and establishing a UN Decade of ESD to continue efforts to re-orient teaching and tea-cher education towards sustainability, with an associated policy guidance, research and evaluation framework to support that.

Nutley, Walter, and Davies (2007, 108–109) regard such instances as ripe for research, given they are typical of attempts by policy entrepreneurs (and particularly researchers) to 'soften up' the system to their own ideas and proposals, and to act as brokers, negotiating amongst key stakeholders, on their own terms, or as part of research organisation (e.g. university or academic network), think tank, or peak body's research wing, for example, an environmental education association or spe-cial interest group. These channels are manifold, direct or indirect and demonstrated in several of the papers put together in this VSI (e.g. Blewitt 2005; Læssøe, Feinstein, and Blum 2013). In this, researchers (sometimes acting as policy entrepre-neurs) draw on personal contacts and interactions to shape perceptions and under-standings of policy production and critique, using social media, conferences and campaigns to try to influence policy, practice or change (such as that allied to the 2015 World Environmental Education Congress). Or they might even dust off old studies to show their continued relevance to a contemporary problem or possible solution to a policy, political impasse or priority …

Our expectation then, rather self-consciously, is that in providing examples and commentary on such matters, the VSI and its editorial inspires renewed interest into the (at times, fickle) relationship between ESE and the dual worlds of possibility and tension that take place both within, and surrounding, their fields of policy and research. We also trust that in what is presented here, cognizant of both the strengths and weaknesses of the articles, that further engagement is prompted on two fronts. First, by those inside the field(s) looking to reimagine and reinvigorate policy research on ESE; but also by those that we believe that ESE research needs most: namely, those standing at the brink and looking in, offering different perspectives, ideas and expertise, and believing that the field's complex terrain of ideas, policy and practice are ripe for cross-fertilisation.

Roots and routes of ESE policy research

Since the inaugural issue of *Environmental Education Research* in 1995, contrast-ing views on how to understand, engage and use policy have become a mainstay of debate within the journal. Early frustrations over differences in research meth-ods, goals and discourse embedded within studies of policy and policy-making have not dissipated over the years. But as the contributions to this VSI show, they have been softened by new perspectives on how ESE research and practice are caught in an ongoing dance with all things 'policy', and relatedly, 'political' – a set of plural and unstable rather than singular and fixed concepts if ever we needed reminding.

As Ozga, Popkewitz, and Seddon (2006, 10) put it:

> Questions about what knowledge is produced and legitimized, how it can be mobilized and used, and whose resource it is (i.e., for which communities it can be a collective resource) are critical not just because they sit at the heart of education research steering but also because they are fundamental to the practical politics of education research.

Of course, no field of practice or its research enjoys an unproblematic or stable relationship with **P**olicy and policies (nor their politics either), especially when we consider broader concerns raised by educational research about policy cycles, policy-making frameworks and communities, and policy actors (see, e.g. seminal contributions on curriculum, such as Ball and Bowe 1992). Moreover, whether the relationship of ESE research to the topic of education/environment/sustainability policy resembles a dance macabre, an intimate tango, a ballet rehearsal, or more of a mosh pit frenzy, seems to be very much a matter of perspective and experience. So in this VSI, we hope to shed light on some of these impressions as well as the clarifications required, by tracing the particular moves afoot, so to speak, in some of the central debates illustrated in this selection from the journal.

In fact, throughout its volumes, it remains clear that the field that the journal addresses is a *highly contentious, shifting and politically sensitive field of scholarship* (see Law and Baker 1997; Ashley 2000; Sund and Öhman 2014). Not only do diverse understandings and foci for policy and policy perspectives form a central part of ESE research, these differences and divergences also act as leverage points for researchers, policy-makers and practitioners with non-coinciding perspectives on how the field(s) (and publications on the topic in academic journals) should develop, let alone be 'steered'.

Kingdon (1984) and Neilson (2001) trace this kind of situation to the separation or integration of three distinct streams running through the policy arena: a *problem stream*, a *policy stream*, and a *political stream*. When these aren't operating in isolation but in concert, that is, a 'policy window' briefly opens, solutions can be coupled to problems and political opportunities, such as having Education, as Goal 4, of the Sustainable Development Goals. Equally, a solution can be offered by specialists in the policy stream to which there is no problem per se, while special interest groups and social movements through to politicians of various stripes may not have the power to craft, let alone, imagine or enact public policy for education, given such vagaries as the policy climate, policy cycles, democratic process, and policy (in)activism.

Such 'policy windows' can also be understood, with inspiration from Hardt and Negri's *Empire* (2000) as 'windows of opportunity'. These open up in an otherwise quite impermeable fabric of society and policy and make it possible, even for a brief moment, to push for change. Windows do not, however, remain open. They have a tendency to close, but as this VSI demonstrates, new ones always appear and offer possibilities that we have yet to imagine, or research.

A case in point – which we have already illustrated in switching between singular and plural – is the discussion embedded within disputes about *ESE policy nomenclature*. This can be seen to centre on the pre-existing and potential clash between competing ideologies and perspectives on the *environmental* and *sustainability* and *educational*, and their various combinations and framings. Down the years, this has occasionally led to harsh criticism in certain communities, particularly of the most recent newcomer, and if it has been sponsored by international rather than local bodies. Other criticisms have included to argue that 'sustainable development' is 'oxymoronic' conceptually and as global policy, or that 'ecological sustainability' or simply 'sustainability' are preferred anchors for localised environmental values as much as for cultural and political reasons. Or simply that sustainable development offers not just a series of potentials but also dangers to education and educators, particularly from an ecopedagogical perspective (see Stables and Scott 2002; Stevenson 2006; Ferreira 2009; Kopnina 2012). Arguably, the concept has also become something of a Trojan horse to instrumentalist, neo-liberal economic agendas (see Connolly 2013; Hursh, Henderson, and Greenwood 2015). But at the same time, such attacks have also been rebuffed by academics with a different worldview, position and self-critical understanding of the long-term possibility of using the sustainability concept in education, as well as to transform it (see Bengtsson and Östman 2015). The policy work required, it is argued, for a 'sustainable education system' is quite different from that required of an 'education system for sustainability' or a 'system of education for sustainability', but this isn't always transparent when 'strawmen' are the targets.

To illustrate further, the UN Decade for ESD arrived in 2005 and marked a key shift in priorities for policy-making, practice development and research, even if it was also later dismissed at its conclusion as little more than fostering 'business as usual' (Huckle and Wals 2015). Be that as it may, for ten years, 'Education for Sustainable Development' (or some variation thereof) was a concept that could neither be ignored nor circumvented in ESE, and in the company of the aforementioned professors, was developed with a clear intent to impact educational policy around the world, and the world itself. It also had the effect of making sustainability and education a commonplace combination in the pages of this and other journals recording research and practice development (see Reid and Scott 2006), in research and development programmes more broadly, and in this and related fields elsewhere (e.g. Network 30 at ECER on ESE research, and Network 8 on research on health education) – however temporary or convenient some of these 'marriages' may have proven to be.

Discussions related to the shifting focus of the ESE field have also found echoes in those on the very purpose of having a research endeavour and community that deals with these issues, even as a subfield of education or environment more broadly, or tied to what can be regarded as an adjectival education, or other combination thereof. In Wales, for example, Education for Sustainable Development has been coupled with Global Citizenship, rather than under the sole banner of ESE – perhaps too, that will change (by separation or divorce?), or for that matter, other 'polyamorous' combinations could be suggested, for example, regarding climate change education as a key component of ESE, and vice versa.

A key point amid this rhetorical and conceptual play though, comes from recognising that the adjectival format often suggests an almost activist *problem-solving orientation* to socially-produced and socially-embedded issues (Cox 1996). Ongoing discussion in this field has considered whether ESE researchers should primarily adopt an activist stance too (see Stables 1998; Blewitt 2005; Mogensen and Schnack 2010; Rudsberg and Öhman 2010). As in other fields, such debate rages over how far 'we/I/they/one' should – or should not – take the level of instrumentalism that this position so easily harbours, even under the guise of a critical approach. Is there a special responsibility of education to push for a certain development shaped by ideals and/or policies? Likewise, must *education* research be *educational* research and *educative* research too – always, everywhere … who by, how, why? The debate has been fierce, and continues, particularly in relation to configuring and possibly recon-figuring 'education's response' to climate change (Læssøe, Feinstein, and Blum 2013). In fact, ESE and its policy research, it has been argued, deal with incredibly important questions: of how we as human beings understand and engage with the environment, climate, and all levels and relations in between – even if it can fail to do so sufficiently and effectively (Stables and Scott 2002; Ferreira 2009; Kopnina 2012).

Some scholarly policy inquiries, with their various strategies, tactics and heuris-tics in this space though, might seem to suggest there are few barriers, even as they remain enmeshed in a political maelstrom. On the one hand, there are international environmental and sustainability-related summits that rarely deliver in practice; on the other, national policy struggles to boost and direct economic growth; and to create a multi-handed beast, yet more considerations, including sincere hopes that through lifelong learning policies and practice, children and adults might actually learn some-thing valuable along the way about the/our/others' environment (and/or sustainabil-ity). In the midst of this we find some researchers questioning the purpose of their existence and practice, if not 'impact' personally, and of their work, if not that of their colleagues, in policy circles (see Van Poeck, Vandenabeele, and Bruyninckx 2014).

Returning to Lingard (2013, 119), the possible and actual uses and abuses of research in education policy shouldn't be ignored here. These range from giving too much weight to one role over another in the policy-research-practice nexus: of research as rationale, justification, ammunition or legitimation of a particular policy direction, or for that matter, in offering a certain vocabulary, grammar and discourse for the ideas and words to be used in the policy domain. Elsewhere, Shulha and Cousins (1997) acknowledge the possibility of the 'justified non-use' of findings and outcomes, if not their 'mischievous use', alongside examples of 'misevaluation' in the first place owing to poor quality outcomes, and 'abuse' through the suppres-sion of potentially useful and high-quality findings. Again, drawing on Orland (2009, 118), Lingard notes:

> To the extent it is relied on at all, educational research is much more likely to be paid attention to by educational policy leaders when it buttresses arguments about particular policy directions or prescriptions *already* being advocated, thus furthering a particular political/policy position. It is research as ammunition not as knowledge discovery.

A sense of this uneasy friction between research and policy can be found at the very core of many of the articles brought together in this VSI (e.g. Stevenson 2006; Rudsberg and Öhman 2010; Sund and Öhman 2014; Bengtsson and Östman 2015). Yet we also anticipate that a rich research field of ESE will never overcome this apparent friction, as it also proves a most productive of grist for activity and further research. As Nutley, Walter, and Davies (2007) put it, there are a number of barriers and enablers to the use of research in policy that can be clustered into four groups (see Box 1).

In general, these highlight the need for reflexive research communities, including their members and critical friends, to give careful attention to:

- the nature of the research;
- the personal characteristics of the researchers and potential research users;
- the links between research and its users;
- the context for the use of research.

Box 1.   Barriers and enablers to the use of research.

The nature of the research
Research is more likely to be used that:
- Is high quality and comes from a credible source
- Provides clear and uncontested findings
- Has been commissioned, or carries high-level political support
- Is aligned with local priorities, needs and contexts
- Is timely and relevant to policy makers' and practitioners' requirements
- Is presented in a 'user-friendly' way – concise, jargon-free and visually appealing

The personal characteristics of researchers and potential research users
- Policy makers and practitioners with higher levels of education or some experience of research are more likely to be research users
- Lack of skills to interpret and appraise research can inhibit research use
- Some individuals may be hostile towards the use of research, or to research more generally
- Researchers may lack the knowledge and skills to engage effectively in dissemination and research use activities

The links between research and its users
- Research use may be inhibited where policy makers and practitioners have limited access to research
- Knowledge brokers – both individuals and agencies – can play an effective 'bridging' role between research and its potential users
- Direct links between researchers and policy makers or practitioners also support research use. Face-to-face interactions and two-way exchanges of information are most likely to encourage the use of research

The context for the use of research
Context plays a key role in shaping the uptake of research
- In policy contexts, research is more likely to be used where:
  o It is aligned with current ideology and individual and agency interests
  o Its findings fit with existing ways of thinking or acting or with other information within the policy environment
  o Open political systems exist
  o Institutions and structures bring researchers and policy makers into contact
  o At a local level, an organisational culture exists that is broadly supportive of evidence use
- In practice contexts, local organisational, structural and cultural issues may limit the use of research, for example:
  o Lack of time to read research
  o Lack of autonomy to implement the findings from research
  o Lack of support – financial, administrative and personal – to develop research-based practice change
  o Local cultural resistance to research and its use
- In research contexts, a number of barriers inhibit the flow of findings to policy makers and practitioners:
  o Lack of incentive or reward for engaging in dissemination and research use activities
  o High value placed on traditional academic journal publications at the expense of 'user-friendly' research outputs
  o Lack of time and financial resources for research use activities
  o A set of attitudes among some academic researchers that dissemination is not part of their role

---

Source: Extended quote adapted from Nutley, Walter, and Davies (2007, 81–83).

History as the new New?

These considerations, of course, are another way of saying that an overly rosy view of the nexus isn't actually that desirable. For a start, it risks being ahistorical, apolitical and uncritical of key features of policy activity, such as the workings of policy communities, advocacy coalitions, epistemic communities, and issues networks in shaping policy and research (Nutley, Walter, and Davies 2007, 106–108). In fact, a critical sense of a field's history is often the first (of many a) victim in the busy life of a researcher. As we have found with our own struggles to hang onto a credible sense of a research field, producing new work and even gaining a workable understanding of some of the many neighbouring fields (while also dealing with the more mundane aspects of meeting up with real world human researchers and having an informed and informative discussion) – these simply remain arduous tasks. Who really wants to sit down and thump through the back catalogue of a research journal?

A recurrent critique though that can be discovered in doing so with *Environmental Education Research*, is that within the ESE field, it is dangerous to predict the Future based on what the Past – and even worse, what the Now – seem to insist on, particularly if this is interpreted as suggesting the only possibility for policy development. Our first of many cautions arising from such efforts on our own part, is: one should not race towards a particular future, while staring into a particular past, particularly given the blinkers of one's own past as a policy researcher. However, as individual and collaborating researchers, we also risk being barred access to both the past and the future if we do not spend time (and with others) discovering as well as re-discovering the history of any research field, and perspectives on that and its complexities, certainties and ambiguities, whatever their fluidity too.

For example, looking into the archives, the trend of producing (mono-disciplinary) research that tells us nothing (much) new about transdisciplinary problems and polyvocal debates, whilst at the same time, resembling (though its logic, methods and conclusions), work done 15–20 years ago, hasn't seriously abated. It remains, however, an important task of any research community to challenge such trends, while also developing a better and shared understanding of a field's past and priorities, as these remain effective tools that enable its furtherance (Reid and Payne 2013).

This is also because the history of any academic field of study is neither static nor stable, and in order to navigate diverse perspectives on what we can learn from its past and its history, we will need to maintain familiarity with the important work and workers that have been published within a field and in a range of outlets over time. In this, re-interpretation is more appropriate than translation, suggest Lauen and Tyson (2009) for policy research, especially when we engage with new projects and ideas *about* and *for* policy, building upon, and challenging, the socially embedded intelligence that a field's collective memory represents.

We do not, however, need to discover everything (new) ourselves, particularly if the time frame for policy (and knowledge to inform and shape that) is 'time sensitive'. We can enjoy the benefits of the hard work of past and new generations of researchers, particularly through their meta-analysis and synthesis work (e.g. Rickinson and Reid 2015; Aikens, McKenzie, and Vaughter, forthcoming), even as we remain mindful of another caution, well illustrated in the work of Læssøe, Feinstein, and Blum (2013), and expressed concisely by Nutley, Walter, and Davies (2007, 37):

> The same body of research may be seen and used very differently by different policy actors within the policy environment; and different groups may manage and fund research in order to use it for their own ends.

So it would be a pity not to find ways, such as through VSIs, to remain open to a carefully conceived possibility of cross-fertilisation – of new research processes and approaches drawing on critical perspectives both *from* and *upon* the work already present within the ESE research field. Indeed, it is impossible to truly move forward without an acute sense of history and how contributions to that act as its 'veins', if not its 'lifeblood'. In fact, the ambition of any researcher within any field, we might argue, should be to go beyond producing the predictable 'new', beating the poor old horse of well-proven methods and conclusions. Rather: aim higher! Aim for the new New! Novel and potentially influential path-breaking ideas are always in vogue. As Alvesson and Sandberg (2014) suggest, a powerful route to these is through reflexive and collective examination of the field: unpacking and challenging the basic assumptions that underpin existing research programmes, and in this case, also with policy processes and their literatures in mind. And with the papers in this VSI, this should offer a good platform to begin or continue this activity on ESE policy research?

Jumping the fences of research fields

Finally for this introduction, and in relation to the role of educational research in particular, we turn to Jill Blackmore's comments, and an attempt to resist an inevitable fate ascribed to particular approaches within a performative context for research. Blackmore (2003, 1) has asked somewhat rhetorically and largely in relation to feminist approaches, is their role to be that of 'policy service, policy critique, technical expert or public intellectual?' Such questions can avoid receiving either-or responses by advancing one that seeks to combine them, that is, in ways that are always already sensitive to the particular policy question or priority or problem in mind. Then it is possible to see ESE policy research as not just a generalised body of activity responding to abstracted questions, but rather as having a range of direct and indirect, immediate and delayed effects on policies, policy-making and policy actors – some of whom, of course, may be researchers, practitioners or members of policy networks and communities.

However, as floated above and in our other introduction to this VSI for the ECER conference (http://www.tandf.co.uk/journals/pdf/education/CEER-VSI-ESE-1. pdf), ESE policy researchers may have an acute lack of will to limit the scope and reach of their work, for a variety of reasons. No area of the social and more-than-social seems to scare off the most intrepid ESE researcher with global(ised) convictions and impact so apparently in reach. Such a situation not only makes for a dynamic and intriguing research field, it also leads to a plethora of different methodologies, theories, epistemologies and ontologies being sucked in to its activities, often in the name of interdisciplinary or transdisciplinary activity. The borders of the field remain fuzzy, with *researchers happily moving between and across this and other fields*, roles, positions and logics – normative, pluralistic and otherwise. This tendency can be applauded to some extent, even as the risk of any emerging vampiric analogy which might also be quickly dispatched. The field of ESE remains strong and vibrant, but is its strength that of insisting on or resisting, an unbridled 'lust' or 'promiscuity' of idea(l)s?

Contributions to this VSI recognise the reality of this tricky possibility: of an 'endarkenment' as much as 'enlightenment' of public policy, so to speak (Weiss 1979). It also offers an open and active invitation to researchers from other fields who might find the perspectives within ESE and its research alluring, if not hard to resist. But can that be to not simply 'perform' or 'colonise' without interaction and enlivening on both sides? In fact, by focusing on policy research and the quarrels it brings about in relation to ESE, some might hope that a VSI both lures and frightens researchers in neighbouring fields with its ongoing struggles, no matter what the particular educational policy terrain to hand.

Citation analysis is one way of exploring this, as for some years now, it has been clear that researchers of ESE have imported ideas, concepts and methodologies quite widely from other researchers, research fields and research programmes, usually carefully, but sometimes imprudently. The deep tool boxes of philosophy, sociology, psychology, and anthropology, for example – including how these relate to notions of knowledge quality, transfer and mobilisation – have been raided over and over again by bands of education researchers wanting to apply the latest or most fashionable ideas to the most pressing questions, conceptually and empirically, linked to environment, sustainability and education. Critique often follows shortly thereafter. Hence our interest in organising the contributing papers for this VSI into groupings that reflect this introduction's key themes, as follows:

- A contentious and politically sensitive field of scholarship.
- What's in a name? Questioning the purposes of ESE in policy and practice.
- ESE as problem solver? Solution-oriented research, policy and practice.
- At the crossroads of research, policy-making and practice: changing roles and positions of ESE policy researchers.

Continuing to witness through the pages of a research journal how such themes relate to general perspectives on education, society, and politics, if not how we deal with this planet, suggests to us that the time has also come for ESE researchers to be more willing to share their own treasure chest and actively engage with the fields that they borrow from. This returns us to questions of policy and education and transition once more, that we deal with further in the editorial. But also to those aforementioned foundational disciplines where insights from the ESE field seem to be more in demand, particularly as issues such as climate change, environmental crisis and regimes of neo-liberal education, continue to draw increasing attention in research and policy communities.

Just imagine what a follow-up VSI could look like in a decade or so …

Disclosure statement

No potential conflict of interest was reported by the authors.

References

Aikens, K., M. McKenzie, and P. Vaughter. (2016). "Environmental and Sustainability Education Policy Research: A Review of Geographic and Thematic Trendsover Time." *Environmental Education Research* 22 (3): 333–359.

Alvesson, M., and J. Sandberg. 2014. "Problematization Meets Mystery Creation: Generating New Ideas and Findings through Assumption Challenging Research." In *Critical Management Research: Reflections from the Field*, edited by E. Jeanes and T. Huzzard, 23–41. London: Sage.

Ashley, M. 2000. "Science: An Unreliable Friend to Environmental Education?" *Environmental Education Research* 6 (3): 269–280.

Ball, S., and R. Bowe. 1992. "Subject Departments and the 'Implementation' of National Curriculum Policy: An Overview of the Issues." *Journal of Curriculum Studies* 24 (2): 97–115.

Ball, S., and S. Exley. 2010. "Making Policy with 'Good Ideas': Policy Networks and the 'Intellectuals' of New Labour." *Journal of Education Policy* 25 (2): 151–169.

Bengtsson, S., and L. Östman. 2015. "Globalisation and Education for Sustainable Development: Exploring the Global in Motion." *Environmental Education Research*, Online First. doi:10.1080/13504622.2014.989960.

Blackmore, J. 2003. "Tracking the Nomadic Life of the Educational Researcher: What Future for Feminist Public Intellectuals and the Performative University?" *The Australian Educational Researcher* 30 (3): 1–24.

Blewitt, J. 2005. "Education for Sustainable Development, Governmentality and Learning to Last." *Environmental Education Research* 11 (2): 173–185.

Connolly, W. 2013. *The Fragility of Things*. Durham, NC: Duke University Press.

Cox, R. 1996. *Approaches to World Order*. Cambridge: Cambridge University Press.

Ferreira, J. 2009. "Unsettling Orthodoxies: Education for the Environment/for Sustainability." *Environmental Education Research* 15 (5): 607–620.

Gordon, I., J. Lewis, and R. Young. 1977. "Perspectives on Policy Analysis." *Public Administration Bulletin* 25: 26–35.

Hardt, M., and A. Negri. 2000. *Empire*. Cambridge, MA: Harvard University Press.

Huckle, J., and A. E. J. Wals. 2015. "The UN Decade of Education for Sustainable Development: Business as Usual in the End." *Environmental Education Research* 21 (3): 491–505.

Hursh, D., J. Henderson, and D. Greenwood, eds. 2015. Environmental Education in a Neoliberal Climate. Special Issue. *Environmental Education Research* 21 (3): 299–318.

Kingdon, J. 1984. *Agendas, Alternatives and Public Policy*. Boston, MA: Little Brown.

Kopnina, H. 2012. "Education for Sustainable Development (ESD): The Turn Away from 'Environment' in Environmental Education?" *Environmental Education Research* 18 (5): 699–717.

Læssøe, J., N. Feinstein, and N. Blum. 2013. "Environmental Education Policy Research –
Challenges and Ways Research Might Cope with Them." *Environmental Education
Research* 19 (2): 231–242.

Lauen, D. L., and K. Tyson. 2009. "Perspectives from the Disciplines: Sociological Contribu-
tions to Educational Policy Research and Debates." In *Handbook of Education Policy
Research*, edited by G. Sykes, B. Schneider, and D. N. Plank, 71–82. New York:
Routledge.

Law, B., and R. Baker. 1997. "A Case Study of Dilemmas and Tensions: The Writing and
Consultation Process Involved in Developing a National Guideline Document for Environmental Education." *Environmental Education Research* 3 (2): 225–232.

Lingard, B. 2013. "The Impact of Research on Education Policy in an Era of Evidence-Based
Policy." *Critical Studies in Education* 54 (2): 113–131.

McKenzie, M., A. Bieler, and R. McNeil. 2015. "Education Policy Mobility: Reimagining
Sustainability in Neoliberal times." *Environmental Education Research* 21 (3): 319–337.

Mogensen, F., and K. Schnack. 2010. "The Action Competence Approach and the 'New'
Discourses of Education for Sustainable Development, Competence and Quality Criteria."
Environmental Education Research 16 (1): 59–74.

Neilson, S. 2001. *IDRC Supported Research and Its Influence on Public Policy: Knowledge
Utilization and Public Policy Processes: A Literature Review*. Ottawa: International
Development Research Centre.

Nutley, S., I. Walter, and H. T. O. Davies. 2007. *Using Evidence: How Research Can Inform
Public Service*. Bristol: The Policy Press.

Orland, M. 2009. "Separate Orbits: The Distinctive Worlds of Educational Research and
Policymaking." In *Handbook of Education Policy Research*, edited by G. Sykes,
B. Schneider, D. Plank, and T. Ford, 113–128. New York: Routledge.

Ozga, J. 2007. "Knowledge and Policy: Research and Knowledge Transfer." *Critical Studies
in Education* 48 (1): 63–78.

Ozga, J., T. Popkewitz, and T. Seddon, eds. 2006. *Education Research and Policy: Steering
the Knowledge-Based Economy*. London: RoutledgeFalmer.

Reid, A., ed. 2015. "Curriculum Challenges for and from Environmental Education." *Journal
of Curriculum Studies*, VSI. http://explore.tandfonline.com/content/ed/jcs-vsi-2015.

Reid, A., and P. Payne. 2013. "Handbooks of Environmental Education Research: For
Further Reading and Writing." In *International Handbook of Research on Environmental
Education*, edited by R. B. Stevenson, M. Brody, J. Dillon, and A. E. J. Wals, 529–541.
New York: Routledge.

Reid, A., and W. Scott. 2006. "Researching Education and the Environment: Retrospect and
Prospect." *Environmental Education Research* 12 (3–4): 571–587.

Rickinson, M., and A. Reid. 2015. "Synthesis of Research in Higher Education for
Sustainable Development." In *Routledge Handbook of Higher Education for Sustainable
Development*, edited by M. Barth, G. Michelsen, M. Rieckmann, and I. G. Thomas,
142–160. London: Routledge.

Rudsberg, K., and J. Öhman. 2010. "Pluralism in Practice – Experiences from Swedish Evaluation, School Development and Research." *Environmental Education Research* 16 (1):
95–111.

Saunders, L., ed. 2007. *Educational Research and Policy Making: Exploring the Border
Country between Research and Policy*. London: Routledge.

Shulha, L., and J. Cousins. 1997. "Evaluation Use: Theory, Research, and Practice Since
1986." *Evaluation Practice* 18 (3): 195–208.

Stables, A. 1998. "Environmental Literacy: Functional, Cultural, Critical. The Case of the
SCAA Guidelines." *Environmental Education Research* 4 (2): 155–164.

Stables, A., and W. Scott. 2002. "The Quest for Holism in Education for Sustainable Development." *Environmental Education Research* 8 (1): 53–60.

Stevenson, R. B. 2006. "Tensions and Transitions in Policy Discourse: Recontextualizing a
Decontextualized EE/ESD Debate." *Environmental Education Research* 12 (3–4):
277–290.

Sund, L., and J. Öhman. 2014. "On the Need to Repoliticise Environmental and Sustainability
Education: Rethinking the Postpolitical Consensus." *Environmental Education Research*
20 (5): 639–659.

Van Poeck, K., J. Vandenabeele, and H. Bruyninckx. 2014. "Taking Stock of the UN Decade of Education for Sustainable Development: The Policy-Making Process in Flanders." *Environmental Education Research* 20 (5): 695–717.

Weiss, C. 1979. "The Many Meanings of Research Utilization." *Public Administration Review* 39 (5): 426–431.

Weiss, C. 1999. "The Interface between Evaluation and Public Policy." *Evaluation* 5 (4): 468–486.

A Case Study of Dilemmas and Tensions: the writing and consultation process involved in developing a national guideline document for environmental education

BARRY LAW
ROBYN BAKER

SUMMARY   *This paper is about the experience of two writers contracted to write a national guideline document on environmental education for the education sector. The focus is on the dilemmas and tensions that arose for the writers in developing a document that was to represent the views of people involved in environmental education across all education sector groups.*

Introduction

IN 1993 a national curriculum document for New Zealand schools was released. This identified seven essential learning areas, the essential skills and the attitudes and values that were to be fostered in schools. While the environment was not specifically identified as one of the learning areas *The New Zealand Curriculum Framework* identified the environment as an important area of study (Ministry of Education, 1993).

In early 1995 we were invited to write a document that provided guidelines for schools for environmental education. These guidelines were to give a rationale for and give direction to programmes in environmental education that aided implementation of *The New Zealand Curriculum Framework* and the curriculum documents were based on the essential learning areas.

Context and Method

The issues discussed in this paper were identified by an analysis of the response data received from individuals during the consultation process. The consultation process was part of the contract arrangements for developing the document and this was achieved by establishing two separate review groups.

The first group was a reference group of six people who all had an academic background in environmental education-related studies. The second group was a diversity of people who represented a range of different sector groups with a specific interest in environmental education. This group covered both the formal and non-formal education sectors.

Data were collected from group one on three separate occasions over a period of six months. This included formal written statements, phone conversations and face to face discussions. Note that summaries were taken during phone and face to face meetings.

Group two data were collected in a one-off written response to a draft document that was sent out to about 100 individuals, approximately two thirds of the way through the contract. This response corresponded with the second consultation with group one.

An overview of the document construction and consultative process is outlined in Fig. 1.

Contract Specifications

The contract specifications were designed by the Ministry of Education (see Fig. 2) and these were discussed with the writers at a preliminary meeting.

The contractual agreement also specified that the writers would produce three milestone reports during the writing process to provide feedback to the Ministry of Education and to highlight any specific issues that arose during the development phase.

This was a constructive process as it helped the writers to clarify some of the dilemmas and tensions that arose and provided a forum to discuss with the Ministry the significance of these concerns and responsibilities for action.

Identification of Dilemmas and Tensions

During the initial development stage we identified two major dilemmas.

The initial dilemma involved the actual nature of the guidelines and the second concerned the place of environmental education within the curriculum.

These dilemmas arose from the discussion and debate between the two of us as we considered the critical feedback from the reference group. Dealing with the dilemmas served to focus our debate, clarify our dual position and certainly assisted in developing a cohesive framework. The dilemmas often became internal arguments for the two of us within the framework of the contract specifications. This could be described as frustrating, but realistically it served as healthy self- and peer-reflection.

The identification of tensions came from unrealistic expectations on both of us from either specific individuals or groups that wanted their own view to be the mainstream agenda. They were not perceived as dilemmas because the problem

1995

January	— Negotiation meeting (Wellington) Ministry of Education/Barry and Robyn
20–21 February	— Development of document framework — Establishment of reference group
28 March	— Meeting with Auckland Branch of the New Zealand Association for Environmental Education (NZAEE) for consultation
11-12 April	— Writers working meeting (Wellington) — Contract signed — First draft of Framework sent to reference group — Letters sent to 78 member/organisation of consultation group
14 April	— Milestone 1 sent to Ministry of Education (four days late) X Dilemma One Policy vs Guidelines (interpreting specification 7) • Tension 3 Indigenous perspective
11–12 May	— Writers working meeting (Christchurch) X Dilemma Two Infusion vs Block course approach
7 June	— Writers working meeting (Wellington)
12 June	— Draft document finished for consultation — Draft document sent to 100 people/organisations (Summary of returned responses by July 2) — Meeting with Ministry of Education to discuss feedback
3 July	— Milestone 2 sent to Ministry of Education • Tension 1 and 2
28 July	— Writers working meeting (Christchurch)
11 August	— Writers working meeting (Wellington)
16 August	— Final draft completed
18 August	— Milestone 3 sent to the Ministry — Final draft document forwarded to the Ministry
18 September	— Contract termination

Fig. 1. Document construction: the process used.

lay outside the framework of the contract. However, these tensions did have the potential to impact heavily on completion and subsequent publication of the document.

Dilemma 1: policy versus curriculum guidelines

The contract title clearly stated curriculum guidelines for environmental education. The specifications then made reference to government policy on the environment and *The New Zealand Curriculum Framework*. Specifications 1–3 (see Fig. 2) clearly refer to policy statements that provide a context for environmental education and a link to the curriculum framework. The first dilemma arose when deciding how much of the document content should indicate Ministry of Education policy on environmental education and how much should provide curriculum guidelines for teachers. It could be argued that the two were not compatible within the framework of one document.

The Ministry is to develop and publish guidelines to explain Government policy related the environment and to assist teachers to integrate environmental issues into the delivery of the curriculum.

The outcome of the policy should be that students develop increased awareness and understanding of issues related to the concept of sustainability and the need to maintain and improve the quality of the environment.

The guidelines should include:

1. A foreword which links the guidelines to the Government's policy on environment, including sustainable developments, and environmental education policy stated in *The New Zealand Curriculum Framework*

2. A statement showing the linkage with *The New Zealand Curriculum Framework* and the achievement objectives in the national curriculum statements.

3. A rationale for environmental education taking into account local, national, and international, perspectives including issues raised in the United Nations Conference on Environment and Development (UNCED), and the Government's environment strategy outlines in *Path to 2010* and set out in detail in *Environmental 2010 Strategy*.

4. A definition of environmental education which recognises that environmental education is a process which develops the understanding, skills, attitudes and values that will enable individuals and the community to contribute towards maintaining and improving the quality of the environment and sustainable development.

5. Key principles for environmental education in schools.

6. A few general aims and some key objectives arising from the aims.

7. Suggestions about cross-curriculum teaching and learning approaches and strategies for environmental education which are appropriate for junior, middle and senior primary school, and junior and senior secondary school.

8. Reference to support materials available produced by government agencies and non-government organisations.

9. Information about the responsibilities of schools and boards of trustees.

10. A listing of resources, recent articles, and publications which could be of assistance to teachers in developing programmes.

In development of the guidelines groups to be consulted should include:

- Colleges of Education, particularly those with environmental education programmes.
- Universities with environmental education courses.

FIG. 2. Specifications for guidelines on environment education.

Comments on the initial draft from both review groups contained comments that challenged us to face this dilemma.

> you need to reduce the amount of policy material in sections 1–3 of the document and concentrate on guidelines on how to teach EE.

> This document clearly needs to be followed with a 'how to' document with sample units of work, how to be effective in a crowded curriculum, etc. I believe this document will lie dusty on the shelf if it is not followed up with additional resources.

> The first sections of this document seem to be legitimising statements rather than focussing strongly enough on desired learning outcomes.

Comments also emphasised the need for more examples to be shown in both sections 'Learning outcomes for environmental education' and 'A teaching and learning process for environmental education'.

The basic dilemma for us was how to produce a document that gave a policy framework for environmental education and so legitimate its inclusion within the curriculum and also provide practical guidance for environmental education programmes. At a time in education where schools are feeling overwhelmed with the developments of new curricula a lack of environmental education policy would just lead to environmental education falling between the essential learning areas. Legitimising environmental education would give those who wanted to see it included in their programme something to justify their claim and also help resource writers develop material around a framework. At the same time, feedback indicated that many educators were primarily seeking guidance for developing classroom programmes.

Adding to this dilemma was the fact that educators in the school sector were unsure of how to interpret a document entitled 'curriculum guidelines'. The more generic meaning of curriculum has been reduced to mean a document constructed in levels with specific objectives, i.e. curriculum now equates to the national curriculum statements.

The general attitudes could be categorised into two groups, those that believed that:

- policy documents sit on shelves and are not used by teachers and guidelines for teaching and learning programmes in environmental education are what the teachers want:
- legitimising environmental education with a Ministry of Education policy document would result in gaining some status for further developments within the whole area, which may include guidelines for implementing environmental education programmes, examples of units, resource development and teacher education programmes.

Accommodating both views was not easy and required a major re-ordering of the document's content so that a context was provided for reflecting current government policy on education and the environment and for giving guidance for implementing environmental education programmes. We highlighted key areas of the document with practical examples to assist teachers who wanted to see 'how' and 'where' environmental education could be a part of the school programme, rather than only emphasising 'why' they should include it.

Dilemma 2: environmental education as separate subject versus multi-disciplinary approach

The second dilemma centred around the notion of environmental education as a block approach or as an infusion model. While many people indicated environmental education should be infused throughout the curriculum, others thought this was a recipe for disaster, as one respondent commented: 'this is a worthy message but in light of the experience of health education over the past decade perhaps over optimistic'. Another respondent directly asked why we hadn't considered the subject approach: 'You mention the integration approach, thematic approach, what about the subject approach to EE'. The cross-curricular thematic approach, while being supported mainly by primary teachers, was questioned by secondary teachers, who focus on a block (subject) approach to teaching. While *The New Zealand Curriculum Framework* is advocating a cross-curricular, thematic and holistic approach, the perception of secondary teachers is that under the present structure this would be difficult. However *The New Zealand Curriculum Framework* under the seven main learning areas does not acknowledge environmental education as a main learning area. Establishing environmental education as a subject area in its own right therefore has limitations within the new framework document. The framework however, clearly identifies environmental education as a major theme that could be infused throughout the curriculum.

The process of critical thinking which resulted from this dilemma highlighted the need to offer options to schools from within the constraints of the curriculum framework document. It should be noted that our personal views could not be reflected in a national document that was to represent the Ministry of Education's position. This resulted in our suggestion that schools who wished to use a block approach formalise a course called environmental education using existing learning outcomes from selected learning areas that related to environmental education. Another suggestion from a member of review group one indicated that: 'a specific learning area may also develop EE programmes and modules in their own right. This will be important in some secondary schools'. For example, a school may wish to establish a course entitled environmental science or environmental health.

Tensions

The tensions that emerged during the writing process were largely due to the multiple perspectives on issues associated with environmental education, lack of appreciation of consultative processes and an apparent lack of understanding of the actual nature of the proposed document, i.e. it was to be an official Ministry of Education publication that was to be signed by the Minister of Education. The document was, of course, influenced by the perspective of the two authors but it was not to be a reflection of our views.

The three major tensions that arose during the consultative process were the result of political issues impacting on the contract. The resolution of these issues lay outside the framework of the writers' contract. While the tensions were dealt with cooperatively between the writers and the Ministry of Education, they highlighted the sensitive and contentious nature of environmental education within the wider political environment.

Tension 1

A number of the responses to the initial draft were very concerned about the lack of apparent 'passion' of the authors: 'The authors need to have a clear and personal vision of what is at stake here, and they need to communicate that vision to the teachers of New Zealand'. However, it was not actually our personal vision that was the issue. Our challenge was to integrate our environmental education understandings within existing government environmental and educational policies. We would acknowledge that the initial draft was certainly more bureaucratic than the final one; but initially we were all too conscious of the need to clearly set the document within existing policy and curricula so that it had a greater chance of being politically acceptable and might be published in a relatively unchanged state.

Tension 2

The draft document was sent to about 100 people and organisations. Much of the feedback was constructive and certainly contributed to the debate between us and informed the many changes we made in the initial draft. Again, there were people who reacted strongly to perceived omissions and did not see the consultative process as an opportunity to contribute. One person rang the Ministry to express his ire that we had not mentioned 'The Resource Management Act', a significant piece of environmental legislation in New Zealand. The complainant was wanting to convey his anger to the Ministry, something that could have been very counter-productive to the viability of the developing document.

Tension 3

A significant area within any environmental development in New Zealand is the Maori perspective. The Treaty of Waitangi recognises the rights of the Maori and this position is given further strength by the fact that the government is a signatory to *The Earth Summit* (Te Puni Kokiri, 1993). The consultation process is always challenged by groups who may have different ways of operating. In this case we were required to work to a very tight time frame and although we were aware that real consultation with the Maori requires face-to-face meetings we relied on written communication only. Even so, it took considerable time to set up a consultative process that ensured that a wide range of perspectives, organisations and people were asked for their contribution. While numerous draft documents were sent out, the feedback was light—supportive but perhaps not really representative. More important, the consultative process was not seen to be owned by the Maori or undertaken in a way that they saw as appropriate. Time will tell if the document is received with some ownership by the Maori who are involved in environmental education through their efforts to manage their own resources.

Conclusions

Education and issues concerning the environment are highly political. The combination of education and the environment offers a particular challenge and this paper highlights the almost irresolvable issues involved in producing guidelines that provide some direction to educators in this field. In particular, it raises the problematic nature of contracting documents that are politically sensitive and combining this with a consultative process where the contractors may not have access to all the potential interest groups. While all this is of great concern, it is encouraging, and somewhat ironic, that the pressure for environmental education is continuing to increase in the non-formal education sector, which is supported by legislation that is environmental, rather than educational.

NOTE

[1] The opinions in this paper are those of the authors and not necessarily those of the Ministry of Education and the Ministry of Education takes no responsibility for the accuracy of the conclusions that the paper reaches.

REFERENCES

MINISTRY OF EDUCATION (1993) *The New Zealand Curriculum Framework* (Wellington, Learning Media).

TE PUNI KIKIRI (1993) *Draft Declaration of the Rights of Indigenous Peoples 1993: background and discussion on key issues* (Wellington, Ministry of Maori Development).

Science: an unreliable friend to environmental education?

MARTIN ASHLEY

SUMMARY   *This article focuses upon the uneasy relationship between science and environmental education. It argues that science probably offers the strongest justification for the adoption of pro-environmental behaviours and policies, but that the relationship between science and environmentalism is strained by conflicts over fundamental values that are apparent in interpretation of the precautionary principle. An understanding of risk and scientific uncertainty is seen as an essential element of citizenship education for a sustainable society. Curriculum design needs to respond to the challenges of living in a risk society. The article argues for changes to the curriculum which lead to a scientific action competence founded in an understanding of the limits of science and an appreciation of the fact that scientists are moral agents who face ethical dilemmas in their work.*

Introduction

The title of this article is derived from Pepper (1996) who describes science as an 'unreliable friend to environmentalism' when he discusses the uneasy relationship that has developed between science and the deeper green wing of environmentalism. This article intends to explore the tensions that exist between environmentalists who espouse causes such as rapid action to reduce greenhouse gas emissions or risks associated with nuclear waste, and scientists who are committed to the principles of reason based upon evidence and a public understanding of this. After considering the nature of the relationship between a science which can appear conservative through its need for sound evidence and an environmentalism which can appear radical through its demands for social and political action, there will be a discussion about how such tensions culminate in the need to invoke value judgements in formulating the precautionary principle. Finally, ways are considered in which science education can move forward as a key partner of environmental education in the light of this.

Some Introductory Thoughts on Friendship and Risk

Pepper's unreliable friendship idea encapsulates the principle that science can be capricious through at one moment supporting the environmentalist's cause whilst at another undermining it. In a similar way, environmentalists sometimes appeal to science for evidence to support their cause, yet at other times are seen to be harshly critical of it when writers such as Capra (1983) or Merchant (1992) attack the whole Baconian project of subjugating nature to humankind's progress.

Magnus Magnusson, in the keynote address to the 1994 Association for Science Conference in Inverness (Magnusson, 1994) described how scientists detect warning signs which tell when the Earth is under stress. 'These signs are discovered, measured and monitored by scientists. They are then analysed and the results made public ...'(p. 8). In this sense, science is a 'friend' to environmentalism. The present levels of political attention given to, for example, the issue of climate change would surely not exist without the substantial input of science. Such scientific explanation is *powerful*, and for this reason, science is potentially not only a friend but also a prized ally of environmentalism. However, scientific explanation is also *provisional*, and herein lies the problem. As Woollacott (1998) reminds us, science must always hold out against absolute conclusions. Science cannot be there, unfailingly allied to the environmentalist's cause, for it must always admit to doubt and alternative possibilities and works, not with certainties, but with probabilities and managed risks.

This uneasy relationship that has thus developed between science and environmentalism crystallises around the *precautionary principle* where the agenda of certain scientists and certain environmentalists may differ. For some environmentalists, particularly those on the deep-green or eco-radical wing, the precautionary principle requires that where there is risk or uncertainty, and the scientific evidence is inconclusive, precautionary action should be guided by value judgements that favour the natural world. It is at this point that the friendship between science and environmentalism becomes strained. Many scientists feel constrained by such considerations as the 'value-free' thesis that seeks to preserve science from contamination by contextual values. Subsequent weaknesses in potential alliances between science and environmentalism are readily exploited by the growing anti-environmentalist movement which also seeks to enlist science as a powerful ally (see, for example, Aldrich-Moodie & Kwong, 1997).

Behind these difficulties lies the legacy of the post-war period of 1945–65 when, as Durant (1998) suggests, science was the consumer's friend. This period was the heyday of deference to the scientific expert. Science had won its 19th century battle for cultural supremacy and, bolstered by astonishing discoveries such as jet-powered aircraft, atomic power and antibiotics was at the apotheosis of its powers as the oracle of all wisdom. The scientific expert was the person who could tell us what to do and shape and guide our behaviour in all circumstances. This, with hindsight, can now be seen to have been an unfortunate period for science. Since 1965, disasters such as DDT, Bopal or Chernobyl have driven an escalating loss of public confidence in science. It is doubtful that, in the year 2000, science remains the consumer's friend to the degree that it was during the 1950s and 1960s.

The crucial point, however, is that it is not so much science that may be in decline as the ideology of technocentric managerialism, the notion that some kind of paternalistic relationship exists between politicians advised by scientific 'experts' and a technologically and scientifically naive general public. Ulrich Beck's seminal analysis of risk society and reflexive modernity (Beck, 1992) has done much to alert scholars to the political consequences of a realisation that science may have gone the way of theology as the infallible guide to what we ought to do. Beck's analysis concerns itself with the equitable distribution of public 'bads' (such as ground water contamination) in a society which is less at the mercy of nature or 'acts of God', but which has created for itself its own risks. Public and democratic responsibility for the management of such risks is seen by Beck as a core element in his vision of reflexivity in a society that has progressed beyond the modernist notion of growing mass consumption on the basis that nobody is responsible for the environmental consequences.

Yet, if it is truly the case that society is in a period of transition to reflexive modernity in which the most difficult dilemmas of the precautionary principle are to be resolved democratically, educators and policy-makers may have a huge task ahead of them. This has been graphically illustrated in the UK recently by the crisis over British beef. The public expectation that a primary role of government was to protect them from risk, in this case from Creutzfeldt-Jacob Disease, (CJD, strongly linked in the public mind with Bovine Spongiform Encephalopathy, the so-called 'mad cow disease' [BSE]), was seriously undermined, and confidence in the joint action of politicians and scientists fell yet further.

As Tindale (1998) has reasoned, the then Conservative Government's assertion that advice about beef would be based upon 'sound science' was hollow and rhetorical. Who, he asks, would suggest that advice about risk should be based upon 'unsound science'? The government's handling of the BSE crisis demonstrated the alarming inadequacy of British politicians in the face of the kind of technologically-generated uncertainty that is the fundamental postulate of Beck's risk society. Central to the BSE crisis was the government's apparent failure even to understand let alone admit to the limits of science. The National Curriculum for England and Wales, in its present form, was conceived by this same government which, grounded in modernism, promoted the notion of science as the ultimate authority. Yet as Giddens (1998) illustrates, this is a lay-person's view of science, it is not the informed view of the community of scientists who are generally far more realistic about risk, uncertainty and the limits of science than politicians whose understanding of science as often as not is gained from the media or even their own memories of school science.

Since the demise of the Major Government, there has come to power in Britain a 'New Labour' which loudly proclaims its commitment to 'modernisation'. Giddens (1998) is cautiously optimistic that Prime Minister Blair understands and is committed to a reflexive modernisation as envisaged by Beck rather than the kind of regression to the modernity of economic growth that was so unfortunately pursued by the Conservatives. Nevertheless, there is little evidence of this in the nature and content of the year 2000 revisions to the English and Welsh National Curriculum. The crisis of British beef is arguably a small, local and relatively inconsequential affair when compared with the potential consequences of rapid and unprecedented (in human history) climate change.

That humanity's response to global climate change might be handled with a comparable degree of competence to the handling of the beef crisis ought surely to figure as one of the highest concerns of citizens. I now proceed to reflect upon the nature of the precautionary principle and the need for an education about this if members of the public are to take more responsibility for their environment, have more realistic expectations of their politicians, and understand better the nature of science.

Values Conflict and the Precautionary Principle

Procrastination over the adoption of precautionary policies in response to the prospect of global warming has been a characteristic of late 20th century politics. O'Riordan's formulation of the precautionary principle 'thoughtful action in advance of scientific proof' (O'Riordan, 1995) would seem to imply a context in which cultural conflict between an inherently conservative science and an inherently impatient eco-radicalism is possible. At the heart of this conflict is the inescapable conclusion that wherever there are conflicts of evidence, or risk and uncertainty are operative, value judgements need to be made in the formulation of policy.

The possibility of policy-making, at whatever level, being dependent upon values rather than rational procedures based upon logical application of scientific knowledge raises the question of relativism. Is scientific knowledge universal and absolute, or is it merely the set of beliefs of a particular social group, the scientific community? In a relativistic world where the beliefs of the scientific community may come into conflict with the beliefs of alternative social groups, such as what one writer has described as the 'technophobic' eco-radical community (Lewis, 1992), a power struggle for the authority on which claims for rightness of action are based might be inevitable. Some scientists prominent in the public eye, such as Richard Dawkins, object to the grounds on which such a power struggle is conducted. In Dawkins' view, the superiority of scientific authority is to be taken as unquestioned (Dawkins, 1995).

Poole (1996) discusses this potential struggle for cultural supremacy and concludes that reactions against grandiose claims that science is the paradigm of rationality and truth are both likely and a threat to science itself. Drawing upon the New Age movement as an alternative set of values, he describes a counter-cultural threat to science which is characterised by the denigration of science itself, an anti-rationalist preference for subjectivism, a relativistic interpretation of knowledge and an orientation to mysticism and holism which paradoxically draws inspiration from pseudoscientific writings about quantum mechanics. Unlike Dawkins (1995), however, Poole admits to the possibility of science having legitimate limits, and to the possibility that there are other valid standards of rationality and other kinds of truth than scientific ones.

Such a view would be concordant with a view that has emerged in the official documentation of the UK government, for example, the National Curriculum Council's 1993 pronouncement that schools 'should encourage their pupils to question the often exaggerated view of the infallibility of science as the only means of understanding the world, and the equally exaggerated view of the inadequacy of religion and philosophy' (NCC, 1993, p. 6). Again, the Schools

Curriculum and Assessment Authority (1995) develop this theme when they claim that 'the perception of science as the only way to understand experience, combined with Enlightenment humanism, had been largely responsible for the demise of the spiritual and moral dimensions of the curriculum' (SCAA, 1995, p. 13). Such statements might be construed as in some ways hostile to science.

One way of understanding these cultural conflicts is to examine the core values that underpin science and eco-radicalism. My contention is that at the heart of both of these cultural communities, there lies what is perceived by the community as an absolute value. This value gives the community its identity and a failure to acknowledge it results in exile from the community. For the community of scientists, the fundamental absolute is a belief in the powerful but provisional nature of scientific truth (Lakatos, 1970; Ruse, 1982; Thagard, 1988). 'Truth', in this context, however, is a dangerous word. The notion that 'the truth' is an abstract object that can be possessed is more probably rooted in pre-20th century theology than 21st century science. Gaukroger (1998), for example, discusses the limits of 'truth' as an absolute value of science and points out that the idea that the value and success of scientific activity is to be explained in terms of its proximity to an abstract conception of 'truth' is deeply problematical. He prefers the concept of justification that he defines as processes that enable us to answer questions in ways that fit the available evidence.

The understanding of truth that this engenders points more towards the processes of science and the value of integrity in relation to those processes. Membership of the community of scientists is dependent upon 'telling the truth' in relation to the available evidence rather than 'possessing the truth'. It is this process-oriented value that lies behind the so-called 'value-free' thesis that is often problematic for science and environmentalism. Curd & Cover (1998) summarise the debate on the value-free thesis by drawing attention to Thomas Kuhn's critical distinction between cognitive and contextual values in science (Kuhn, 1996). Kuhn's cognitive values of accuracy, consistency, scope, simplicity and fruitfulness are process-oriented values that allow us to judge scientific theories. Contextual values, on the other hand, are said to be the norms, beliefs and interests that are unrelated to the cognitive aims of science.

Gross examples of the influence of contextual values might be the continuous attack on relativity theory undertaken by Soviet physicists on the grounds of its incompatibility with the official doctrine of dialectical materialism (Stachel, 1990), or the anti-Semitic bias of German science during the Nazi era. It is a less gross, but still problematical influence of contextual values that so concerns Pepper (1991). There can be little doubt that 'the environment' is a context for scientific activity. Can science, therefore, proceed within this context and be free of contextual values? Pepper is perplexed and sets up a polarity between ecocentric and technocentric science, thereby undermining the notion that there is one kind of 'good' science and raising again the possibility of cultural relativism in science.

The fact that it is possible for scientists publicly to disagree about, for example, the degree to which global warming has human causes, leads Pepper to question the extent to which scientific processes are as objective as sometimes claimed. Surely, he argues, 'objective' processes should have arrived at greater consensus than is often the case with environmental issues? He points out that in the 20th century, the scientific research which was or was not done—and the technological developments which stemmed from it—was essentially selected according to whether or not it supported the ideologies and purposes of particular groups.

How can we know whether 'good' science is being practised, and what kind of environmental science would thus count as 'good' science? Curd & Cover (1998) seem to imply an orthodox view of 'good' science in which the exclusion of contextual values is the ideal. Is this a realistic basis, however, for science to answer some of our most pressing environmental questions? An alternative might be to consider, as does Thagard (1988), the type of transgression that would result in exile from the scientific community and condemnation of one's activities as 'pseudoscience'. A prime candidate for such exile might be Whitcomb & Morris (1961) and their so-called 'creation science'. Creation science can only proceed once its would be practitioners have affirmed their possession of 'the truth' by allegiance to a dogmatically asserted absolute—that creation was a unique and supernatural act. Thagard condemns astrology, Freudian analysis and Marxism as pseudosciences for similar reasons:

> ... the community of practitioners makes little attempt to develop the theory towards solutions of the problems, shows no concern for attempts to evaluate the theory in relation to others, and is selective in considering confirmations and disconfirmations. (p. 32)

Where, then, does environmental science stand? Is it 'good' science, or is it pseudoscience? There are, as Pepper points out, different kinds of environmental science. In discerning 'good' science, however, we might search for the existence of any fundamental absolutes which are prerequisites for community membership and which might be associated with a conflict between cognitive and contextual values. Pepper himself reminds us that to belong to the community of eco-radicals, one must first assent to the absolute value of nature as a guide to all decision-making (Pepper, 1996). He reminds us of the 'deep-green' tendency to define sets of ecological absolutes as referents for all action, whilst remaining either silent or relativist on social issues and dismissive of any form of science or technology which is unrelated to ecological concerns.

For committed eco-radicals, there is no dilemma over the interpretation of the precautionary principle. The belief in the intrinsic value of nature and the inherent 'rightness' of natural processes ensures that a value judgement in favour of the nature preserving option will always be made when determining how the precautionary principle should be interpreted. This provides an attractively (to some) simple solution to an intractably complex problem, much in the way that creationism provides an attractively simple solution to the intractably difficult problem of how we all came into existence and what the purpose of our existence might be. The solutions are simple, and to a degree, workable, but are they authentic?

Masters (1993) extols the virtue of what he calls ancient science. Ancient science seeks to discover the secrets of nature on the grounds that nature cannot be improved and is therefore a model of 'rightness'. We can, according to this view, appeal to the way nature works for guidance about what we ought to do. Szerszynski (1996) however provides a comprehensive analysis of the shortcomings of such an approach. He points out, furthermore, that it is itself a modernist assumption that nature is determinable and describable without reference to human projects and languages. The eco-radical appeal to nature as an absolute model of rightness which therefore can reliably tell us what to do is itself a product of the modernism that assumes scientific knowledge can attain towards a perfectible reflection of natural reality.

The conclusion to which arguments such as these all seem to point is that we cannot escape responsibility for those of our actions that have environmental consequences. Given that so many of these consequences are the result of the way the public has embraced science and its technological products, the public has to develop a more responsible attitude to science. A scientific education for all that is more likely to result in such responsibility therefore has to be a key objective for environmental education. The next section of this article considers ways in which such improvements in scientific education might come about.

Towards Scientific Action Competence in a Risk Society

If we are to provide an authentic education for the 21st century, we will, at some stage, have to recognise that arguments such as those described will need to be presented to pupils. The English and Welsh National Curriculum as it stands is, in practice, a socially reproductive curriculum of 'no change', informed almost exclusively by the political short-term and economic and materialistic aspirations and values of the 20th century. One starting point for the development of a transformative curriculum more likely to lead to a serious political will to move towards sustainability might be the acknowledgement of the partiality of the way in which science is presented by this curriculum.

Relatively few school pupils will ever become acquainted with the anti-science writings of eco-feminists such as Carolyn Merchant (Merchant, 1992), who remain marginal to the dominant ideology of mainstream culture. Almost all pupils, however, are presented with a view of science that is still largely influenced by logical positivism, reductionism and the 'value-free' thesis. It is, furthermore, a curriculum that is driven primarily by the goal of selection for university entry. Little has changed since Bernstein (1971) wrote of his collection code in which the aim of discrete curriculum subjects was to 'socialise' learners into the university driven hierarchy of those subjects. A school science which is geared to the selection, at age 16, of the minority of pupils who will study 'hard' sciences as a preparation for university entry, is unlikely to be a science which is capable of developing those friendships with other disciplines which may be necessary to create educated citizens who can react rationally to the precautionary principle.

What sort of response to this possibility is appropriate from educators? The most fundamental point of this article is that it cannot be a technophobic or anti-scientific response. Curriculum designers are right to be wary of capitulating to any of the relativist, subjectivist or anti-rationalist pressures from eco-radical idealists. A 'more-of-the-same' approach to the science of modernism, however, would be equally inappropriate. The science of reflexive modernity is a science of uncertainty and a science with limits. It is, moreover, an inherently more democratic form of science. It is not the science of university researchers who see no need to communicate with the public, nor the science of technocentric managerialism in which 'experts' tell the politicians what to do.

If there are to be acknowledged limits to science, however, the curriculum needs to reflect appropriate responses to this. This means a curriculum that prepares for responsible participation in a democracy in which public competence in ethical reasoning and moral responsibility complement the public understanding of science. In constructing such a curriculum, we need to be alert to the fact that, whilst there are regressive voices that desire, for whatever reason, to reassert the science of modernity, there are equally voices that call for regression in the field of ethics and morality. Blake (1997) demonstrates convincingly that much of the recent furore over the desire to include spiritual and moral development in the UK National Curriculum is rooted in a naive desire to regress to the imagined golden age of premodern ethics. The criticisms by SCAA (1995) of rational humanism associated with the Enlightenment have led some to argue that the response must be to rediscover or reassert what existed before the Enlightenment.

He continues to argue that ethical decisions about how we should live need a political dimension grounded in the reflexive analysis of risk and uncertainty. This is the reality for which the curriculum must prepare pupils. What might such a curriculum look like? Millar & Osborne (1998) have proposed significant changes to the science curriculum. They point out that many young people perceive the purpose of the scientific endeavour substantially in terms of its technological products, whilst remaining ignorant of the value and values of science outlined at some length earlier in this article. They are critical of the grounding of the present curriculum in the process of selection for higher study and argue instead for a curriculum, up to age 16, of general scientific literacy made accessible through what they call 'explanatory stories'.

By this term, they mean that science has an account to offer in response to questions such as 'How do we catch diseases?' It is possible, they argue, to answer such questions in accessible narrative form without degradation of the quality of scientific knowledge. They contend that a narrow focus on detail, further obscured by a numerical rather than narrative approach, has led to science education losing sight of the major ideas that science has to tell. They aim, amongst other things, to teach pupils why scientific ideas are valued and how scientific ideas underlie the rationale behind decision-making in such areas as personal diet, medical problems or energy use.

There are likely to be hazards in experimentation with a story-based science curriculum, however, not least because science is not the whole story. The precautionary principle is, after all, an acknowledgement of the limits of science. Ultimately, it needs to be clear to pupils where the boundaries of scientific knowledge and ethical responsibility in the face of uncertainty lie. Wittingly or unwittingly, the possibility of a subjective bias reflecting the culture or politics of the science storyteller is likely to be greater, and ultimately the authority of science thereby diminished.

Jickling & Spork (1998) have recently critiqued education for the environment, and their exposure of the degree to which practices akin to little more than indoctrination have become common is alarming. Some means of guarding against a passive approach in which the pupil is simply the recipient of the values and world view of the storyteller, however well intentioned, is needed.

Bishop & Scott (1998) argue for what they describe as scientific action competence. They draw on Brickhouse et al. (1993) in acknowledging that most school science is firmly rooted in positivistic philosophies with the consequence that little attention is paid to aspects of science education relating to the development of competence. They quote the example of the development of a school compost heap in order to investigate the effect of moisture and nutrient input on the rate of compost production and the quality of the end product. They claim that, through this, the environmental problem of the waste of organic materials within the school is resolved, and that pupils can follow a formal scientific investigation.

The greatest potential of an action competency model is probably to be found in the way it creates the need for scientific knowledge to address a genuine environmental problem perceived by the pupils. Another example cited is the creation of a school wildlife pond, where scientific action competence is necessary to create a stable ecological community. There remains, however, a gap between school compost heaps and ponds, however worthy these may be, and global issues such as climate change.

That this gap needs some kind of bridging is illustrated graphically by new research currently under design at the University of the West of England, Bristol. In preliminary questioning of 11 year-old pupils about whether they will face any risks associated with global warming, 40.4% of respondents so far agreed that 'there might be a slight risk but that it's so far in the future it's not worth worrying about'. This compares with the next highest category where 36.1% rated that there is 'enough risk to justify everybody having good lessons about it at school'. Early indications of work with older pupils would seem to indicate that the first view is also likely to feature strongly in the thinking of these pupils.

How, then, can this challenge be addressed without reverting to crude behaviourism or largely discredited forms of moral persuasion through exaggerated threat? The approach currently under investigation at UWE is that of the development of pupil-scientist partnerships. The aim is to bridge the gap between 'school science' where, it would appear, the notion of truth possession and certainty would seem still to dominate the prescribed curriculum and the world of 'real science', where risk, uncertainty and limits to knowledge are increasingly regarded as the norm. If, in pursuing this goal, pupils are brought into contact with practising scientists and, through this come to the realisation that scientists themselves have moral principles and are frequently confronted in their work by ethical dilemmas, then steps towards a curriculum for reflexive modernity may well have been taken.

A priority in the UK identified by the New Labour Government, which came to power in 1997, is the linking together of schools, libraries and other educational organisations via a government-sponsored national computer network known as the National Grid for Learning. When universal access to this is achieved, highly significant technological developments such as 'new literacies' and a communicative capacity that brings the community of school pupils into a hitherto unimagined contact with the community of scientists may be achieved. The possibilities for the development of extended scientific action competence through partnerships between scientists and school pupils are exciting. A crucial difference between the original Habermas view of communicative competence (Habermas, 1984, 1987) and the emerging Beck view of risk society is the possibility of the emergence of the ethics of reflexive modernity through the creation of a new shared understanding. School pupils may not be able to halt the processes of climate change, but they will be able to participate in the process of setting priorities for adapting to climate change (Smith, 1997).

They will participate with their eyes open and they will know that global warming is not a problem for the generation after them but a responsibility they share with the community of scientists now. Perhaps then, their expectations of politicians will change, and the decline in political interest amongst the young that so troubled the authors of the Crick Report (Crick, 1998) will be reversed.

Conclusion

If the present National Curriculum is allowing significant numbers of pupils to grow up with the view that global warming is a problem far in the future which need not trouble them, then there is some doubt that these pupils are being prepared for adult life in the 21st century. Preparation for adult life in the 21st century has to include an element of risk literacy and an understanding of the limits of science. It also has to include an education in the philosophy, values clarification and citizenship skills that will be needed for competent and responsible participation in a risk society. Whilst writers such as Wynne (1992) usefully remind us, science has in the past been its own worst enemy in promoting the modernist cult of the technocratic managerial elite, the time has surely come to end any estrangement of science and environmental concern.

A new vision for a National Curriculum is needed. This will be a vision of a curriculum for a 21st century of reflexive modernity. It will not have much place for the yearnings for regression to modernity in science and premodernity in ethics that have characterised the closing decades of the 20th century. It will promote the public understanding of science and its limits as a vital function of effective and full democratic citizenship. It will use new communications technologies to forge friendships between the community of scientists and the community of school pupils. Through such new friendships it will develop the humility and respect towards the created world that the eco-radical community has sought for so long. There is no reason why socio-cultural sources of environmental concern as diverse as romanticism or religious belief cannot be part of this, for scientists can be romantics or religious believers as well as scientists. Perhaps, then, even the eco-radical community may one day be included in this new friendship.

REFERENCES

ALDRICH-MOODIE, B. & KWONG, J. (1997) *Environmental Education* (London, Institute of Economic Affairs).

BECK, U. (1992) *Risk Society, Towards a New Modernity* (London, Sage).

BERNSTEIN, B. (1971) On the classification and framing of educational knowledge, in: M. YOUNG (Ed.) *Knowledge & Control: new directions for the sociology of education* (London, Collier MacMillan).

BISHOP, K. & SCOTT, W. (1998) Deconstructing action competence: developing a case for more scientifically-attentive environmental education, *Public Understanding of Science*, 7(3), pp. 225–236.

BLAKE, N. (1997) Spirituality, anti-intellectualism, and the end of civilisation as we know it, in: R. SMITH & P. STANDISH (Eds) *Teaching Right and Wrong: moral education in the balance* (London, Trentham).

BRICKHOUSE, N., STANLEY, W. & WHITSON, J. (1993) Practical reasoning and science education: implications for theory and practice, *Science and Education*, 2(4), pp. 363–375.

CAPRA, F. (1983) *The Turning Point: science, society and the rising culture* (London, Flamingo).

CRICK, B. (Chairman) (1998) *Education for Citizenship and the Teaching of Democracy in Schools* (London, QCA).

CURD, M. & COVER, J. (1998) *Philosophy of Science: the central issues* (London, Norton).

DAWKINS, R. (1995) *River Out of Eden* (Oxford, Oxford University Press).

DURANT, J. (1998) Once the men in white coats held the promise of a better future ... in: J. FRANKLIN (Ed.) *The Politics of Risk Society* (Cambridge, Polity Press).

GAUKROGER, S. (1998) Justification, truth and the development of science, *Studies in History and Philosophy of Science*, 29A(1), pp. 97–112.

GIDDENS, A. (1998) Risk Society: the context of British politics, in: J. FRANKLIN (Ed.) *The Politics of Risk Society* (Cambridge, Polity Press).

HABERMAS, J. (1984) *Theory of Communicative Action. Vol. 1. Reason and the Rationalisation of Society* (Cambridge, Polity Press).

HABERMAS, J. (1987) *Theory of Communicative Action. Vol. 2. Lifeworld and System: a critique of functionalist reason* (Cambridge, Polity Press).

JICKLING, B. & SPORK, H. (1998) Education for the environment: a critique, *Environmental Education Research*, 4(3), pp. 309–327.

KUHN, T. (1996) *The Structure of Scientific Revolutions*, 3rd edn (Chicago, University of Chicago Press).

LAKATOS, I. (1970) Falsification and the methodology of scientific research programmes, in: I. LAKATOS & A. MUSGRAVE (Eds) *Criticism and the Growth of Knowledge* (Cambridge, Cambridge University Press).

LEWIS, M. (1992) *Green Delusions: an environmentalist critique of radical environmentalism* (Durham, Duke University Press).

MAGNUSSON, M. (1994) I've started so I'll finish. Keynote address to ASE Scotland Conference, Inverness, *Education in Science*, 163, June 1995, pp. 8–10.

MASTERS, R. (1993) *Beyond Relativism: science and human values* (London, University Press of New England).

MERCHANT, C. (1992) *Radical Ecology* (New York, Routledge).

MILLAR, R. & OSBORNE, J. (1998) *Beyond 2000: science education for the future* (London, King's College School of Education).

NATIONAL CURRICULUM COUNCIL (1993) *Spiritual and Moral Development: a discussion paper* (London, HMSO).

O'RIORDAN, T. (1995) Environmental science on the move, in: T. O'RIORDAN (Ed.) *Environmental Science for Environmental Management* (Harlow, Longman).

PEPPER, D. (1991) *The Roots of Modern Environmentalism* (London, Routledge).

PEPPER, D. (1996) *Modern Environmentalism. An introduction* (London, Routledge).

POOLE, M. (1996) *Beliefs and Values in Science Education* (Buckingham, Open University Press).

RUSE, M. (1982) *Darwinism Defended: a guide to the evolution controversies* (Reading, PA, Addison-Wesley).

SCHOOLS CURRICULUM AND ASSESSMENT AUTHORITY (1995) *Education for Adult Life: the spiritual and moral development of young people* (London, DfEE).

SMITH, J.B. (1997) Setting priorities for adapting to climate change, *Global Environmental Change*, 7(3), pp. 251–264.

STACHEL, J. (1990) The theory of relativity, in: R. OLBY, G. CANTOR, J. CHRISTIE & M. HODGE (Eds) *Companion to the History of Modern Science* (London, Routledge).

SZERSZYNSKI, B. (1996) On knowing what to do, in: S. LASH, B. SZERSZYNSKI & B. WYNNE (Eds) *Risk, Environment & Modernity: towards a new ecology* (London, Sage).

THAGARD, P. (1988) Pseudoscience, Chapter 9, in: *Computational Philosophy of Science* (Cambridge, MA, MIT Press).

TINDALE, S. (1998) Procrastination, precaution and the global gamble, in: J. FRANKLIN (Ed.) *The Politics of Risk Society* (Cambridge, Polity Press).

WHITCOMB, J. & MORRIS, H. (1961) *The Genesis Flood: the biblical record and its scientific implications* (Michegan, Grand Rapids).

WOOLLACOTT, M. (1998) Risky business, safety, in: J. FRANKLIN (Ed.) *The Politics of Risk Society* (Cambridge, Polity Press).

WYNNE, B. (1992) Misunderstood misunderstanding: social identities and the public uptake of science, *Public Understanding of Science*, 1(3), pp. 281–304

On the need to repoliticise environmental and sustainability education: rethinking the postpolitical consensus

Louise Sund and Johan Öhman

This article draws attention to the possibilities of the ongoing philosophical discussion about cosmopolitan universal values in relation to the normative challenges in environmental and sustainability education (ESE). The purpose of this paper is to clarify the philosophical problems of addressing universally sustainable responsibilities and values in ESE. Our arguments draw inspiration from the work of three poststructuralist scholars: we explore how Butler develops her claim that universal assertion requires a cultural translation, how Mouffe exposes the political in universal claim and how Todd argues that education needs to introduce students to a political language that enables them to critically reflect on their own and other groups' values and actions. In the concluding part, we suggest the following guidelines for rethinking ESE: unmasking the political dimension, re-politicising education, seeing beyond the relativist and objectivist divide and using passion as a moving force.

Introduction

For decades, attention has been drawn to the normativity of an environmental and sustainability education (ESE) that bases its understanding on and embraces universal aspects and ethical ideals. The problem with universal values and how to address them is neither new nor unique for the field of ESE. Such a discussion can also be found in current debates in related disciplines such as cultural studies (Andreotti 2006), climate change ethics (Gardiner 2004), environmental ethics (Kronlid and Öhman 2013) and feminist ethics (Todd 2009a).

Especially, within the philosophical perspective of cosmopolitanism[1] and cosmopolitan education, there has been considerable debate about the relation between universal claims and cultural and human diversity.[2] In response to this debate, feminist philosopher Butler (1995, 1996, 2000a, 2000b), political theorist Mouffe (1993, 1996, 2000, 2005, 2008) and educational philosopher Todd (2003, 2008, 2009a, 2009b, 2010) have developed vital critique of universal claims from poststructural perspectives and have also suggested alternative ways of dealing with the new global challenges. The *purpose* of this paper is to clarify the philosophical problem of addressing universally sustainable responsibilities and values in ESE. Our arguments draw inspiration from the work of these poststructuralist scholars.

From a poststructural perspective, there is no ground separated from human practice that we can turn to in order to find criteria for our values. The difficulty of finding a final ground does not mean that there is no need for universal values. On the contrary, Laclau (1996) – to whom Butler, Mouffe and Todd relate in different ways – holds that the universal is absolutely essential for any kind of *political* interaction and explains that 'the impossibility of universal ground does not eliminate its need: it just transforms the ground into an empty place which can partially be filled in a variety of ways (the strategies of this filling is what politics is about)' (158). In other words, universal ideals and values cannot be abandoned, because they are essential aspects of political life.

In what follows, we explore how Butler develops her claim that universal assertion requires a cultural translation, how Mouffe exposes the political in universal claim and how Todd argues for the need to introduce students to a political language that enables them to critically reflect on their own and other groups' values and actions.

We argue that the critique of Butler, Mouffe and Todd enhances and extends previous contributions to discussions about universalism and normativity in ESE by offering a radical and political critique of universal values without abounding the practical need for such values. In the concluding part of the article, we therefore suggest a number of guidelines for an ESE practice which constitutes an alternative to a values education that is driven by and strives to inculcate preconceived universal values by repoliticising education and dealing with universal values as part of the educational process.

Normative challenges in ESE

A global and future-oriented ethics[3] can be discerned in international policy documents concerning environmental and sustainable issues and education, for example, the Brundtland Report (World Commission on Environment and Development 1987) and others. Several of these documents bear traces of cosmopolitan universalism and rational morality. One example is the Earth Charter (2000), with its fundamental ethical principles for building a sustainable and shared society, which has had a strong impact on ESE. The global network, the Earth Charter Initiative, was both an important influence on and an active partner of United Nations Educational, Scientific and Cultural Organization (UNESCO) in supporting the UN Decade of Education for Sustainable Development (2005–2014). Although there are no explicit references to the Charter, it is clear that the Johannesburg Declaration (World Summit on Sustainable Development [WSSD] 2002) borrows language from the Charter on the theme 'Making it happen': 'We commit ourselves to act together, united by a common determination to save our planet, promote human development and achieve universal prosperity and peace' (Paragraph 35, WSSD 2002). In 2003, UNESCO adopted a resolution that recognised the Earth Charter (2000) as an important ethical framework for sustainable development. The charter suggests that:

> [W]e must decide to live with a sense of universal responsibility, identifying ourselves with the whole Earth community as well as our local communities. We are at once citizens of different nations and of one world in which the local and global are linked. Everyone shares responsibility for the present and future well-being of the human family and the larger living world.

The UNESCO report, *Universalism and ethical values for the environment* (2010), adds to the idea of establishing 'a framework for pluralist environmental values' and concludes that there are possibilities of finding common values and even universally agreed ethics through dialogue among 'cultural communities' with different value systems, ethical outlooks and contrasting ways of living together.

Based on the above brief description of some of the important policy documents, ESE can be regarded as an 'ethical education' that embraces universal aspects and concepts (Sund and Öhman 2011) or, as described by Schlottmann (2008), 'education with the adoption of an ethical framework as its aim' (208). However, we see problems with such an education – on two interlinked counts. First, it renews a classical *democratic problem* – whether or not the state should promote certain 'desirable' values through compulsory education. Second, it also brings to the fore an *ethical problem* – whether or not there is any external foundation for our values. Also, if values are culturally contextual and variable – are educators and education policy-makers then left with relativist positions and arguments? In the following, we expand on how these two problems have been addressed in the ESE research debate.

The democratic problem

The relationship between democracy and education has concerned philosophers and educationalists since ancient times. This issue has also been thoroughly dealt with by democratic theorists like Dewey (1916/1980), Gutmann (1987), Englund (2000), Säfström and Biesta (2001), and more recently by Biesta (2011). The democratic problem is here defined as the paradox between the double educational assignment to foster free, autonomous subjects and at the same time transfer particular ethical values and dispositions to future generations.

Several debaters have highlighted the democratic problem that is associated with an ESE practice based on a specific ethics.

In the 1990s, a debate about the nature and purpose of the ESE field occurred where some researchers criticised socially critical accounts of strong democracy 'for the environment' in education (cf. Jickling 1992; Jickling and Spork 1998; Sauvé 1999). Jickling and Spork (1998) described education for the environment as indoctrination for a particular social vision and they argued that such an approach to education does not handle values issues professionally and has universalising tendencies that seek to marginalise other approaches. In a response, Fien (2000) argued that their critique overlooks many philosophical and pedagogical aspects of socially critical approaches to education and that education informed by critical theory has a central political role to play in helping to create more sustainable forms of development.

In a similar philosophical line of thinking, Payne (1997, 133) argued that 'the locus of understanding, explanation and praxis "for the environment" should be "in here, with me and you" rather than "out there, somewhere, to be found, identified, studied and solved"'. Payne's claim for embodied, situated and direct environmental learning experiences is an important reminder that environmental problems are not only philosophical but also practical since people, through their everyday actions (in the community, the classroom, the home, etc.) and interaction with the environment, are part of these issues.

Fundamental discussions about normativity and whether it is possible for a liberal state to conduct or promote specific environmental and sustainable values in compulsory education without it conflicting with the assumption of its neutrality have been spearheaded by researchers like Dobson (2003), Bell (2004), Hailwood (2005) and Schinkel (2009). For example, Schinkel (2009, 509) asks: 'if the state is to abstain from endorsing or favouring particular conceptions of the good life, can it legitimately make compulsory for all schools a type of education that explicitly tries to *form* rather than just inform pupils?'.

Jickling and Wals (2008) respond to this question with a definite 'no' when it comes to what they call the 'expert-driven' concept of education for sustainable development (ESD) as presented by UNESCO. In ESD, they discern a homogenising tendency that promotes a neo-liberal agenda. The authors criticise consensus thinking as an approach to complex issues like sustainable development in an educational practice, because they contend that it would only have an opposite effect on education. Jickling and Wals accordingly claim that ESD turns education into a political tool that promotes a certain ideology which excludes other possibilities and, thus, leaves less space for action and autonomous thinking. Educational philosopher Biesta (2011) follows a similar line of thinking in his reflections on citizenship education in countries around the world. Biesta sees a tendency for education to be mobilised by policy-makers in order to promote certain knowledge claims about what a good citizen is, and what and how individuals need to learn to become good citizens. Biesta argues that if these knowledge claims are seen as relatively uncontested, there is a risk that education will lead to a 'domestication' of citizens, that is, individuals learn a particular knowledge and the task of education is merely to reproduce the existing political order.

In response to normative approaches, several authors have claimed that participatory perspectives should be a significant feature of ESE (see Öhman and Öhman 2013). Participatory approaches focus on a communicative turn (cf. Säfström 1999; Englund, Öhman, and Östman 2008) and the democratic mission of an education that involves diverse interest groups, supports free opinion-making and enhances students' competences to act (cf. Fien 1995; Huckle 1999; Jensen and Schnack 2006; Lundegård and Wickman 2007; Vare and Scott 2007; Jickling and Wals 2008; Öhman 2008, 2009). These claims are largely in line with an educational approach to environmental and sustainability issues that is regarded as pluralistic. A pluralistic tradition can be seen as a postfoundational (Stables 2001; Marchart 2007) perspective on normative approaches which argues that society cannot be grounded in a final foundation. Such a perspective is characterised by an effort to mirror the variety of opinions on sustainability informing the contemporary debate about different questions and problems relating to the future of our world.

To some extent, the participatory turn in education solves the democratic problem, although we are still faced with what we refer to as the ethical problem in education when addressing questions of universalism.

The ethical problem

The ethical problem concerns the philosophical difficulty of finding reliable arguments for the existence of an external and eternal foundation to which we can anchor our moral beliefs. One aspect of this ethical problem lies in what Bernstein (1983, 16) refers to as Cartesian anxiety: the fear of a complete relativism if the right and the good are arbitrary constructions. From a pragmatist perspective, both Bernstein (1983) and Rorty (1980, 1982/2003) have criticised this either-or dichotomy and the search for a fixed foundation for our knowledge. Rorty (1980, 178) argued that 'there is no way to get outside our beliefs and our language' and from this follows that 'the True and the Right are matters of social practice'. Later Rorty (1982/2003, xix) also said that we cannot 'step outside our skins', criticising attempts to get back behind language to find something which 'grounds' it. Rorty thus stresses the difficulty of neglecting particular differences and the lived realities of individuals and claiming that universal values and norms are independent of particular practices.

Within the field of ESE, this is not a new problem. Ten years ago, Gough (2002, 1233) addressed similar terrain when he problematised 'what do environmental educators *mean* when they say they are "thinking globally"' (1217) – a phrase that he claimed was coined in the 1970s and became a self-evident truth 10 years later. Deploying feminist and postcolonial scholars, he criticises the position that a culturally transcendent environmental science is possible and instead suggests 'that "thinking globally" in science and environmental education might best be understood as a process of creating transnational "spaces" in which scholars from different localities collaborate in reframing and decentring their own knowledge traditions and negotiate trust in each other's contributions to their collective work'(Gough 2002, 1233). Lotz-Sisitka and Schudel (2007) add to the debate about the postmodern critique of universalising approaches in education because, like Gough, they see that discussions about values and ethics in education also concern the environmental education research field: 'The contours of the debate on how values education should be approached in environmental education presents an ongoing site of struggle as educators seek to find ways of engaging with normative, value-based questions in ways that are not (a) utopianist /universalising, or (b) relativist and situated' (249).

A similar struggle to that mentioned by Lotz-Sisitka and Schudel is also possible to discern in the tension between the universal and the particular. The contextuality of ESD-related issues and the importance of using non-western values and traditions to inform the development of ESD curricula is described by Wals (2009, 16), who underlines that:

> Although both the challenge of sustainable development and the call for ESD is worldwide, there is a general understanding that the local realities and manifestations of 'unsustainability' are often quite different and deeply rooted in local histories and political and cultural traditions.

Using this same line of thinking, McKenzie (2012) highlights the problem of educational sustainability policies that articulate that 'we' supposedly share a vision for a sustainable future without considering or exploring how ways of life are constructed locally in relation to places, their inhabitants, their histories and their futures. 'Rather than an assumed global "common sense", this requires local "good sense" enabled through a more careful exploration of the interscaler relationships of people to place/space' (McKenzie 2012, 171). McKenzie also points to the problem that the critique that has been raised so far revolves around failures related to the implementation of universally desirable goals in international agreements and that little attention has been directed to critical policy studies and alternative educational forms and processes in sustainability education:

what needs to be critiqued is not that everyone should have access to quality education, but rather the assumptions of what it should entail, and that it should necessarily be institutionalized, print-based, individualistic, and otherwise promoting western and neoliberal values. (168)

The above scholars within the ESE research field all relate to the ethical problem, in that their positions revolve around a number of philosophical questions: Is there a set of values that can be defended and justified as universal? How, in that case, do universal values relate to local commitments and concerns deeply rooted in tradition? And what role should universal values play in the field of ESE? These philosophical questions are important to relate to, since they have implications for how we teach sustainable issues that inevitably involve conflicting values and interests (cf. Lundegård and Wickman 2007).

The ethical problem also points to an increasing need for a nuanced framework for ethical analyses. In a recent edition of this journal, Kronlid and Öhman (2013) suggested an environmental ethical conceptual framework that facilitates environmental ethical analyses within ESE which 'acknowledges the complexities of environmental moral conundrums that all students face' (1). Among other things, they argue that such a framework can provide researchers with opportunities for comparative reflections on various environmental ethics positions.

As argued previously, ESE is based on principles that underlie sustainability (UNESCO 2005), which means that such an education can easily end up in universal ideals. Here, we can see parallels with the cosmopolitan idea that there are universal values and a morality that we all share. Below we outline a qualified, philosophical discussion concerning universal and particular values that has been taking place for many years within the perspective of cosmopolitanism. This discussion is important in order to understand the radical and political critique of universal approaches in education that we will later elaborate on. We begin this enquiry by briefly introducing the approaches to cosmopolitan education suggested by the philosopher and cosmopolitan educator Martha Nussbaum, a defender of a strong cosmopolitan universalism in education, and by the philosopher Appiah (2005, 2006), who stresses that local customs and beliefs are to be respected in so far as they do not conflict with a minimal (but essential) set of universal moral principles. We then turn to the poststructural and feminist criticism that has addressed the effects and limits of universalism and emphasised the political in the articulation of universal claims.

A cosmopolitan move in education

The term cosmopolitanism has been used since the Classical Greek era to describe the idea that all human beings belong to a single community. Also, in education, there has been an increase in the number of programmes and approaches that reintroduce 'the citizen of the world' as the education ideal (cf. Nussbaum 1997, 2010; Appiah 2005, 2006; Hansen 2008; Kemp 2011). Nussbaum (2010) argues for an education that cultivates certain capacities and addresses cultural blind spots, which, she claims, requires a normative view of how human beings ought to relate to one another. In other words, good education has a democratic purpose and promotes certain universal values. This claim has led to a debate between those who defend universal values in education and those who take a more critical position. A more intermediate stance towards cosmopolitan universalism is taken by Appiah (2005), who recommends a version he calls rooted cosmopolitanism. In *Cosmopolitanism* (2006), he names this position as partial cosmopolitanism, which is an intertwining of two strands: the recognition of our responsibility for *every human being* (the vast abstract humanity) and that we should value *particular human lives* (since human beings are different and we can learn from each others' differences) (xv). According to Appiah, the problem with universal cosmopolitanism is that it appeals to universality over locality and to Appiah there is no conflict between local partialities and universal morality (xviii). Appiah's rooted cosmopolitanism appears to suggest that it does not have to be either/or, but that you can both be a part of your local place and a part of a broader cosmopolitan community. In this sense, Appiah takes a more critical stance towards universal cosmopolitanism than Nussbaum. Appiah (2006) also reminds us that we cannot reach a final consensus on values, since some are – and should be – universal and some are local, and the model he advocates is that of conversations between people. Conversation has particular implications for education and here Appiah advocates a 'cosmopolitan curiosity', that is, that we take an interest in other people's lives and arguments – not in order to come to any agreement but because this will help us get to know the other person. His advice is to start with the things that people share in a cross-cultural conversation: 'We can learn from one another; or we can simply be intrigued by alternative ways of thinking, feeling, and acting' (97).

According to its critics, there are important problems with the above type of cosmopolitan move in education. Pourgouris (2010) sees two problems. The first is that it is based on idealism – the bottom line in Appiah's reasoning is that we share enough to overcome human differences in that we agree on certain universal values. Thus, Appiah believes that we will eventually arrive at a number of shared beliefs if we are given the chance to engage with others. The second problem is that if Appiah's cosmopolitanism is to work, it must always depend on the nation to respect local traditions. Pourgouris (2010) claims that, however, noble such a position might seem, it negates the existing and real friction between the 'cosmos' and the 'nation'. Strand (2010) also illustrates how Appiah's moral cosmopolitanism, which is grounded in liberalism, advocates commitment towards a global social contract and is prescriptive as to how universal values can unite us across our differences.

A development of the criticism offered by Pourgouris and Strand can be found in the feminist and poststructural critique of the universal ideals of cosmopolitanism and cosmopolitan education. In the remainder of this article, we draw inspiration from the writings of Judith Butler and Chantal Mouffe and argue for an emphasis on the political nature of articulating values. We will also follow Sharon Todd, who focuses on what is at stake in the *process* of learning from otherness and emphasises the importance of disagreement in educational practice. By deepening the philosophical criticism of universal claims, Butler, Mouffe and Todd – together with scholars who add to their debate – offer ways of dealing with the ethical dilemma. By drawing on Butler, Mouffe and Todd, our aim is to problematise the difficulties of warranting universal values and to suggest ways out of relativism.

Radical and political critique of universal values in education

Rethinking universality in society

One of the most important critics to challenge universal and abstract claims is Judith Butler, who has written extensively on feminism, political philosophy and ethics. The core of Butler's argument is that universal concept cannot be understood as separate from power relations circulating in society. Butler (2000a) sees that there is a dual perspective, or a mutual exchange between the universal and the particular, and that universal claim is contaminated precisely by the concretion from which it seeks to differentiate itself (19). Connecting power relations to the processes of exclusion/inclusion, Butler argues that in an attempt to name what is common to all, universality requires the exclusion and negation of the particularity (the specific and living) on which it rests.

The implication of Butler's view of assimilating the particular into the universal is that a transcultural notion of the universal will be stained by the cultural norms it intends to transcend. No claim to universality can be made outside cultural norms, and therefore, the universal is culturally variable (Butler 1996). From this, it follows that 'there is no cultural consensus on an international level about what ought and ought not to be a claim to universality, who may make it, and what form it ought to take' (2000a, 35).

What Butler (2000a) points to here is a paradox of universality, where the universal is always articulated in a particular context, and she argues that an articulation of the universal is a political claim – it is neither exclusively universal nor exclusively particular. The way to relate a particular claim to one that is universal is not by a violent clash between them, but rather one of 'establishing *practices of translation* among competing notions of universality' (Butler 2000b, 167). In the act of translation, the one who has been excluded from the universal concept will haunt the concept until it changes. Butler (2000a, 11) further explains 'that haunting becomes politically effective precisely in so far as the return of the excluded forces an expansion and rearticulation of the basic premises of democracy itself'. Through the practice of *cultural translation* – a term borrowed from Bhabha (1994) – the universal claim is scrutinised and 'the alterity within the norm' is exposed, and this pressure and challenge from outside finally leads to a rearticulation of the universal claim (Butler 1996, 50).

Considering the problem of universality, Butler finds that this opens up a new possibility, namely a contingent and open process of translation that can be regarded as a democratic struggle. In this sense, the act of cultural translation can bring about something politically new as it exposes the limits of the dominant perspective of society.

Butler is seen as a strong interrogator of metaphysical foundations and even as an anti-universalist by her strongest critics (Nussbaum 1999). This, we believe, misunderstands Butler's framing of the debate that the universal is culturally variable. Foundations are not something that we can, or should, do away with. On the contrary, in an answer to Nussbaum (Butler 1996), and in the essay *Contingent Foundations* (1995),[4] she both claims and explains that:

> The point is not to do away with foundations, or even to champion a position that goes under the name of antifoundationalism. Both of those positions belong together as different versions of foundationalism and the sceptical problematic it engenders. Rather,

the task is to interrogate what the theoretical move that establishes foundations *authorizes* and what precisely it excludes or forecloses. (Butler 1995, 39)

What Butler is saying here is that the difficulty of substantiating the universal does not mean that there is no foundation, but rather that we have to try to relieve the term universality of its foundationalist weight and instead see it as politically produced and contingent.

Exposing the political dimension of democratic politics

In her critique of a 'postpolitical' world and a striving for universal consensus, Chantal Mouffe (2005) is, like Butler, a strong critic of cosmopolitan visions. Her main point is that we have to face our society in a *political* way. By that she means grasping its pluralistic character and the conflicts that pluralism entails, and not ducking for dissent, conflicting values and interests. For that reason, Mouffe (2008) warns against the illusion of a cosmopolitan project and of establishing global acceptance of universal values and a 'dream of unification of a world achieved by transcending the political, conflict and negativity' (465).

By the political, Mouffe (2005) refers to the dimension of antagonism that is inherent in human relations and society; the 'pluriverse' we inhabit (cf. Lyotard 1984). Mouffe (1996) claims that a democratic society will never be free of antagonism and without exclusions and says that it is an illusion to think that it is possible to establish a 'we' that does not imply the existence of a 'them'. Once we accept that, we can envisage democratic politics in different ways.

Here, we can see parallels with Butler's (2000a) thoughts about exclusion/inclusion. Butler and Mouffe both claim that there is no consensus without exclusion, no norm without an exception – only by defining a 'they' can a 'we' be established. Like Butler, Mouffe (2000, 2005) questions a political foundation that believes in the possibility of rational thinking that tries to establish a sphere of consensus without exclusion. Such ideas hide the political dimension and thus forego the political process. Alternatively, they both claim that political foundations must be contested, because it is impossible for all diverse values to be reconciled. They also acknowledge conflict and dissensus as important features of the political.

If this is the critique of some form of realisation of a cosmopolitan vision, what kind of model does Mouffe advocate? In *The Democratic Paradox* (2000), Mouffe develops her idea of an agonistic model of democracy, where on the one hand she makes clear the key role of conflict and on the other hand underlines the limits of pluralism. In *On the Political* (2005), she clarifies that:

> The agonistic approach does not pretend to encompass all differences and to overcome all forms of exclusions. But exclusions are envisaged in political and not in moral terms. Some demands are excluded, not because they are declared to be 'evil', but because they challenge the institutions constitutive of the democratic political association. (Mouffe 2005, 120f.)

Here, Mouffe (2005) argues for 'a shared symbolic place' (121), where opponents confront each other in a democratic debate. She also defends her position by explaining that: 'adversaries do fight – even fiercely – but according to a shared set of rules, and their positions, despite being ultimately irreconcilable, are accepted as legitimate perspectives' (52). Disagreement between adversaries with whom we share a common adhesion to the principles of liberty and equality – but differ as to how these ideals can and should be fulfilled – is both necessary and important Mouffe (2005) holds and underlines the repoliticisation of the conflictual perspective and argues that a problem nowadays is that the difference between us 'is being played out in the moral register' rather than being political (75).

A central aspect of Mouffe's (2005) approach is the crucial role of passion as the moving force in politics. Mouffe criticises a democratic model that wants to regulate passion to a private sphere in order to make rational consensus possible, because she regards political passion as that which is mobilised in the creation of collective identity. This is to underline that when people act politically, and for example cast their vote, they are moved by much more than simply the defence of their interests, rationality or morality. Mouffe (2005) argues that: 'There is an important affective dimension in voting and what is at stake there is a question of identification' (25). To envisage politics as a rational process of negotiation among individuals not only obliterates the political, 'it is also to neglect the predominant role of passions as moving forces of human conduct' (1993, 140). Taking the affective dimension of politics into account is explained by Mouffe (2005) as follows:

> Mobilization requires politicization, but politicization cannot exist without the production of a conflictual representation of the world, with opposed camps with which people can identify, thereby allowing for passions to be mobilized politically within the spectrum of the democratic process. (24f.)

In order to act politically, Mouffe sees a need for people 'to identify with a collective identity which provides an idea of themselves that they can valorise' (2005, 25). That is, a conflictual representation of the world, with opposed positions with which people can identify, provides collective identities that can mobilise political passion. In Mouffe's view, downplaying the importance of political opposition is dangerous, because this would give way to a process of individualisation (as opposed to partisan interests based on collective interests) and the 'moralisation' of politics (75).

Relating back to a previous discussion about cosmopolitanism and shared values, Mouffe (2005) takes an anti-cosmopolitan position when she argues that collective identities always entail a 'we/they' discrimination (5) and that difference is a prerequisite for the existence of an identity. To some extent, collective identity as described by Mouffe does involve something shared – not in the cosmopolitan sense that all human beings belong to a single community and share a global identity, but in the sense of shared values of liberty and equality (121). As the survival of a pluralist democracy depends on collective identities understanding and interpreting issues differently, Mouffe argues that it is an illusion to believe in cosmopolitanism, since it eliminates conflicts and thereby the political dimension.

Although Butler and Mouffe open up new ways of understanding complex issues, we believe that in order to consider our problem – what kind of role universal values should play in an educational practice – we need to turn to a scholar who has a similar political orientation to universal ideals but who also problematises how we can understand and use universal values in an educational context. We therefore turn to Sharon Todd's ideas about how a political orientation to cosmopolitan approaches in education offers education a *political,* rather than a dialogical language for understanding conflicts of interest in educational practice.

Facing imperfection in education

The possibility of contingent foundations in the plural that undergo acts of cultural translation, as suggested by Butler, is picked up by Todd (2009a), who suggests that instead of 'cultivating' or 'promoting' humanity, education should seek to *face* humanity without doing away with dissonance and conflict (2009a, 8f.). What Todd's work so well expresses is that if we educate for universal ethics – or unquestionable and shared values – and deal with the interconnected issues facing us by avoiding differences and imperfection, the danger is that we will not take pluralism seriously. Drawing on political theorist Hannah Arendt's line of argumentation, Todd points to the fact that we should be vigilant about education turning into a political tool: 'In educating *for* humanity, we run the risk of creating for children a world that does not respond to it *as it is*, and create instead a harmonious image of what we adults *want the world to be*' (2009a, 16).

According to Todd and Säfström (2008), educational models that aim to promote respect often centre on creating a conflict-free atmosphere through appeals to deliberation, conversation and consensus. In relation to that, the authors argue that certain relations of conflict are necessary for the very existence of democratic politics and can inform education in promoting better ways of living together. In their opinion, it is not that a Habermasian-inspired deliberative model has nothing to offer in terms of establishing discursive procedures for taking certain decisions. Rather, they claim that 'as a model for actually engaging and confronting competing "truth claims", values, and perspectives, it fails to sustain the diversity upon which democracy itself rests'. Biesta (2011), who elaborates on the same issues, sees a danger of education becoming a process in which those who wish to take part have to meet certain entry conditions, such as a commitment to values and norms on which everyone is supposed to agree and argues that this *masks the political dimension of education.*

This criticism of consensus-orientated approaches is in line with Todd's (2009a) suggestion that when responding to normative dilemmas in education, we need on the one hand to challenge our ideals and on the other to avoid cynicism. Dealing with this tension seriously – refraining from 'cultivating' people in a Nussbaumian sense and at the same time acknowledging diversity – and locating it in the classroom is an approach towards pluralistic education and an education of humility. Todd (2009a) argues that we cannot import universal principles into education in the belief that students will secure justice and responsibility by abiding by normative rules. On the contrary, education needs to introduce students to a political language that enables them to rethink their own and other groups' situated values and actions. Borrowing the term 'conflictual consensus' from Mouffe (2005), Todd (2009a, 114) explains that

> this means helping students to reframe expressions of conflict as constituting we/they relations – relations which are continually shifting and contingent – and to help them recognize that the point is not to win the argument, or to eschew the passions of others, but to live in that fragile and unstable space of 'conflictual consensus'.

As we have tried to stress, the relation between ethics and education is complex and, in discussions about moral education, there is the risk that education is treated as an instrument for ethics. Such education sees ethics as a particular kind of knowledge that brings with it a change in how one lives. The dilemma as Todd sees it is that 'ethics still enters education from the outside' (2003, 5). Although Todd does not suggest that universal values are irrelevant for how we live together, she does caution against seeing education as an instrument for a particular ethical position:

> When it comes to ethics, the danger is that whether one teaches ethics as a set of abstract principles, or attempts to teach ethical relations (such as empathy) in order to lead students to interact more appropriately, or teaches through modelling an example, education risks becoming a form of rhetoric, a practice in the art of persuasion that already presumes that those who are subject to it do not already know what they need to in order to act morally. (2003, 7)

Todd introduces a way of thinking about the relation between ethics and education in which ethics is something other than acting on knowledge. Learning *about* otherness – in order to understand or to be more responsible – does not lead to better ethical reflections. Instead, Todd argues, we need to place openness and vulnerability at the core of relationality and shift the focus to what is at stake in the *process* of learning from otherness in such relations. Thus, it is through critical reflection in situated contexts that we undergo change, provoked by others in all their differences.

Conclusions and discussion

Addressing universal values in ESE

The purpose of the above exposition of a poststructural criticism of universalistic approaches in education is not to dismiss the possibilities of ESE, but to emphasise that one of the greatest challenges now facing the development and implementation of ESE is the search for balanced ways of dealing with values and normativity in education. The strength of the critique – we believe – is that Butler, Mouffe and Todd avoid the programmatic path and offer new and different ways of thinking about the tension between the universal and the particular with a focus on the political. The above argumentation on how universal claims need to be translated has a significant bearing on how ESE teachers, curriculum designers and educational policy-makers can relate to policies that are driven forward by world organisations in their educational practice. When organisations like UNESCO and national syllabuses suggest that certain universal values are desirable to educate for, there is a risk that we will fail to see the limits of educational thought. Presenting universal values uncritically is to obscure the power relations that are built into them. We therefore mean that it is essential to think about universal values as a *question* for education, and not simply as a solution or an abstract justification for it.

The critique of cosmopolitanism advises us to try to move away from instrumental methods for sustaining the future world and instead turn towards an inquiry into the ethical grounds of our responsibility by recognising the multiplicity of competing notions of universality. In other words, we cannot escape the idea of universal values, but should try to see them as *part of the educational process rather than as educational goals*. In essence, in this paper, we argue that ESE needs to focus on what happens in the educational process of learning, and it is in that context that we propose an alternative philosophical perspective that acknowledges *the political* in this process. One of the crucial aspects of this perspective is to avoid turning environmental and sustainable issues into moral issues of good and evil and thus *moralise the political*.

Educational guidelines for future ESE

Below we suggest four guidelines – or areas of change – for future ESE that takes the radical and political critique of universal values in education into account: *unmasking the political dimension, repoliticising education, seeing beyond the relativist and objectivist divide* and *using passion as a moving force.* We introduce these guidelines – described below – to exemplify how to deal with universal values as part of the educational process.

Unmasking the political dimension

By way of introduction, we discussed the democratic problem in ESE and pointed to understandings of the intersection between values and democracy as well as responses to the problematic relationship between the two. Van Poeck and Vandenabeele (2012) also contribute to this debate by emphasising the importance of presenting issues of sustainable development as matters of public concern, instead of focusing on the acquisition of individual competences. Wals (2010) exemplifies the democratic problem when reflecting on some recurrent tendencies in ESE research in Scandinavia that can be described as emancipatory, pluralistic, participatory and dialogic[5]:

> It is suggested that these tendencies are quite crucial, but are also at odds with the increasing sense of urgency in dealing with sustainability challenges and a corresponding temptation to revert to instrumentalism. At the same time elevating these tendencies to norms or universal principles is internally inconsistent with the principles themselves. (2010, 143)

We also exposed the *political* nature of the articulation of universal sustainable claims. Here, we agree with Mouffe (2005) that any cosmopolitan world order – and any educational approach we may add – that assumes a form of consensus overlooks the fact that power relations are constitutive of the social and that conflict and antagonism cannot be eradicated. The critique of universalistic approaches in education is that in an attempt to find values on which we all agree; these approaches mask existing power relations. If we import preconceived universal sustainable values and principles into education, we thus run the risk of *depoliticising* education.

These thoughts can be related to the current discussion in ESE research and to the paradox described by Van Poeck, Vandenabeele and Wals above. Instead of seeing environmental and sustainable universal values as things that determine political claims or policies, universal values should be regarded as products of political practice. In addition, we also need to envisage the environmental and sustainable problems facing our societies in a political way.

Repoliticising education

An overall mission of the UN Decade of ESD is to integrate universal sustainable values and principles into education (UNESCO 2005). With the Earth Charter (2000), the idea is that, through forms of dialogue and identification with the whole world community, we can resolve conflicts and reach mutual understanding. Although this mission seems to be solely good, we argue that such a cosmopolitan approach is not able to provide the political perspective that is required today.

What we can learn from Butler, Mouffe and Todd is how to treat the articulation of the universal as a political claim that comprises power relations. We can also allow for the possibility that conflict may appear and provide a space in which differences can be expressed and students can wrestle with these confronting viewpoints. Seen in this light, power relations and issues of disagreement, both in the classroom and in the political arena, are essential for critical studies in ESE. Here, we side with Ruitenberg (2009), who argues that Mouffe's work has important implications for the ways in which we educate students to disagree and to regard their opponents in political conflicts as adversaries rather than moral enemies. Drawing on both Butler and Mouffe, Todd (2009a) focuses on the educational processes of negotiation and translation. She suggests that dealing seriously with human pluralism in education means making difficulty of judgement a central part. This includes acknowledging that the issue of how we adjudicate between rights and particular contexts lies at the heart of 'thinking cosmopolitan' – or in Mouffe's words, how we confront and face our differences in a way that grasps the nature of the political in an agonistic way.

Several recent studies from Swedish ESE research support this poststructural critique of the need to repoliticise education. Öhman and Öhman (2013) show how ESE practices that are based on the concept of sustainable development run the risk of being consensus oriented, thereby hiding ideological conflicts. They argue that it is important for teachers to create opportunities for students to get involved in discussions so that they can both discover and experience the differences and conflicts that are embedded in issues related to sustainable development. Examples of such discussions can be found in Lundegård and Wickman (2007, 2012). In their analysis of 2007, they showed how conflicts of interest came to light during the course of a student dialogue concerning the environment, while their more recent article (2012) focuses on how those taking part in student dialogues pointed to three human conflicts of interest and offered each other the opportunity *to act as political subjects* in relation to them. The creation of a subject is regarded as the result of a political encounter with different values, and the study points to how the political subject emerges at the same time as the other outlines a human conflict of interest for an individual to take a stand against. Lundegård and Wickman's findings relate to Mouffe's thoughts about the return of the political and how we need to rethink education as an approach that challenges the myth of the unitary subject. We are in fact multiple and contradictory subjects and, as a result of an encounter, a new political subject emerges that lacks a clear identification.

Seeing beyond the relativist and objectivist divide

In the introduction to this paper, we raised the ethical problem concerning the difficulty of warranting a set of educational values and norms and the risk for relativism if we abandoned them. Here, we would like to emphasise that the contributions of Butler, Mouffe and Todd play an important role in seeing beyond the relativist and objectivist divide. Postfoundational criticisms such as those argued by Butler, Mouffe and Todd have pointed to the difficulty/impossibility of theoretically deciding whether universal values correspond to any permanent foundation or not. They claim that there are no positions outside our language, culture and life, since universal values are always particular to a specific culture. From a postfoundational perspective, the right and the good are things that human beings establish in practice and in relation to certain purposes in their activities. ESE can accordingly be seen as one of those democratic practices where such values are confirmed. This means that values are not arbitrary, because, as Rorty (1982/2003, 166) holds, 'one cannot find anybody who says that two incompatible opinions on an important topic are equally good'. Thus, relativism is really only a problem if you assume that there exist external foundations to which values can be anchored. The important thing to discuss in ESE is therefore rather the *practical consequences* of dealing with the ethical dimension of environmental and sustainability issues in different ways (see Öhman 2007, 2008). The cultural dependence of universal values does not mean that we have to reject the idea that these values can play an important role in the educational process. However, we have to scrutinise the functions they have in our culture, look for functional equivalents in other cultures and ask ourselves 'whether other cultures do not give different answers to the same question' (Mouffe 2005, 126).

Valuing and exchanging various ideas should thus be an important aspect of ESE practice because this makes it possible for students to make meaning of contradictory knowledge. It also increases their understanding of unfamiliar values and establishes certain views of environmental and sustainability issues in a pluralistic discussion.

A recent empirical example of the impossible ideals involved in constructing meaning is Lysgaard's (2012) analysis of NGOs' ideals of a better and more sustainable society. Here, we can see parallels with Lysgaard's study and the poststructural criticism that we have presented, especially that developed by Todd (2009a). The philosophical grounding of (a sustainable) ethics should not only be preconceived 'universal ideals' but should also include that which is imperfect about ourselves and needs to be faced: the unsustainable, the irresponsible, etc. As in Butler's work (2000a), this study points to the fact that we need to navigate between our ideals and everyday actions that are perceived as bad, bearing in mind that this translation might be an attempt to deal with the inherent contradictions of our lives.

Lysgaard (2012) shows that although the possibilities of reaching these ideals are slim; they still serve a purpose in that they create meaning for the individual subject. In the study, the concept of *Bad Practice* is developed as an important coping strategy to keep the subject from doing the impossible: 'Stepping, with eyes wide open, into the void of the chaotic surrounding world, with all its wrongs and randomness' (200). Lysgaard shows how Bad Practice serves a double purpose in the sense that it is a coping strategy but also a facilitator of enjoyment, as the subject also needs to live the very opposite life of a truly sustainable one, consuming and producing waste.

Using passion as a moving force

According to Hicks and Bord (2001), very little attention has been paid to the affective dimension of learning ESE issues. This, they claim, is due to the enlightenment heritage of rationalism. They argue that learning about global issues should also involve an emotional response:

> This appears to occur when knowing shifts from being something intellectual and detached to a personal and connected knowing. /.../ Most importantly the emotional responses experienced by students need to be accepted and seen as part of a shared experience. (415f.)

Here, we also would like to stress the non-rational aspect of sustainable issues and the importance of confronting moral problems in real life, since the majority of moral problems can neither be avoided by rational planning nor solved by intellectual process of consideration.

An empirical example is Lundegård's (2008) illumination of the role that emotions and passion play in students' discussions about the environment and sustainable development and their constitutive of political subjects. In his study, Lundegård shows how during a dialogue students create emotional and aesthetic relations to the world and that these relations lead to the students taking a stand for or against a certain issue.

Öhman and Östman (2008) argue that emotional and spontaneous reactions are an essential part of human moral life. They mean that students therefore should be encouraged to express and share their personal moral reactions as this provide opportunities for them to understand the diverse varieties of moral problems and to learn to respect the deeply personal, moral emotions that people show in different situations, even though these emotions may not always be possible to explain or defend by rational argument. To systematically try to inculcate a certain way of reacting would, on the other hand, intrude upon the students' personal sphere and expose ESE to the dangers of indoctrination.

With reference to Mouffe and Todd, and with the above examples from scholars within the field of ESE, we would like to stress the importance of passion and emotion in the field of education and education policy. Passion has a political dimension that is important to emphasise in education, especially when consensus-orientated approaches in education run the risk of falling short in terms of acknowledging the political. Todd (2003) discusses a relation to the other that considers students' affective responses to the encounter with knowledge and agrees with Mouffe that consensus-orientated approaches 'fail to take account of the passionate commitments that factor into contesting and competing points of view and interests' (Todd 2009a, 103).

Thus, both Mouffe and Todd stress that we should not remove passion from politics and education, because in order to mobilise passion, people (students) need to experience democratic confrontation. Also, according to Mouffe (2005, 28), 'democratic politics needs to have a real purchase on people's desires and fantasies and that, instead of opposing interests to sentiments and reason to passions, it should offer forms of identifications conducive to democratic practices'. Both Todd and Mouffe underline the importance of dealing with conflicts *passionately* and that we can relate to an ESE that aims towards dealing with environmental and sustainable issues that confront students with conflicts and plurality, that is, issues that affect students deeply.

Concluding remarks

The critique of cosmopolitanism advises us to try to move away from instrumental methods for sustaining the future world and instead turn towards an inquiry into the ethical grounds of our responsibility by recognising the multiplicity of competing notions of universality. In other words, we should take universal values into consideration in education and see them as a part of the educational process, rather than as educational goals.

Important aspects to be considered when developing ESE are how universal sustainable ideals are culturally translated in specific environments and that dissonant political and ethical voices need to be reflected in the educational encounter. A central challenge for ESE practitioners is, accordingly, how to create opportunities for students to get involved in discussions so that they can discover and experience the differences and conflicts that are embedded in issues related to sustainable development (cf. Lundegård and Wickman 2007, 2012; Rudsberg and Öhman 2010; Öhman and Öhman 2013). We believe that the position developed by Butler, Mouffe and Todd – being mindful of different voices and allowing for uncertainty and disagreement – can offer ESE a political language. If ESE is understood as a *political project* comprising dissonant and conflicting voices, it would be an important contribution to its development or transformation.

Acknowledgements

We thank the contribution of the SMED (Studies of Meaning-making in Educational Discourses) research group, and the helpful support of anonymous reviewers.

Notes

1. For a special issue on 'Cosmopolitanism in the Making', see *Studies in Philosophy and Education* 29 (2).
2. A cosmopolitan orientation on environmental and sustainability education has also been developed by scholars from the social sciences; see, for example, Beck (2006) and Dobson (2003).
3. Also referred to as principles of intra- and intergenerational equity.
4. The essay was first published 1991 in *Praxis International* 11 (2).
5. For a special issue on environmental and sustainability education with a focus on research in Scandinavia, see 'Democracy and values in environmental and sustainability education: research contributions from Denmark and Sweden', *Environmental Education Research* 16 (1).

References

Andreotti, V. 2006. "Theory Without Practice is Idle, Practice Without Theory is Blind: The Potential Contributions of Post-Colonial Theory to Development Education." *Development Education Journal* 12 (3): 7–10.
Appiah, K. A. 2005. *The Ethics of Identity*. Princeton: Princeton University Press.
Appiah, K. A. 2006. *Cosmopolitanism: Ethics in a World of Strangers*. New York: Norton.
Beck, U. 2006. *The Cosmopolitan Vision*. Cambridge: Polity Press.

Bell, D. 2004. "Creating Green Citizens? Political Liberalism and Environmental Education." *Journal of Philosophy of Education* 38 (1): 37–53.

Bernstein, R. J. 1983. *Beyond Objectivism and Relativism: Science, Hermeneutics, and Praxis*. Oxford: Blackwell.

Bhabha, H. K. 1994. *The Location of Culture*. London: Routledge.

Biesta, G. J. J. 2011. "The Ignorant Citizen: Mouffe, Rancière, and the Subject of Democratic Education." *Studies in Philosophy and Education* 30 (2): 141–153.

Butler, J. 1995. "Contingent Foundations: Feminism and the Question of 'postmodernism'." In *Feminist Contentions: A Philosophical Exchange*, edited by S. Benhabib, J. Butler, D. Cornell and N. Fraser, 35–58. New York: Routledge.

Butler, J. 1996. "Universality in culture." In *For Love of Country: Debating the Limits of Patriotism – Martha C. Nussbaum with Respondents*, edited by J. Cohen, 45–52. Boston, MA: Beacon Press.

Butler, J. 2000a. "Restaging the Universal: Hegemony and the Limits of Formalism." In *Contingency, Hegemony, Universality: Contemporary Dialogues on the Left*, edited by J. Butler, E. Laclau and S. Žižek, 11–43. London: Verso.

Butler, J. 2000b. "Competing Universalities." In *Contingency, Hegemony, Universality: Contemporary Dialogues on the Left*, edited by J. Butler, E. Laclau and S. Žižek, 136–181. London: Verso.

Dewey, J. 1916/1980. "Democracy and Education." In *The Middle Works, 1899–1924, Volume 2: 1925–1927*, edited by J. A. Boydston. Carbondale, IL: Southern University Press.

Dobson, A. 2003. *Citizenship and the Environment*. Oxford: Oxford University Press.

Englund, T. 2000. "Rethinking Democracy and Education: Towards an Education of Deliberative Citizens." *Journal of Curriculum Studies* 32 (2): 305–313.

Englund, T., J. Öhman, and L. Östman. 2008. "Deliberative Communication concerning Sustainability and Security: A Habermas Inspired Approach." In *Sustainability and Security within Liberal Societies*, edited by S. Gough and A. Stables, 29–48. London: Routledge.

Fien, J. 1995. "Teaching for a Sustainable World. The Environmental and Developmental Education Project for Teacher Education." *Environmental Education Research* 1 (1): 21–34.

Fien, J. 2000. "'Education for the Environment: A critique' – An Analysis." *Environmental Education Research* 6 (2): 179–192.

Gardiner, S. M. 2004. "Ethics and Global Climate Change." *Ethics* 114 (3): 555–600.

Gough, N. 2002. "Thinking/Acting Locally/Globally: Western Science and Environmental Knowledge in a Global Knowledge Economy." *International Journal of Science Education* 24 (11): 1217–1237.

Gutmann, A. 1987. *Democratic Education*. Princeton: Princeton University Press.

Hailwood, S. 2005. "Environmental Citizenship as Reasonable Citizenship." *Environmental Politics* 14 (2): 195–210.

Hansen, D. T. 2008. "Curriculum and the Idea of a Cosmopolitan Inheritance." *Journal of Curriculum Studies* 40 (3): 289–312.

Hicks, D., and A. Bord. 2001. "Learning about Global Issues: Why Most Educators Only Make Things Worse." *Environmental Education Research* 7 (4): 413–425.

Huckle, J. 1999. "Locating Environmental Education between Modern Capitalism and Postmodern Socialism: A Reply to Luce Sauvé." *Canadian Journal of Environmental Education* 4 (1): 36–45.

Jensen, B. B., and K. Schnack. 2006. "The Action Competence Approach in Environmental Education." *Environmental Education Research* 12 (3–4): 471–486.

Jickling, B. 1992. "Why I don't Want My Children to Be Educated for Sustainable Development." *Journal of Environmental Education* 23 (4): 5–8.

Jickling, B., and H. Spork. 1998. "Education for the Environment: A Critique." *Environmental Education Research* 4 (3): 309–327.

Jickling, B., and A. E. J. Wals. 2008. "Globalization and Environmental Education: Looking Beyond Sustainability and Sustainable Development." *Journal of Curriculum Studies* 40 (1): 1–21.

Kemp, P. 2011. *Citizen of the World: The Cosmopolitan Ideal for the Twenty-First Century*. Amherst, NY: Humanity Books/Prometheus Books.

Kronlid, D. O., and J. Öhman. 2013. "An Environmental Ethical Conceptual Framework for Research on Sustainability and Environmental Education." *Environmental Education Research* 19 (1): 21–44.

Laclau, E. 1996. *Emancipation(S)*. London: Verso.

Lotz-Sisitka, H., and I. Schudel. 2007. "Exploring the Practical Adequacy of the Normative Framework Guiding South Africa's National Curriculum Statement." *Environmental Education Research* 13 (2): 245–263.

Lundegård, I. 2008. "Self, Values and the World – Young People in Dialogue on Sustainable Development." In *Values and Democracy in Education for Sustainable Development – Contributions from Swedish Research*, edited by J. Öhman, 123–144. Stockholm: Liber.

Lundegård, I., and P.-O. Wickman. 2007. "Conflicts of Interest: An Indispensable Element of Education for Sustainability." *Environmental Education Research* 13 (1): 1–15.

Lundegård, I., and P.-O. Wickman. 2012. "It Takes Two to Tango: Studying How Students Constitute Political Subjects in Discourses on Sustainable Development." *Environmental Education Research* 18 (2): 153–169.

Lyotard, J.-F. 1984. *The Postmodern Condition. A report on knowledge*. Minneapolis: University of Minnesota Press.

Lysgaard, J. G. 2012. *The Educational Desires of Danish and Korean Environmental NGOs*. PhD diss., Aarhus University.

Marchart, O. 2007. *Post-Foundational Political Thought: Political Difference in Nancy, Lefort, Badiou and Laclau*. Edinburgh: Edinburgh University Press.

McKenzie, M. 2012. "Education for y'all: Global Neoliberalism and the Case for a Politics of Scale in Sustainability Education Policy." *Policy Futures in Education* 10 (2): 165–177.

Mouffe, C. 1993. *The Return of the Political*. London: Verso.

Mouffe, C. 1996. "Deconstruction, Pragmatism and the Politics of Democracy." In *Deconstruction and Pragmatism*, edited by C. Mouffe, 1–12. London: Routledge.

Mouffe, C. 2000. *The Democratic Paradox*. London: Verso.

Mouffe, C. 2005. *On the Political*. London: Routledge.

Mouffe, C. 2008. "Which World Order: Cosmopolitan or Multipolar?" *Ethical Perspectives* 15 (4): 453–467.

Nussbaum, M. C. 1997. *Cultivating Humanity: A Classical Defence of Reform in Liberal Education*. Cambridge, MA: Harvard University.

Nussbaum, M. C. 1999. "The Professor of Parody: The Hip Defeatism of Judith Butler." *The New Republic* February 22: 37–45.

Nussbaum, M. C. 2010. *Not for Profit: Why Democracy Needs the Humanities*. Princeton: Princeton University Press.

Öhman, J. 2007. "The Ethical Dimension of ESD – Navigating Between the Pitfalls of Indoctrination and Relativism." In *Drivers and Barriers for Learning for Sustainable Development in Pre-School through High School and Teacher Education*, edited by I. Bjorneloo and E. Nyberg, 43–47. Paris: UNESCO Education Sector.

Öhman, J. 2008. "Environmental Ethics and Democratic Responsibility A Pluralistic Approach to ESD." In *Values and Democracy in Education for Sustainable Development – Contributions from Swedish Research*, edited by J. Öhman, 17–32. Stockholm: Liber.

Öhman, J. 2009. "Sigtuna Think Piece 4: Climate Change Education in Relation to Selective Traditions in Environmental Education." *Southern African Journal of Environmental Education* 26: 49–57.

Öhman, J., and L. Östman. 2008. "Clarifying the Ethical Tendency in Education for Sustainable Development Practice: A Wittgenstein-Inspired Approach." *Canadian Journal of Environmental Education* 13 (1): 57–72.

Öhman, J., and M. Öhman. 2013. "Participatory Approach in Practice: An Analysis of Student Discussions about Climate Change." *Environmental Education Research* 19 (3): 324–341.

Payne, P. 1997. "Embodiment and Environmental Education." *Environmental Education Research* 3 (2): 133–153.

Pourgouris, M. 2010. "Rey Chow and the Hauntological Spectres of Poststructuralism." *Postcolonial Studies* 13 (3): 275–288.

Rorty, R. 1980. *Philosophy and the Mirror of Nature*. Oxford: Princeton University Press.

Rorty, R. 1982/2003. *Consequences of Pragmatism (Essays: 1972–1980)*. Minneapolis: University of Minnesota Press.

Rudsberg, K., and J. Öhman. 2010. "Pluralism in Practice: Experiences from Swedish Evaluation, School Development and Research." *Environmental Education Research* 16 (1): 95–111.

Ruitenberg, C. W. 2009. "Educating Political Adversaries." *Studies in Philosophy and Education* 28 (3): 269–281.

Säfström, C. A. 1999. "On the Way to a Postmodern Curriculum Theory – Moving from the Question of Unity to the Question of Difference." *Studies in Philosophy and Education* 18 (4): 221–233.

Säfström, C. A., and G. J. J. Biesta. 2001. "Learning Democracy in a World of Difference." *The School Field* 12 (5/6): 5–20.

Sauvé, L. 1999. "Environmental Education between Modernity and Postmodernity: Searching for an Integrating Educational Framework." *Canadian Journal of Environmental Education* 4 (1): 9–36.

Schinkel, A. 2009. "Justifying Compulsory Environmental Education in Liberal Democracies." *Journal of Philosophy of Education* 43 (4): 507–526.

Schlottmann, C. 2008. "Educational Ethics and the DESD. Considering Trade-Offs." *Theory and Research in Education* 6 (2): 207–219.

Stables, A. 2001. "Who Drew the Sky? Conflicting Assumptions in Environmental Education." *Educational Philosophy and Theory* 33 (2): 245–256.

Strand, T. 2010. "The Making of a New Cosmopolitanism." *Studies in Philosophy and Education* 29 (2): 229–242.

Sund, L., and J. Öhman. 2011. "Cosmopolitan Perspectives on Education and Sustainable Development – Between Universal Ideals and Particular Values." *Utbildning Och Demokrati [Education and Democracy]* 20 (1): 13–34.

The Earth Charter. 2000. "Earth Charter Commission." Accessed May 25, 2012. http://www.earthcharterinaction.org/content/pages/Read-the-Charter.html

Todd, S. 2003. *Learning from the Other: Levinas, Psychoanalysis and Ethical Possibilities in Education*. Albany, NY: State University of New York Press.

Todd, S. 2008. "Facing Humanity: The Difficult Task of Cosmopolitan Education." Paper presented at the annual international conference of the Philosophy of Education Society of Great Britain, Oxford, UK, March 28–30.

Todd, S. 2009a. *Toward an Imperfect Education: Facing Humanity, Rethinking Cosmopolitanism*. Boulder, CO: Paradigm Publishers.

Todd, S. 2009b. "Universality and the Daunting Task of Cultural Translation: A Response to Penny Enslin and Mary Tjiattas." *Journal of the Philosophy of Education Society of Great Britain* 43 (1): 18–22.

Todd, S. 2010. "Living in a Dissonant World: Toward an Agonistic Cosmopolitics for Education." *Studies in Philosophy and Education* 29 (2): 213–228.

Todd, S., and C. A. Säfström. 2008. "Democracy, Education and Conflict: Rethinking Respect and the Place of the Ethical." *Journal of Educational Controversy* 3 (1). Accessed June 3, 2012. http://www.wce.wwu.edu/Resources/CEP/eJournal/v003n001/a012.shtml

United Nations Educational, Scientific and Cultural Organization (UNESCO). 2005. *United Nations Decade of Education for Sustainable Development (2005–2014): International Implementation Scheme*. Paris: UNESCO.

United Nations Educational, Scientific and Cultural Organization (UNESCO). 2010. *Universalism and Ethical Values for the Environment*. Bangkok: UNESCO.

Van Poeck, K., and J. Vandenabeele. 2012. "Learning from Sustainable Development: Education in the Light of Public Issues." *Environmental Education Research* 18 (4): 541–552.

Vare, P., and W. A. H. Scott. 2007. "Learning for a Change: Exploring the Relationship Between Education and Sustainable Development." *Journal of Education for Sustainable Development* 1 (2): 191–198.

Wals, A. E. J. 2009. *Learning for a Sustainable World: Review of Contexts and Structures for Education for Sustainable Development*. Paris: UNESCO.

Wals, A. E. J. 2010. "Between Knowing What is Right and Knowing That is It Wrong to Tell Others What is Right: On Relativism, Uncertainty and Democracy in Environmental and Sustainability Education." *Environmental Education Research* 16 (1): 143–151.

World Commission on Environment and Development. 1987. "Our Common Future: Report of the World Commission on Environment and Development." Accessed May 3, 2012. http://www.un-documents.net/wced-ocf.htm

World Summit on Sustainable Development (WSSD). 2002. "Johannesburg Declaration on Sustainable Development." Accessed June 21, 2012. http://www.un-documents.net/jburgdec.htm

Education policy mobility: reimagining sustainability in neoliberal times

Marcia McKenzie, Andrew Bieler and Rebecca McNeil

This paper is concerned with the twinning of sustainability with priorities of economic neoliberalization in education, and in particular via the mobility or diffusion of education policy. We discuss the literature on policy mobility as well as overview concerns regarding neoliberalism and education. The paper brings these analyses to bear in considering the uptake of sustainability in education policy. We ask to what extent sustainability as a vehicular idea may be twinning with processes of neoliberalization in education policy in ways that may undermine aspirations of, and action on, environmental sustainability. Toward the end of the paper, we draw on data from an empirical study to help elucidate how the analytic frames of policy mobility can inform our analyses of the potential concerns and possibilities of sustainability as a vehicular idea. In particular, we investigate how sustainability and related language have been adopted in the policies of Canadian post-secondary education institutions over time. The paper closes by suggesting the potential implications of the proceeding analyses for policymakers, practitioners, and researchers concerned with sustainability in education policy.

This paper is informed by trajectories of work in critical policy scholarship or policy sociology in education (e.g. Ball 1994, 1997; Dale 1999; Ozga 2000; Rizvi and Lingard 2010), as well as by interdisciplinary research on policy diffusion and transfer, and in particular, policy mobility (e.g. Peck and Theodore 2010a; Peck 2011a; Temenos and McCann 2013). We explore the shifts in theoretical perspective and methodological orientation that are required to analyze neoliberalism and sustainability as 'vehicular ideas' (Temenos and McCann 2012) and follow the uptake and mobility of policy concerned with sustainability[1] in Canadian post-secondary education institutions.

Our understanding of policy includes policy texts, but also broadly considers the contexts and consequences influencing their development and enactment. As Lingard and Ozga (2007) suggest, a process/text definition of educational policy 'indicates the politics involved in the production and implementation of a policy and in the actual purposes and language of the policy text' (2). We are concerned with these politics and their potentially productive and/or constraining effects on how sustainability is being conceived and mobilized in and through educational policy.

In this paper, we focus particularly on factors that may be influencing where and how sustainability is being taken up in post-secondary education policy, including in relation to processes of neoliberalization. We appreciate the cautions made against uses of 'neoliberalism' as a 'blunt, omnibus category' that can 'reproduce a narrowed analytical and political gaze;' as well as the arguments for nonetheless considering its distinctive hegemonic aspects across diverse settings and variations (Peck 2013, 17, 10). Analyses of the impacts of neoliberalization on education policy within specific locations and across sites have been ongoing over the past several decades (e.g. Ball 1994, 1998, 2013; Olssen and Peters 2005), with many concerned about 'the increasing colonization of educational policy by economic policy imperatives,' including neoliberalism (Ball 1998, 122).

Some researchers have also examined the shift to the language of 'sustainable development' or 'sustainability' in relation to economic policy priorities. For example, While, Jonas, and Gibbs (2004) have suggested the uptake of this lexicon in policy can provide a 'sustainability fix,' or in other words, support an 'organization of economic interests, institutional capacities, and political positions that allows development to proceed despite economic and ecological crises and in the face of growing popular concerns about the state of the environment' (Temenos and McCann 2012, 4). There seems little doubt that sustainability is a 'vehicular idea' (McLennan 2004; Temenos and McCann 2012) or a 'floating signifier' (Gonzalez-Gaudiano and Nidioa Buenfil-Burgos 2009), which can be taken up in different ways toward various means. Vehicular ideas are distinguished by their hermeneutic and contextual flexibility, by their ability to balance between discursive exclusivity and vague open-endedness, by their robust capacity to reabsorb opposition, evolve with the times, and move across sites (McLennan 2004, 488–489), which, more cynically, can serve to propel or greenwash economic interests. More optimistically, the terminology of sustainability can be powerful because of its ability to allow for coalition building and for 'moving things on' (Temenos and McCann 2012). The analysis of sustainability as a 'vehicular idea' requires consideration of both sides of this potentiality, which aligns with calls for both typological, observational analysis of such vehicular notions and attention to their normative characteristics (McLennan 2004, 494). For example, we can observe the uptake and use of various types of sustainability discourse, such as the three pillars definition, but we should not lose sight of the norms and ideologies that may be articulated with various types in particular policy-making contexts.

We bring these trajectories together in our concerns with the pairing of sustainability with priorities of economic neoliberalization in education, and in particular via the mobility or diffusion of education policy. We are interested in shifts from language of 'environment' to 'sustainable development' and 'sustainability' over the past several decades and explore the concerns and possibilities of the mobility of these terms and their associated meanings in education policy. We ask to what extent sustainability as a vehicular idea may be twinning with processes of neoliberalization in educational policy in ways that may undermine aspirations of, and action on, environmental sustainability. In doing so, we build on earlier work that has begun to examine the relationships among sustainability, neoliberalization, policy mobility, and education (e.g. Jickling and Wals 2008; Hursh and Henderson 2011; McKenzie 2012; Sylvestre, McNeil, and Wright 2013). Toward the end of the paper, we draw on data from an in progress empirical study to help elucidate how the analytic frames of policy mobility can inform our analyses of the potential concerns and possibilities of sustainability as a vehicular idea. In particular, we investigate how sustainability and related language have been adopted in the policies of Canadian post-secondary education institutions over time. The paper closes by suggesting the potential implications of the proceeding analyses for policymakers, practitioners, and researchers concerned with sustainability in education policy. We first begin with a discussion of sustainability as a 'vehicular idea' in relation to the developing literature on policy mobility.

The mobility turn and policy research

'It sometimes seems as if all the world is on the move' (Urry 2007, 3). The movement of vehicular ideas, like Richard Florida's creative city model or municipal sustainability fixes (Peck 2012; Temenos and McCann 2012), can be interrogated through the lens of the mobility turn in the social sciences and humanities. This 'turn' focuses on the immense scale of movement of objects, people, and ideas across the globe. It takes a stance that embraces epistemological exchange across disciplines and proposes a transformation of the social sciences away from static paradigms, where roots are favored at the expense of routes, in order to explore expanded metaphors of movement (Cresswell 2006; Frello 2008; Urry 2007). 'The term "mobilities" refers not just to movement but to this broader project of establishing a "movement-driven" social science in which movement ... as well as voluntary/temporary immobilities, practices of dwelling and "nomadic" place-making are all viewed as constitutive of economic, social and political relations' (Buscher, Urry, and Witchger 2011, 4). This project seeks to explain the complex relationships between mobilities, moorings (like airports or conference centers), spatial scales, and practices of place-making, in order to describe how social worlds, like sustainability policy-making, are in part 'made in and through movement' (Buscher, Urry, and Witchger 2011, 13). This paradigm marks a shift away from the historical focus of social scientific research on face-to-face relationships within spatially propinquitous communities, and toward an analysis of the multiple, the distributed, the fleeting, and the complex interdependencies between corporeal, communicative, and physical travel that variously shape what we have come to call 'globalization' (Buscher, Urry, and Witchger 2011). This turn is less defined by any overarching theoretical orientation than by a renewed empirical sensitivity to the movement of materials and ideas. This sensitivity attends not only to the global flow of vehicular ideas like 'sustainability,' but also to the flow of these ideas within and across national, regional, or local contexts.

This mobility turn is currently informing debates in critical policy research. The study of policy mobility and mutation is a relatively recent development in this field, partly building out of earlier scholarship in political science on policy diffusion and transfer. Providing an overview of various stages of the diffusion and transfer literature from the 1960s and onwards, Peck (2011a) suggests aspects of these literatures that continue to be relevant and useful in policy analysis and those which appear to have become outdated in more recent contexts of globalized networks of travel and technology. Table 1 provides an overview of differences identified by Peck (2011a) between the transfer–diffusion literatures and those developing, so far mainly within urban and economic geography, under the label of policy mobilities.

Table 1. Policy transfer vs. policy mobilities (adapted from Peck 2011a, 775).

	Policy transfer	Policy mobilities
Theoretical scale	Methodological nationalism	Mobility turn: global flow of policy across nations, regions, and places
Origins	Disciplinary: political science	Transdisciplinary: geography, political science, sociology, urban planning, and expanding, i.e. environmental education research
Epistemology	Positivist/rationalist	Postpositivist/constructivist
Privileged object	'Successful' transfers	Policies in motion/interconnection: continuous transformation and mutation
Social action	Instrumental: bounded rationality	Strategic: embedded calculation
Dynamic	Frustrated replication of best (or better) practices	Contradictory reproduction of connected but unevenly developing policy regimes
Spatiality	Sequential diffusion	Relational connection
Mode of explanation	Reification of essentialized design features	Contextually sensitive analysis of emergent capacities
Politics of knowledge	Abstracts from politics of knowledge and practice	Problematizes politics of knowledge and practice

Across these approaches, the interest is on how policies are instituted (i) over time, and (ii) over space, and (iii) which factors may be influencing temporal and spatial trends. Policy transfer–diffusion literatures have been concerned with how policy developed in one region or nation spreads to other locations over time, outlining geographic clustering (being influenced by one's neighbors) and networks (being influenced by the networks one participates in) as factors in the diffusion of a policy from its location of origin to other locations (Dale 1999; Weyland 2005). Temporally, diffusion has been suggested to occur on a bell curve, beginning with an innovation and slow uptake until policy uptake surges in popularity and eventually tapers off. The phase at which a government or institution may adopt a policy – either as an early adopter, within the peak of its popularity, or as a laggard – is suggested by the diffusion literature to be related to *why* the policy was adopted, or its mechanisms of uptake.

While a range of discussions of mechanisms of uptake exist in the transfer–diffusion literatures, a predominant approach is to consider the four classifications such as emulation, learning, competition, and coercion (Garrett, Dobbin, and Simmons 2008; Shipan and Volden 2008, 2012). 'Emulation' can be understood as the voluntary adoption of policy already in place elsewhere based on information passed through social channels. This may take the form of copying the strategies of powerful or successful actors or institutions, 'expert theorization' in which there is coalescence around favored solutions which are then 'sold' through various channels, or learning from peers where policy is borrowed from locations which share political or cultural affinities (Peck 2011a). 'Learning' describes circumstances where policies are adopted after observing their impact in another institution or jurisdiction (Shipan and Volden 2008). However, critical policy research has suggested that 'learning' is more prevalent among locations which share ideology and belief systems, making it difficult to isolate from emulation and other forms of transfer. As Peck (2011a) suggests: 'the near impossibility of rationally determining "success" or "failure" outside the framework of particular policy paradigms and belief systems means that learning behavior remains in the eye of the beholder' (787). The mechanism of 'competition' refers to cases where a policy is adopted due to a perception that it confers a competitive economic advantage, while 'coercion' can be understood as pressure or encouragement to adopt a policy from an outside source with some influence or power, such as a government funding body, and can take the form of required trade practices or economic sanctions (Shipan and Volden 2008). In his review of research in these areas, Peck (2011a) concludes that of the four mechanisms, emulation and competition appear to be the most prevalent, often acting in combination and operating through 'powersoaked epistemic networks' (788).

Indeed, such networks are a focus in the policy mobilities literature recently developing in urban and economic geography, which critiques frameworks of policy transfer–diffusion on the grounds that they focus on policies as discrete objects which can indeed be 'transferred' in whole to other locations (Prince 2012). Instead, the mobilities literature suggests that policies, in so far as they move from one location to another, often as bits and pieces, are also necessarily transformed through that process of movement and translation (Peck and Theodore 2010a). Rather than tracing policy from a particular point of origin to locations elsewhere, mobilities approaches also understand policy creation and mobilization as more dispersed or as not necessarily having a clear center or point of origin. This latter shift suggests the impacts of the globalization of policy practice, where policies are circulating globally with greater speed, 'aided by new communications technologies and a growing cadre of cosmopolitan policy advocates' (Peck and Theodore 2010a, 172).

We can analyze this globalization of policy practice by dissecting the relationships between five 'interdependent "mobilities" that produce social life organized across distance,' including corporeal travel, physical movement, imaginative travel, virtual travel, and communicative travel (Buscher, Urry, and Witchger 2011, 5). While inquiry may focus on any one of these areas, the mobility turn underlines the specific interdependencies between them, including corporeal travel of policy actors for meetings; imaginative travel effected through policy tourism or marketing campaigns; virtual travel via video conferences; communications via face-to-face meetings, social media, texts, mobile phone; and the actual movement of the bits and pieces of policy (Buscher, Urry, and Witchger 2011, 5). There has been some attention to the complex interrelationships between the multiple mobilities involved in the movement of policy. For instance, McCann (2011) outlines the role of local policy actors (policy professionals and civil society groups), the 'global policy consultocracy,' and informational infrastructures in policy mobilization processes (114). Conferences, seminars, fact-finding trips, 'policy tourism,' computer networks, blogs, social media, and other sites of connection provide venues of policy mobility, while measurement data such as indicators, storytelling, and related 'inscription devices' such as maps, charts, tables, and power point slides help policy 'carriers' or 'travelling technocrats' (Dale 1992; Larner and Laurie 2010) 'construct, legitimate, and propel specific policy models through and across scales' (Temenos and McCann 2012, 2).

The substance of the work undertaken by such carriers, traveling technocrats, and other mediator intellectuals is the 'facilitation' of spaces for dialog, like conferences, and platforms for selling ideas, like websites, so they become more accessible for particular policy-making networks (Osborne 2004, 441). Thomas Osborne (2004) argues that this style of intellectual labor is part of a broader shift away from the grand ideas and positivistic expertise of the ivory tower, and toward a more facilitative style of work that focuses on the production of flashy, vehicular ideas that are responsive to specific policy networks, think tanks, and media landscapes. Typically, this labor in ideas aims to exert political influence through networks and the creation of new networks, which marks a decisive shift away from the advisory policy expert who exerted influence through personal relationships with decision makers (Osborne 2004, 433).

This focuses on policy actors, locations, and techniques adds conditions of knowledge production and circulation to consider in examining the movement of policy and removes the nation state as the primary agent in the production and uptake of policies as in some earlier approaches to policy transfer–diffusion (Temenos and McCann 2013). This is part of a broader shift away from methodological nationalism within the new mobilities paradigm (Buscher, Urry, and Witchger 2011), wherein sociologist Ulrich Beck (2006) argues for a methodological cosmopolitanism to interrogate the contradictory and coerced effects of cosmopolitanization (or globalization) on everyday life and politics. This perspective directs our attention to the ways in which policy actors may be responding simultaneously to *both* regional *and* global policy-making networks and to the tensions and contradictions that come along with these blurred boundaries of cosmopolitanization (Beck 2006). This also suggests the significance of researching across multiple spatial scales and to the continuing significance of place-based contexts in the development of policy (McKenzie 2012). McCann (2011) emphasizes that a mobilities approach builds on longer standing traditions in geography (e.g. the work of David Harvey and Doreen Massey), which have understood place 'in terms of fixity and mobility; relationality and territoriality' (112). This suggests an attention to both the circulatory infrastructures and interconnections among 'somewhat "unbounded" state and state actors' while simultaneously focusing on the continued importance of territorial embeddedness (Temenos and McCann 2013, 346–347). Responding to critiques of the potential overemphasis on mobility in social analyses, Peck (2011a) likewise suggests that studies of policy mobility must embed understandings of mobility in the situated realities of policy-making frames, rule regimes, and institutional environments. We would add that the situated contexts need also to include longer histories of empire and the colonization of land and peoples (Tuck and McKenzie 2015).

Indeed, these situated contextual factors are understood to play a considerable role in policy uptake, with existing policy/politics suggested by some as largely determining new policy adoption. As every policy serves some interests more than others, there are no simple solutions of 'best' policy, but rather more complex underlying factors that influence which policies may be developed, emulated, or passed on (Temenos and McCann 2013). Discussing cross-national policy borrowing or transfer, Halpin and Troyna (1995) suggest that policy adoption has much more to do with legitimating other related policies within the country of adoption than to with the success, however defined, of the policy in other locations. Citing research by Whitty and Edwards (1992), they outline how elected politicians and officials are 'more likely to be interested in a borrowed policy's political symbolism than its details' (307). Likewise, Peck and Theodore (2010b) suggest how policy models that extend and affirm dominant paradigms and consolidate powerful interests are more like to travel. Furthermore, the style of ideas-work that supports the development of these kinds of models remains tied at the heels to ideologies of 'innovation' and 'enterprise' (Osborne 2004). Thus, the mobility of policy may have more to do with ideology than to do with rational or technical decision-making (Peck 2011b).

In sum, the study of policy mobilities is concerned with how policy is formed and modified through policy techniques and actors in situated and mobile locations and emphasizes the study of politics and power as they relate to policy.

Neoliberalization and mobile policies

Located within and spurring on these 'messier geographies' of 'fast policy' (Peck and Theodore 2010a, 2010b), neoliberalism is now part of the contextual landscape within which other policy considerations are undertaken in many regions of the world. If we hope to follow the networks or actors behind policy mobility, we will need to undertake an in-depth analysis of the politics of neoliberalism. We take four points from related work on processes of neoliberalization as central to our discussion here: (1) Neoliberalism is not dead: Despite discussions of what next 'after neoliberalism' following the 2008 financial crisis, it is clear that there has been further entrenchment of neoliberal rationalities in public policy, including educational policy, in Canada and elsewhere around the globe (Peck, Theodore, and Brenner 2012). (2) Neoliberalism is variegated: Or in other words, it takes specific forms in different locales, and thus, there is no one form of 'neoliberalism.' It is important to thus describe and analyze neoliberalization processes in relation to particular sites and situations, rather than discussing 'neoliberalism' in sweeping catchall ways (Brenner, Peck, and Theodore 2010; Peck 2013). (3) Thus, it is not as simple as to say 'neoliberalism did it:' As Peck (2013, 8) outlines, while 'analytically inconvenient,' neoliberalism should be understood to operate alongside of and in hybridity with a range of other forces, which may also, or more so, be influencing the policy contexts (for example, globalization). Part of the variation in neoliberalization in differing contexts is due to the other political and policy trajectories it comes into contact with. (4) Despite these caveats regarding approaching neoliberalism as a frame of analysis, it is also useful to understand the 'commonalities and connections across (local) neoliberalisms' in considering the political contexts into which other policies may be taken up (or not) (Peck 2013, 11), including those of sustainability in post-secondary education.

Common manifestations of neoliberalism include the extension of market-based competition as well as commodification processes into many realms of social life, including education (Peck, Theodore, and Brenner 2012; McKenzie 2012). The new 'competition state' or 'enterprise society' then operates strategically in relation to the globalization of economy through distributed forms of governance. Resulting impacts in education include a rescaling of political authority from an emphasis on the state to that of a 'global education policy field,' which is constituted through measures of comparative performance as well as via networks of politicians and policy makers with similar 'policy dispositions and related epistemic communities' (Lingard 2011, 368). A second impact of neoliberal governance on education is the turn to 'new public management,' or the application of private sector management practices in the public sector, including in administering education (Klees 2008; Lingard 2011). Reframing educational institutions and bodies as competitive entities, a focus of accountability and auditing enables oversight at a distance and fosters a culture of performativity. A third common aspect of neoliberal educational forms is increasing privatization of education, including of educational policy and policy processes. These trends are affecting post-secondary education specifically through new forms of management and auditing, the commodification of teaching and research, amplification of relations of competition, increasing privatization of campuses and research priorities, and an overall growing emphasis on measurable outputs (Davies, Gottesche, and Bansel 2006; Olssen and Peters 2005).

Returning to earlier discussions of policy mobility, one can see the ways in which neoliberalism both spreads through the circulatory systems of policy mobility as well as influences the situated institutional environments and rule regimes in which other 'mobile policies' may be developed or introduced. Indeed, Peck, Theodore, and Brenner (2012) suggest that the circulatory systems of policy operate 'across a now deeply neoliberalized terrain, from which promising local models are variously seeded, scaled up, and stylized for emulation, more often than not under the aegis of multilateral agencies, private consultancies, and expert networks' (279). Thus, neoliberalization acts as a filter for other policy initiatives or models, resulting in policies 'strongly skewed in favour of market-oriented rationalities and practices' (279). Such policy models are thus carriers of globally endorsed presumptions and are represented as replicable policy technologies, with both designs and outcomes viewed as transferable from place to place. This leads to the worry that:

> policy models pre-emptively disrupt what would otherwise be much more variegated, 'local' policy debates, (re)shaping the very terms in which such debates are constructed. This has the (desired) effect of further depoliticizing the policy-making processes through the circulation of prefabricated solutions, traveling in the disarmingly, apparently 'neutral' and post-ideological form of evaluation techno-science and best practice pragmatism. (Peck, Theodore, and Brenner 2012, 283)

In these ways, we worry that neoliberalization is filtering not only how education is conceptualized and shaped through policy (Davies and Bansel 2007; Peters 2001), but also how sustainability in education is understood and addressed. In the following section, we discuss 'sustainability' as it articulates with neoliberalism and global policy flows.

The twinning and mobility of neoliberalism and sustainability in education policy

The 'pan global rhetoric' of sustainability[2] in education has been suggested to be deeply susceptible to neoliberal influence (Huckle 2008) in that it can maintain a façade of green politics while allowing for the persistence of neoliberal relations to the environment (Irwin 2007). The neoliberalization of sustainability in education policy has been suggested as evident in the failure to engage with the ecological limits to growth in the so-called sustainability focus of corporate social responsibility work in schools (Manteaw 2008, 122), and in the curtailment of progress on sustainability education in particular national or regional contexts (Huckle 2008; McKenzie 2012). Some suggest that '[e]ducation is becoming more deeply connected to economic and security projects that are highly invested in projects pushing unrestricted economic growth … in areas of science and technology, military/security apparatuses, and resource acquisition' (Pierce 2013, 17). To unpack this neoliberalization of sustainability in education policy, we might learn from analyses of economistic framings of 'sustainability' in other areas of environmental policy. Coffey and Marston (2013) show how the reform agenda of ecologically modern discourses, where sustainability is at least still tied to environmental goals, may be co-opted by the neoliberal framing of sustainability in exclusively economic terms. They conclude that policy strategies that combine these discourses are 'flawed because, in commodifying nature, limiting the nature and magnitude of change required, and placing responsibility to act on to individuals, they offer a constrained understanding of the challenge of sustainability and what needs to be done' (196). This suggests how neoliberal framings of sustainability can be subtly masked through their ad hoc synthesis with other environmental policy discourses. The worry is that in these kinds of ways, the enterprise society of neoliberalism is bringing 'sustainability' into its fold at a moment when '[t]he tensions of capitalism are being played out on a global, biospheric scale and thus implicate the future of life on earth' (Cooper 2008, 49).

The global orientation of sustainability-related terminologies and the movement or stasis of various understandings (González-Gaudiano 2005; Irwin 2007) demand in-depth research into the mobilities, moorings, definitions, and policy routes that allow for the movement of particular understandings of sustainability and the immobility of others. Why do particular understandings of 'sustainability' get to move across nations and institutions, while other conceptualizations are immobilized? The complexity of this query may be interrogated by considering mobility not only as a physical and communicative phenomenon but, also, as a discursive and ideological process that shapes the kinds of ideas or actors that get to move and those which are rendered immobile (Frello 2008). This directs our attention to the ways in which language shapes the mobility or immobility of particular understandings of sustainability, which we interrogate by considering the competing or facilitatory discourses that variously shape its meaning in policy (Jørgensen and Philips 2002). Thus, if we are going to direct our research imaginations to a future beyond the high carbon societies of the neoliberal period (Urry 2011), we need to remain mindful of the versions of 'sustainability' that we draw upon to forecast preferable futures and remain vigilant to its' co-optation.

This can be explored further by considering sustainability as a vehicular idea, which foregrounds a number of interrelated concerns. First, the ways in which 'sustainability' gives substance to new kinds of cognitive labor in environmental policy-making, which we can analyze by following the facilitative labor (Osborne 2004) of various carriers and technocrats as they move through powerful epistemic networks (Peck 2011a). Second, its role as a 'floating signifier' (González-Gaudiano 2005; Gonzalez-Gaudiano and Nidioa Buenfil-Burgos 2009) with rather diffuse meanings across the discourses that gather under its name, which can potentially mask the persistence of powerful ideologies like the invisible hand of the free market under variegated conditions of neoliberalization (Irwin 2007; Peck 2013). The policy discourses through which this masking unfolds are incredibly complex, due to the disparate and diffuse connotations that have latched onto this floating signifier.

Third, we can analyze the role of sustainability policy goals in depoliticizing local policy debates. For instance, Temenos and McCann (2012) outline the ways in which mobile and neoliberal policies can frame thinking on local issues, including in relation to which solutions might be sought or developed in relation to sustainability policy. Other definitions of the problem and associated solutions can then be left outside the conversation to the point where they are unable to be thought or raised. They suggest how sustainability as a policy goal or concept can at times be used in these ways, to frame issues in a manner that is both open and at the same time delimits the range of possible ways forward (Temenos and McCann 2012, 1393). Temenos and McCann (2012) suggest that 'The utilization of vehicular ideas like sustainability allows sometimes sudden breaks in policy direction to appear almost seamless, natural, and inevitable, or alternatively, mask the fact that not much beyond the surface has changed' (1402). As a 'vehicular idea' or mobile policy goal, sustainability and related terms can be understood to be formulated with purposive ambiguity or mutability so as to be able to move quickly between policy-making sites. And unlike moral or theoretical vocabularies, vehicular ideas with their multiple interpretations have a more limited shelf life: 'They serve to make things happen at a particular time, after which their time may be up' (McLennan 2004, 435).

Finally, the notion of sustainability as a vehicular idea also highlights the ways in which the language and power of neoliberalism bring 'sustainability' on board in a variety of consensual and depoliticized ways that 'fix' the terms of debate around local environmental issues (Temenos and McCann 2012) and mask the persistence of market liberalization (Irwin 2007). This can be analyzed as part of a broader depoliticization of the policy process and politics generally, which Swyngedouw (2010) describes as 'structured around the perceived inevitability of capitalism and a market economy as the basic organizational structure of the social and economic order, for which there is no alternative' (215). In an analysis of the transition from environmental education to education for sustainability in New Zealand, Ruth Irwin (2007) argues that the framing of the 'invisible hand' of the free market by the metaphorical vehicle of 'sustainability' serves to perpetuate a calculative, instrumental relationship to the earth (Irwin 2007). She argues, 'the metaphor of the market gets subsumed in the rhetoric of 'sustainability' and *all factors* are absorbed into the enframing rubric of potential resource' (11). Thus, there is increasing evidence that certain types of sustainability discourse are depoliticized in policy-making processes, in ways that foreclose imagining or constructing a future that is more just and environmentally sustainable than what neoliberalism has to offer, including in education (Irwin 2007; Temenos and McCann 2012; Coffey and Marston 2013). The remainder of this paper suggests the ways in which sustainability may be functioning as a 'vehicular idea' in the context of initial data from a national study of sustainability in the educational policy of post-secondary institutions in Canada.

Researching sustainability in the education policy of post-secondary institutions

As part of the contextual dynamics of Canadian political and institutional factors, and in the context of this special issue, we are concerned with the extent to which processes of neoliberalization may be active in how sustainability is understood in education, and to what extent these two ideas may be traveling together in their global mobility and local uptake. Our discussion here draws on year one data collected from the 220 accredited post-secondary institutions in Canada[3] based on their publicly available policy documents and websites (see Beveridge et al. forthcoming). Of the 220 institutions, 110 had sustainability policies or plans (hereafter referred to jointly as 'policies'). In our analysis of the policies, the most frequent terms used in the policy titles were as follows: environment (49 uses), sustainable development (38 uses), and sustainability (41 uses).[4] For the purposes of this discussion, we are focusing on the language used in the titles and sustainability definitions in order to begin to examine the mobilities of the aims and language of the policies. Building on our discussion of sustainability as a vehicular idea, we ask to what extent the conceptions of sustainability in education policy texts may be keeping up with the neoliberal times.

Figure 1 shows temporal changes in the terms used in the sustainability policy titles, with earlier policies more commonly using the terminology of environment and sustainable development, with these terms decreasing in usage as the term sustainability emerged in the mid-2000s. The width of the bars indicates the relative number of policies developed in a given year, with most current policies developed after 2002. Sustainability is the most frequently used term in the titles of policies created over the past five years. Of the 110 institutions with sustainability policies, 69 policies included definitions of the terminology used in the policy titles. While a number of the definitions were environment-specific or specifically used the language of sustainable development in alignment with the policy titles, almost a third of the policies included a definition of sustainability which included a focus on the natural environment, society, and economy, or what is often called a 'three pillars' definition of sustainability (Sneddon, Howarth, and Norgaard 2006). Given the suggested emergence of sustainability as a dominant terminology, in what follows, we examine the definitions in the policies to extend an analysis of sustainability as a potential vehicular idea. In particular, we discuss three pillars definitions and ask how the priorities of neoliberalization may be shaping the construction of 'sustainability' as defined in these post-secondary education policies.

The three pillars are often introduced in the literature as a nested concept – the largest circle being the 'natural environment,' which the 'society' circle is then placed within, and 'economy,' is in turn, as part of society (Adams 2006, 2). They are placed in this hierarchy based on the understanding that without a natural environment human beings would not exist, and without a society to create it, there would be no economy. However, within the policies reviewed, there was no mention of any hierarchy or prioritization of these three elements. We might attend to the ideological

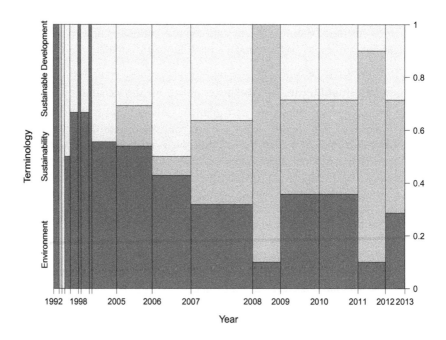

Figure 1. Policy title terminology by year and displaying relative number of policies per year (from Beveridge et al. forthcoming).

implications of this indeterminateness: Is an invisible hand supposed to organize coordination between the three pillars? The vagueness of this type of sustainability definition corroborates our understanding of it as a vehicular idea (McLennan 2004). We can read the elasticity of this three pillars definition as suggesting that sustainability, like environmental education before it, has become a 'floating signifier' with diverse meanings in each of the numerous discourses that gather under its umbrella (Gonzalez-Gaudiano 2005, 248). This purposive ambiguity is an important variable to consider in studying mobility, since it is the indeterminateness of vehicular ideas that allows them to travel quickly across policy-making sites (Temenos and McCann 2012) and 'move with the times' (McLennan 2004, 488–489).

In addition, we also want to draw attention to the segmentation of the 'pillars' and as a result, the boundaries that are established between them. As Gough and Scott (2006) write,

> it is important not to mistake a convenient representation of something for the thing itself. There are no clear boundaries between environment, society and economy, and each is fundamentally dependent on the other … Thus, the solid lines by which this model is normally divided are very misleading. (276)

The division of sustainability into three spheres can thus also be read as a kind of boundary maintenance activity, wherein the blurry boundaries between these domains are hardened at the policy-making level. The segmentation of these areas as 'pillars' can reduce reflection on the meaning of sustainability in one of these areas from the perspective of the other: for example, reflection on the meanings of 'economic sustainability' from the perspective of 'environmental sustainability' or the latter in relation to 'social sustainability.' Whereas the nested hierarchy model implies at least some reflection on the interrelationship of the three pillars, the absence of any such model in the definitions themselves leaves open for any one area to take priority in moving toward 'sustainability.'

Returning to the discussion of the previous section regarding the potential twinning of sustainability with neoliberalism, three pillar definitions thus run the risk of enabling sustainability as a vehicular idea in problematic ways. It can function both as a floating signifier through its ambiguity (anything goes), as well as enabling sustainability to be 'fixed' in certain ways through the creation of the boundaries between pillars (i.e. giving priority to a particular pillar). This enables sustainability to get onto the policy-making table as it is seen as flexible and not in conflict with economic and political priorities of neoliberalization and practically can result in situations where, for example, a local administrator believes they can appropriately check off policy requirements to address sustainability if they have done work on economy, society, *or* environment. The boundaries of the three pillar definitions can thus insulate the economy pillar from those of social and environmental sustainability, enabling a form of neoliberal sustainability (Coffey and Marston 2013). If the boundaries around the three pillars are allowed to harden, and there are no structures for critical reflection on their interrelations, there runs the risk of a relative dominance of a neoliberal framing of sustainability within such policy definitions. While we recognize this discussion is based only on sustainability definitions in the policies and not on an analysis of the full policies or of practices in institutions,[5] it is intended to provide an example of concerns about the twinning of sustainability with neoliberalism in education policy, as well as to help generate further questions and modes of analysis for researching how such definitions of sustainability become prioritized and mobilized.

In closing the discussion of this research, the initial analysis suggests that increasing numbers of post-secondary institutions in Canada are developing sustainability-related policies and that increasingly frequently, the terminology used to name these policies is 'sustainability.' While this may appear promising on the surface, peeling back just one layer to look at how sustainability is defined in these policies, suggests that priorities of neoliberalization may travel with and into how sustainability is conceptualized. Further analysis is needed to determine the extent to which this may be borne out in the policies in their full, as well as to consider more nuanced questions of mobility and uptake, such as to what extent sustainability networks, policy actors, virtual communications, or other conduits of mobility are facilitating the ways in which sustainability is adopted in localized contexts as well as how regional or municipal policies and priorities may also be influencing the specifics of how sustainability is articulated and practiced. We see shifts in the language of sustainability-related policy over time as shown in Figure 1, but there are also trends in the language and definitions used regionally, as well as in the numbers of institutions within various provinces/territories which have policies (see Beveridge et al. forthcoming). The terminology used in international or national policies and declarations, assessment bodies such as the Association for the Advancement of Sustainability in Higher Education (AASHE) or Cégep-Vert in Québec, or the UN-affiliated Regional Centers of Expertise in Education for Sustainable Development, are some of the factors which may be influencing the movement and translation of particular versions of sustainability. Claims of a sustainability focus are also increasingly a selling point in attracting students, faculty, and funders (Kerr and Hart-Steffes 2012, 12), in an age where post-secondary institutes operate in conditions of commodification and market-based competition (Davies, Gottesche, and Bansel 2006). In the worst case scenario of institutional greenwashing, sustainability policies and related high level initiatives such as signing of declarations may function as 'sustainability fixes' (While, Jonas, and Gibbs 2004), in which there is an appearance of taking steps toward protecting the environment while the higher prioritization given to economic considerations in the institution as a whole means that little may have changed. In a better case scenario, the ever growing focus on sustainability in post-secondary education is an opportunity for 'moving things on' (Temenos and McCann 2012) through the institutional prioritization of environmental considerations.

Implications for research

Given these multiple potentialities of sustainability in education policy in current conditions of mobile neoliberal policy-making, we are left with questions of the possible implications for policy-making, practice, and research. Or more specifically, if we consider the mobility of both neoliberal and sustainability policy, how can we guard against their inevitable pairing? If neoliberal forms of capitalism are increasingly tied to biological life through our dependence on extractive science and technology (Castree 2007; Pierce 2013), disassociated three pillar versions of sustainability which do not require the disruption of the logics of neoliberalism seem wholly inadequate. In a national political context which has lost even the veneer of sustainability,[6] the elasticity of the three pillars definition with its ability to 'keep up with the times' is not promising.

We suggest that an exploration of policy mobility can be helpful in considering how and why certain ideas travel and in enabling more intentionality in which ideas are taken up, or possibly ruptured. Guarding against being mere neoliberal 'network dopesters' (Peck 2012, 25), we can then better ask which actors, associations, and policies we are mobilizing and why. Such analytic frames also enable us to better consider the value, not only of mobile policies, but those which are also community and place specific. With an orientation to policy which considers the contexts or origins of policy as well as its enactment through practice, we propose the following kinds of questions that may be asked about the origins and mobilities of education policy:

- Can the policy or policy mandate be traced to a beginning, and if so, who was responsible for its genesis and the writing of the text?
- What are the typical and unconventional routes followed by sustainability-related education policy in their movement from one institution to another or from one country to another?
- How are sustainability-related education discourses synthesized with other policy agendas and discourses, and what are the effects of such hybrid policy discourses?
- How is sustainability articulating in relation to neoliberalization in local contexts?
- How does the mobility of sustainability-related education policy intersect with community and place-based 'policies' of sustainability education?
- What are the most significant moorings (retreats, conference centers) and platforms (websites, magazines, journals, etc.) for the development, branding, and selling of sustainability-related education policy or alternatively for dissensus and dialog?
- What are the various roles played by different policy actors, both locally at an institutional level, but also across institutions and nations through global policy networks?
- How can environmental education researchers engage diverse communities in the process of reimagining the meaning and scope of sustainability-related policy in education?

Although beyond the scope of the current paper, another host of detailed questions surrounds the related sphere of policy enactment or practice – in what happens on the ground in particular institutions and communities as policies are adopted and interpreted in local contexts, including in relation to how policies are combined, modified, resisted, and otherwise informed by situated actors, places, and practices (Bowe, Ball, and Gold 1992; Ball, Maguire, and Braun 2012).

Much of the existing research on policy mobilities focuses on unique urban planning, social, or health policy initiatives which can then be traced in their uptake across different locales – for example, workfare policies in the US (Peck and Theodore 2010b) or urban design policies such as smart growth or business improvement districts as they have spread globally (McCann and Ward 2012). Likewise, the uptake of sustainability in educational policy can be studied to better understand when and where various terminology and models emerged and the means through which they have become more distributed and with what effects (Ball and Junemann 2012). Methodologies for studying policy mobilities are still nascent, but have tended toward qualitative ethnographic and case study approaches which 'follow the policy' within and across sites (McCann and Ward 2012; Peck and Theodore 2010a). McCann (2011) advocates for 'global ethnographies' that study relationships between sites while maintaining one site as the primary perspective (121). Temenos and McCann (2013) suggest that most policy mobilities work to this point has largely employed '"standard" qualitative case study methods' (351) and that there is additional need for more detailed empirical research. McCann (2011) also suggests the value of analyzing policy documents and websites to better understand the structural and historical contexts within which policy mobilities have emerged and are active, as well as the potential of quantitative methods in examining some data (122). Finally, mobile methods also involve following the actors and their techniques (Buscher, Urry, and Witchger 2011), honing a deep familiarity with the specific techniques used by actors to organize the movement of policy.

By better understanding how current sustainability policies in education emerge, travel and are adapted in particular national or regional contexts, including in convergence or divergence with processes and discourses of neoliberalization, we can perhaps offer more critical and imaginative interventions in how sustainability is mobilized in education (McKenzie 2009). Arguably, we need a rupture or dissensus with the limited terms of debate around 'sustainability' in education policy, which we might imagine as a widening and redistribution of those who have a say in the unfolding of depoliticized education policy (Stevenson 2013). Philosopher Rancière (2009) says 'dissensus brings back into play both the obviousness of what can be perceived, thought and done, and the distribution of those who are capable of perceiving, thinking and altering the coordinates of the shared world' (49). A dissensus with consensual understandings of sustainability would involve a radical reconfiguration of who is able to have a voice and of what is expressible in public discourse around 'sustainability' in education policy. It will require drawing upon many dynamic understandings and practices of social, cultural, and environmental sustainability (Stoekl 2007; Dillard, Dujon, and King 2009; Monani 2011) in order to move beyond these neoliberal times.

Acknowledgments

Our thanks to Kathleen Aikens, Laurie Lidstone, Philip Vaughter, and Tarah Wright for their contributions to the development of the methods and the collection of the data referred to in this paper and to project manager Nicola Chopin for her very capable and constant support.

Funding

This publication draws on research from the Sustainability and Education Policy Network (SEPN), supported by a Partnership Grant from the Social Sciences and Humanities Research Council of Canada [grant number 895-2011-1025], Principal Investigator Dr. Marcia McKenzie. For more information, visit www.sepn.ca.

Notes

1. We understand 'sustainability' here as any policy that takes up the natural environment in some capacity, including in relation to social, economic, culture, health, and other factors. While we are concerned with the various ways sustainability terminology is engaged, we have limited the scope to those cases which include some reference to and consideration of environment.

2. We focus on the terminology of sustainability in this paper; however, in some cases, similar issues arise and have been discussed in relation to 'sustainable development' and other sustainability-related terminology. We draw on this broader literature in our discussion of sustainability.
3. Data were collected in 2012 from all 220 post-secondary institutions in Canada accredited with the Association of Universities and Colleges of Canada (AUCC) and the Association of Canadian Community Colleges (ACCC).
4. Policies which focused on sustainability goals but did not include any of the above terms in their titles totaled 6. Some policy titles included more than one of the terms, and thus, the numbers add up to more than 110.
5. For a content analysis of the policy documents of 50 of the 220 post-secondary institutions in Canada, see Vaughter et al. (forthcoming).
6. The Canadian federal government under Prime Minister Stephen Harper has revoked the protection of 99% of Canada's waterways and dismantled federal agencies responsible for environmental science and environmental assessment over the last several years to facilitate oil and tar sands development (Land 2013).

References

Adams, W. M. 2006. *The Future of Sustainability: Re-thinking Environment and Development in the Twenty-first Century.* Report of the IUCN Renowned Thinkers Meeting, January 29–31, The World Conservation Union.

Ball, S. J. 1994. *Education Reform: A Critical and Post-Structural Approach.* Buckingham: Open University Press.

Ball, S. J. 1997. "Policy Sociology and Critical Social Research: A Personal Review of Recent Education Policy and Policy Research." *British Educational Research Journal* 23 (3): 257–274.

Ball, S. J. 1998. "Big Policies/Small World: An Introduction to International Perspectives in Education Policy." *Comparative Education* 34 (2): 119–130.

Ball, S. J. 2013. *The Education Debate: Policy and Politics in the Twenty-first Century.* 2nd ed. Bristol: Polity Press.

Ball, S. J., and C. Junemann. 2012. *Networks, New Governance, and Education.* Bristol: Policy Press.

Ball, S. J., M. Maguire, and A. Braun. 2012. *How Schools Do Policy: Policy Enactments in Secondary Schools.* London: Routledge.

Beck, U. 2006. *Cosmopolitan Vision.* Malden, MA: Polity.

Beveridge, D., M. McKenzie, P. Vaughter, and T. Wright. (2015). "Sustainability in Canadian Post-Secondary Institutions: An Analysis of the Relationships among Sustain-ability Policy Initiatives and Geographic and Institutional Characteristics." *International Journal of Sustainability in Higher Education*, 16 (5): 611–638.

Bowe, R., S. J. Ball, and A. Gold. 1992. *Reforming Education and Changing Schools: Case Studies in Policy Sociology.* London: Routledge.

Brenner, N., J. Peck, and N. Theodore. 2010. "After Neoliberalization?" *Globalizations* 7 (3): 327–345.

Buscher, M., J. Urry, and K. Witchger. 2011. *Mobile Methods*. New York: Routledge.

Castree, N. 2007. *Neoliberal Environments: A Framework for Analysis*. Manchester: Manchester University. http://www.socialsciences.manchester.ac.uk/PEI/publications/wp/documents/Castree.pdf.

Coffey, B., and G. Marston. 2013. "How Neoliberalism and Ecological Modernization Shaped Environmental Policy in Australia." *Journal of Environmental Policy & Planning* 15 (2): 179–199.

Cooper, M. 2008. *Life as Surplus: Biotechnology & Capitalism in the Neoliberal Era*. Seattle, WA: University of Washington Press.

Cresswell, T. 2006. *On the Move: Mobility in the Modern Western World*. New York: Routledge.

Dale, R. 1992. "Recovering from a Pyrrhic Victory? Quality, Relevance and Impact in the Sociology of Education." In *Voicing Concerns: Sociological Perspectives on Contemporary Education Reforms*, edited by M. Arnot and L. Barton, 201–207. Wallingford: Triangle Books.

Dale, R. 1999. "Specifying Globalization Effects on National Policy: A Focus on the Mechanisms." *Journal of Education Policy* 14 (1): 1–17.

Davies, B., and P. Bansel. 2007. "Neoliberalism and Education." *International Journal of Qualitative Studies in Education* 20 (3): 247–259.

Davies, B., M. Gottsche, and P. Bansel. 2006. "The Rise and Fall of the Neo-Liberal University." *European Journal of Education* 41 (2): 305–319.

Dillard, J., V. Dujon, and M. C. King. 2009. *Understanding the Social Dimension of Sustainability*. New York: Routledge.

Frello, B. 2008. "Towards a Discursive Analytics of Movement: On the Making and Unmaking of Movement as an Object of Knowledge." *Mobilities* 3 (1): 25–50.

Garrett, G., F. Dobbin, and B. A. Simmons. 2008. "Conclusion." In *The Global Diffusion of Markets and Democracy*, edited by B. A. Simmons, F. Dobbin, and G. Garrett, 344–360. New York: Cambridge University Press.

Gonzalez-Gaudiano, E. 2005. "Education for Sustainable Development: Configuration and Meaning." *Policy Futures in Education* 3: 243–250.

Gonzalez-Gaudiano, E., and R. Nidioa Buenfil-Burgos. 2009. "The Impossible Identity of Environmental Education: Dissemination and Emptiness." In *Fields of Green: Restorying Culture, Environment, and Education*, edited by M. McKenzie, P. Hart, H. Bai, and B. Jickling, 97–108. Cresskill, NJ: Hampton Press.

Gough, S., and W. Scott. 2006. "Education and Sustainable Development: A Political Analysis." *Educational Review* 58 (3): 273–290.

Halpin, D., and B. Troyna. 1995. "The Politics of Education Policy Borrowing." *Comparative Education* 31 (3): 303–310.

Huckle, J. 2008. "An Analysis of New Labour's Policy on Education for Sustainable Development with Particular Reference to Socially Critical Approaches." *Environmental Education Research* 14 (1): 65–75.

Hursh, D. W., and J. A. Henderson. 2011. "Contesting Global Neoliberalism and Creating Alternative Futures." *Discourse: Studies in the Cultural Politics of Education* 32 (2): 171–185.

Irwin, R. 2007. "'After Neoliberalism': Environmental Education to Education for Sustainability." Paper presented at the Philosophy of Education Society of Australasia, Wellington, New Zealand.

Jickling, B., and A. E. J. Wals. 2008. "Globalization and Environmental Education: Looking beyond Sustainable Development." *Journal of Curriculum Studies* 40 (1): 1–21.

Jørgensen, M. W., and L. J. Philips. 2002. *Discourse Analysis as Theory and Method*. London: Sage.

Kerr, K. J., and J. S. Hart-Steffes. 2012. "Sustainability, Student Affairs, and Students." *New Directions for Student Services* 137: 7–17.

Klees, S. J. 2008. "A Quarter Century of Neoliberal Thinking in Education: Misleading Analyses and Failed Policies." *Globalisation, Societies and Education* 6 (4): 311–348.

Land, L. 2013. *A Summary of Current Federal Legislative Amendments Affecting First Nations*. Accessed March 23. http://www.oktlaw.com/wp-content/uploads/2013/01/summaryconcerns.pdf.

Larner, W., and N. Laurie. 2010. "Travelling Technocrats, Embodied Knowledges: Globalising Privatisation in Telecoms and Water." *Geoforum* 41: 218–226.

Lingard, B. 2011. "Policy as Numbers: Ac/Counting for Educational Research." *The Australian Educational Researcher* 38: 355–382.

Lingard, B., and J. Ozga, eds. 2007. *The RoutledgeFalmer Reader in Education Policy and Politics*. New York: Routledge.

Manteaw, B. 2008. "When Businesses Go to School: Neoliberalism and Education for Sustainable Development." *Journal of Education for Sustainable Development* 2 (2): 119–126.

McCann, E. J. 2011. "Urban Policy Mobilities and Global Circuits of Knowledge: Toward a Research Agenda." *Annals of the Association of American Geographers* 101 (1): 107–130.

McCann, E. J., and K. Ward. 2012. "Assembling Urbanism: Following Policies and 'Studying Through' the Sites and Situations of Policy Making." *Environment and Planning A* 44 (1): 42–51.

McKenzie, M. 2009. "Scholarship as Intervention: Critique, Collaboration, and the Research Imagination." *Environmental Education Research* 15: 217–226.

McKenzie, M. 2012. "Education for Y'all: Global Neoliberalism and the Case for a Politics of Scale in Sustainability Education Policy." *Policy Futures in Education* 10 (2): 165–177.

McLennan, G. 2004. "Travelling with Vehicular Ideas: The Case of the Third Way." *Economy and Society* 33 (4): 484–499.

Monani, S. 2011. "At the Intersections of Ecosee and Just Sustainability: New Directions for Communication Theory and Practice." *Environmental Communication: A Journal of Nature and Culture* 5 (2): 141–145.

Olssen, M., and M. A. Peters. 2005. "Neoliberalism, Higher Education and the Knowledge Economy: From the Free Market to Knowledge Capitalism." *Journal of Education Policy* 20 (3): 313–345.

Osborne, T. 2004. "On Mediators: Intellectuals and the Ideas Trade in the Knowledge Society." *Economy and Society* 33 (4): 430–447.

Ozga, J. 2000. *Policy Research in Educational Settings: Contested Terrain*. Buckingham: Open University Press.

Peck, J. 2011a. "Geographies of Policy: From Transfer-diffusion to Mobility-mutation." *Progress in Human Geography* 35 (6): 773–797.

Peck, J. 2011b. "Global Policy Models, Globalizing Poverty Management: International Convergence or Fast-Policy Integration?" *Geography Compass* 5 (4): 165–181.

Peck, J. 2012. "Recreative City: Amsterdam, Vehicular Ideas and the Adaptive Spaces of Creativity Policy." *International Journal of Urban and Regional Research* 36 (3): 462–485.

Peck, J. 2013. "Explaining (with) Neoliberalism." *Territory, Politics, Governance* 10: 1–24.

Peck, J., and N. Theodore. 2010a. "Mobilizing Policy: Models, Methods, and Mutations." *Geoforum* 41: 169–174.

Peck, J., and N. Theodore. 2010b. "Recombinant Workfare, across the Americas: Transnationalizing "Fast" Social Policy." *Geoforum* 41: 195–208.

Peck, J., N. Theodore, and N. Brenner. 2012. "Neoliberalism Resurgent? Market Rule after the Great Recession." *South Atlantic Quarterly* 111 (2): 265–288.

Peters, M. 2001. "Education, Enterprise Culture and the Entrepreneurial Self: A Foucauldian Perspective." *Journal of Educational Enquiry* 2 (2): 58–71.

Pierce, C. 2013. *Education in the Age of Biocapitalism: Optimizing Educational Life for a Flat World*. New York: Palgrave Macmillan.

Prince, R. 2012. "Metaphors of Policy Mobility: Fluid Spaces of 'Creativity' Policy." *Human Geography* 94 (4): 317–331.

Rancière, J. 2009. *Aesthetics and Its Discontents [Malaise dans L'esthétique]*. English ed. Malden, MA: Polity Press.

Rizvi, F., and B. Lingard. 2010. *Globalizing Educational Policy*. London: Routledge.

Shipan, C. R., and C. Volden. 2008. "The Mechanisms of Policy Diffusion." *American Journal of Political Science* 52 (4): 840–857.

Shipan, C. R., and C. Volden. 2012. "Policy Diffusion: Seven Lessons for Scholars and Practitioners." *Public Administration Review* 72 (6): 788–796.

Sneddon, C., R. B. Howarth, and R. B. Norgaard. 2006. "Sustainable Development in a Post-Brundtland World." *Ecological Economics* 57: 253–268.

Stevenson, R. 2013. "Researching Tensions and Pretensions in Environmental/Sustainability Education Policies: From Critical to Civically Engaged Policy Scholarship." In *International Handbook of Research on Environmental Education*, edited by R. B. Stevenson, M. Brody, J. Dillon, and A. E. J. Wals, 147–155. New York: Routledge.

Stoekl, A. 2007. *Bataille's Peak: Energy, Religion and Postsustainability.* Minneapolis, MN: University of Minnesota Press.

Swyngedouw, Erik. 2010. "Apocalypse Forever? Post-political Populism and the Spectre of Climate Change." *Theory, Culture & Society* 27 (2–3): 213–232. doi:10.1177/026327640 9358728.

Sylvestre, P., R. McNeil, and T. Wright. 2013. "From Talloires to Turin: A Critical Discourse Analysis of Declarations for Sustainability in Higher Education." *Sustainability* 5 (4): 1356–1371.

Temenos, C., and E. McCann. 2012. "The Local Politics of Policy Mobility: Learning, Persuasion, and the Production of a Municipal Sustainability Fix." *Environment and Planning a* 44: 1389–1406.

Temenos, C., and E. McCann. 2013. "Geographies of Policy Mobilities." *Geography Compass* 7 (5): 344–357.

Tuck, E., and M. McKenzie. 2015. *Place in Research: Theory, Methodology, and Methods.* New York: Routledge.

Urry, J. 2007. *Mobilities.* Malden, MA: Polity Press.

Urry, J. 2011. *Climate Change and Society.* Malden, MA: Polity Press.

Vaughter, P., M. McKenzie, L. Lidstone, and T. Wright. (2016). "Campus Sustainability Governance in Canada: A Content Analysis of Post-secondary Institutions' Sustainability Policies." *International Journal of Sustainability in Higher Education*, 17 (1): 16–39.

Weyland, K. 2005. "Theories of Policy Diffusion Lessons from Latin American Pension Reform." *World Politics* 57 (2): 262–295.

While, A., A. E. G. Jonas, and D. C. Gibbs. 2004. "The Environment and the Entrepreneurial City: The 'Sustainability Fix' in Leeds and Manchester." *International Journal of Urban and Regional Research* 28: 549–569.

Whitty, G., and T. Edwards. 1992. "School Choice Policies in Britain and the USA: Their Origins and Significance." Paper Presented at the Annual Meeting of the American Educational Research Association, San Francisco, California, April.

The Quest for Holism in Education for Sustainable Development

ANDREW STABLES and WILLIAM SCOTT

SUMMARY *'Sustainable development' is a 'paradoxical compound policy slogan' (Stables, 1996), of a type rhetorically constructed to appeal simultaneously to apparently opposed interest groups, and is widely recognised to be a contested notion. Indeed, structuralist and post-structuralist theories hold that no terms can have uncontested, stable meanings—even 'education'. Notwithstanding, environmental education (EE) has often been associated with a quest for a holistic worldview. This is despite the fact that the monological view of truth implied in such a quest, assuming absolute understanding (and thus enabling total control over nature), has been cited as contributing to the development of the ecological crisis.*

'Sustainable development' can, however, remain a regulative ideal for environmental educators, as long as it is acknowledged that it has no absolute legitimation. Human reflexivity remains capable of reworking the cultural traditions which have shaped late modernity with reference to such a regulative ideal, albeit variously recognised. The quest for holism remains one voice in a continuing dialogue, or series of simultaneous and sometimes overlapping dialogues, about the environment and the human relationship with it.

In *Tintern Abbey* (1798), William Wordsworth writes compellingly of 'Something far more deeply interfus'd/Whose dwelling is the light of setting suns/ And in the round ocean, and the living air/And the blue sky, and in the mind of man.' The literature of the time, both poetic and philosophical, is replete with a sense of wonder at the sublime grandeur and totality of Nature. We find it in Hegel, in the Kantian sublime, in the natural history of Humboldt, and in Keats' famous dictum that 'Beauty is Truth, Truth Beauty;/That is all ye know on Earth, and all ye need to know.'

'Yes,' remarked one of our undergraduate tutors of this Keatsian truism, 'but what does it *mean*?'

High Romanticism, very much a Northern European phenomenon (as, it might be argued, was the Green movement of the latter years of the 20th century) was the expression of a cultural and historical moment, no less than was the Industrial Revolution, in opposition to which it found its *raison d'être*. It speaks to us powerfully now, not only through its legacies, including ecology and respect for the human condition, but because we live still in a world riven, to a large extent, by the sometimes conflicting consequences of a scientific technology that 'murders to dissect' (to use another phrase from Wordsworth) and of its counter-forces of intuition, mysticism, community and a sense of wholeness. However, we shall argue that an appeal to holism in environmental and sustainable development education (SDE), across the broad spectrum of the application of these phrases, is problematic on three fronts: first, that the serious intellectual quest for holism was never itself sustainable; second, that there are no stable conceptions to which holism can be attached; and, third, that 'sustainable development' as a idea is itself highly ambivalent. In place of a naïve cross-curricular approach to SDE, we shall argue for disciplined environmental literacies, in the sense of a series of reflexive critiques of the human–nature relationship in each of the language-games that the curriculum promotes: in other words, we argue for SDE as within-disciplinary rather than cross-disciplinary concern.

It is possible to construe our argument as not anti-holistic at all, but merely pluralistic. We are, to this degree, sympathetic to Roy Bhaskar's call for an 'integrative and structured pluralism ... [acknowledging the] distinctions and connections between objects of scientific enquiry' (Bhaskar, 1986, pp. 106). Bhaskar, however, also warns against 'Monism/holism [that] spurns distinctions and is typical of positivistic philosophies of science' (1986, pp. 106). Our argument is against that which Lyotard (1983) has identified as the totalising tendency of modern thought, and a naïve faith in that which Derrida has decried as the Platonic 'metaphysics of presence': in other words, in this case, the assumption that at the heart of all our discourses about nature, there is an essential nature that we can know in some absolute sense. We are opposed to a holistic approach to SDE that assumes we should be aiming for a single and uncontested set of understandings and for complete consensus concerning future action.

Our first contention is that we cannot undo the historical process that led, particularly during the 19th century, from Humboldt's idealistic vision of the unity of Nature and the mind of Man to the post-Darwinian specialisation of the disciplines. In fact, a desire to understand the workings of Nature by means other than the intuitive has, of course, characterised the whole of the Western project, and has equally and, it would seem, inevitably been characterised by epistemological conflict. If there is much in Hegel which takes from the idealistic rationalism of Plato and has informed Arcadian visions through three millennia, there is also much in Darwin and the whole enterprise of Western science which is owed to the empirical bent of Plato's most famous pupil, Aristotle. Holism vs. atomism; rationalism vs. empiricism; faith vs. doubt. If modern humans rest their Being in such dualities, then it must also be the case that blind faith is always undesirable: while the quest for holism may remain a regulative ideal, the way to attaining it can never be clear. A post-structuralist view—and our argument is, in that sense, post-structuralist—might hold that we can transcend the dualisms of logocentric thinking, but not through adherence to anything with a clear or fixed referent meaning.

There is no single concept which can serve as the focal point of some new integrated discipline of, or 'for', SDE. As Rom Harre and others have pointed out (Harre *et al.*, 1999) the discourse of 'Greenspeak', however well intentioned, is prone to the most unprincipled borrowings from conflicting traditions: for instance, in the crude mixing of notions of palaeontological, cultural and personal time in the generation of a sense of imminent ecological crisis. Even 'Nature' is inherently unstable. To Shakespeare, human or divine Nature served as the touchstone for understanding all other forms of life: in *The Tempest*, the half-man, half-monster Caliban is described as 'a born devil, on whose nature/Nurture can never stick'; in contemporary vernacular, 'nature' generally refers to the non-human elements of the biosphere (though we still speak of 'human nature', in other contexts); in the 'natural sciences', specifically the physical sciences, nature can escape the organic entirely and becomes the play of abstract forces. However, at least the disciplines, by attempting to be true to themselves (though forever prone to change), enable some degree of clarity of thinking.

Our final objection concerns the phrase 'sustainable development', increasingly formalised as the aim of environmental education. Critical discourse analysts, such as Norman Fairclough (1995) regard compound terms such as 'sustainable development' as 'nominal compounds' with high 'ambivalence potential'; one of the authors of the present article has called such terms 'paradoxical compound policy slogans' (Stables, 1996). The argument is that, in democratic societies, politicians must find ways of appealing to previously diverse interest groups; to do this, they resort to the creation of compound terms which embrace what are otherwise opposite aspirations: 'parity' and 'esteem', 'multicultural' and 'society', 'equality' and 'opportunity', 'sustainability' and 'development'. Of course, one can argue that the new compound distils the best from each contributing element; certainly, one must acknowledge the various forms of good that have been done by those committed, in their own ways, to such regulative ideals as these—but regulative ideals they must remain, in that their ability to guide action is not linked to any clear referent meaning. There can never be any total consensus about how 'sustainability' can be married to 'development', though there can certainly be lively debate both around theoretical ideas and around explorations of sustainable development education. The gap between policy sloganising and policy implementation is very great, as politicians and educationalists forget to their peril, as at each stage those implementing a policy have their own 'secondary elaborations of belief' (Corson, 1988). 'Sustainable development' can never be pinned down without losing all its rhetorical power.

The Development of Disciplined Environmental Literacies

There being no 'one correct way of doing it' is not tantamount to a rejection of any means of making sense of how humanity–non-human nature relationships can be studied within each existing discipline. We have argued elsewhere (e.g. Stables, 1998; Stables & Scott, 1999; Stables & Bishop, 2001) that a disciplined view of environmental literacy, taking a broad view of text to include everything with which we engage semiotically, provides a useful framework for curriculum planning that valorises the potential diversity of curricular responses to the environmental and ecological crisis. As with print literacy, we can conceive of different levels, or types, of environmental literacy, such as functional, cultural and critical, and can examine how each of these might apply to the study of any particular subject without compromising or distorting it. In the study of history, for example, students can learn about the transformations of landscapes and their regional, national and global implications pre- and post-Industrial Revolution, and about how previous societies experienced and coped with their own crises of sustainability. While much historical work does not focus on societies within their natural contexts in this way, some does, notably the French *Annales* historian, Fernand Braudel, who distinguishes 'event time' from the '*longue duree*' defined, most markedly, by changes in climate, to which human beings have responded with various degrees of technological success. (For summary, see Lechte, 1994.) More recently, Simon Schama's *Landscape and Memory* (1995) charts changes in landscapes which have long had important roles in European and American culture. In literary studies, students can look at how natural setting and character are mutually implicated in works of poetry and fiction. There is a growing corpus of ecocriticism. Lawrence Buell, for example, has produced criteria for classifying nature writing, considering issues such as the implication of setting in the development of character (1995, pp. 6–7). The study of biology can examine how changes in our understanding of the natural world, from before Darwin to the mapping of the genome, can be associated with our changing views of the nature of humanity; in chemistry, students can learn about the implications of the laws of thermodynamics for energy usage; in physics, the same can be done with reference to our place in the universe, and the cultural shifts associated with, for example, Galileo, Newton and Einstein.

The development of such environmental literacies (please note the use of the plural) does not, of course, guarantee the saving of the planet from ecological destruction, but nothing does. While the emphasis in much environmental education to date has been narrowly teleological, we argue that really useful education, at least in the Western tradition, never accepts a monological view of the truth and the clear end-points one can associate with it, and that real personal change (which may, indeed, help to save the planet from ecological destruction, directly or indirectly by making us *behave* differently) can only be effected through an education that problematises and acknowledges multiple voices. Paradoxically, education for the whole child requires an acknowledgement that there is no whole truth.

This begs the question of how teachers can be prepared to develop such disciplined environmental literacies.

Over the last 20 years or so, there has been no shortage of advice and direction to teachers and teacher trainers about the nature of the professional development needed to prepare teachers and schools to deal with the, often vaguely expressed, environmental and ecological crises facing society. Inevitably, most of this has been set out under the heading of *environmental* education with only recently the notion of sustainable development (sustainability) becoming a significant factor—and even then without the concept's being problematised. Most of the work on teacher training within environmental education stems from UNESCO'S International Environmental Education Programme (see, for example, Hungerford *et al.*, 1988) arising directly from the imperative that teacher education in environmental education should be the 'priority of priorities' (re-emphasised in UNESCO–UNEP, 1990). For historical reviews of these developments, see Tilbury (1992) and NAAEE (1994); for an analytical critique of their limitations, see Oulton and Scott (1995). The OECD's ENSI (Environmental Education in Schools Initiative) has also been significant in generating both theory and practice in relation to environmental teacher education (see, for example, Kyburz-Graber & Robottom, 1999). In a previous article, Scott (1996) has attempted to draw these developments together. In other recent work linking sustainability and teacher professional development, (see, for example, Shallcross et al., 2000) there continues to be a tendency to address sustainability issues from within an environmental education framework, implicitly seeing education related to sustainability/sustainable development as an extension of environmental education and, as such, as being conceptually relatively unproblematic, although administratively, of course, it remains complex.

However, much of the complexity derives from attempts to develop a cross-curricular or multi-disciplinary approach in contexts which are either dominated (in secondary schools) or heavily influenced (in primary/middle schools) by structures which are organised conceptually, managerially and temporally around single disciplines. Whitty et al. (1994) have developed a critique of recent attempts within the UK to promote cross-curricularity. We have already set out a number of reasons for a within-discipline approach to environmental literacy so that reflexive critiques of the human–nature relationship can be made with maximum clarity in the discipline-structured curriculum in order that a useful framework for curriculum planning, which encourages a diversity of responses to the environmental and ecological crises, can be provided. There is another, pragmatic reason, which is that to do so is to work with the grain of school life and teacher professional development. Teachers, especially in secondary schools, are nurtured at school, in higher education and in teacher training through disciplines, and their work is similarly structured. It is what they know and profess. If this needs to evolve, it had better be approached from within the confidence of the discipline.

It might be argued that for a discipline to develop environmental literacy, a suitable conceptual framework is necessary; that is, a prior interpretation of sustainable development as a regulatory ideal is required. We have already suggested, through examples, a number of different issues that might be explored from within disciplinary bases. To what extent do we need a structure that will allow teachers to explore these issues for themselves? This might not be definitive or even broadly accepted; indeed, given the field, a degree of tentativeness adds to usefulness as it encourages critique and acknowledges, and thus valorises, the possibility of plural perspectives. We shall now consider two approaches, the first less radical than the second. In the first, a framework is provided which can be used differentially within disciplines; in the second, no such generic framework is considered appropriate.

In terms of the first approach, it might be considered that such a framework is provided by the work of the Higher Education 21 initiative (HE21, 1999) which sets out seven key sustainability concepts, a series of process values (Crick, 1999) supporting 'sustainability solutions', and three sets of draft learning outcomes relating to 'effective sustainability teaching'. The key concepts are:

- Interdependence—of society, economy and the natural environment, from local to global
- Citizenship and stewardship—rights and responsibilities, participation and cooperation
- Needs and rights of future generations
- Diversity—cultural, social, economic and biological
- Quality of life, equity and justice
- Sustainable change—development and carrying capacity
- Uncertainty and precaution (acknowledgment of the limits of our knowledge: not to act unless the impacts are known)

The issue is not so much whether these *are* the key concepts, or whether there are *seven* of them; rather, it is whether the framework which they provide can act as a starting point for the development of within-discipline interpretations of a functional, cultural and critical environmental literacy.

Our more radical approach, by contrast, holds that a within-disciplinary approach should not be based on any such outside framework as, almost by definition, the imposition of such a framework alters the primary agenda of the discipline. After all, the humanity–nature relationship is already explored in many ways in curriculum subjects; we have already cited examples of what does, and what easily could, happen with respect to this. As part of the EU-funded project, 'The Development of Environmental Awareness through Literature and Media Education', a collaboration between the universities of Bath, Ghent and Oporto, we developed five foci, with a view to developing environmental awareness through literature and media education methods such that what emerged was 'good literature/media teaching' *as well as*, as opposed to *in the service of* environmental education; in other words, we did not wish to reduce the role of literature to one of the expression or clarification of either ecological or their related social issues (Bishop *et al.*, 2000). The foci were developed from an analysis of the ways in which good literature and media teaching interrelate the ideas of text, human interests and nature. The foci were as follows:

(1) The development of understanding of environmental issues through the study of literary and media texts. Teachers provoking thinking and discussion of environmental issues as part of the study of both classic literary texts and media texts, such as feature films, reflecting a broad cross-section of European traditions, whether or not these are principally texts overtly concerned with what we might call 'environmental issues'.
(2) The study of literary and media texts specifically concerned with the environment. Developing teachers' ability to address such texts critically, in order to enable students both to compare and contrast the treatment given to issues in differing texts and to evaluate such texts in terms of their effective handling of the issues.
(3) The creation of literary and media texts relating to environmental issues. Providing help for teachers in enabling students to produce good quality texts about environmental issues, and helping them to evaluate their and others' work critically.
(4) The study of aspects of the environment itself as text. It is possible to adopt a very broad definition of text which incorporates, at the very least, crafted

landscape features such as parks and gardens, and which, in its extreme form, can even be held to include purely 'natural' landscapes.

(5) The re-creation and enhancement of the environment with reference to aesthetic considerations. As an extension of (4), examining ways in which environmental conservation, repair and improvement can be carried out with reference to aesthetic considerations as well as to the notion of the environment as a cultural and social construct.

In summary: according to our first approach, frameworks such as those provided by the Panel's key concepts, the work of the HE21 project, or, for example, by the Learning for a Sustainable Environment project (UNESCO, 1997), are useful in helping teachers and others to think through what amounts to the reinterpretation of their disciplines in light of a sustainable development agenda. Here, a teacher development priority must be the generation of means whereby teachers can begin to engage with ideas which will very likely lie beyond their experiences of working within their disciplines.

However, the arguments underpinning the creation of frameworks such as those to which we have referred are rarely spelt out in policy documents. It might be argued that only the most highly motivated teachers and teacher-trainers will make the effort to come to grips with frameworks from outside their disciplines that have apparently been imposed upon them without clear explication of their rationales; these are exacting conditions for success. To follow this line is to move towards arguing for our second approach in preference: that what we should be about is examining, in a vaguely Foucauldian way, the various ways in which each discipline construes, and has construed, the human–nature relationship. Such an approach is uncertain, but, we would argue, no more uncertain in its outcomes than the first approach, which assumes a false consensus regarding sustainable development.

REFERENCES

BHASKAR, R. (1986) *Scientific Realism and Human Emancipation* (London, Verso).

BISHOP, K., REID, A., STABLES, A., LENCASTRE, M., STOER, S. & SOETAERT, R. (2000) Developing environmental awareness through literature and media education: curriculum development in the context of teachers' practice, *Canadian Journal of Environmental Education*, 5, pp. 268–286.

BUELL, L. (1995) *The Environmental Imagination: Thoreau, nature writing and the formation of American culture* (Cambridge, MA, Belknap Press).

CORSON, D. (1988) Making the language of education policies more user-friendly, *Journal of Education Policy*, 3(3), pp. 249–260.

CRICK, B. (1999) The presuppositions of citizenship education, *Journal of Philosophy of Education*, 33(3), pp. 337–352.

FAIRCLOUGH, N, (1995) *Critical Discourse Analysis: the critical study of language* (London, Longman).

HARRE, R., BROCKMEIR, J. & MUHLHAUSLER, P. (1999) *Greenspeak: a study of environmental discourse* (London, Sage).

HE21 (1999) *Sustainable Development Education: teacher education specification* (London, Forum for the Future).

HUNGERFORD, H.R., VOLK, T.L., DIXON, B.G., MARCINKOWSKI, T.J. & ARCHIBALD, P.C. (1988) *An Environmental Education Approach to the Training of Elementary Teachers: a teacher education programme*. International Environmental Education Programme. Environmental Education Series No. 27 (Paris, UNESCO–UNEP).

KYBURZ-GRABER, R. & ROBOTTOM, I. (1999) The OECD–ENSI Project and its relevance for teacher training concepts in environmental education, *Environmental Education Research*, 5(3), pp. 273–292.

LECHTE, J. (1994) *Fifty Key Contemporary Thinkers: from structuralism to postmodernity* (London, Routledge).

LYOTARD, J.-F. (1983) *The Postmodern Condition: a report on knowledge* (Manchester, Manchester University Press).

NAAEE (1994) *Developing a Framework for Environmental Educator Performance Standards*. National Standards for Environmental Education Project Working Paper 3 (Troy, OH, North American Association for Environmental Education).

OULTON, C.R. & SCOTT, W.A.H. (1995) The Environmentally Educated Teacher an exploration of the implications of UNESCO–UNEP's ideas for pre-service teacher education programmes, *Environmental Education Research*, 1(2), pp. 213–231.

SCOTT, W.A.H. (1996) The environmentally-educating teacher: a synthesis of an implementation theory for pre-service courses, *Australian Journal of Environmental Education*, 12, pp. 53–60.

SCHAMA, S. (1995) *Landscape and Memory* (London, Harper Collins).

SHALLCROSS, T., O'LOAN, K. & HUI, D. (2000) Developing a school-focused approach to continuing professional development in sustainability education, *Environmental Education Research*, 6(4), pp. 363–382.

STABLES, A. (1996) Paradox in educational policy slogans: evaluating equal opportunities in subject choice, *British Journal of Educational Studies*, 44(2), pp. 159–167.

STABLES, A. (1998) Environmental literacy: functional, cultural, critical. The case of the SCAA guidelines, *Environmental Education Research*, 4(2), pp. 155–164.

STABLES, A. & BISHOP, K. (2001) Strong and weak conceptions of environmental literacy, *Environmental Education Research*, 7(1), pp. 89–97.

STABLES, A. & SCOTT, W. (1999) Environmental education and the discourses of humanist modernity: redefining critical environmental literacy, *Educational Philosophy and Theory*, 31(2), pp. 145–155.

TILBURY, D. (1992) Environmental education within pre-service teacher education: the priority of priorities, *International Journal of Environmental Education and Information*, 11(4), pp. 267–280.

UNESCO–UNEP (1990) Environmentally educated teachers, the priority of priorities?, *Connect*, 15(1), pp. 1–3.

UNESCO (1997) *Learning for a Sustainable Environment* (Griffith University, UNESCO Asia-Pacific Centre of Educational Innovation for Development).

WHITTY, G., ROWE, G. & AGGLETON, P. (1994) Discourse in cross-curricular contexts, *International Studies in Sociology of Education*, 4(1), pp. 25–42.

Tensions and transitions in policy discourse: recontextualizing a decontextualized EE/ESD debate

Robert B. Stevenson

Introduction

For many scholars (see Smyth, 1995; Tilbury, 1995; Fien & Tilbury, 2002; Hopkins & McKeown, 2002) the emergence of the discourse of education for sustainable development (ESD) over the past 15 or so years is viewed as a progressive transition in the field, along similar lines to the positive portrayal of prior historical transitions from nature study to conservation education to environmental education (Stevenson, 1987). Two claimed advancements represented by this new discourse are identified by Smyth (1995) as: (1) the replacement of a problem (or negative) orientation associated with environmental education by a contrasting positive orientation of ESD; and (2) a shift from an almost exclusive focus on environmental concerns without attention to social and human development issues (in environmental education), to the inclusion of social and economic development alongside the environmental dimension (in ESD). The conceptual superiority of ESD is continually claimed despite the acknowledgement by many of the same authors of the definitional problems of the term 'sustainable development' (SD), principally its fuzziness or ambiguity which has led to multiple, often contradictory interpretations. Given these tensions in the concept that is foundational to ESD, questions then arise as to how such tensions play out in the discourse of ESD, and the extent to which such a policy orientation can provide a helpful framework for thinking about practice and making a transition away from environmental education.

In this vignette I first examine Smyth's (1995) and Bonnett's (2002) different positions on the potential for clarifying the ambiguities and contradictions of the concept of sustainable development, before focusing on Smyth's two claims. Central to both this issue of clarifying meanings of sustainable development and Smyth's second claim is the polarization of viewpoints on the human–environment connection which, drawing in part on Bonnett's different philosophical perspective, I argue is limiting. Finally, in looking ahead to address the policy–practice tensions in environmental education and ESD, I argue for contextualizing policy discourses by engaging educators in their co-construction.

Sustainable development as an ambiguous goal

An examination of the discourse, including the purposes and characteristics, of ESD requires a consideration of how sustainable development itself is conceptualized (Scott, 2005). The concept of sustainable development, first introduced by the World Conservation Strategy (IUCN *et al.*, 1980) but given international currency by the World Commission on Environment and Development or Brundtland Report (1987) and then by Agenda 21, has been variously described as imprecisely defined, ambiguous, socially and culturally contested, and therefore subject to both a wide range of interpretations (Fien & Tilbury, 2002) and internal contradictions (Bonnett, 2002). This ambiguity or fuzziness is seen by some as advantageous in promoting reflection and dialogue and allowing for the development of a consensus about sustainable development (Pezzey, 1989), while others describe it as an example of a 'paradoxical compound policy slogan' (Stables & Scott, 2002) that enables people with widely different views to accept it to some degree but without agreeing on any of the underlying philosophical and political issues which remain obscured and in tension. The authors of the Brundtland Report seem to acknowledge some of these concerns in indicating that their statement of sustainable development raises as many questions as it answers, but they argued that it represents ideals and implied that certain issues of ambiguity and uncertainty will be addressed as the concept is put into practice while other new problems and potentials are likely to be revealed in the process.

While both Smyth and Bonnett acknowledge the problematic nature of the concept, Bonnett is less optimistic than Smyth and the Brundtland Commission about the possibility of achieving clarity and identifies three major issues (semantic, ethical and epistemological) with sustainable development as a policy goal. He argues that ethical questions—such as 'How is any ethical dimension to be grounded?'—and epistemological questions—such as 'How are we to judge which actions will positively contribute to sustainable development?'—are far from a satisfactory resolution. Meanwhile, Smyth believes that the lack of clarity should—and therefore presumably can—be avoided, especially by educators who should be clear what they mean when using the term. While acknowledging the importance of educators constructing their own understanding of sustainable development, it should be recognized that this requires considerable time and effort on the behalf of the educators if the extensive debates in the literature are any indicator of the complexity of the issues involved.

Not only is conceptual clarity missing but so also are illustrative examples or 'case histories' which could provide support materials for educators. Although there is a vast and burgeoning literature on some aspects of sustainable communities, such as sustainable agriculture and the design of energy efficient systems, materials are not currently accessible or available to most educators in a form that is relevant to primary and secondary students or that can be readily adopted for use in school classrooms. Building an environmentally sustainable society would seem to require some vision of what it would look like, but such visions are difficult to find on a societal scale although more limited visions might be gleaned from efforts within many countries to create more sustainable communities. Describing how sustainable individual life-styles and community practices can be shaped into a wider sustainable society is a difficult and risky proposition. McKeown and Hopkins (2003) acknowledge that both the means to and the ends of sustainability are unknown, but argue that if we understand what is unsustainable about current lifestyles, then we should be able to clearly identify what is sustainable. The task of creating such a vision is however complicated by the unanswered (and perhaps unanswerable) question: What is to be sustained? (Bonnett, 2002). Educators do not need a vision to adopt, but do need to construct, preferably through a thoughtful process of critical inquiry, reflection and dialogue, their own understanding of sustainable development that can guide them in their curriculum planning and teaching. After all, it is their own understanding of this concept that will shape their pedagogical practices in ESD. In the absence of such understanding, teachers are likely to find it difficult to help young people acquire a sense of their place in co-constructing a sustainable society.

The tripartite conceptualization and contradictions of sustainable development

Although definitions and visions are elusive, one of the few points of consensus is that the concept of sustainable development unites—or more accurately, attempts to unite—social, economic and environmental factors (Summers *et al.*, 2003) into a 'triple bottom line' (Scott, 2005). One advantage of this conceptual model is that 'it reduces a complex and elusive notion to more familiar and manageable proportions' that fit into existing disciplinary and institutional structures (Gough, 2002, p. 71). Yet there is the problem of fragmenting knowledge construction and problem solving, especially given that the world doesn't function in neat categories. Additionally, the shift in the debate from environmental issues to sustainable development 'presup-poses the validity of pursuing economic, social and environmental aims in tandem' (Stables & Scott, 2001, p. 133). This assumption has been challenged philosophi-cally, in particular in the 2001 special issue of *Educational Philosophy and Theory*, and, to some extent, politically as a strategy for increasing Government attention to environmental concerns, especially in developing or countries of the South (Gonza-lez-Gaudiano, 2005). In a political context, priorities are always established and historically, at least since the Second World War, economics has been 'the primary focus of public policy as well as of individual and public choices' (Henderson, 1996,

p. 7). Despite evidence of heightened global problems such as climate change, environmental considerations continue to be subordinated to economic ones.

Some writers also argue that sustainable development has been conceptualized to maintain the economic status quo and current socio-economic structures—paradoxically, the very structures that appear to have created our current ecological problems are seen as part of the solution (Rees, 1992). For example, Rees points out that *Our common future* assumes that economic growth is the primary vehicle for addressing both poverty and environmental sustainability. In the first case, an expanded economic pie is seen as enabling the poor to eventually obtain an adequate share; an argument that not only is contrary to the evidence that economic growth in the past has not eradicated poverty but only created a greater share for the rich, but it also avoids political debate and inevitable conflicts about a more equitable (re)distribution of incomes and resources. Second, it is highly questionable whether industrial production can be expanded without further degradation to the environment. Despite the widely-held and continuing belief that economic growth and/or markets can provide the means to correct environmental problems, there is as yet little evidence to support such a relationship (with the exception of a reduction in sulphur dioxide emissions in rich industrialized nations achieved through emissions trading) (Martinez-Alier, 1999).

Yet a positive contribution of the sustainable development discourse, according to Smyth, is 'its adoption of humankind into the system it sets out to conserve' (1995, p. 10). Certainly, issues of human development are related to issues of environment. For far too many people in the world, a sustainable lifestyle involves 'the most basic of securities, such as food, water, sanitation, freedom from violence' (p. 11). Thus, a concern for the human condition, in addition to the environmental condition, is much needed, even overdue. However, human survival and economic growth are dependent on energy and material resources that are extracted from natural ecosystems (Rees, 1992). In other words, the economy is not only intertwined with, but also wholly dependent on, natural capital and ecological limits. Although many of these limits cannot, at least as yet, be established with any degree of certainty, it is clear they exist (Scott, 2005). Rather than seeking a balance across the economic, social and environmental arenas, 'the real bottom line is the ecological integrity of the biosphere' (Scott, 2005, p. 2). Given that prevailing patterns of development are unsustainable, we must learn how—and why we need—to live on 'the interest generated by remaining stocks of natural capital' (Rees, 1992, p. 25). Despite its imprecise measures, the concept of ecological footprints, for example, offers one way for teachers to engage students concretely in examining why current lifestyles, at least in countries of the North, are unsustainable.

At the same time, however, efforts to live within these limits can be pursued at the continued expense of the poor and the powerless. In addition to the ecological imperative, there is a moral imperative to alleviate human suffering and provide basic material well-being for all humankind. Therefore, I would argue these two imperatives constitute an alternative double bottom line. Economic development is not an imperative because it should be viewed only as a means of contributing to human development and not what it has become, an end in itself. Furthermore, political measures, such as redistribution of wealth, although often considered politically unpalatable, are possible for achieving the dual goals of living within environmental limits without human suffering.

What then are the implications for ESD of these issues surrounding conceptions of sustainable development? If there is a danger that sustainable development can conceal rather than reveal the tensions in pursuing economic development while sustaining environmental quality and relieving human suffering, then why might ESD be seen by some as a progressive transition from environmental education? That question needs to be examined within the context of arguments about the limitations of environmental education.

Environmental education and the problem orientation concern

The emphasis in the environmental education policy documents that were widely promulgated after the inter-Governmental conferences in Belgrade (1976) and Tbilisi (1977) can be read as more focused on the environment than on human development and such issues as poverty, standard of living, and human rights (McKeown & Hopkins, 2002), although these issues are included. Nevertheless, prior to the emergence of ESD, some argued that environmental education is intimately connected to development, human rights and peace education (Greig et al., 1987), while similarly social transformation-oriented environmental educators have argued for 'interrogating the relationship between environmental issues and gender, race and class' (Russell, 1997, p. 38). Where the Tbilisi statements referred to 'environment', Agenda 21 substituted 'environment and development' (Gough, 1997), suggesting a transition to a greater concern for social and economic concerns. Others (see Sauvé, 1996; Gonzalez, this issue), however, have pointed out that the human dimension was discussed in the Belgrade and Tbilisi reports and therefore, ask 'what is really new about ESD?' The answer seems to be more one of emphasis than new substance, although this change of emphasis is troubling to many who feel it devalues environmental considerations and that we need to recover the environmental concerns embedded in environmental education. As Spring (2004) puts it, a key concern here is that the ESD discourse maintains an instrumental and anthropocentric worldview and excludes consideration of an eco-centric or bio-centric perspective.

A second difference in emphasis that is viewed as significant by the advocates of the ESD discourse relates to policy. The policy objectives and principles for environmental education emphasized that its goals should focus on the development of students' problem solving, critical thinking, decision-making and participation skills in addressing environmental issues and actively working toward the resolution of environmental problems (Tbilisi Declaration, 1978). These internationally agreed upon policy statements underlie the second conclusion reached by Smyth (1995) that the character of environmental education has been associated with environmental problems, including global issues (such as acid rain, the greenhouse effect, climate change) which are complex and subject to 'continuing scientific development'. He argues that this focus in environmental education on environmental problems has two significant limitations: (1) it presents a negative rather than positive or healthy state as the norm; and (2) it leads educators, who have to try and make sense of these issues, to frequently over-simplify and reach hasty judgments about these issues.

Smyth's explanation for his first concern is that a focus on the environment as problems may be counter-productive, especially in working with children, and that a healthy state should be presented as normal with problems viewed as 'injuries, diseases or maladjustments' that need to be treated and corrected. This conclusion is supported by teachers who have expressed concerns about the negative effects on students of teaching about environmental disasters (Cross, 1998; Hicks, 2002; Christenson, 2004). However, there seems to be an additional implicit assumption that adopting a positive orientation means that students will become (or at least more likely to become) motivated to learn about and take actions to improve the environment. This assumption is questionable given that studies on student motivation have indicated that a positive approach is not sufficient to engage students, especially older children and adolescents, in learning (Brophy, 1987). Intrinsic interest, a sense of ownership of the work, a challenging task, and connections to the real world—especially their own lives—have each been reported as more important factors for student engagement (Newmann, 1990; Stevenson, 1990).

With regard to Smyth's second limitation to the problem-based conceptualization of EE, no doubt there is a tendency among many teachers, often supported by topics listed in curriculum guidelines and the availability of related curriculum materials, to focus on the kind of complex, well publicized and commonly accepted global environmental problems that he identifies. The press for coverage—whereby teachers try to squeeze everything they think is important and worth knowing into their curriculum—and the press for right answers (in response to the perceived demands of standardized tests in many countries) frequently results in the reduction of these issues to oversimplified and discrete facts and concepts and leaves a perception that action, albeit limited, is being taken on these issues in schools. But to what extent can this legitimate concern be attributed to a problem orientation to education and the environment? Are other explanations, such as the kind of problems selected and the way in which they are treated in schools, more compelling?

As I have argued elsewhere (Stevenson, 1997), an alternative approach is the intensive, in-depth study of fewer, less complex, local environmental problems or issues that connect to students' lives. This approach is more likely than the transmission of discrete environmental facts and concepts to develop more important and enduring outcomes, such as critical thinking capacities for analyzing and interpreting human–environment relationships and the value positions underlying environmental issues. Research in the ENSI project in Europe (Elliott, cited in Robottom, 1992; see also Elliott, 1995), and on promoting higher order or critical thinking in the USA (Onosko & Newmann, 1994) lends support about the impact of this approach and furthers understanding of how teachers can emphasize such inquiries. Similarly, research on problem-based learning (PBL) suggests the potential of a problem orientation to developing flexible understanding and skills for lifelong learning about complex issues (Hmelo-Silver, 2004). If we agree that education has a responsibility 'to develop a critical approach to what is communicated to us by others and also to what we perceive ourselves' (Smyth, 1995, p. 5), then a problem orientation with the kinds of pedagogical thinking and practices revealed by the above research is one way that this goal can possibly be achieved. On the other hand, the disciplinary structure of secondary education, a curriculum organization around pre-specified outcomes, the expectations for a teacher-directed pedagogy, and the demands for individual assessment of student learning, present teachers with a number of significant challenges in pursuing this approach.

The above alternative would seem to fit with what Bonnett terms a 'democratic approach', something which he questions in terms of the sufficiency of pure rationality in understanding environmental issues given both the power of 'exploitative and consumerist motives' to override any rational or logical decisions and the non-rational role of spirituality and identification (e.g., with place and peer groups) in shaping many people's decisions about environmental issues. Although non-rational factors play an important role in policy decision-making, these factors can be addressed pedagogically as part of the process of formulating a moral code on environmental issues and in critically appraising the values involved in different positions on environmental policy issues. Of course, as evidenced in Smyth's later report on the failure to implement a national ESD strategy in Scotland (Lavery & Smyth, 2003), non-rational political factors can play a major role in environmental education policy decisions. So, while rationality alone cannot account for most environmental and educational decisions, environmental education processes need not exclude the consideration of non-rational factors; however, there is often a tendency for educators to do so, for example, K-12 teachers avoiding political dimensions (Cross, 1998), and university teachers, especially perhaps scientists, steering clear of the spiritual.

ESD as a positive goal

How then, according to Smyth, does ESD address the limitations of environmental education he identified? The emergence of the concept of sustainable development is viewed by Smyth (1995) as a major advancement for its proactive, rather than reactive, approach to the environment, by 'aiming to prevent problems arising rather than cleaning up afterwards' (p. 10). Others, similarly, have claimed that a focus on sustainability has brought a strong futures orientation with the result that 'we no longer start with problem-solving but with envisioning a better quality of life and considering how we can achieve it' (Tilbury, email communication, 2003). This focus is seen as a clear transition from or 'move away from the 'doom and gloom' scenarios which dominated much of environmental education work in the 1980s' (*ibid.*) and is illustrated by a case study of ESD programmes in Germany. Arguing the need for 'a more hopeful modern ecological modernization scenario' rather than a 'fear scenario' of environmental degradation and resource depletion, De Haan and

Harenberg have developed a framework for supporting ESD in schools across Germany that is based on the belief 'that people can create and plan for the future in an optimistic way, rather than looking backwards or viewing the future or people's capacity pessimistically' (Reid & Nikel, 2004, p. 12; see also De Haan, 2006, and other contributors to that special issue of *Environmental Education Research* focused on environmental education and ESD projects, development and research in a range of German-speaking countries). Underlying De Haan and Harenberg's belief is a conception of competence in decision-making and planning that will assist the individual to master unpredictable situations and to model 'one's own future and the future of a community together with others' (Reid & Nikel, 2004, p. 13). To achieve this competence, three major lesson planning and organizational principles are proposed by De Haan and Harenberg: interdisciplinary knowledge (emphasizing, for example, creativity, multiple ways of knowing, and systemic and holistic thinking), participatory learning (through such projects as sustainability audits and student environmental businesses), and innovative school structures (e.g., enabling cooperation with the community) (*ibid.*).

No doubt, there is a more positive orientation to a focus on the proactive question of how can we ensure sustainable communities and societies in the future, rather than an emphasis on how to solve current environmental problems. And, education, as Cross (1998) observes, is intended to be 'basically an optimistic activity, an investment in the future' (p. 47). However, not only must we determine the ends and nature of a more sustainable society, but we also need to explore the origins and consequences of current unsustainable practices (Hicks & Holden, 1995). In other words, we can't address a vision of a sustainable society without simultaneously considering the present state of our environmental health, including existing problems that need to be tackled. Stated another way, the concept of sustainability is founded on the belief that there is a problem in viewing progress as represented by economic growth unconstrained by any ecological limits. So while ESD may be futures oriented, it raises serious questions about that future, as well as about the present status quo (Sterling, 2001, 2004). A pedagogical question concerns the appropriate starting point—is it the present (negative) situation, or a future (optimistic or pessimistic) vision? Note that this is not a choice between the solution of present environmental problems or the prevention of future ones, as both should be examined.

A second issue for education is the need to balance the development of individual competency and agency, which is necessary but not sufficient for creating sustainable societies, with attention to collective agency, such as the role of social movements, and the politics of social change. Educational institutions traditionally have been far more focused on and effective in individual development than in fostering the collaborative skills needed by community groups and social movements in political organizing and advocacy. Work on a humanities curriculum for citizen action skills (Newmann *et al.*, 1977), participatory or citizen action research and liberatory pedagogy (Freire, 1993), participatory learning to achieve *Gestaltungskompetenz* or citizen competence (Reid & Nikel, 2004; De Haan, 2006), and Danish action competence in environmental education (Jensen, 2002), all offer important ideas for educators in contributing to the development of collective agency.

Rather than his concern that environmental education can over-simplify issues in addressing environmental problems, in this case a positive or 'position of normality' approach, Smyth expresses a concern that ESD demands a simplification which can only be achieved 'from a high level of understanding of how the healthy system is constituted, and therefore requires that scientists and educators should work more closely together to produce acceptable interpretations' (Smyth, 1995, p. 10). Not only is current knowledge on that very question contested and 'subject to continuing scientific development', as Smyth notes, but there is the practical challenge of creating time and opportunities for teachers, at least in K-12 schooling, to work with scientists and develop such sophisticated understandings of the complexity of the issue of what represents a healthy sustainable system.

If ESD overcomes what are perceived to be significant limitations of the problem-orientation of environmental education, and if, as Smyth claims, the central principle in ESD of intergenerational equity 'is a successful means of encouraging people to think positively about vital issues' (p. 10), then the expectation should be that ESD becomes more prevalent in schools than environmental education has been. Yet, thus far, there is no reported evidence for this in primary and secondary schools or in post-secondary education. On the other hand, its limited implementation should not be surprising given not only the practical challenges described above, but also the problems, like EE, of implementing such a radical ideology and pedagogy (Spring, 2004) that challenges dominant political and ideological interests and structures, as well as the purposes and structures of schooling (Stevenson, 1987).

The human–environment problematic

Smyth refers to the inevitable tensions between human and environmental qualities as the main objectives or priorities of both environmental education and ESD. He attributes part of the problem of helping people understand the human–environment connection to the original motivation for environmental education to conserve the natural environment which shaped the connotation of the term 'environment'. Even today, he argued, many people still define the environment as 'green', or comprising only nature, and therefore see it as separated from their own lives, rather than an extension of them, making it difficult to address the impact of human behavior. A task of environmental education, Smyth believed, is to correct this situation and help people understand 'the totality of what we live in, natural or constructed, spatial, social and temporal' (p. 4) and the connections between their own behavior and the environment. Few environmental educators I imagine would argue with this task which is particularly pertinent given that teachers need to try and make connections to students' lives.

The problem is that an underlying assumption of the modern/industrial world-view is that humans as a species stand above and separate from the natural world (Smith, 1992; Bowers, 1993; Spring, 2004). Even the accumulation of enormous quantities of technical information has failed to enhance our 'understanding of our connections with and dependence on nature' (Plant, 1995, p. 260), both as individuals and societies. As a result, this industrial/technological and anthropo-centric worldview has remained a part of the hidden curriculum of schooling (Orr, 1994).

Many writers, therefore, have argued that a paradigm shift is required from an anthropocentric to an eco- or bio-centric worldview. This alternative worldview, however, risks divesting us of our humanity in not recognizing our unique capacity to construct views of reality or worldviews which themselves must in some sense be anthropocentric since 'the non-human can only be defined in human terms' (Gough et al., 2000, p. 44). Bonnett (2002) offers a similar critique of the eco-centric view as failing to account for the special role of human consciousness. The binary polariza-tion of perspectives, however, limits the possibilities to the extremes of a duality. Instead, Bonnett proposes a position which is neither anthropocentric in 'seeing our relationship with the environment as properly oriented around human interests or wants, nor eco-centric in the sense of subsuming us in, or subordinating us to, some greater whole' (p. 17) but 'locates the essence of sustainability in the nature of human consciousness itself' (p. 18). Rejecting instrumental conceptions of sustainable devel-opment and its treatment as a policy goal, he proposes thinking of sustainability as a frame of mind with a focus on human flourishing. He argues, drawing on Heidegger, that 'alienation from nature and from self are highly interrelated and key to our ability to knowingly despoil the environment' (p. 18). If we value ourselves, then we will value that which we believe supports us. Thus, part of the task of education for sustainability, he proposes, is to reconnect people to their origins, what sustains them and their love of themselves.

Another way out of the binary is offered by Stephen Gough and his colleagues who, drawing on Buell's eco-criticism criteria for judging the environmentalism of a piece of writing, argue that 'a partially eco-centric viewpoint is possible, which to some extent transcends the dominant anthropocentric perspectives of the established disci-plines' (Gough et al., 2000, p. 45). They seek a more balanced—and to which I would add a more dialectic—position between anthropocentric and eco-centric worldviews in conceptualizing the human–environment relationship.

While making sense for societies concerned with post-material quality of life issues, I question the extent to which this task can speak to individuals and communities whose daily energies must be devoted to their livelihood and survival. Nevertheless, Bonnett's conceptualization of sustainability reminds us that environmental educa-tion and ESD cannot be effectively separated from other aspects of education, such as personal or self-development and the development of habits of mind. Just as the need to link or unite the social, economic and environment has been recognized in sustainable development, ESD has to be linked with individuals' development of self-concept, literacy, critical thinking, and citizenship, and so forth. Unfortunately, current standards-based accountability reforms throughout most of the western world are resulting in a predominant emphasis on literacy and numeracy, in many cases to the detriment of some of these other areas.

Looking ahead

The policy discourse of ESD, like that of environmental education, has generally been constructed by policy-makers and academics as an abstraction decontextualized from contexts of practice and to be enacted by others, namely educators who have not participated in the formulation of the goals and concepts. The consequences include: (1) a tendency to reify the discourse; (2) a de-emphasis on issues of pedagogy and politics in enacting ESD in local settings; and (3) a 'gap between policy sloganizing and policy implementation [that] is very great' (Stables & Scott, 2002, p. 55).

A view of sustainable development as a 'salvation narrative' that represents the way for society to be rescued from environmental and social destruction, along with its prominence in international conferences, risks reifying ESD policy. The reification of international policy discourse can imply an unquestioning faith in so-called 'experts' and authorities, in centralized global institutions and inter-Governmental agreements, and in top-down approaches to educational reform. Yet the discourse in the field needs to be continually and reflexively re-conceptualized (Plant, 1995), but not just by academics and policy-makers. Discourse should also be informed by practitioners and practice in diverse cultural contexts.

While policy discourse can provide a framework for local initiatives, decontextualized international policy statements must be recontextualized, after being mediated through national, provincial/regional and local policies (related both specifically to ESD and generally to educational reform) by educators at the local level. Environmental education and ESD have been described as 'the most all encompassing educational ideology' and 'the most radical pedagogy shaping global society' (Spring, 2004, p. 100). This description highlights both the reason why environmental education and ESD are very thin on the ground, especially in K-12 schooling, and why they challenge existing hegemonic interests and structures. The process of learning to live within ecological limits without human suffering must include uncovering the ideologies and power relationships that underlie the discourses of sustainable development. Consequently, local initiatives and responses are often highly political: a situation with which many teachers are uncomfortable (Cross, 1998). The process and politics of negotiating changes in rhetoric and policy are far easier than, and very different from, the process of negotiating and enacting changes in practices. In the latter case, the changes themselves are much harder to make, not only because they require changes in behaviour, but also because they also have repercussions for, and challenge vested interests in, maintaining the status quo.

If ESD is concerned with a process of learning how to live within environmental limits—by, for example, reducing our ecological footprints—with all humankind having sustainable livelihoods, then most educators have much to offer the discourse owing to their contextualized knowledge of learning and learners. For example, they have important perspectives on ways in which the human–environment relationship can be treated from their own disciplinary and experiential background, and young people's need for hope and a sense of place and purpose might be addressed. Educators, therefore, can contribute to such important questions as: How can issues of environment and development be connected to students' lives? How can linkages be made from ESD to other areas of education? What kinds of discourse and practice create more of a sense of optimism than pessimism among children and adolescents about the possibilities of a sustainable future? And, how do local externalities shape their willingness and capacity to work with students in inquiries into conflict-ridden social and environmental issues?

In the decade ahead, there is a need for identifying and creating spaces for engaging educators in the discourse so it is constructed *with* them rather than *for* them and is contextualized historically, pedagogically and politically. We might look reflexively at southern Africa where there 'has been a greater concern to foster participatory perspectives in both school and community contexts' (O'Donoghue & Russo, 2004, p. 343). These perspectives include engaging educators in the research process and viewing the research process itself as part of social and environmental transformation. I look ahead to a transition from the provision of policy on what ESD should be, to co-constructing and recontextualizing policy discourses. There certainly will be continuing tensions and more transitions in the educational future, but what the new transitions and tensions will be are as uncertain as the nature and process of constructing sustainable communities and societies. In both cases the imperative is to learn our way forward.

References

Bonnett, M. (2002) Education for sustainability as a frame of mind, *Environmental Education Research*, 8(1), 9–20.

Bowers, C. (1993) *Education, cultural myths, and the ecological crisis: toward deep changes* (Albany, NY, SUNY Press).

Brophy, J. (1987) Synthesis of research on strategies for motivating students to learn. *Educational Leadership*, 45(2), 40–48.

Christenson, M. (2004) Teaching multiple perspectives on environmental issues in elementary classrooms: a story of teacher inquiry, *Journal of Environmental Education*, 35(4), 3–16.

Cross, R. (1998) Teachers' views about what to do about sustainable development, *Environmental Education Research*, 4(1), 41–53.

De Haan, G. (forthcoming) The German BLK 21 Programme: education for sustainable development, *Environmental Education Research*, 12(1).

Elliott, J. (1995) Reconstructing the environmental education curriculum: teachers' perspectives, in: Centre for Education Research and Innovation, *Environmental learning for the twenty-first century* (Paris, OECD), 13–29.

Fien, J. & Tilbury, D. (2002) The global challenge of sustainability, in: D. Tilbury, R. Stevenson, J. Fien & D. Schroeder (Eds) *Education and sustainability: responding to the global challenge* (Geneva, IUCN), 1–12.

Freire, P. (1993) *Pedagogy of the oppressed* (New York, Continuum).

Gonzalez-Gaudiano, E. (2005) Education for sustainable development: configuration and meaning, paper presented at the *UQAM Seminar*, Montreal, Canada

Gonzalez-Gaudiano, E. (2006) Environmental education: a field in tension or in transition? (This issue.)

Gough, A. (1997) *Education and the environment: policy, trends and the problem of marginalisation* (Melbourne, Australian Council for Educational Research).

Gough, S. (2002) Increasing the value of the environment: a 'real options' metaphor for learning, *Environmental Education Research*, 8(1), 61–72.

Gough, S., Scott, W. & Stables, A. (2000) Beyond O'Riordan: balancing anthropocentrism and ecocentrism, *International Research in Geographical and Environmental Education*, 9(1), 36–47.

Grieg, S., Pike, G. & Selby, D. (1987) *Earthrights: education as if the planet really mattered* (London, Kogan Page).

Henderson, H. (1996) *Building a win-win world: life beyond global economic warfare* (San Francisco, Berrett-Koehler).

Hicks, D. (2002) *Lessons for the future: the missing dimension in education* (London, Routledge-Falmer).

Hicks, D. & Holden, C. (1995) Exploring the Future: a missing dimension in environmental education, *Environmental Education Research*, 1(2), 185–193.

Hmelo-Silver, C. E. (2004) Problem-based learning: what and how do students learn?, *Educational Psychology Review*, 16(3), 235–66.

Hopkins, C. & McKeown, R. (2002) Education for sustainable development: an international perspective, in: D. Tilbury, R. Stevenson, J. Fien & D. Schroeder (Eds) *Education and sustainability: responding to the global challenge* (Geneva, IUCN), 13–24.

IUCN, UNEP & WWF (1980) *World conservation strategy* (Gland, IUCN).

Jensen, B. (2002) Knowledge, action and pro-environmental behavior, *Environmental Education Research*, 8(3), 325–334.

Lavery, A. H. & Smyth, J. C. (2003) Developing environmental education, a review of a Scottish project: international and political influences, *Environmental Education Research*, 9(3), 359–383.

Martinez-Alier, J. (1999) Environmental justice (local and global), in: F. Jameson & M. Miyoshi (Eds) *The cultures of globalization* (Durham, Duke University Press), 312–326.

McKeown, R. & Hopkins, C. (2003) EE#ESD: defusing the worry, *Environmental Education Research*, 9(1), 117–128.

Newmann, F. (1990/91) Authentic work and student engagement, *National Center on Effective Secondary Schools Newsletter*, 5(3), 2–3.

Newmann, F., Bertocci, T. & Landsness, R. (1977) *Skills in citizen action: an English- social studies program for secondary schools* (Stokie, IL, National Textbook Company).

O'Donoghue, R. & Russo, V. (2004) Emerging patterns of abstraction in environmental education: A review of materials, methods and professional development perspectives, *Environmental Education Research*, 10(3), 331–351.

Onosko, J. & Newmann, F. (1994) Creating more thoughtful learning environments, in: J. N. Mangieri & C. Collins-Block (Eds) *Creating powerful thinking in teachers and students: diverse perspectives* (Fort Worth, Texas, Harcourt Brace), 27–49.

Orr, D. (1994) *Earth in mind: on education, environment, and the human prospect* (Washington, DC, Island Press).

Pezzey, J. (1989) *Definitions of sustainability* (London, CEED).

Plant, M. (1995) The riddle of sustainable development and the role of environmental education, *Environmental Education Research*, 1(3), 253–266.

Rees, W. (1992) Understanding sustainable development, in: B. Hamm, G. Zimmer & S. Kratz (Eds) *Sustainable development and the future of cities*. Proceedings of an international summer seminar, Bauhaus Dessau, 7–14 September 1991, 17–40.

Reid, A. & Nikel, J. (2004) Towards evaluating the theory and practice of participation in environmental education?, paper presented at the *Annual Meeting of the American Educational Research Association*, San Diego, April 12–16.

Robottom, I. (1992) Matching the purposes of environmental education with consistent approaches to research and professional development, *Australian Journal of Environmental Education*, 8, 133–146.

Russell, C. (1997) Approaches to environmental education: Towards a transformative perspective, *Holistic Education Review*, 10(1), 34–40.

Sauvé, L. (1996) Environmental education and sustainable development: a further appraisal, *Canadian Journal of Environmental Education*, 1, 7–34.

Scott, W. (2005) ESD: What sort of education? What sort of learning? What sort of decade?, invited paper presented at the *Danish Opening Conference for the United Nations Decade of Education for Sustainable Development*, 10–11 March, Copenhagen, Denmark. Available online at: www.ubu10.dk/konf/english.htm (accessed 15 September 2005).

Smith, G. (1992) *Education and the environment: learning to live with limits* (Albany, NY, SUNY Press).

Smyth, J. C. (1995) Environment and education: a view of a changing scene, *Environmental Education Research*, 1(1), 3–20.

Spring, J. (2004) *How educational ideologies are shaping global society: intergovernmental organizations, NGOs, and the decline of the nation state* (Mahwah, NJ, Lawrence Erlbaum Associates).

Stables, A. (2001) Who drew the sky? Conflicting assumptions in environmental education, *Educational Philosophy and Theory*, 33(2), 245–256.

Stables, A. & Scott, W. (2001) Editorial, *Educational Philosophy and Theory*, 33(2), 133–135.

Stables, A. & Scott, W. (2002) The quest for holism in education for sustainable development, *Environmental Education Research*, 8(1), 53–61.

Sterling, S. (2001) *Sustainable education: re-visioning learning and change* (Totnes, Green Books for the Schumacher Society).

Sterling, S. (2004) *Whole systems thinking as a basis for paradigm change in education: explorations in the context of sustainability*. Ph.D. thesis, University of Bath. Available online: http://www.bath.ac.uk/cree/sterling.htm (accessed 15 September 2005).

Stevenson, R. (1987) Schooling and environmental education: contradictions in purpose and practice, in: I. Robottom (Ed.) *Environmental education: practice and possibility* (Geelong, Victoria, Deakin University Press), 69–81.

Stevenson, R. (1990) Engagement and cognitive challenge in thoughtful social studies classes: a study of student perspectives, *Journal of Curriculum Studies*, 22(4), 329–341.

Stevenson, R. (1997) Developing habits of environmental thoughtfulness through the in-depth study of select environmental issues, *Canadian Journal of Environmental Education*, 2, 183–201.

Summers, M., Corney, G. & Childs, A. (2003) Teaching sustainable development in primary schools: an empirical study of issues for teachers, *Environmental Education Research*, 9(3), 327–346.

Tilbury, D. (1995) Environmental education for sustainability: defining the new focus of environmental education in the 1990s, *Environmental Education Research*, 1(2), 195–212.

World Commission on Environment and Development (1987) *Our common future* (Oxford, Oxford University Press).

Unsettling orthodoxies: education for the environment/for sustainability

Jo-Anne Ferreira

In this paper I employ Foucault's notion of governmentality to reflect on a debate that occurred in the pages of this journal some 10 years ago. I argue that their exchanges indicate ways in which various positions are engaged in a struggle for dominance in this field, and how particular strategies are used to legitimate and maintain these positions. My purpose is not to propose a new orthodoxy – or even to critique those we have – but rather to raise questions about how the unquestioned 'that-which-is' of orthodoxies comes to be, and their effects. I also suggest that as environmental educators and researchers, we need to work harder to unsettle more often the taken-for-granted in environmental education so that we remain alert to our own easy acceptance of orthodoxies. Without this, we risk our exhortations to those we seek to educate – to think critically, to question assumptions, and so forth – becoming empty rhetoric if we are not practising these ourselves – examining our own, as well as others', assumptions and practices.

Introduction

About 10 years ago, in the pages of *Environmental Education Research*, Bob Jickling and Helen Spork (1998) argued that 'education *for* the environment' had become nothing more than a slogan, past its use-by date, and in need of retirement. John Fien (2000), long an advocate of 'education *for* the environment', responded to these charges by arguing that Jickling and Spork had provided only a partial interpretation of this approach, attributing this to their lack of reflexivity over their own ideological stance, and failure to see that the 'liberal' position (which he argued they subscribed to) dominates environmental education.

In this paper, I seek to re-examine this debate, to understand how this is indicative of what I see as the development of 'education *for* the environment' as orthodoxy within the field of environmental education, in the realm of theory if not practice. While some may see this as a return to an old debate, I think it timely to revisit it now, for two reasons. First, it is quite difficult to see the various positions that govern our thinking as they occur and while they still appear as possible solutions to our problems. It is, however, somewhat easier to identify and examine these 'historically'. Second, we are halfway through the United Nations Decade of Education for Sustainable Development (UN DESD). While some may question whether 'education *for* the environment' is (or, for that matter, has been or ever was) an orthodoxy for the field, the grounds for investigating such a claim are readily illustrated in recent shifts in the terminology employed within the field. For example, the naming of the UN Decade as 'education for sustainable development', and its focus on an education through which individuals and societies can 'learn the values, behaviour and lifestyles required for a sustainable future and for positive societal transformation' (UNESCO 2007, 2) is a strong indicator of the orthodoxy of the notion that environmental education should be *'for'* something – namely, preparing individuals to be socially critical in order that they are willing and able to bring about 'societal transformation' (ibid.). Readers may also question an apparent conflating of 'education *for* the environment' with 'education for sustainable development' or 'education for sustainability'. However, I argue that while many have shifted their focus from environmental education to education for sustainability, this shift seems to have occurred despite the concerns raised by some environmental education scholars (see Stevenson 2006; Jickling and Wals 2008; Nomura and Abe 2009).[1] Thus, I point to some of the immediate similarities between 'education for sustainable development' and 'education *for* the environment', such as their shared goal of a society transformed into a sustainable society, and their shared belief that the goal of education is to enhance the capacities of individuals so that they can bring about personal and social change – be this 'for sustainable development' or 'for sustainable lifestyles', as the ultimate goal of each is respectively articulated (see Jickling and Wals 2008).

I also think it is timely to reflect on why the debate between Jickling, Spork and Fien bubbled to the surface and then disappeared without a trace, and how this may be an indication of the ways in which discourses compete with one another for positions of dominance within knowledge domains such as environmental education. The purpose here is not to comment on the veracity or otherwise of the authors' respective claims, nor to critique or valorize either a 'socially critical' or a 'liberal' approach to environmental education. I do not wish to contribute to the debate by providing evidence to either support or refute the 'truth' of either position or the claims they make. Neither do I offer a reading of the 'what' or even the 'why' of these positions.

Instead I take a more novel approach of examining the 'how' of these positions: how do positions compete for dominance in a field and, most importantly, how do these positions have effects that govern what it is possible to think and what it is possible to do in environmental education. Such a reading is important because, as Nikolas Rose (1999, 9) reminds us, 'concepts are more important for what they do than for what they mean' and we seem to most often discuss what concepts contain, signify and mean (for those who develop them and those who interpret and/or critique them) rather than what they do, that is, the effects they have. Thus I offer this reading not as a critique of either position but in the spirit of 'generous scholarship', of which Russell (2006) speaks, in and for the field.

I begin by further outlining the similarities I see between 'education *for* the environment' and 'education for sustainability', before turning to some of the indications that 'education *for* the environment' can be seen (theoretically at least) as an orthodoxy for the field.

'Education *for* the environment'

There are a range of defining characteristics underpinning 'education *for* the environment' that its proponents argue will lead to the empowerment of individuals and the transformation of social structures. According to Fien, these are:

- the development of a critical environmental consciousness;
- the use of critical thinking and problem-solving skills;
- the development of an environmental ethic;
- the development of political literacy; and
- 'critical praxis', that is, teaching strategies that are consistent with the goals of 'education *for* the environment' (1993, 12, 50–75).

These characteristics display a commitment to identifying and recognizing underlying ideological stances and to adopting a new ideology. According to Tilbury (1995), one of the leading advocates of 'education for sustainability' (who has also been a strong advocate of 'education *for* the environment' in the past), 'education for sustainability' also focuses on empowering individuals and transforming social structures, through an education that:

- is relevant in that it deals with contemporary issues of concern to the learner;
- is holistic in addressing environmental issues and in teaching and learning;
- not only teaches about values but also teaches values, in this case 'an environmental ethic which has sustainable living at its core' (1995, 201);
- is issues-based, to allow for an 'exploration of moral, social and political values required for the development of an environmental ethic' (1995, 202);
- has an action-orientation, both in encouraging learners to take actions to bring about change in their own lives and in their communities, and in promoting the use of active teaching and learning strategies; and
- involves critical education, that is, an education that develops socially critically and political literacy skills, essential, she argues, to 'achieving "sustainability"' (1995, 204).

At face value, these are remarkably similar in their intent and focus to the characteristics outlined by Fien, and to those later outlined in the UNESCO Johannesburg definition of 'Education for Sustainable Development' as 'a concept that encompasses a new vision of education that seeks to empower people of all ages to assume responsibility for creating a sustainable future' (UNESCO 2002, 5). Each description articulates a shared belief that education should enable (either through 'empowering' or 'enhancing capacity') the sort of social change that will bring into being a sustainable society and/or future.

Governments have also – perhaps surprisingly – taken up the social change orientation of 'education *for* the environment'. For example, the Australian government argues that 'environmental education for sustainability involves' the rather lofty and paradoxical[2] goal of 'developing the kinds of civic values and skills that empower all citizens to be leaders in the transition to a sustainable future' (Australian Government and Curriculum Corporation 2005, 8) and more recently: 'Through information and awareness, but more importantly by building people's capacity to innovate and implement solutions, education for sustainability is essential to re-orienting the way we live and work and to Australia becoming a sustainable society' (Australian Government 2009, 3). Such a desire on the part of a government indicates that the discourse of 'education *for* the environment', with its vision of empowering individuals to transform themselves and their worlds now so that they can have sustainable societies in the future, has become the unquestioned 'that-which-is' – the orthodoxy – in environmental education in Australia, so much so that it is even a goal that the government aspires to. Is this an indication that the view that environmental education should empower individuals to bring about social change is now orthodox in our field? Indeed, could it even be suggested that the way in which the word *for* is no longer italicized in the terms 'education for sustainable development' or 'education for sustainability' provides another indication that the notion of 'education *for*' is now orthodox?

Towards an analytics of government perspective

How we come to such a remarkable situation – where a position of critique of the norm becomes the norm – is intriguing, especially for a position so focused on social transformation as 'education *for* the environment' is. Is it really the case that even governments, traditionally seen as the opponents of social change and against the empowerment of the people, are supporting and indeed promoting such a position?

To explore these matters further, in this paper I draw on ideas encapsulated in Michel Foucault's (1991) notion of governmentality. Three key concepts underpin the notion of governmentality: *power, knowledge* and *the self.* These concepts, as framed by Foucault, present an understanding of power not as repressive but as consisting of productive power relations, as dispersed outside of the state, and as productive of new truths and capacities. They offer an understanding of what Foucault refers to as 'power/ knowledge', where knowledge is both essential to the exercise of power and a product of power. They also offer an historical and cultural understanding of the self that allows the ways in which power, knowledge and the self are intimately and distinctively inter-connected within societies with liberal modes of rule to be understood. As I aim to show, these ideas provide a way for us to grapple with understanding how a position of critique is able to become that of orthodoxy.

Foucault challenges traditional conceptions of power by claiming that power is not held only by those who are *in* power but is rather dispersed and operates through *relations of power*. For Foucault, power cannot be reduced to 'an institution, a structure or a certain force with which people are endowed; [but is rather] the name given to a complex strategic relation in any given society' (in Gordon 1980, 236). Power here is 'quite different from and more complicated, dense and pervasive than a set of laws or a state apparatus' (Foucault 1980a, 158). Power relations are not simply uni-directional and linear, in the way that power exercised by 'the state' over 'the people', or the potential power of 'civil society' over 'the state', are often conceived. Nor does power originate from a single source: it is not 'built up out of "wills" (individual or collective), nor is it derivable from interests' (Foucault 1980b, 188). Neither is it unified in intent or in effect. Rather, Foucault argues that 'power in its exercise goes much further, passes through much finer channels, and is much more ambiguous' (1980c, 72) than those accounts which claim that power originates from a single source would have. Such relations of power exist inside, outside and alongside the state.

Foucault's investigations of the history of our present ways of knowing and doing in a range of institutions and situations demonstrates how relations of power and their concomitant mechanisms are dispersed through a range of governmental systems and agencies, as well as through organizations, bodies of knowledge and individuals thought to be outside the realm of the state. Power here then does not refer only to the exercise of political power. What Foucault's studies offer to environmental education is a way to understand how power operates both inside and outside the realms of the state or other political structures within modern liberal modes of governance. Grasping this, however, entails letting go of an understanding of power as the exclusive domain of the few – the powerful – and of the exercise of power as repressive and linear.

The key contribution Foucault's studies offer in this regard, I would suggest, is that the relationship between *power* (as productive not as repressive and as dispersed outside of 'the state'); *knowledge* (where knowledge is the product of power as well as essential to the exercise of power); and *the self* (as both an object of power/knowledge and a subject of power/knowledge) is made evident. The notion of 'governmentality' (Foucault 1991) – our 'mentalities' or thoughts about how we govern ourselves and how we govern others – acts as a shorthand for these key propositions and understandings.

In undertaking the analysis in this paper, I use a quasi-methodological approach referred to as 'an analytics of government'. Foucault himself only ever spoke retrospectively of methodological issues and did not articulate a single or clear methodology or set of methods for his work. As O'Farrell (2005, 50) notes, 'Foucault continually changed and refined his concepts, not only on a major scale, but in very minute and subtle ways, something which makes his work extremely difficult to systematize for the purposes of a methodical and wholesale application'. Foucault's initial ideas about how to undertake studies of our 'govern-mentalities' have underpinned efforts by Foucault scholars – in particular the Anglo-Foucauldians (see Dean 1994, 1999, 2007; Kendall and Wickham 1999; Miller and Rose 2008; Rose 1999) – to develop a methodological framework for examining governmentality 'in action', referred to now as an analytics of government. An analytics of government is thus a means for investigating practices that direct conduct, and for investigating the forms of thought or mentalities that guide such practices (Dean 1999, 36–40).

It is important to note that an analytics of government does not search for ultimate goals or transcendent principles that should or should not direct the ways in which we govern and are governed. It does not propose new, utopian solutions. Instead, such an approach is concerned with gaining purchase on governmental regimes by clarifying their forms of thought – their mentalities – and by examining the effects of these at their point of application. Thus an analytics of government does not seek to understand discourses linguistically or to undertake micro-level critical analyses using linguistic methodologies. Rather, it is a form of philosophical enquiry interested in understanding the formation of discourses, how they become legitimate, how they are distributed, how they maintain their legitimacy, and what effects they have on how we think about and seek to govern our own conduct and the conduct of others. In short, such an analysis does not provide glossy or easy answers to problems but instead provides new, often troubling, insights that challenge us to think differently about problems.

Such an analytics of government perspective then, offers a means for exploring how environmental education as a discipline is engaged in exercises of power through the generation of a range of positions that come to be, through a process of internal struggle within the field, seen as truths or orthodoxies. As truths or orthodoxies they are often unquestioned as their truth seems self-evident, or is so embedded as 'that-which-is' that we seldom question them. These orthodoxies are important to examine not to prove them 'wrong' or 'untrue' but in order to understand how they work as rationalities of rule that govern how things can be thought, understood and done in environmental education. Positions, once they have gained the status of truth or orthodoxy, are thus not only exercises of power that seek to challenge and critique, but also exercises of power that work to govern thought and practice within a field. This is because such orthodoxies carry with them a range of semi-normative prescriptions that work to include, exclude and govern what it is acceptable (possible) to think, and what it is acceptable (possible) to do, in environmental education.

There are many ways in which orthodoxies come to be established, legitimated, maintained, and distributed in a field. In this paper, I examine only one instance that I read as the legitimation and maintenance of 'education *for* the environment' as orthodoxy in and for the field of environmental education.[3] Such an examination is important as it helps us to 'interrogate the "rationality" of the present' (Gordon 1980, 242), that is, to illuminate how certain points of view have become 'normal', 'everyday' and 'obvious' in our thinking and practices. In this way we might better understand, for example, how we have come to, in many settings, see 'education *for* the environment' – that is, education that seeks social transformation through individual empowerment – as the most, perhaps only, legitimate approach to environmental education.

Discourse struggles

One of the methodological techniques through which to make visible the establishment of a position as orthodoxy is an examination of the power relations evident in 'discourse struggles' within a field of endeavor. In illustrating my argument that 'education *for* the environment' has come to be accepted as orthodoxy in our thinking – or mentality – about how best to 'do' environmental education, this paper describes one instance of a struggle that has taken place in environmental education over whether environmental education should be '*for* the environment', that is, a way to empower individuals to transform their society into a sustainable one. This debate has occurred largely between those who are deemed – by each other and by themselves – to hold 'critical' and 'liberal' philosophical positions on education. A case in point of this debate can be found in the Jickling and Spork (1998) and Fien (2000) papers.

The Canadian scholar, Bob Jickling, has been vocal in challenging the notion that education more generally, and environmental education in particular, should be '*for*' empowering individuals to transform social structures. Jickling's argument is that 'education *for* the environment' is more activism than education, with its focus on educating towards a particular mindset and set of values (see Jickling 1991, 1992, 2005). Jickling's position is that we should not 'apply the term education to the achievement of some particular end' and that education 'transcends immediate instrumental values such as the advocacy of a particular sort of behaviour' (Jickling 1991, 172). Therefore, he argues, 'while it may be important for citizens to promote changes in attitudes and behaviours, this must not be confused with our work as educators' (Jickling 1991, 171). For Jickling, education is something other than – and more than – simply training people to take on a particular point of view or particular sets of practices. His critique then, is with what he sees as the 'deterministic' nature of 'education *for* the environment'.

In contrast, Fien (see Fien 1993, 1997, 1999/2000, 2000, 2002) and others (see Palmer 1998; Tilbury 2004; van Rossen 1995) have argued that the goal of environmental education should be to empower individuals to transform society. Such socio-critical environmental educators argue that this is not to be achieved through training people to take on a particular point of view, as Jickling claims, but through an education that seeks to develop a critical consciousness, political literacy and an environmental ethic, through the use and development of critical thinking and socially critically teaching and learning strategies (Fien 1993, 12, 50–75).

These two positions have engaged directly with one another in the Jickling and Spork (1998) and Fien (2000) papers. In 1996, Jickling and Spork presented a paper at the American Educational Research Association (AERA) conference in New York titled 'Environmental education for the environment: Retained or retired?' (Jickling and Spork 1996). In a revised version of this paper, published in 1998, they argue that the term 'education *for* the environment' needs to be retired as it has become a slogan (Jickling and Spork 1998). They also claim that there has been very little critique in environmental education of Arthur Lucas' (1979) categorization of environmental education as education '*about, in* or *for*' the environment, to the point that each of the prepositional forms have become mere slogans. In particular, they argue that the term 'education for the environment' is used uncritically, that is, 'interpreted literally' (Jickling and Spork 1998, 311). Their problem with this is that terms can 'acquire different meanings and serve new purposes' (Jickling and Spork 1998, 311). In supporting this claim, they use as an example the shift that has occurred since the initial use of the term by Lucas – as a 'descriptive' protocol to distinguish it from education *about* and *in* the environment – to its later use by its advocates as an 'analytical standard' or evaluative protocol (Jickling and Spork 1998, 312), as Fien does, for example, in arguing that identifying underlying ideologies helps to provide a means for developing a framework to elaborate 'characteristics by which environmental education programmes can be scrutinized for their counter-hegemonic potential' (Fien 1993, 11).

The effect of the term being used as an analytical standard troubles Jickling and Spork. They argue that 'continued analytical use (see Fien, 1993) can lead to exclusiveness and serve to entrench [the] perception' that only 'education *for* the environment' is 'correct' environmental education (Jickling and Spork 1998, 312). In addition, they argue that what they see as the sloganistic use of 'education *for* the environment' lacks clarity, imposes a particular moral viewpoint, and discourages and confines discussion within the field. They argue that the term thus needs to be retired not only because it has become a slogan but also because its language reflects the values and predilections of activists, not educators. For them, 'continued popular use of the term runs the risk of encouraging non-educative activities' (Jickling and Spork 1998, 323).

For Jickling and Spork, any approach to education that claims to be critical and encourage critical thinking but that has a pre-determined outcome is problematic:

> The crux of the problem is, however, structural. When we talk about 'education for the environment' we imply that education must strive to be 'for' something external to education itself. Unfortunately, there is an oxymoronic quality embedded in this construction. If we want students to examine ideologies, criticize conventional wisdom and participate in cultural criticism and reconstruction, then we must accept that they may well reject the externally imposed aim that has been pre-selected for them. If we are serious about education, we should, in the first place, put aside *our* most promising visions for the future. Moreover, if we really want to open students' minds to alternative worldviews, it makes little sense to steer them, however gently, towards a particular vision. The prepositional use of 'for' ultimately leads, therefore, to either a literal or programmatic interpretation which is, in our view, deterministic. (Jickling and Spork 1998, 323–4; emphasis in original)

The issue not addressed by Jickling and Spork, however, is how and in what ways education can be anything other than the achievement of some particular end, even if this is as nebulous as a 'well-rounded' or 'educated' person, or the development of citizens or critical thinkers.

Despite their criticisms of 'education *for* the environment', Jickling and Spork do acknowledge that it has been useful in drawing attention to the social and political aspects of environmental problems, and as a practical framework for those seeking to empower themselves and/or their students to act for the environment:

> On the positive side, it is important to recognize that activities labeled 'education for the environment' have helped to place, and keep, the political dimension of issues on the environmental education agenda. As thinking about the term has developed, the socially critical dimension of environmental education has been illuminated and has thus helped to give life to this field in the face of conservative influences. The term and its various stipulations has also been a useful tool for teachers and other practitioners for discovering overlooked dimensions of their work. A critique such as ours must acknowledge and value these contributions. (Jickling and Spork 1998, 323)

It is finally their contention, though, that these positive features are outweighed by the negative impacts of the sloganistic and analytical use of the term. To provide a sound educational experience, Jickling and Spork maintain, environmental educators need to:

> ... acknowledge that shaping the future does not consist of being led to adopt some alternative vision. Rather, it involves the more indeterminate process of examining and recasting society. If we acknowledge that education should be free of specified ends, then we are ultimately led to challenge the way in which 'education for the environment' operates to predetermine educational aims. (Jickling and Spork 1998, 325)

As noted previously, what Jickling and Spork fail to address is that education – be it that provided by state, church or independent schools – is purposive: to form and shape particular types of persons, for example, 'critical thinkers'. As Hunter (1994) noted in his history of education in western liberal societies, all education seeks to govern our conduct by teaching us how to self-govern our conduct. For the purposes of the argument I am posing here, however, the claimed 'truth' of either of these positions of principle is of less interest to my argument than their *effects*.

What happened next?

When the Jickling and Spork paper first appeared as a conference presentation at AERA in 1996, there was great interest in the issues raised, with for example, discussion groups held in the UK following the AERA conference that included discussion of the paper. Unsurprisingly, advocates of the 'education *for* the environment' approach were quick to respond. For example, Joy Palmer, who at the time was a leading researcher in the field and author of key environmental education texts, argued thus:

> Surely it is important to retain goals and terms that have actually served and continue to serve the critical function of assisting teachers and other practitioners to discover overlooked and important dimensions of environmentalism. I would actually go further than this, and say that an understanding of the phrase 'education for the environment'... has been the bedrock stimulus for the practical development of environmental education

programmes in classrooms around the world. ... Countless students and teachers have found the use of the word 'for' in relation to the environment most helpful when coming to grips with criticism of conventional wisdom, consideration of alternative worldviews and formulation of attitudes and values that will enable us to recast society for the better. ... To lose sight at this stage of the *accepted terminology* is to lose sight of important research findings that reveal the critical role of 'in the environment' and 'about the environment' experiences in terms of illuminating an understanding of actions 'for the environment'. ... Surely the... language of the field of environmental education similarly awaits the appropriate time for reformulation. (Palmer 1998, 238–9; my emphasis)

From an analytics of government perspective, Palmer's argument illustrates two interesting issues: how proponents of particular positions – despite the status or standing of the position within a field – retain a capacity to see their position as the position of challenge and oppositional criticism, not as the orthodoxy; and how such proponents seek, through their responses, to maintain their position of dominance by simply declaring, for example, 'now is not the appropriate time'.

Fien's (2000) response argued that Jickling and Spork had presented only a partial interpretation of 'education *for* the environment', one driven by their own beliefs:

Thus, [Fien's] article addresses Jickling and Spork's concern that education for the environment is a universalizing discourse that seeks to marginalize other approaches. It does this by showing how it may be Jickling and Spork's lack of reflexivity over their own ideology of education which leads them to construct such a partial interpretation of education for the environment. (Fien 2000, 179)

For Fien, Jickling and Spork's argument 'is not of education for the environment as it has been developed in the literature but of a partial reading that has been constructed through an unacknowledged but, nevertheless, ideologically motivated and literal textual reading' (Fien 2000, 186). Fien contrasts what he sees as a failure on the part of Jickling and Spork to reflect on their own beliefs and ideology with 'the way many practitioners of a critical education for the environment have been open in describing the approach as an integration of 'red–green' environmentalism *and* socially–critically approaches to education' (2000, 181). The effect of such a claim is that it provides Fien with a more principled position than Jickling and Spork's.

In understanding the range of mechanisms of power that operate to legitimize and maintain orthodoxies, it is significant to note here that Fien's response takes the form of a moral critique. For Fien, it is Jickling and Spork's 'lack of reflexivity', their 'lack of openness about their own ideological dispositions', that is the problem (Fien 2000, 181). Moreover, two of the hallmarks of the socio-critical stance underpinning 'education *for* the environment' are 'reflexivity and self-critique' (Fien 2000, 184), thus making it impossible, from this perspective, that 'education *for* the environment' could be constraining debate in environmental education. Indeed, Fien argues that 'education *for* the environment is based upon and embodies education *in* and *about* the environment' (Fien 2000, 183), and as such, is not deterministic or purposive but rather inclusive of all environmental education approaches. In support of his argument, he cites a passage from his 1993 text, *Education for the environment: Critical curriculum theorising and environmental education,* which talks about the type of reflective and self-critical work one needs to undertake as a 'transformative intellectual', work such as:

... actively theorizing upon one's own environmental and educational ideologies ... This is one of the secrets of success in being a transformative intellectual. There are others of course, including perseverance and hard work, constantly being open to ideas and constructive critique, political literacy and a keen eye for strategic opportunities, and courage, skill and patience in dealing with the arguments and possible complaints of those whose teaching serves the interests of the Dominant Social Paradigm. However, the hallmark of a transformative intellectual is her and his 'inner life', that commitment to ecological and social justice and transformation, which is sustained not only by moral outrage (and we do need our share of that) but also by the habit of critical reflection upon one's views and work. (Fien 1993, 98, in Fien 2000, 185)

What is clear here – when we look at it through a governmentality lens – is the rationality of rule evident in this quote: to be a critical environmental educator who is also a transformative intellectual – and thus not one who 'serves the interests of the Dominant Social Paradigm' (ibid.) – one must ensure that one is capable of, and practices to the point of forming a habit, reflexivity and self-critique. Put simply, this statement illustrates a 'govern-mentality': it indicates that one should be a transformative intellectual (the self as object), and the practices to follow to be a transformative intellectual (the self as subject). When we have the 'mentality' that it is necessary to be critically reflexive, this has an effect on what we do as environmental educators, to ourselves and to others such as our students. In undertaking and encouraging such practices, we work to govern our own and others conduct. Thus it is an example of a mentality that governs how we think and how we act in environmental education.

It is perhaps worth noting here that the practices of reflexivity and self-critique have a religious history, arguably one that has been more connected to governing and reforming conduct than it has been to fostering emancipation and liberation. Indeed, Fien is correct in referring to this type of work as habit-forming as it is work that fashions a new type of persona: the self-governing, and self-regulating, transformative intellectual. However, what he misses is that this work occurs within the limits of the normative prescriptions imposed by socio-critical theory.[4] It is such normative prescriptions that work to govern how we think and how we act in environmental education.

Moreover, not only are such prescriptions normative, but successfully so in environmental education: there is little critique of an environmental education that seeks to empower individuals to transform society, and even less critique of the concepts of reflexivity, democracy, social justice, empowerment or transformation. Foucault's studies make clear the ways in which the setting in which an orthodoxy is located helps to legitimize and maintain it. We now live in a time, for example, when it is politically incorrect – almost impossible – to critique concepts such as democracy, empowerment and citizenship without being accused of 'walking with the devil on the dark side'. This setting – and its attendant normativities – allows Fien to accuse his detractors of failing to be reflexive, while at the same time failing to acknowledge the normativity of his own position. Fien is partly able to make such a charge because it is unlikely that – at this moment in our history – many will speak out against the desirability of these things. To re-iterate, this is not to imply that such practices are 'bad' or should not be used in environmental education but rather to suggest that such practices – when linked to positions of principle – work to govern and shape our conduct – and it is because of this 'power' that we need to be alert to the *effects* of our govern-mentalities.

Fien concludes his paper with the suggestion that we need to better understand why scholarly disputes are a part of academic culture. He argues that he is 'increasingly coming to see Foucault's notion of discourse as power/knowledge as an important way of explaining this' (Fien 2000, 188). His understanding of Foucault's concept of power/knowledge leads him to argue that:

> ... it could be that the critique presented by Jickling and Spork (1998) represents not a critique of education *for* the environment, *per se*, but an attempt to control the influence of critical environmental education through the power/knowledge of liberal educational and environmental discourses. ... Their desire to control discourse in environmental education is also revealed by their attempts at limiting who is entitled to speak about the field. Numerous examples of this are found in the paper. For example, Jickling and Spork allege that several Canadian educators are 'refusing to engage in serious discussion' as they 'champion the conversion of environmental education into "education *for* sustainable development"'. Two techniques for controlling discourse are evident in this brief passage. One is Jickling and Spork's failure to declare their own positions within environmental education debates and, thereby, attempt to construct themselves as disinterested commentators... The second technique of control evident in this passage is the attempt to marginalize the voices of other researchers through the use of loaded terminology, in this case, through the use of terms such as 'serious discussion', 'champion' and 'conversion'. The use of such vocabulary may be interpreted as an attempt to construct others as unworthy commentators who 'champion' ideas, rather than 'argue' for them, who want to 'convert' environmental education rather than 'reorient' it towards sustainability, and whose work cannot be described as a 'serious discussion'. (Fien 2000, 188)

From a governmentality perspective, Fien has correctly read the situation. However, he fails to signal that he himself is a part of this power relation (as am I in writing this article and engaging with this debate). Rather, Fien seems to situate 'education *for* the environment' as somehow standing outside of this power relation, as the voice oppressed by the dominance of liberal educational and environmental discourses. He may well be correct about which position dominates thinking in the field, although I have put a contrary position here. However, as I noted at the beginning of this paper, my interest is not in seeking to claim one or other position of principle as 'true'. Rather, my aim in writing this article is to illustrate that it is difficult for us to understand the effects of positions of principle when they become orthodox – 'that-which-is' – as their 'obviousness' makes it difficult for us to question them.

Thus Jickling, Spork and Fien, in engaging in this debate, are all working to 'control discourse in environmental education' (Fien 2000, 188), as am I, to some extent, in writing this article. The great insight that Foucault offers is that we are all constantly engaged in these power relations and that none of us sit outside them. What is interesting to me, in seeking to understand the effects that various positions have on governing thinking and practice within a field, is why Jickling and Spork chose not to respond to the Fien article, despite claiming in their 1998 article that they wanted to encourage debate in the field about this issue. In seeking to understand why Jickling and Spork did not respond, I asked them. According to Spork (personal communication, 2008) it was not because she felt proven wrong by Fien's arguments in his 2000 paper, but because she thought the discussion would quickly degenerate if they responded and that she preferred to leave it open for others in the field to respond. None did in this or other journals. According to Jickling (personal communication, 2007) he was actively discouraged from responding to Fien's article in *Environmental Education Research* by a then member of this journal's editorial team. Despite their different explanations, the interesting issue given the burden of this paper in trying to understand relations of power is why only Palmer (1998) and Fien (2000) responded to the Jickling and Spork call for the field to debate the issue. Did everyone agree with Palmer and

Fien's response and feel there was nothing more to say? Were people afraid of possible repercussions from being seen to be speaking out for one or the other side of the debate? Or could it be that this is another remarkable feature of such discourse struggles, that when a position is orthodox, alternative positions struggle to find additional supporters, or at least supporters who will 'speak publicly' (see also Russell 2006). Could it be that through such strategies orthodoxies come to be maintained and so to govern what can be thought – and what can be said – within a field?

Conclusion

In conclusion, the reading I have undertaken in this article offers one way for us to think about orthodoxies and their alternatives in our field. I am not arguing for one or another orthodoxy – indeed whichever position manages to become dominant will become orthodox and remain so until there is enough critique of it for its position of dominance to be challenged. What an analytics of government reading of this debate helps to illustrate, however, is not that one discourse has become orthodox as an inevitable result of the 'correctness' or 'truth' of its principles but rather that it has, for a moment, won a battle between competing discourses. Indeed, in unsettling 'that-which-is', I hope I have demonstrated that 'education *for* the environment' may not be 'the truth' but simply a rationality or mentality that currently rules or governs contemporary environmental education thought and practice.

Proponents of an orthodoxy will no doubt not see or understand their position in such governmental terms. However, when governmental terms – such as understanding orthodox approaches to environmental education as rationalities of rule – are adopted, certain new emphases emerge that allow us to jettison an orthodoxy's self-understanding in favour of a different – perhaps more precise and accurate – understanding of how we as environmental educators govern our own – and govern others – thought and practice. The point of such an unsettling of 'that-which-is' is that it offers a reminder that we need to remain vigilant in environmental education to our own rhetoric – and vigilant of the ways in which such rhetoric is indicative of rationalities of rule through which we are governed and through which we seek to govern others, that is, of our own 'govern-mentalities'. It is only through making these visible that we are able to reflect on their effects on our thoughts and practices, and to consider whether to keep using them or seek to change them.

Acknowledgements

I wish to thank the reviewers of this paper for their very thoughtful and detailed suggestions as well as Professors David Saunders and John Fien for discussing this paper with me.

Notes

1. These concerns relate to the various conceptualizations of sustainable development and sustainability (in particular the primacy of the economy and economic development) and the philosophies and ideologies underpinning them, as well as the effects of these on the development of uncontextualized education for sustainability/sustainable development policies and practices.
2. Can *all* be leaders in the transition to a sustainable future?
3. See Nomura and Abe (2009) on the development of the UN DESD from a political opportunities perspective.
4. For an earlier account, also in *Environmental Education Research*, see Walker (1997).

References

Australian Government and Curriculum Corporation. 2005. *Educating for a sustainable future: A national environmental education statement for Australian schools.* Canberra: Australian Government Department of the Environment and Heritage.

Australian Government. 2009. *Living sustainably: The Australian government's national action plan for education for sustainability.* Canberra: Department of Environment, Water, Heritage and the Arts.

Dean, M. 1994. *Critical and effective histories: Foucault's methods and historical sociology.* London: Routledge.

Dean, M. 1999. *Governmentality: Power and rule in modern society.* London: Sage Publications.

Dean, M. 2007. *Governing societies: Political perspectives on domestic and international rule.* Maidenhead: Open University Press and McGraw-Hill Education.

Fien, J. 1993. *Education for the environment: Critical curriculum theorising and environmental education.* Geelong, Vic.: Deakin University.

Fien, J. 1997. Stand up, stand up and be counted: Undermining myths of environmental education. *Australian Journal of Environmental Education* 13: 21–6.

Fien, J. 1999/2000. Education, sustainability and civil society. *Australian Journal of Environmental Education* 15/16: 129–31.

Fien, J. 2000. 'Education for the environment: A critique': An analysis. *Environmental Education Research* 6, no. 2: 179–92.

Fien, J. 2002. *Education and sustainability: Reorienting Australian schools for a sustainable future,* Tela Papers,No. 8. Melbourne: Australian Conservation Foundation.

Foucault, M. 1980a. The eye of power. In *Power/knowledge, selected interviews and other writings 1972–1977, by Michel Foucault,* ed. C. Gordon, 146–65. Hertfordshire: Harvester Wheatsheaf.

Foucault, M. 1980b. The history of sexuality. In *Power/knowledge, selected interviews and other writings 1972–1977, by Michel Foucault,* ed. C. Gordon. 183–93. Hertfordshire: Harvester Wheatsheaf.

Foucault, M. 1980c. Questions on geography. In *Power/knowledge, selected interviews and other writings 1972–1977, by Michel Foucault,* ed. C. Gordon. 63–77. Hertfordshire: Harvester Wheatsheaf.

Foucault, M. 1991. Governmentality. In *The Foucault effect: Studies in governmentality with two lectures by and an interview with Michel Foucault,* ed. G. Burchill, C. Gordon, and P. Miller. 87–104. Chicago: The University of Chicago Press.

Gordon, C. 1980. Preface and afterword. In *Power/knowledge, selected interviews and other writings 1972–1977, by Michel Foucault,* ed. C. Gordon, vii–x, 229–260. Hertfordshire: Harvester Wheatsheaf.

Hunter, I. 1994. *Rethinking the school: Subjectivity, bureaucracy, criticism.* St. Leonards, NSW: Allen and Unwin.

Jickling, B. 1991. Environmental education and environmental advocacy: The need for a proper distinction. *Canadian Issues* 13: 169–75.

Jickling, B. 1992. Why I don't want my children to be educated for sustainable development. *Journal of Environmental Education* 23, no. 4: 5–8.

Jickling, B. 2005. Education and advocacy: A troubling relationship. In *Environmental education and advocacy: Changing perspectives of ecology and education,* ed. E.A. Johnson, and M. Mappin. 91–113. Cambridge: Cambridge University Press.

Jickling, B., and Spork, H. 1996. Environmental education for the environment: Retained or retired? *American Educational Research Association conference.* New York: American Educational Research Association. Unpublished conference paper.

Jickling, B., and Spork, H. 1998. Education for the environment: A critique. *Environmental Education Research* 4, no. 3: 309–27.

Jickling, B., and Wals, A. 2008. Globalization and environmental education: Looking beyond sustainable development. *Journal of Curriculum Studies* 40, no.1: 1–21.

Kendall, G., and Wickham, G. 1999. *Using Foucault's methods.* London: Sage Publications.

Lucas, A. 1979. *Environment and environmental education: Conceptual issues and curriculum implications.* Melbourne: Australian International Press and Publications.

Miller, P., and Rose, N. 2008. *Governing the present: Administering economic, social and personal life.* Cambridge: Polity Press.

Nomura, K., and Abe, O. 2009. The education for sustainable development movement in Japan: A political perspective. *Environmental Education Research* 15, no. 4: 483–96.

O'Farrell, C. 2005. *Michel Foucault.* London: Sage Publications.

Palmer, J. 1998. *Environmental education in the twenty-first century: Theory, practice, progress and promise.* London: Routledge.

Rose, N. 1999. *Powers of freedom: Reframing political thought.* Cambridge: Cambridge University Press.

Russell, C. 2006. Working across and with methodological difference in environmental education research. *Environmental Education Research* 12, nos. 3/4: 403–12.

Stevenson, R. 2006. Tensions and transitions in policy discourse: Recontextualizing a decontextualized EE/ESD debate. *Environmental Education Research* 12, nos. 3/4: 277–90.

Tilbury, D. 1995. Environmental education for sustainability: Defining the new focus of environmental education in the 1990s. *Environmental Education Research* 1, no. 2: 195–212.

Tilbury, D. 2004. Environmental education for sustainability: A force for change in higher education. In *Higher education and the challenge of sustainability: Problematics, promise and practice,* ed. P. Corcoran, and A.E.J. Wals, 97–112. Dordrecht: Kluwer Academic Press.

UNESCO. 2002. *Education for sustainability: From Rio to Johannesburg: Lessons learned from a decade of commitment.* Paris: UNESCO.

UNESCO. 2007. *Highlights on DESD progress to date, January 2007.* Paris: UNESCO.

van Rossen, J. 1995. Conceptual analysis in environmental education: Why I want my children to be educated for sustainable development. *Australian Journal of Environmental Education* 11: 73–81.

Walker, K. 1997. Challenging critical theory in environmental education. *Environmental Education Research* 3, no. 2: 155–62.

Education for sustainable development (ESD): the turn away from 'environment' in environmental education?

Helen Kopnina

This article explores the implications of the shift of environmental education (EE) towards education for sustainable development (ESD) in the context of environmental ethics. While plural perspectives on ESD are encouraged both by practitioners and researchers of EE, there is also a danger that such pluralism may sustain dominant political ideologies and consolidated corporate power that obscure environmental concerns. Encouraging plural interpretations of ESD may in fact lead ecologically ill-informed teachers and students acculturated by the dominant neoliberal ideology to underprivilege ecocentric perspective. It is argued that ESD, with its focus on human welfare, equality, rights and fair distribution of resources is a radical departure from the aim of EE set out by the Belgrade Charter as well as a distinct turn towards anthropocentrically biased education. This article has two aims: to demonstrate the importance of environmental ethics for EE in general and ESD in particular and to argue in favour of a return to instrumentalism, based on the twinned assumptions that the environmental problems are severe and that education of ecologically minded students could help their resolution.

Introduction

There is a growing body of literature about the relationship between environmental education (EE) and education for sustainable development (ESD) (e.g. Johnson 2011; Wesselink and Wals 2011) as well as pluralistically driven tensions within each of EE and ESD (e.g. Læssøe and Öhman 2010; Reid and Scott 2006; Stevenson 2006). Some authors argue that ESD is not likely to replace EE but become one of the (important) goals of it (e.g. McKeown and Hopkins 2003, 123), ESD is a dominant perspective of EE (Sauvé, 29) or EE has in fact become ESD (e.g. Ärlemalm-Hagsér and Sandberg 2011; Eilam and Trop 2010). Important distinctions between the goals of EE were made by Lucas (1979) 'in', 'about' or 'for' the environment in order to avoid misunderstandings about the intended type of EE. Similarly, distinctions were drawn between ESD, sustainable development education, learning for sustainability and 'education for sustainability'. According to Huckle (1983) and Robottom (1987), 'education for the environment' has generated powerful images, which have resonated with educators seeking empowerment and new directions to enable inquiry into socio-political dimensions of EE (e.g. Ferreira [2009] account and the criticism of the socially critical perspective is instructive for these distinctions).

Reflecting upon these distinctions, recent editions of *Environmental Education Research* were entirely devoted to theoretical deliberations about ESD as well as international case studies. Researchers from South Africa (Volume 10, Number 3, 2004); German-speaking countries (Volume 12, Number 1, 2006); Denmark and Sweden (Volume 16, Number 1, 2010) and Iceland (Volume 17, Number 3, 2011) addressed ESD in specific socio-cultural settings. These studies also emphasize the inherent complexity and diversity of use of the term 'environment' (what is and what is not included in it?) and examine how the very definition of 'sustainability' (what is to be sustained?) fits within the broader history, issues and purposes of EE. As opposed to earlier nature or conservation study that used to dominate EE practices in the early 1970s, infinitely complex forms of 'environment' (including the entire biosphere or just the species; including or excluding humans as part of an ecosystem, seeing 'nature' or 'wilderness' as socially constructed or considering 'acculturated' human landscapes such as urban gardens to be 'natural environ-ments') have been outlined in recent debates. The author will examine the implica-tions of the shift towards ESD against the background of environmental ethics and will consider four areas outlined by Wesselink and Wals (2011, 77–8) within which a shift occurs: the institutional, content, purpose and process domains of education.

When addressing case studies of ESD, the distinction is made between theory and practice, as well as elementary and higher forms of education. Often, empirical studies discussing the practice of ESD at elementary schools are associated with goals of raising environmental as well as social awareness among children. In the case of vocational or higher education students, the goal of ESD is more akin to developing knowledge and skills necessary for participation in the 'green economy' envisioned by the top-down promoters of ESD such as United Nations Educational, Scientific, and Cultural Organization (UNESCO). The role of large international institutions as well as national education policy-makers in determining the aims of ESD (in the simplest instrumental sense of 'what should ESD aim to achieve?' or 'making something matter') may be very different from those goals formulated by practitioners and/or theorists of ESD.[1] For the purpose of this article, however, we shall concentrate on the 'generic' discussion of ESD, as it is presented in recent publications of *Canadian Journal of Environmental Education* (e.g. Sauvé 2005) and *Journal of Curriculum Studies* (e.g. Jickling and Wals 2007) and *The Journal of Environmental Education* (e.g. Eilam and Trop 2010).[2]

This article has two broad aims instructed by the openly ecocentric position of the author. One aim is to demonstrate the importance of environmental ethics for EE in general and ESD in particular. The second aim is to argue in favour of return to instrumentalism, based on two assumptions: that the (anthropogenically created) environmental problems are severe and objective and that education of ecologically minded future generations could help their resolution (Kopnina 2011a). The author will develop an argument that recent ESD debate does not fully realize the problem-atic nature of economic development for the ecological health of the biosphere. Plu-ral perspectives on ESD can lead practitioners into an essentially anthropocentric paradigm which can be counter-productive to the effort of fostering environmentally concerned citizenry.

Plural perspectives and ecocentrism

It is argued that there is a need for deliberation about ESD, both in terms of its overall aim, theoretical and methodological orientations (e.g. Jensen and Schnack 1997). Some authors imply that unless ESD and generally the discourse on sustainable development (SD) stay open to opinions and debates of educators, it risks becoming indoctrination, a mindless and autocratic repetition of official definitions and limiting standards (Wals and Jickling 2000). Research on ESD is presently dominated by the calls for pluralistic, emancipatory or transactional forms of education that encourage co-creation of knowledge (e.g. Scott 2002; Stables and Scott 2002; Stevenson 2006) and encourage multiple perspectives and critical dialogue on the very concept of SD and ESD (Gough and Scott 2007; Wals 2007).

A related development is viewing ESD as a subjective, interpretive and context-dependent domain (e.g. Jickling 2009; Læssøe and Öhman 2010). Criticism of the concept of SD or educational forms and content within ESD does not necessarily have to be understood solely by reference to specific theoretical positions, but can also be seen in terms of the diverse ways that human beings react morally, encounter different norms and conduct ethical reflection. This position is well summed up by Öhman (2006, 149) who argues that the question is not whether the criticism (of ESD) is correct or not in absolute terms but rather whether the opinions and perspectives have significance in people's lives.

In this article, the author will argue that not only should different perspectives on EE and/or ESD have significance in people's lives, they should (in a way of moral obligation espoused by moral discourse underlying ESD) also have a significance in the world where not only human lives and welfare are at stake. Despite very productive and dynamic debates about what ESD is or should be, there is an 'elephant in the room' very few of current academic debates seem to be addressing. The key concern here is that ESD presents a radical change of focus from prioritizing environmental protection towards mostly social issues, which may or may not be related to environment. While the moral obligation in regard to the poor in the 'developing' world is acknowledged by most ESD theorists (e.g. Stevenson 2006), moral obligation for caring about other species or the entire ecosystems is less often part of ESD discourse.

While some scholars regard the tension between sustainability and development as a universal dilemma (e.g. Læssøe and Öhman 2010; Lewis 2005; Mosse 2005; Oliver-Smith 2010), other scholars seem to be turning towards a kind of post-modern, relativistic, hermeneutic, interpretive view of the very notion of education and agency. Some scholars have argued that the diverse nature of the questions, issues and problems facing advocates of sustainability in higher education requires a willingness to adopt an eclectic approach to the choice of research methodologies as well as empirical analytical, interpretive, critical and post-structural paradigms (Fien 2002). The tension between different approaches to EE, namely the instrumental (in the sense of EE serving particular ends) and the more pluralistic or emancipatory (in a sense of EE privileging transactional and dialogical forms of decision-making characterized by indeterminism and co-creation) leads to a paradox:

> On the one hand there is a deep concern about the state of the planet and a sense of urgency that demands a break with existing non-sustainable systems, lifestyles, and routines, while on the other there is a conviction that it is wrong to persuade, influ-

ence, or even educate people towards pre- and expert-determined ways of thinking and acting. (Wals 2010, 150)

Wals (2010, 143) argues that there is the need to reflect on and expose the implicit normativity of ESD and discusses central concepts in the articles dealing with ESD, including democracy, pluralism, the public good, agency, self-determination, and 'competence'. These central concepts, often related to the notions of relativism and uncertainty, are at odds with the increasing sense of urgency in dealing with sustainability challenges and a corresponding temptation to revert to instrumentalism.

In the article titled 'Environmental education research: to what ends?' Jickling (2009, 213) has inquired about the broad aim of EE and reflected upon the intersection of education and ethics. In reflecting upon philosophical assumptions of what education is or should be, Jickling argues against the post-structuralism claims that education has no meaning and no ends, other than the ones that are subjectively ascribed to it. After cautioning about perils of prescribing research agendas, Jickling suggests that in EE, key normative questions exist at the intersection of 'education' and 'ethics', and that they point to an area of research that deserves more attention. Jickling argues that normative questions need to be recognized as important areas of inquiry and that the most value-laden ideas concern 'ethics' and 'education'. Remarkably, while Jickling (2009, 215) does discuss the interceptions of ethics and environmental ethics, as well as ethics and education, he does not address environmental ethics in relation to EE.

Transition from EE to ESD: perspective from environmental ethics

Since the 1960s, education has also been increasingly linked to environmental management and international development efforts. In 1968, the UNESCO Biosphere Conference in Paris issued a declaration that there was a worldwide awareness of the field of EE. EE was then defined as

> the process of recognizing values and clarifying concepts in order to develop skills and attitudes necessary to understand and appreciate the inter-relatedness among man, his culture, and his biophysical surroundings. Environmental education also entails practice in decision making and self-formulation of a code of behaviour about issues concerning environmental quality. (Quoted in Palmer 1998, 5)

The Belgrade Charter – A Global Framework for EE (UNEP and UNESCO 1976) – and The Tbilisi Declaration (1977) had as their aims educating people to be aware of, concerned and actively involved in working towards the resolution of environmental problems and preventing new ones. The early proponents of EE emphasized that EE has as its goal a positive change in human relationship with nature. In the prospects, one of the earlier academic texts on EE, Chiappo (1978) argued

> Environmental education ... should be critical in fostering awareness of the social and political factors of the problem, and creative in helping to establish a new ethic of liberation. In this latter respect, EE should favour a return to harmony with nature in order to redress the balance of the ecosystem and to enable man's full potential to flourish. The aim should be to bring about a radical change in man's relation with nature ... and to give emphasis to the relationship of belonging, replacing the anthropocentric world-view by an ontocentric worldview ... What is needed, at bottom, is a

transcendent humanism, starting from a biological and spiritual context in which the historical struggle for liberation forms part of the open-ended encompassing whole, just a biological evolution and the energy of matter dynamically incorporates the succession of species and flourishes in its diversification. (Chiappo 1978, 460)

The 1992 publication of Chapter 37 of Agenda 21 suggested that a balance must be found between addressing the needs of the environment and those of humankind. Agenda 21 signals the introduction of SD discourse as well as ESD into school curricula throughout the world.

While the earlier forms of EE, such as naturalist, systematic, scientific, value-centred, or holistic perceived the environment as nature, system, object of study or field of values, ESD conceives environment as 'resource for economic development or shared resource for sustainable living' (Sauvé 2005, 34). United Nations *Decade for Education for Sustainable Development* (2005–2014) encompasses action themes, including overcoming poverty, gender equality, health promotion, environment, rural development, cultural diversity, peace and human security and sustainable urbanization (UNESCO 2005). While the earlier forms of EE embodied by UNESCO's *International Environmental Education Program* (1975–1995) could be generally characterized by concern with 'ecological justice', defined by Low and Gleeson (1998) as 'justice between human beings and the rest of the natural world', the Educating for a Sustainable Future programme focuses on environmental justice, which concerns the distribution of environmental benefits and burdens among human beings. While the Belgrade Charter is more focused on the environment than on human development, emphasizing the need of environmental protection from human activities, ESD only places further emphasis on human rights issues rather than offering any new substance (Smyth 1995).

Case studies of ESD curriculum indicate the shift towards democratic issues with the goal of contributing to promotion of SD, recognizing that a sustainable economy is closely linked to the conservation of natural resources and the equitable sharing of resources (Sauvé 2005, 29). We may reflect on how institutional context is influenced by content and aim formulated at national level. What does the process of interpretation from 'prescribed' curriculum imply for the practice of EE of which ESD may have become a part? These questions can be generalized to different national and institutional settings in which ESD is taught.

Environmental ethics literature poses the question as to the extent to which only loss in human life and welfare should be the basis of political action and moral concern, and whether human 'progress' should also take into account the consequences for non-human species. An important basic distinction may be drawn between the 'functions of' natural capital and the 'functions for' humans which it generates[3] (Eckins 2011, 636). The value bases for environmental concern address a number of basic assumptions about the intrinsic value assigned to humans and non-human entities; as well as belief in human progress and ability to solve all problems. Environmental sociologists, Dunlap and Van Liere (1978) and Dunlap and Catton (1979), described western dominant worldview (with its possibly global dominance over other worldviews), characterized by human exceptionalism paradigm in which humans may be seen as 'part of nature' and yet 'above nature' and thus exempt from natural constraints (or able to solve environmental problems through human ingenuity). In this dominant paradigm, while human dependency on natural resources is largely acknowledged, and while human place in the natural system is seen as 'interdependent', the intrinsic value of 'nature' and the moral imperative of humans to address non-human needs (in some cases, the very survival of entire species) is rarely part of this paradigm. In other words, while social and environmental concerns are certainly closely related in the case of dominant ESD discourse, the balance between human and natural worlds is largely lost.

This concern is exacerbated by the recent calls for the pluralistic perspectives (e.g. Öhman 2006; Wals 2010). Multiple perspectives and visions might be less democratic then they appear as the discourse on SD is dominated by the international organizations such as the United Nations, financiers such as World Bank and the International Monetary Fund and large non-governmental organizations (NGOs) (Lewis and Kanji 2009; Lewis and Mosse 2006) and with corporatists seeking to exert their influence through the development of curricula (Crossley and Watson 2003; Jickling 2009, 214).

The most obvious anthropocentric position can be illustrated by the Biblical quotation:

> Let us make man in our image, after our likeness and let them *have dominion over* the fish of the sea, and *over* the fowl of the air, and *over* the cattle, and *over* all the earth and *over* every creeping thing that creepeth upon the earth. (Genesis I, 26)

In contrast, ecocentric theorists like Leopold (1949/1987) postulated that humans should protect the biotic community by eschewing self-interest and acting for the good of other species. Based on Leopold's Land ethic, Dunlap and Van Liere (1978) introduced the idea of non-anthropocentric (ecocentric) altruism into environmental concern. Ecocentric or biospheric altruists extend concern beyond the human boundary and acknowledge intrinsic value of other species.

Eckersley (1992, 33) considered ecocentrism and anthropocentrism to be '... the opposing poles of a wide spectrum of differing orientations towards nature', acknowledging mixed value systems in between in her later work (Eckersley 2002, 2004). These gradations in the shades of green may be placed on a continuum between deep and shallow ecology (Næss 1973) indicating degrees of strong and weak anthropocentrism and weak and strong ecocentrism. In the context of development 'shallow ecology movement' can be seen as a 'fight against pollution and resource depletion', with the central objective of 'the health and affluence of people in the developed countries'. In this lighter shade of green, the values assigned to nature are instrumental in character, in the sense that the concern for environment is limited to promoting the satisfaction of human wants and needs, both in material and aesthetic terms (Mathews 1994). Proponents of shallow ecology worry about the environmental problems, which affect humans, such as overexploitation of natural resources and pollution. However, according to their critics, they do not ask 'deep' questions about ecological relationships and the origins of environmental problems, leaving the basic structures of advanced industrial societies intact (Lundmarck 2007). Following more 'deep green' perspectives, the environmental crisis calls for revision of major political, economic and social systems (Devall 1993) and re-examination of an anthropocentric dominant western worldview (DWW) in which humans are seen as superior to nature and able to solve all environmental problems (Dunlap and Catton 1979).

If anthropocentrism in all of its shades is optimistic regarding human capacity to cope with environmental problems, ecocentrism's proponents take a more sceptical stance (Naess 1973). The 'deep ecology movement' endorses 'biospheric egalitari-anism', the view that all living things are alike in having intrinsic value, indepen-dent of their utilitarian usefulness to humans, thus embedding environmental ethics debate in the sphere of political theories of justice. While the scope of this article does not allow for discussion of theories pertaining to political liberalism and eco-logical justice, suffice is to say that many theorists agree that democratic liberalism is incompatible with non-anthropocentric ecologism, as at its foundation, liberalism is concerned with the lives of individual humans, not with plant and animal species (Conglianese 1998, 56 in Bell 2006, 207). More moderate political thinkers see the relationship as not necessarily incompatible but potentially problematic (e.g. Bell 2006; Eckersley 2002). The fundamental point is that if EE in general and ESD in particular are not instrumental in the basic goal of making environment matter to students, ecological perspective might be simply lost. In line with Callicott's (1990) 'The case against moral pluralism' and 'Moral monism in environmental ethics defended' (1999), it may be possible that pluralism weakens our moral obligations towards non-human species. It needs to be noted that there are many 'shades of green' present in the anthropocentric and ecocentric continuum. However, the dif-ferences in the context and scale, debates and levels of consensus generated in sub-fields such as social ecology or ecofeminism do not negate the fact that 'with a variety of theories at our disposal, each indicating different, inconsistent, or contra-dictory courses of action we may be tempted to espouse the one that seems most convenient or self-serving in the circumstances' (Callicott's 1990, 155). Are we (EE researchers and practitioners) not actually denying them (students of EE and/or ESD) the opportunity to actually learn (to care) about and contribute to the resolu-tion of environmental problems by suggesting that all perspectives are subjective and (in the most relativist sense) equally valid?

Using environmental (rather than general ethics, as Jickling 2009 proposes) insights, we may ponder the implications of pluralistic approach for fostering what Wals (2010, 150) termed a 'planetary consciousness'. Without the deep ecology per-spective, can the aim of the Belgrade Charter (to educate students that are aware of, and concerned about, the environment and its associated problems, and which have the knowledge, skills, attitudes, motivations and commitment to work individually and collectively towards solutions of current problems and the prevention of new ones) be achieved?

Paradoxes of SD and ESD

The empirical dilemma in regard to SD in general can be summed up in the ques-tion whether human equality and prosperity as well as population growth can be achieved with the present rate of natural degradation (Rees 1992). Rees suggests that expanding the 'economic pie' to include the most dispossessed, will necessarily include even more natural resources being consumed. Since the material saturation level as witnessed by western consumers is 'unsustainable', the negative spiral of increasing needs for resources and depletion is not likely to cease. The oxymoronic goal of both promoting development through economic growth, re-distribution of wealth and keeping the health of the ecosystem intact, the internalization of the ideas of 'development' poses new ethical challenges (Shoreman-Ouimet and Kopn-ina 2011).

In line with Dunlap and Van Liere (1978) and Dunlap and Catton's (1979) inquiry into the DWW in environmental sociology, Bowers (1993) formulated an underlying assumption of the modern/industrial worldview that humans as a species stand above and separate from the natural world. In regard to ideas of SD and corporate responsibility, Scott (2005) proposes that rather than seeking a balance across the economic, social and environmental arenas, the 'real bottom line is the ecological integrity of the biosphere' (Scott 2005, 2).

Environmental protection in SD discourse is seen as an afterthought to all other pressing human issues such as equality, fair distribution of natural resources (*sic!*), and human rights, the key concern is that the discourse on SD maintains an instrumental and anthropocentric worldview (Kopnina and Keune 2010; Kopnina and Shoreman-Ouimet 2011). Concerns with depletion of resources, equity in distribution of resources, concerns about human health and welfare exclude consideration of an ecocentric perspective (Spring 2004). Anthropocentric perspective does not necessarily exclude the interests of non-human species, but non-human-oriented interests are likely to be marginalized (Dunlap and Catton 1979). On the other hand, while the ecocentric perspective is not necessarily exclusive of social concerns (aside from 'very deep green' variety, humans are positioned within the 'nature' domain and are seen as part of the bio- or eco-sphere), there is empirical evidence that people with ecocentric orientation are more likely to protect the environment independent of its value to humans (Thompson and Barton 1994; Kortenkamp and Moore 2001). While the inclusion of the ecocentric perspective is logical in a truly pluralistic system which represents interests and priorities of different stakeholders in cosmopolitan democracy (Eckersley 2002), empirical evidence of many governments' and citizens' failure to address issues such as rapid biodiversity loss may indicate that non-anthropocentric perspective is either under-represented (due to the current power balances within neo-liberal democratic societies) or simply too weak in comparison to anthropocentric interests. Recent calls of ESD scholars for plural representations and democratic debates are not likely to lead to the inclusion of ecocentric perspectives that favours interests of non-human species independent of their value to humans, and may in fact unintentionally support the dominant post-industrial neo-liberal anthropocentric discourse.

In the recent qualitative study of pre-school teachers' comprehension of SD, Ärlemalm-Hagsér and Sandberg (2011) have noted that SD is seen as a holistic approach, an environmental issue or a democratic issue with the particular emphasis on 'fundamental topics' that do not concern ecological issues. These issues include four categories: children's views, social relations, gender equality and cultural diversity. For example, one teacher is quoted as saying: 'In my pre-school the most fundamental parts of working with SD are human rights, democracy, gender equality, morals and ethics' (Quoted in Ärlemalm-Hagsér and Sandberg 2011, 194). Another example is ESD curriculum in Iceland described by Jóhannesson et al. (2011), emphasizing social and economic aspects of development and evoking environment only in relation to either environmental problems that effect humans or environmental *social* justice. Environment in such a discourse often comes as an afterthought, or only in connection with human interests, as in 'health and environment' or 'poverty and pollution' and environmental protection is not seen as in any way liked to intrinsic value of non-human species. According to the Founder and President of Sea Shepherd Conservation Society Paul Watson (2012),

> Racism and Sexism... are social issues but they are not issues relevant to the survival of the biosphere... I think that speciesism is a far more serious issue. Human discrimination against practically every other species on this planet has resulted, is resulting and will continue to result in mass extinctions, extirpations and diminishment. Whereas racism is acknowledged, speciesism is not even given a moment's thought by most people. It is willfully and arrogantly ignored.

In other words, while human rights are taken for granted, while the rights of other species are reduced to 'protection of natural resources'.

SD as a concept has been described as contradictory and socially and culturally contested. Many authors have suggested that the fuzziness and contradictions are not only acceptable but desirable as transformative debates on sustainability are then made possible (e.g. Jickling and Wals 2007). While multiple perspectives on SD are possible and desirable and although democratic forms of learning are certainly welcome, the dominant, mainstream discourse on SD masks inherent anthropocentric bias. The real danger of ESD is that it confuses the teacher and the student about inherent contradictions of 'having your cake and eating it' approach. The most fundamental paradox of SD can be summed up in its oxymoronic goal of both promoting development through economic growth and re-distribution of wealth and keeping the health of the ecosystem – including humans – intact.[4]

While human and environmental domains are intimately intertwined as acknowledged by most environmental ethics thinkers, ESD debates tend to emphasize environmental concerns in relation to human welfare. Social and environmental interdependency is often framed within the context of human needs, deconstructing 'nature' or 'wilderness' in terms of 'natural resources' rather than finding a true balance between human and non-human needs.

In sum, two points of concern need to be stressed. The first concern is that the pluralistic perspectives might not be truly democratic as the discourse on SD is dominated by the perspectives of the political and corporate elites. If we consider the power of political or corporate elites and the apparently global (although unequal) influence of industrial capitalism in shaping the discourse on development, with its clear emphasis on human welfare, how can we guarantee that pluralistic perspectives will lead students to develop ecocentric values?

What light do we shine on things the moment we qualify them as 'resources'? ... A resource is something that achieves its purpose only when it is transformed into something else: its own value evaporates before the claims of higher interests ... Our perception has been trained to see the lumber in a forest, the mineral in a rock, the real estate revenue in a landscape ... What we term a resource is placed under the jurisdiction of production ... (Sachs and Esteva 2000, 77–8 in Sauvé 2005, 15).

ESD is still dominated by the industrial worldview and has 'remained a part of the hidden curriculum of schooling' (Orr 1994). Corporatists have sought to 'exert their influence through the development of school curricular and teaching aids' (Jickling 2009, 214). Læssøe (2010) emphasized that the ecological modernization theory still dominates much of ESD and that without inclusion of dissenting perspectives, deliberative communication tends to only strengthen the hegemony of dominant discourse. This implies that there is no guarantee that dialogical, open and pluralistic in-class discussions will not be influenced by these dominant anthropocentric corporatist perspectives.

The second concern is that pluralistic approach to education may simply not address ecocentric perspectives. Eckersley (2002, 29), in reflecting upon the strengths and weaknesses of moral pluralism approach to environmental politics reflects that there is nothing in the environmental pragmatist method of inquiry that would guarantee any special representation rights to non-human species in cases when there are no human advocates to represent them. Despite the diversity and nuances of the ethnically or gender-specific perspectives, moral pluralists or environmental pragmatics tend to be conservative and take too much as a given, as we avoid critical inquiry into 'the big picture' (such as environmental degradation), and do work with rather than against the grain of existing structures and discourses (such as those that are prevalent in real-world liberal democracies) and facilitate 'interest accommodation' in the context of prevailing alignment of social forces. It accepts path dependency of institutional design, and prefers incrementalism over any radical overhaul of social institutions precisely because the latter are disruptive and likely to generate conflict of a kind that makes agreement much more difficult (Eckersley 2002, 32–3).

Encouraging plural interpretations of ESD and opening it up for democratic debate may in fact lead to allowing corporate and political elites as well as ecologically ill-informed (or simply uninterested) student-citizens to exclude ecocentric perspective from considerations. From the deep ecology perspective, 'pluralism' represents the 'voice' of a single species and marginalizes the voice of the 'eco-advocates' as just one of many perspectives. The true biospheric justice would resonate with 'voices' of non-human species, which are in the majority, based on a simple ethical assumption that all species – and individuals – want to survive.

Implications for the ESD research and practice

The tensions between EE and ESD can be summarized in four distinctive domains: the institutional, content, purpose and process (Wesselink and Wals 2011, 77). Key activities within the institutional domain are engaging in continuous quality improvement, sharing and developing expertise with other institutions, as well as be proactive attitude towards working with government (e.g. Læssøe 2010). The *content domain* reflects highly diversified perspectives regarding the relationship between EE and education for SD (e.g. Hesselink et al. 2000) or conceives the relationship as problematic (e.g. Jickling and Wals 2007). The third is the *purpose domain*, which is related to the preferred goal orientation of EE. The final domain is the *processes domain*, characterized by the shift in emphasis from transmissive learning towards more transformative and pluralistic social learning.

Within the *institutional* domain, EE or ESD curriculum needs to be clearly articulated and embedded within local institutional context. Within institutional domain, as one of the reviewers of the draft of this article has pointed out, context and scale are important 'relativizers' of the way a discourse about EE or ESD might 'trickle down' or 'percolate up' and be practised circumstantially. Nations where ESD is practised differ greatly in their socio-political priorities, as do the forms of democracy surrounding their educational institutions, as well a host of other historical, socio-cultural, political, ecological and economic factors. ESD might be more appropriate in some circumstances (for example, the issues concerned with reproductive health in developing countries); while EE might be more appropriate in others (the issues concerned with consequences of high level of consumption in more affluent western societies). Diversity of institutional settings does not imply a student–teacher dyad in a formal setting but can also be interpreted in the context of wider socio-cultural influences in which both formal and informal learning takes place (e.g. see recent work of anthropologists in the field of EE: Anderson forthcoming; Efird 2011; Kopnina 2011a, 2011b, 2012). Internal tensions within EE or ESD are persistently intensified by the hyper-individualized susceptibilities generated by the neo-liberal pragmatists. These differences in institutional domain call for critical 'sociology' of knowledge generation or production in EE and ESD within the neo-liberal corporate institutions both in 'developed' and 'developing' countries where academic capitalism has traction, as well as 'anthropology' of cultural differences in educational contexts. Harnessing sociology's methodological focus on conceptualization and modelling of concern for social patterning, as well as anthropology's emphasis on in-depth ethnographic study as well as expertise in cultural comparison, investigation of EE and ESD in institutional domain opens up opportunities for further research.

The author is more concerned about too much ambiguity in the generalized *content* domain. Assuming that the recently published articles in academic journals concerned with developments in ESD can be useful to educational practitioners, the author's concern with pluralistic perspectives is that ecocentrism – particularly in the deeper shade of green – is under-represented. While pluralistic views are not necessarily all anthropocentric, the position of deep ecology espoused by the Belgrade Charter does not seem to be the subject of this pluralistic discussion. The apparent lack of discussion of the significance of deep green perspective can confuse the educators about the purpose of EE or ESD and thus render curriculum related to subjects such as SD ineffective. In regard to the *content* domain of EE or ESD curriculum, the author is sceptical of how highly diversified pluralistic perspectives are going to lead the students to more pro-environmental perspectives and actions. While social, participatory and action competence in educational approaches can be very beneficial to the *process* – or methodology – of EE and/or ESD as it actively engages students into the ongoing debates, the danger of abandoning the *purpose* of EE or ESD in addressing environmental problems is of greatest concern. In Breiting and Mogensen (1999) argumentation for action competence in EE, Rickinson's (2003) enquiry-based learning, or Chawla and Cushing's (2007) essay on the importance of strategic learning in EE all call for clear objectives and ends in order to make EE and ESD effective in addressing environmental problems.

In Sauvé's (2005) terms, the critical question about conservation from EE point of view can be 'How to avoid conservation education remaining instrumental?' The question that the author wants to raise in this article is: 'Why should environmental education NOT be instrumental?' The obvious answer to this that instrumental education – or education for something – does not fit with liberal democratic tradition. In his many publications on the subject, Jickling (1992, 2009) and Jickling and Spork (1998) reflected on implications of instrumentalism in education in general and education for environment or for SD in particular. The authors expressed doubts whether education in general can be – or should be – non-instrumental, and pointed out the salience of nominative questions in EE and ESD. Critics have argued, however, that all 'education' – be it that represented in policy, by curricula, in pedagogy and through assessment cannot be normatively neutral (e.g. Fien 2000; Wals 2007). Also, Jickling and Spork do not critically address the normative consideration of EE within the context of the 'strong' to 'weak' versions of democracy. In his critique of Jickling and Spork's concern that education for the environment is a universalizing discourse that seeks to marginalize other approaches, Fien accuses the authors of the lack of reflexivity over their own ideology of education and encourages the critical pedagogy of education for the environment (Fien 2000).

In line with Callicott (1990), the author argues that the embrace of democratic, deliberative or moral pluralism carries a danger of lapsing into indecisive relativism as philosophical contradictions and dubious political and economic priorities may not lead to the enhancement of ecological values. Also, liberal democracy seems to be influenced by the corporate elite and their current powerful, short-sighted and profit-driven regime of production (Dryzek 1992). It has been argued that despite evidence of heightened global problems, 'environmental considerations continue to be subordinated to economic ones' (Stevenson 2006, 280). Liberal democracy typically promotes weak sustainability (Ward 2008) and there is nothing inherent about democracy that guarantees environmental protection (Lidskog and Elander 2010). Pluralistic approach to education may simply not address or under-represent ecocentric perspectives. While plural perspectives do not exclude ecocentrism, deep ecology has been mentioned only in passing in any aforementioned publications of EE journals, suggesting that the majority of ESD scholars are of lighter shade of green. Plural perspectives and democratic representation do not guarantee ecological protection as the underlying concerns may still be anthropocentric.[5]

Another concern is that liberal democracy may be in part influenced not just by government politics and socio-cultural values, but also by corporate elite, such as international financial organizations and multinational corporations or MNCs (Crossley and Watson 2003). There is evidence that formal ESD in 'developed' countries is dominated by UNESCO guidelines for the development of curriculum (http://www.unesco.org/new/en/education/). As Blum (2009) has noted, powerful NGOs may also play a significant role in how educational programmes are structured. It is especially important to understand the role of these organizations and their educational programming in the local context because NGOs have been at the root of community development for the last several decades, and as such they are located precisely at the intersection of powerful interests in (environmental) education (Blum 2009, 718). According to Wesselink and Wals (2011), some in EE are quite critical of adopting the language and models of the corporate world. In evoking the term 'environmental justice', for example, the mainstream discourse on SD, and NGOs that support 'development', for example, may give low priority to environmental protection and privilege economic growth and equal distribution of natural resources. The negative effects of development and 'progress' are often underplayed (Bodley 2008). The use of corporate or development language and models could easily transform EE into a neo-liberal project that undermines everything socially critical EE stands for (Jones and Moore 1993).

Many scholars have pointed out that there is a danger of marginalizing the field of EE by policy-makers, environmentalists and broad-spectrum funding bodies (Reid 2003; Reid and Scott 2006; Rickinson 2001, 2003). One way to avoid this marginalization is to state clear the purpose of EE, rather than obscure it by either conflating it with a number of predominantly social issues unrelated to environment (or only related to it in purely instrumental terms), or by encouraging continuous re-definition, re-contextualizing and re-negotiation of EE. Considering the severity of present environmental problems, the rapid extinction of species of plants and animals, such departure from 'environment' in 'environmental education' and apparent shift towards ESD is worrisome.

Aside from Spring (2004), few theorists have systematically pointed out the problem of anthropocentric approach advocated by mainstream ESD in the institutional, content, purpose and process domains. Concerns expressed in Jickling's article addressing proponents of ESD remain:

> I want them to realize that there is a debate going on between a variety of stances, between adherents of an ecocentric worldview and those who adhere to an anthropocentric worldview. I want my children to be able to participate intelligently in that debate. To do so, they will need to be taught that those various positions also constitute logical arguments of greater or less merit, and they will need to be taught to use philosophical techniques to aid their understanding and evaluation of them. (Jickling 1992, 8)

In the article by Jickling and Spork (1998) addressing these concerns, the authors reflect:

> To enable the success of our students, we need to acknowledge that shaping the future does not consist of being led to adopt some alternative vision. Rather, it involves the more indeterminate process of examining and re-casting society. If we acknowledge that education should be free of specified ends, then we are ultimately led to challenge the way in which 'education for the environment' operates to predetermine educational aims. We believe that the creation and adoption of a promising new environmental vision should instead be viewed not as an aim of education, but as one of the logical and practical outcomes of an educational process. And, we believe such an education offers most hope to those who wish to create promising new visions. (Jickling and Spork 1998, 325)

I agree that the endless contestation of new and alternative perspective should not be the aim of education. However, I fundamentally disagree that EE should be free of specified ends. The refusal to realize the urgency of environmental problems and the possible great benefit of EE in fostering aware, concerned and skilled citizenry that is prepared to prevent them mean the refusal to address the world outside of the anthropocentric vision of it. As one of the referees of this article has argued, understanding of multiple perspectives expressed by, social(ist) ecologists, eco-feminists, deep or shallow ecologists can contribute to understanding of education's complicity in reproducing the 'environmental crises'. In Callicot's argument, pluralism provides no basis for determining which one of multiple incompatible principles to follow in any given circumstance and results in the dissolution of moral responsibility for non-human species for it leads to the scepticism and nihilism he associates with 'deconstructive postmodernism' (Callicott 1990, 1999). Within the field of EE where each perspective (re)constitutes the other, researchers of ESD may need to further elaborate the implications of multiple perspectives upon educational policy, curriculum theory and development and pedagogical strategies within a normative reflexivity about neo-liberal democracy noting the naturalization of the anthropocentric paradigm. In line with Dunlap and Catton's (1979) critique of the dominant western paradigm that led sociologists to treat modern societies as 'exempt' from ecological constraints, continuous prioritization of anthropocentric (or shallow ecology) perspective in dominant theorizing about ESD can lead to the denial of any aim of EE in addressing severe problems such as rapid extinction of species and drastic reduction of biodiversity in recent decades.

Conclusion

In this article, we have argued that pluralistic, liberal or emancipatory approach to education signals scholarly departure from the 'real-world' dilemmas concerned with environmental degradation and an escape from necessity of using education as a tool of acquisition of knowledge and skills that would enable future generations to address urgent environmental problems. ESD represents the shift towards greater anthropocentric orientation in EE. Implications of ESD anthropocentrism were examined in the light of environmental ethics theory and its implications as to the efficacy of the present ESD in fostering young people's care for environment. Despite the very productive and dynamic debates about what ESD is or should be, there is a real danger of losing 'environment' from the aim of EE.

The ESD debate is more salient than just conceptual or philosophical disagreements about nominative domains and differences in perspectives. At the time of unprecedented loss of biodiversity and many other well-known examples of environmental degradation, academic relativism about ESD might in fact be undermining the efforts of educating citizens in the importance of valuing and protecting the environment.

The danger of pluralistic interpretations of ESD is that it may confuse the teachers and the students about the inherent problems and contradictions of SD. While promoting environmental justice that concerns the distribution of environmental benefits and burdens among humans, ESD undermines ecological justice between humans and the rest of the natural world. Without the inclusion of the ontocentric or ecocentric perspective in EE, we may not be too optimistic about the fate of environmental protection and about the long-term welfare of humanity. The early understandings of EE that focused on the protection of natural environment should not be lost in ESD that seems to amplify anthropocentric concepts that often put people and profit before the planet.

As for the potential future direction of this debate, the consequent contributors to the ESD debate are encouraged to deal more emphatically with the intersecting reconstitutions of the ideas and practices of both environment and education, irrespective of how these imperatives might have been manipulated by the discourses of sustainability and the neo-liberal drivers of the unsustainable politics of sustainability. Acknowledging the potential difficulty of advocating deep ecology position (and accusations of ethical 'environmental determinism'), the author's hope is that ESD theorists will consider implications of this position for educative capacity to test theory and ethics off each other.

While academic discussions between EE theorists and practitioners provide an example of engaged deliberative democracy, degradation of environment in the face of rapid industrialization and population growth is continuing to accelerate. The limits to growth seem to be forgotten by the liberal enlightened EE scholars who seem to be increasingly engaged in academic debates about the dangers of dogmatic thinking and declarations of support for democracy and participation. It seems that EE theorists might be failing to see the (still standing) forest behind the (receding) trees.

Notes

1. Also, it needs to be emphasized that environmental, conservation or whatever type of education related to conservation or development is not necessarily taught as such but integrated within general curriculum such as biology or history. This implies that while 'official' ESD and debates about it might be transforming themselves, EE in 'traditional' capacity defined by Belgrade Charter has stayed in its present capacity. This article targets EE theorists as well as practitioners who do consciously engage with the specified subject of ESD.
2. We need to acknowledge, however, that there might be significant differences at the 'grass root' level of practice of ESD – both as far as goals and orientation, as well as level of educational programmes within ESD is concerned. Also, not everything that may be characterized as 'sustainable development' in the curriculum is taught as part of a specific course – for example, at the level of middle school, children could be taught about issues such as poverty and agriculture within regular history or society courses.
3. The functions 'of' (such as the life-support functions of ecosystems) are independent of people. The 'functions for' people all contribute directly in some way to human welfare by acting as inputs to, or waste absorbers from, the economy, others help to maintain human health, or contribute to other aspects of human welfare.
4. Although the scope of this article does not allow for a review of all the positive aspects of ESD discourse, the author is careful not to throw a baby out with the bath water. It needs to be emphasized that advances in conceptualizations and operationalization of ESD have led to a number of very useful developments, both in theory and in practice. Participation and action competence research (e.g. Breiting and Mogensen 1999; Jensen and Schnack 1997) provides excellent perspectives on how new generation of global citizens can be truly engaged and active in the enterprise of sustainability. Breiting (2009) and Jóhannesson and colleagues (2011) argue that education should focus on empowerment for democratic engagement and on teachers becoming capable of handling controversial issues with learners. In advocating the political model for EE, Chawla and Cushing (2007) argue that students need to learn not only about environmental and social equality issues, but also to learn to recognize the power centres that influence environmental and social change and understand the processes by which they operate.
5. For instance, in 1994, as much as 62% of a representative sample of the Swedish public fully approved of the idea of giving constitutional protection to the rights of animals and plants to life and reproduction (Lundmark 1998, 149). However, Lundmark reflected in the later article, if people were also asked to choose between different valuables, to judge the outcome of potential conflicts between rights, or even to see the rights of animals and plants in relation to interests such as employment, health care, macroeconomic stability, the result is likely to be totally different (Lundmark 2007).

References

Anderson, E.N. Forthcoming. Tales best told out of school: Traditional life-skills education meets modern science education. In *Anthropology of environmental education*, ed. H. Kopnina. New York, NY: Nova Science.

Ärlemalm-Hagsér, E., and A. Sandberg. 2011. Sustainable development in early childhood education: In-service students' comprehension of the concept. *Environmental Education Research* 17, no. 2: 187–200.

Bell, D.R. 2006. Political liberalism and ecological justice. *Analyse and Kritik* 28: 206–22.

Blum, N. 2009. Teaching science or cultivating values? Conservation NGOs and environmental education in Costa Rica. *Environmental Education Research* 15, no. 6: 715–29.

Bodley, J.H. 2008. *Victims of progress*. Lanham, MD: Altamira Press.

Bowers, C. 1993. *Education, cultural myths and the ecological crisis: Toward deep changes Albany*. New York, NY: SUNY Press.

Breiting, S. 2009. Issues for environmental education and ESD research development: Looking ahead from WEEC 2007 in Durban. *Environmental Education Research* 15, no. 2: 199–207.

Breiting, S., and F. Mogensen. 1999. Action competence and environmental education. *Cambridge Journal of Education* 29, no. 3: 349–53.

Callicott, J.B. 1990. The case against moral pluralism. *Environmental Ethics* 12, no. 2: 99–124.

Callicott, J.B. 1999. Moral monism in environmental ethics defended. In *Beyond the land ethic: More essays in environmental philosophy*, 171–83. Albany, NY: State University of New York Press.

Chawla, L., and D. Cushing. 2007. Education for strategic environmental behaviour. *Environmental Education Research* 13, no. 4: 437–52.

Chiappo, L. 1978. Environmental education and the Third World. *Prospects, A Quarterly Review of Education. UNESCO* 8, no. 4: 456.

Crossley, M., and K. Watson. 2003. *Comparative and international research in education: Globalisation context and difference*. London: RoutledgeFalmer.

Devall, B. 1993. *Living richly in an age of limits: Using deep ecology for an abundant life*. Salt Lake City, UT: Gibbs Smith.

Dryzek, J.S. 1992. Ecology and discursive democracy: Beyond liberal capitalism and the administrative state. *Capitalism, Nature Socialism* 3, no. 2: 18–42.

Dunlap, R., and W. Catton. 1979. Environmental sociology. *Annual Review of Sociology* 5: 243–73.

Dunlap, R.E., and K.D. Van Liere. 1978. The new environmental paradigm: A proposed measuring instrument and preliminary results. *The Journal of Environmental Education* 9, no. 4: 10–9.

Eckersley, R. 1992. *Environmentalism and political theory: Towards an ecocentric approach*. New York, NY: UCL Press.

Eckersley, R. 2002. Environmental pragmatism, ecocentrism and deliberative democracy: Between problem-solving and fundamental critique. In *Democracy and the claims of nature*, ed. B. Pepperman Taylor and B. Minteer, 49–69. Lanham, MD: Rowman and Littlefield.

Eckersley, R. 2004. *The green state rethinking democracy and sovereignty*. London: MIT Press.

Eckins, P. 2011. Environmental sustainability: From environmental valuation to the sustainability gap. *Progress in Physical Geography* 35, no. 5: 629–51.

Efird, R. 2011. Learning the land beneath our feet: An anthropological perspective on place-based education in China. In *Environmental anthropology*, ed. H. Kopnina and E. Shoreman-Ouimet, 253–66. New York, NY: Routledge.

Eilam, E., and T. Trop. 2010. ESD pedagogy: A guide for the perplexed. *The Journal of Environmental Education* 42, no. 1: 43–64.

Ferreira, J. 2009. Unsettling orthodoxies: Education for the environment/ for sustainability. *Environmental Education Research* 15, no. 5: 607–20.

Fien, J. 2000. 'Education for the environment: A critique' – an analysis. *Environmental Education Research* 6, no. 2: 179–92.

Fien, J. 2002. Advancing sustainability in higher education: Issues and opportunities for research. *International Journal of Sustainability in Higher Education* 3, no. 3: 243–53.

Gough, S., and W. Scott. 2007. *Higher education and sustainable development: Paradox and possibility*. Abingdon: Routledge.

Hesselink, F., P.P. van Kempen, and A.E.J. Wals. 2000. *ESDebate: International on-line debate on education for sustainable development*. Gland, Switzerland.

Huckle, J. 1983. Environmental education. In *Geographical education: Reflection and action*, ed. J. Huckle, 43–68. Oxford: Oxford University Press.

Jensen, B.B., and C. Schnack. 1997. The action competence approach in environmental education. *Environmental Education Research* 3, no. 3: 163–79.

Jickling, B. 1992. Why I don't want my children to be educated for sustainable development. *Journal of Environmental Education* 23, no. 4: 5–8.

Jickling, B. 2009. Environmental education research: To what ends? *Environmental Education Research* 15, no. 2: 209–16.

Jickling, B., and H. Spork. 1998. Education for the environment: A critique. *Environmental Education Research* 4, no. 3: 309–28.

Jickling, B., and A.E.J. Wals. 2007. Globalization and environmental education: Looking beyond sustainable development. *Journal of Curriculum Studies* 40, no. 1: 1–21.

Jóhannesson, I.Á., K. Norðdahl, G. Óskarsdóttir, A. Pálsdóttir, and B. Pétursdóttir. 2011. Curriculum analysis and education for sustainable development in Iceland. *Environmental Education Research* 17, no. 3: 375–91.

Johnson, S. 2011. Review of *Higher education and sustainable development: Paradox and possibility,* by Stephen Gough and William Scott. *Environmental Education Research* 17, no. 2: 281–4.

Jones, L., and R. Moore. 1993. Education, competence and the control of expertise. *British Journal of Sociology of Education* 14, no. 4: 385–97.

Kopnina, H. 2011a. Educating for environmental justice. In *Sage green education series,* Vol. 7, ed. P. Robbins, J. Newman, and J.G. Golson. Thousand Oaks, CA: Sage.

Kopnina, H. 2011b. What about that wrapper? Using consumption diaries in green education In *Environmental anthropology today,* ed. H. Kopnina and E. Shoreman-Ouimet, 118–39. New York, NY: Routledge.

Kopnina, H. 2012. *Anthropology of environmental education.* New York, NY: Nova Science.

Kopnina, H., and H. Keune. 2010. *Health and environment: Social science perspectives.* New York, NY: Nova Science.

Kopnina, H., and E. Shoreman-Ouimet. 2011. *Environmental anthropology today.* New York, NY: Routledge.

Kortenkamp, K.V., and C.F. Moore. 2001. Ecocentrism and anthropocentrism: Moral reasoning about ecological commons dilemmas. *Journal of Environmental Psychology* 21: 1–12.

Læssøe, J. 2010. Education for sustainable development, participation and socio-cultural change. *Environmental Education Research* 16, no. 1: 39–57.

Læssøe, J., and J. Öhman. 2010. Learning as democratic action and communication: Framing Danish and Swedish environmental and sustainability education. *Environmental Education Research* 16, no. 1: 1–7.

Leopold, A. 1949/1987. *A Sand county almanac and sketches here and there.* New York, NY: Oxford University Press.

Lewis, D. 2005. Anthropology and development: The uneasy relationship. In *A handbook of economic anthropology,* ed. James G. Carrier, 472–86. Cheltenham: Edward Elgar. http://eprints.lse.ac.uk/253/.

Lewis, D., and N. Kanji. 2009. *Non-governmental organisations and development.* London: Routledge.

Lewis, D., and D. Mosse, eds. 2006. *Development brokers and translators: The ethnography of aid and agencies.* Bloomfield, CT: Kumarian Books.

Lidskog, R., and I. Elander. 2010. Addressing climate change democratically. Multi-level governance, transnational networks and governmental structures. *Sustainable Development* 18, no. 1: 32–41.

Low, N., and B. Gleeson. 1998. *Justice society and nature: An exploration of political ecology.* London: Routledge.

Lucas, A.M. 1979. *Environment and environmental education: Conceptual issues and curriculum implications.* Melbourne: Australian International Press and Publications.

Lundmark, C. 1998. *Eco-democracy. A green challenge to democratic theory and practice.* Umeå: Umeå University Press.

Lundmark, C. 2007. The new ecological paradigm revisited: Anchoring the NEP scale in environmental ethics. *Environmental Education Research* 13, no. 3: 329–47.

Mathews, F. 1994. *The ecological self.* London: Routledge.

McKeown, R., and C. Hopkins. 2003. EE ≠ ESD: Defusing the worry. *Environmental Education Research* 9, no. 1: 117–28.

Mosse, D. 2005. *Cultivating development: An ethnography of aid policy and practice.* London: Pluto Press.

Naess, A. 1973. The shallow and the deep: Long-range ecology movement. *A Summary, Inquiry* 16: 95–9.

Oliver-Smith, A. 2010. *Defying displacement: Grassroots resistance and the critique of development.* Austin, TX: University of Texas Press.

Orr, D. 1994. *Earth in mind: On education, environment, and the human prospect.* Washington, DC: Island Press.

Palmer, J.A. 1998. *Environmental education in the 21st century: Theory practice, progress and promise.* New York, NY: Routledge.

Rees, W. 1992. Understanding sustainable development. In *Sustainable development and the future of cities*, Proceedings of an international summer seminar, ed. B. Hamm, G. Zimmer, and S. Kratz, 17–40, Bauhaus Dessau, September 7–14, 1991.

Reid, A. 2003. Sensing environmental education research. *Canadian Journal of Environmental Education* 8: 9–30.

Reid, A., and W. Scott. 2006. Researching education and the environment: Retrospect and prospect. *Environmental Education Research* 12, no. 3: 571–87.

Rickinson, M. 2001. Special issue: Learners and learning in environmental education: A critical review of the evidence. *Environmental Education Research* 7, no. 3: 208–320.

Rickinson, M. 2003. Reviewing research evidence in environmental education: Some methodological reflections and challenges. *Environmental Education Research* 9, no. 2: 257–71.

Robottom, I. 1987. Towards enquiry-based professional development in environmental education. In *Environmental education: Practice and possibility*, ed. I. Robottom. Geelong: Deakin University Press.

Sauvé, L. 2005. Currents in environmental education: Mapping a complex and evolving pedagogical field. *Canadian Journal of Environmental Education* 10, no. 1: 11–37.

Scott, W. 2002. Education and sustainable development: Challenges, responsibilities, and frames of mind. *Trumpeter* 18, no. 1: 123–34. http://trumpeter.athabascau.ca/index.php/trumpet/article/view/123/134 (accessed May 26, 2011).

Scott, W. 2005. ESD: What sort of education? What sort of learning? What sort of decade? Invited paper presented at the Danish Opening Conference for the united Nations Decade of Education for Sustainable Development, March 10–11, in Copenhagen, Denmark. www.ubu10.dk/konf/english.htm.

Shoreman-Ouimet, E., and H. Kopnina. 2011. Introduction: Environmental anthropology yesterday and today. In *Environmental anthropology today*, ed. H. Kopnina and E. Shoreman-Ouimet, 1–34. New York, NY: Routledge.

Smyth, J.C. 1995. Environment and education: A view of a changing scene. *Environmental Education Research* 1, no. 1: 3–20.

Spring, J. 2004. *How educational ideologies are shaping global society: Intergovernmental organizations, NGO's, and the decline of the state.* Mahwah, NJ: Lawrence Erlbaum.

Stables, A., and W. Scott. 2002. The quest for holism in education for sustainable development. *Environmental Education Research* 8, no. 1: 53–60.

Stevenson, R. 2006. Tensions and transitions in policy discourse: Recontextualising a decontextualised EE/ESD debate. *Environmental Education Research* 12, no. 3–4: 277–90.

The Tbilisi Declarion. 1977. Intergovernmental conference on environmental education. Organized The United Nations Education, Scientific, and Cultural Organization (UNESCO) in cooperation with the U.N. Environment Programme (UNEP). Tbilisi, Georgia (USSR) from October 14-26, http://www.gdrc.org/uem/ee/tbilisi.html.

Thompson, G.S.C., and M.A. Barton. 1994. Ecocentric and anthropocentric attitudes toward the environment. *Journal of Environmental Psychology* 14: 149–57.

United Nations Educational, Scientific and Cultural Organization (UNESCO). 2005. *United nations decade of education for sustainable development (2005–2014).* Framework for the international implementation scheme. 32 C/INF.9. http://unesdoc.unesco.org/images/0013/001311/131163e.pdf (accessed May 2011).

United Nations Environment Programme (UNEP) and United Nations Educational, Scientific and Cultural Organization (UNESCO). 1976. The Belgrade Charter. http://unesdoc.unesco.org/images/0001/000177/017772eb.pdf; http://www.medies.net/_uploaded_files/The-BelgradeCharter.pdf.

Wals, A.E.J. 2007. *Social learning: Towards a sustainable world*. Wageningen: Wageningen Academic.

Wals, A.E.J. 2010. Between knowing what is right and knowing that is it wrong to tell others what is right: On relativism, uncertainty and democracy in environmental and sustainability education. *Environmental Education Research* 16, no. 1: 143–51.

Wals, A.E.J., and B. Jickling. 2000. Process-based environmental education seeking standards without standardizing. In *Critical environmental and health education: Research issues and challenges*, ed. B.B. Jensen, K. Schnack, and V. Simovska, 127–48. Copenhagen: The Danish University of Education, Research Centre for Environmental and Health Education.

Ward, H. 2008. Liberal democracy and sustainability. *Environmental Politics* 17, no. 3: 386–409.

Watson, P. 2012. Clarification on where director Paul Watson stands on various issues. http://www.ecospherics.net/pages/wonw.htm (accessed January 14, 2012).

Wesselink, R., and A.E.J. Wals. 2011. Developing competence profiles for educators in environmental education organisations in the Netherlands. *Environmental Education Research* 17, no. 1: 69–90.

Öhman, J. 2006. Pluralism and criticism in environmental education and education for sustainable development: A practical understanding. *Environmental Education Research* 12, no. 2: 149–63.

Environmental Literacy: functional, cultural, critical. The case of the SCAA guidelines

ANDREW STABLES

SUMMARY   *The author has argued elsewhere for an increased role for linguistics and literary studies within environmental education. Here he argues that the tripartite division of literacy skills as functional, cultural and critical can be useful in both planning and evaluating programmes of environmental education. As exemplification of the latter, the model is applied to a brief discussion of the School Curriculum and Assessment Authority (SCAA) guidelines for environmental education in England. It is concluded that these offer opportunities for teachers to develop all three kinds of environmental literacy, but with an emphasis on skills development which must largely be seen as functional.*

Background and Rationale

The term 'environmental literacy' has been used hitherto in the environmental education literature, but while it has been given working definitions, these have not been derived directly from a systematic engagement with literacy debates within language and literature studies. As part of the American work on 'standards', Roth (1992) provides a framework for environmental literacy with relation to knowledge, affect, skills and behaviour at three levels of competence (nominal, functional and operational). For UNESCO, Marcinkowski (1991) provides a set of nine statements which amount to what environmental literacy might be taken to be, relating to knowledge, understanding, attitudes and active involvement. In Scotland curriculum planners have included environmental literacy as one of the four goals of 'environmental citizenship' (Scottish Office, 1993), defining it in terms of 'knowledge and understanding of the components of the system' (p. 4). While each of these definitions of environmental literacy might have its practical uses, none is overtly grounded in the primary academic debate about the nature of literacy.

In essence, the case for regarding environmental education as the development of a kind (or of certain kinds) of literacy is a very simple one: the environment is moulded by human hands, is susceptible to action predetermined by human value systems and cultural norms and is, therefore, appropriately studied using approaches derived from the arts and humanities as well as from the sciences. This simple argument can be elaborated in a number of ways.

First, work in a number of disciplines in recent years has tended to give increased emphasis to the role of humanity is shaping the natural environment. To give two examples, Schama (1995) explains how areas of assumed wilderness have been shaped by human culture over a millennium, while McKibben (1990) goes further in claiming, more controversially, that no natural event or place on Earth is free from human intervention.

Second, the disciplines associated with the study of language have seen their scope broadened throughout the 20th century, so that terms such as 'language', 'text' and 'discourse' have been open to broader interpretation than in the 18th and 19th centuries and language has increasingly been seen not just as the vehicle, but as the subject of philosophy and social theory (Stables, 1996a,b).

Third, in relation to the above, 'literacy' has become a catchword in relation to many areas outside that of the acquisition of reading print-based text. The London Institute of Education runs a Masters degree programme in 'literacies'; the phrases 'computer literacy' and 'technological literacy' are frequently encountered. By reference to the first and second points above, a case can be made for defining the ability to make sense of the world around us and our relationship with it as environmental literacy.

Finally, in fields other than education links have already been drawn between the language arts and environmental studies. The author recently attended the first British conference on Literature and the Natural Environment, at the University of Wales, Swansea. Such conferences began in the early 1990s in the USA, where a journal (*Interdisciplinary Studies in Literature and Environment*) exists to develop the field. There are already some significant works of ecocriticism (e.g. Bate, 1991; Buell, 1995).

It is clear from the above that there are a number of justifications for considering the development of environmental awareness and agency in relation to the development of our reading, linguistic and cultural awareness and skills. It is the purpose of the remainder of this paper to show what this means in practice and to relate the insights gained therefrom to the initial analysis of a key environmental education policy document in England and Wales.

Functional, Cultural and Critical Literacies

As has been stated, many kinds of literacy have been identified. In relation to language development, however, whence the term derives, it is common to distinguish between functional, cultural, critical and, sometimes, academic literacies (Williams & Snipper, 1990). The last-mentioned refers specifically to the ability to deal with written texts in the registers common to academic writing; thus academic literacy is deemed necessary for academic advancement. Academic literacy will not be treated as a separate type for the purposes of this paper, as its scope is narrower than that of the others and it could, arguably, be seen as embodying aspects of each of them, particularly, perhaps, the cultural.

Functional Literacy

Functional literacy is the ability to decode what is encoded within the black marks on the white paper into intelligible words, phrases and clauses and to understand their literal meaning on a superficial level. Functional literacy, for example, allows you to read a sign bearing an instruction, such as 'Stop!' and to act upon it. It allows you to read a story, but does not account for whether you can draw any implications from it. Functional literacy (with relation to print) can therefore be taught through the learning of phonic rules. It is not directly concerned with reading for meaning. However, it does involve the ability to recognise the surface meaning of words and phrases in context: for instance, to understand 'stop' in constructions such as 'pull out the organ stop', 'forgot to use a full stop' and 'Danger—Stop!'. Statistics concerning rates of literacy and illiteracy generally relate to functional literacy and obscure the fact that what it takes to be functionally literate varies considerably from time to time and place to place. (Consider, for example, the level of print literacy needed to 'function' as a farm worker in the 19th century and as a computer operator in the 20th; Williams & Snipper, 1990.)

Cultural Literacy

Unlike the above, cultural literacy is a phrase directly attributable to one man. The work of E.D. Hirsch (1987) had an enormous effect on literacy teaching in the USA and a considerable effect elsewhere, not least because of the author's closeness to the Reagan administration. (J.S.Simmons, in Marum, 1996, gives a fascinating account of the development of the USA literacy curriculum during the 1980s, with particular reference to this issue.) Hirsch actually produced a list of 'what every American needs to know', on the assumption that social and cultural cohesion depends on the ability to understand the significance American society places on, for example, Thanksgiving; not merely its existence as, say, a public holiday. Like functional literacy, cultural literacy is, in a sense, passive: it is the ability to know the received wisdom about some cultural event or institution rather than to make meaning for yourself. However, it is a powerful idea, the ramifications of which can be seen in the various ways in which governments around the world have begun, or continued, to use national curricula to reinforce national identities (Marum, 1996).

Critical Literacy

Critical literacy implies the ability to make sense in your own terms of the ideational potential of a text. It includes the ability to 'get behind' the text to interpret it in terms of its ideological underpinnings: to distinguish, for example, between factual account, polemic and propaganda. 'Critical' here is used in a double sense. On the one hand it has a long pedigree in the liberal–humanist tradition of literary criticism, in which the 'critical appreciation' of texts demanded an extended personal response and evaluation of the text as work of art: an exploration of the reader's initial affective response. On the other hand, it can refer to Habermas's concept of 'critical-emancipatory' knowledge (Habermas, 1987), whereby the reader responds to the text not merely as a naive individual who can only 'interpret', albeit for practical ends, but as one who *understands* the cultural, social and political forces that shape the text and can therefore guard against being taken in by it. Because of this dual use of the term 'critical' (the personally engaged as opposed to the socially critical), late 20th century readings of texts have varied from the overtly personal to the apparently dispassionate and deliberately political: Marxist readings, feminist readings, ecofeminist readings and so on. For the purposes of this paper 'critical literacy' will be held to relate to both liberal–humanist and the socially critical perspectives, i.e. to that kind of literacy which involves active exploration of significance and meaning.

What Does it Mean to be Functionally, Culturally and Critically Environmentally Literate?

We now consider each of the above briefly in relation to environmental knowledge, awareness and skills.

Functional Environmental Literacy

Functional print literacy can be measured by objective tests, which can be purely summative or may be diagnostic if subjected to miscue analysis, which analyses reader's errors. Functional literacy is not just a matter of knowing what words mean, but of being able to *find out* what they mean in the context of whole sentences by the use of phonic and contextual cues. Functional literacy also involves being able to read words referring to commonplace abstractions (beauty, goodness, fear, etc.). It involves literal comprehension.

Functional *environmental* literacy must, therefore, refer not only to the ability to remember what an oak tree is, but to recognise one; not only to recognise several trees within a given area, but to know whether they form part of a wood or an area of parkland. Functional environmental literacy must also involve the ability to ascertain, from contextual cues, what something half known is likely to be: for instance, to make an informed guess, using observation, at the types of woodland flower within a beech copse overlying chalk rather than an oak wood on more acid soil. Functional literacy is not, therefore, a mere prerequisite to more advanced forms of literacy, but involves a series of complex skills and an accumulation of knowledge which has unlimited capacity for growth. Arguably, much science education in schools focuses chiefly on what is defined here as functional literacy, whether or not this entirely reflects intentions. Certainly, its role in environmental education should not be underestimated.

Both cultural and critical literacy are impossible without functional literacy. Just as the ability to decode print is a prerequisite to the development of deeper levels of comprehension of the passage to be read, so is knowledge of the natural world a condition of the development of awareness of environmental issues and of the ability to take effective action.

However, functional environmental literacy is not enough because it does not, of itself, engage the learner (though many learners may already be highly motivated) and it does not engage either with the crucial notion of what the environment *means*, either to others or to the learner. Environmental education, therefore, must never abandon its scientific knowledge base, but must always move beyond it, so that scientific knowledge is used to inform what are essentially human value judgements. In terms of environmental literacy, we must acknowledge the importance of the functional but place it alongside the cultural and see both as conditions of the critical, as only critical environmental literacy can facilitate effective environmental action.

Cultural Environmental Literacy

Cultural literacy refers to the ability to understand the significance that society attaches to cultural icons. Such icons include, of course, living natural objects: national parks; the Californian redwood; the English oak. An increased cultural environmental literacy would be gained by a reading of Schama's *Landscape and Memory*, in which the author discusses a series of landscapes of rich significance to contemporary societies (including part of the Eastern European forest, the English Greenwood and the Californian redwoods) in terms of cultural history with respect to the ways in which these landscapes have been viewed, used and reshaped over a millennium. One of the abiding impressions gained from a reading of *Landscape and Memory* is that the landscapes in question have often been strongly shaped by cultural and social forces throughout the period in question. Schama effectively dispels the still partly held misconception, for example, that much of England was covered with virgin forest until the last couple of hundred years.

On one level, a degree of cultural environmental literacy merely enables one to recognise the significance of natural images in human culture, along with some recognition of why and to whom they are significant: the American bald eagle or the white dove of peace, for example. However, it also allows for an understanding of why the landscape itself is as it is, shaped not merely by climate, glaciation and topography, but by arguments about enclosure, the need for timber and patterns of land ownership dating back many centuries. While functional environmental literacy develops knowledge of what natural things are, cultural environmental literacy enables us to explain why they are there when the causes are clearly not simply geological or climatic with no apparent human intervention.

Cultural literacy depends on a degree of acceptance of cultural hegemony: it links the learner with a dominant value system. The culturally literate individual in England will know what is implied by the term 'heart of oak' or understand the English Lake District as a kind of symbol of Wordsworthian Romanticism, even though these conceptions may be more associated with English 'high culture' than with popular culture, as well as having no scientific basis. Cultural literacy refers more to cultural heritage than to cultural analysis. The subtitle of Hirsch's book is 'What every American needs to know'. Insofar as cultural literacy is empowering, it empowers by giving the learner access to socially powerful perspectives; cultural literacy alone does not enable the learner to act upon that knowledge, once acquired. Effective action requires critical literacy.

Critical Environmental Literacy

Critical literacy is the ability to understand the text on a deeper and more creative level: the ability to discuss the use of genre in context, to question the motives and ideology of the text and to explore and develop a personal (and broader social) response to it. Critical environmental literacy must then imply the power to develop an understanding of the factors that contribute to environmental change and to have a view on how to further oppose that change in a way which can be translated into action. Critical environmental literacy involves the ability to explore questions such as: 'What does [a place or an issue] mean to me?'; 'What does it mean to us, or to others?'; 'What are the consequences of carrying on in this way [in relation to this place or this issue]?'; 'Should we act differently, and if so how?'; 'How do we translate our values into effective action, and are our values themselves ready for change as a result of what we now know or feel?'.

As has been stressed above, critical literacy cannot be effectively developed without good levels of both functional and cultural literacy, though the latter are arguably pointless without the former. Critical environmental literacy relies on functional environmental literacy because both environmental debate and environmental action rely on information. Critical environmental literacy relies on cultural literacy not simply because environmental debate and action need to be grounded in an awareness of the norms and values of, say, national cultures, but because influence on environmental change demands an understanding of the norms and values of the *dominant* culture.

The Limitations of the Model

There is no suggestion in this paper that more commonly adopted environmental education paradigms should suddenly be abandoned in favour of an approach which looks at the environment as if it were print-based text: merely that a greater emphasis on such an approach might enrich environmental education, not least by incorporating the aesthetic, the ethical and the cultural at both the discussion and action planning stages (see also Stables, 1996a).

Two obvious objections to such a position might be raised, which are dealt with one by one below.

The first might run as follows: intellectual sophistry might justify the argument that, under certain circumstances, environment can be seen as text, but this does not justify approaches relating to print-based text being applied to reading the environment.

The theoretical case has been argued fully elsewhere (Stables, 1996a, 1997), but it seems pertinent to reiterate two central points here. Firstly, even if only certain kinds of 'environment' (e.g. the garden) can rightly be seen as text, there is still scope for work of this sort in these contexts. In fact, however, when one adopts this approach the borderline between 'textual' and 'non-textual' landscape becomes increasingly blurred (Stables, 1995): it is extremely difficult to draw a clear borderline between what should and what should not be defined as text when many 20th century thinkers have problematised the previously easily held distinctions between things-in-themselves and symbols (i.e. things standing for other things). Even the conception of texts as humanly constructed artefacts is challenged by structuralist and post-structuralist literary theory: Barthes' assertion in 1968 of the 'death of the author' leaves meaning as something no longer fixed in a text by an omniscient creator (unless we consider the divine), but as something we ourselves ascribe to the signifies that constitute our cultural worlds (Stables, 1997).

Nevertheless, the tripartite literacy model used above was not devised with reference to 'reading the world' and it is always wise to recall Wittgenstein's powerful argument that false philosophical problems can arise when terms are used outside the language games of which they are normally a part (Wittgenstein, 1987). There are some crucial differences between reading print-based text and reading the environment. Essentially, functional literacy must have a much narrower scope in the former case than the latter and must, presumably, be much easier to acquire to a high level: our knowledge of print-based texts is bound to be less than our knowledge of the whole physical world. Secondly, cultural literacy could be said to be relatively more important in the former case than the latter, since all print-based texts are unarguably cultural artefacts, whereas some or most (or maybe all) landscapes and landscape features are partially so. Thirdly, in relation to this, critical literacy has been developed as a term with respect to things which can unarguably be seen as expressions of ideology or the specifically human condition; the degree to which we are wise to comment evaluatively on, say, the effects of glaciation is clearly rather less. On the other hand, when we consider current environmental issues (and environmental education exists to help present and future generations deal with these issues) the situation is very different. It would be impossible to conduct effective debate about road building, the European Common Agricultural Policy, mineral extraction or global warming without considerable attention to ideology and human motive.

A second objection to the model might be that, while it may be possible to apply this model to environmental education, it is of limited value so to do, since environmental problems require scientific analysis and scientifically based solutions.

In response to this, there is no doubt that environmental education could not operate effectively purely as an arts or humanities subject. However, all environmental issues are essentially either human issues or issues viewed from a human perspective. Many of the key terms of the environmental debate, including 'balance' and 'sustainability' are terms relating to human values. Science must inform our choices, but they cannot be made without reference to ethical, and often aesthetic, considerations. Thus the arts and humanities, or 'cultural studies', should have a role to play in informing decisions about environmental action. As we shall see below, English National Curriculum guidelines are intended to prepare students to make responsible, and not merely informed, choices for a sustainable future.

Specifically, the contribution of the 'environmental literacy' approach might be greatest in the following areas:

(i) in understanding how and why approaches to the environment have changed and developed over time (e.g. Bate, 1991);
(ii) in ensuring that choices about environmental action take into account ethical and aesthetic, as well as scientific considerations with respect to their likely consequences (i.e. to consider the question 'What will this actually *mean* for us/others/nature?').

Environmental Literacies and the SCAA Guidelines

What follows is not intended as a detailed critique of the National Curriculum guidelines for England (SCAA, 1996), less still a hostile critique, since the guidelines offer many examples of noteworthy practice to teachers and schools determined to pursue an aspect of the curriculum which is given very little weighting in terms of school inspection and accountability. The purpose is merely to show how the model can be applied to the evaluation of a curriculum policy document by reference to some isolated, but hopefully representative, examples from the text.

The document opens with some quotations from important government sources: the Secretary of State for Education and Employment, the Secretary of State for the Environment and a 'British Government Panel on Sustainable Development'.

What is particularly interesting about these initial quotations is the emphasis the government ministers put on what is defined here as critical environmental literacy.

> Gillian Shephard: We need to be aware, as individuals, of how our own choices about a myriad of everyday things can influence the quality of life ... choices with a real relevance to school pupils ... They will have to understand just how great or how small are the risks of environmental change associated with different policies.
>
> John Gummer: ... And sustainable development pressures on these young people will not go away. We need to involve them in the issues now, and help them gain ownership of some of the solutions. (SCAA, 1996, Foreword)

This emphasis is retained in the Aims of the Guidelines (p. 2), particularly in Aims 2 and 3:

> (2) encourage pupils to examine and interpret the environment from a variety of perspectives—physical, geographical, biological, sociological, economic, political, technological, historical, aesthetic, ethical and spiritual;
>
> (3) arouse pupils' awareness and curiosity about the environment and encourage active participation in resolving environmental problems.

What is interesting in the body of the document as a whole is that this emphasis on critical environmental literacy is not maintained. The overall weighting of the exemplar materials which comprise the bulk of the document is on functional environmental literacy. Similarly, arts and humanities subjects, excluding geography, are not given the same weighting as scientific and technical subjects, excluding geography. Each example specifies, in bold print, the subject areas to which it contributes. A crude count reveals the overall numbers as follows: arts/humanities (excluding geography), 16 (including several references to English because the activity involves the practising of English skills); mathematics/science/technical subjects (excluding geography), 39. This bias is neither necessarily conscious nor does it detract from the usefulness of the exemplar materials; however, it does reflect an assumed emphasis within environmental education programmes. Alongside this, the exemplar materials do not place the same emphasis on the development of critical (or cultural) environmental literacy that the ministerial statements would seem to have urged. Indeed, the balance of the Aims (quoted in part above) is not reflected elsewhere in the documentation. The 'Management Issues' section, for example, (pp. 5–11) does not really expand on the critical elements within the Aims, but instead concentrates on generic features of good curriculum planning, on auditing (but not really evaluating the 'critical' element) and on locating sources of further information. Throughout the document, the term 'education about the environment' is used for the sake of ease (though there is a full explication of this towards the beginning) and this might be seen as encouraging functional and cultural, rather than critical, environmental literacy.

It is beyond the scope of this paper to undertake a detailed analysis of the exemplar materials. They embody, as has been stated, excellent environmental education practice and may prove of considerable use to teachers. While they cover all aspects of environmental literacy, they do not, however, place the same emphasis on the critical that might be expected from the opening of the document. At one point a figure shows how the subject departments of a particular school identified the relevant areas of their own subject orders to the teaching of environmental education (p. 33). Here the emphasis is *entirely* on the functional. Even the inclusions from English ('writing for a range of purposes and audiences' and 'developing pupils' ability to write poetry') seem to be mechanistic and to avoid consideration of the ethical, the culturally historical or the aesthetic. Indeed, it is arguably in the subject orders of the National Curriculum themselves (relevant sections of which are quoted on pp. 44–57) that the genesis of this emphasis on the functional lies. Here there is very little emphasis on either the cultural or the critical, though the examination requirements for religious education (not National Curriculum orders in the strict sense, but quoted in the Guidelines *in lieu*) contain potentially challenging objectives in this respect, including 'learning about Jewish teaching on *tikkum olam* (mending the world) and how this affects contemporary Jewish attitudes towards green issues' and 'identify and promote exploration of, and reflection upon, questions about the meaning and purpose of life' (p. 57). Little in the geography orders, in contrast, seems designed to promote either cultural or critical environmental literacy: an exception is 'considering the issues that arise from people's interaction with their environment' (p. 53).

Conclusion

As previously stated, the above comments on the SCAA guidelines do not aspire to a full analysis. The intention is merely to show that the threefold classification of environmental literacy into functional, cultural and critical can be of use in evaluating, and thus reformulating, environmental education syllabuses and courses. Specifically, in this case, the question is raised as to whether government ministers' intentions to promote critical environmental literacy are reflected in the curriculum guidelines and statutory orders for which they are effectively responsible. The argument remains that the roles of the aesthetic, the ethical and the cultural continue to be underplayed within environmental education and that considering environmental education in terms of literacies can go some way to redressing this imbalance.

REFERENCES

BATE, J. (1991) *Romantic Ecology: Wordsworth and the environmental tradition* (London, Routledge).

BUELL, L. (1995) *The Environmental Imagination: Thoreau, nature writing and the formation of American culture* (Cambridge, MA, Belknap Press).

HABERMAS, J. (1987) *Knowledge and Human Interests* (Cambridge, Polity Press).

HIRSCH, E.D. (1987) *Cultural Literacy: what every American needs to know* (Boston, MA, Houghton Mifflin).

MARCINKOWSKI, T. (1991) The relationship between environmental literacy and responsible environmental behavior in environmental education, in: M. MALDAGUE (Ed.) *Methods and Techniques for Evaluating Environmental Education* (Paris, UNESCO).

MARUM, E. (Ed.) (1996) *Children and Books in the Modern World* (London, Falmer).

MCKIBBEN, B. (1990) *The End of Nature* (Harmondsworth, Penguin).

ROTH, C. (1992) *Environmental Literacy: its roots, evolution and direction in the 1990s* (Columbus, Ohio State University).

SCAA [SCHOOL CURRICULUM AND ASSESSMENT AUTHORITY (UK)] (1996) *Teaching Environmental Matters through the National Curriculum* (London, HMSO).

SCHAMA, S. (1995) *Landscape and Memory* (New York, NY, Random House).

SCOTTISH OFFICE (1993) *National Strategy for Environmental Education in Scotland* (Edinburgh, HMSO).

STABLES, A. (1995) Text riddles, *The Use of English*, 47(1), p. 18.

STABLES, A. (1996a) Reading the environmental as text: literary theory and environmental education, *Environmental Education Research*, 2, pp. 189–195.

STABLES, A. (1996b) Studying education as text: parameters and implications, *Westminster Studies in Education*, 19, pp. 5–13.

STABLES, A. (1997) The landscape and the death of the author, *Canadian Journal of Environmental Education*, 2, pp. 104–113.

WILLIAMS, J.D. & SNIPPER, G.C. (1990) *Literacy and Bilingualism* (New York, NY, Longman).

WITTGENSTEIN, L. (1987) *Philosophical Investigations* (Oxford, Blackwell).

Education for Sustainable Development, governmentality and *Learning to Last*

John Blewitt

As Education for Sustainable Development (ESD) slowly moves up the UK Government's policy agenda, practical implementation issues are increasing in significance. This paper offers a retrospective reflective account of a major national ESD initiative, *Learning to Last*, funded by the Quality and Standards Directorate of the Learning and Skills Council. At the centre of the *Learning to Last* experience was a tension between a managerialist approach to project development, common within the Learning and Skills sector, and an ecological, networked and synoptic methodology more in keeping with and sympathetic to the values of ESD. Applying the concepts of 'governmentality' and new public management, *Learning to Last* is viewed as a target and output driven initiative offering restricted opportunities for creative development and conceptual learning. Only with a more reflective and reflexive engagement with sustainability and learning will the possibilities of achieving a more sustainable future and of negotiating our 'society of government' be realised.

Introduction

The UK Government's tenuous commitment to connecting sustainable development to lifelong learning, skills and educational development has been hesitantly articulated by government departments, quasi-autonomous non-governmental organisations and regional bodies since the late 1990s (Blewitt, 2002a). The idea that Education for Sustainable Development (ESD) may involve a radical departure from certain practices current within education policy-making and implementation (Sterling, 2001) was partially acknowledged in the work of the Government's advisory Sustainable Development Education Panel, particularly its draft ESD strategy titled *Learning to last* (Department of Environment, Food and Rural Affairs [Defra], 2003), and the publication of the House of Commons Environmental Audit

Committee's report, *Learning the sustainability lesson* (Environmental Audit Committee, 2003). The Department for Education and Skills's (DfES) *Sustainable development action plan for education and skills* (2003), prompted by some intensive lobbying from environmental and development education groups, such as the Environmental Association for Universities and Colleges, Council for Environmental Education, Development Education Association, Forum for the Future and the mobilising effect of the state-financed *Learning to Last* initiative, did not address the issue of paradigmatic change.[1] The attempts to nudge governmental discourses on education and training towards an engagement with sustainability were clearly shaped by the managerialist governmentality dominating public affairs since the late 1980s.

The Learning and Skills Council (LSC)/Learning and Skills Development Agency (LSDA) *Learning to Last (LtL)* initiative, originally titled Dissemination of Good Practice in Sustainable Development Education, took place in two short phases between March to September 2001 (Phase 1) and January to June 2003 (Phase 2). Each phase involved 11 projects largely based around further education colleges or other post-16 learning and training providers. The Quality and Standards Directorate of the Government's Learning and Skills Council funded these projects. They were project managed by the Learning and Skills Development Agency, who commissioned me as the research evaluation consultant. The research evaluation methods I adopted included in-person, semi-structured interviews with project coordinators, site visits, document and institutional policy analyses, review of interim project reports, network meetings including group discussions with project workers focusing on critical incidents and significant learning experiences derived from the projects. Discussions within steering group meetings also helped shape the final reports.

This paper offers a retrospective reflective account (Wise, 1979) of the initiative's management, learning, monitoring and evaluation processes. For Wise, 'retrospection' is about accumulating practical knowledge, making sense of experience through narrative and other analytical forms that may in turn be further shaped by practice and communicated to colleagues working in similar and related fields. In this way, educators may be positioned to learn from experience, identify what is significant and develop new insights, which both confirm the veracity of the initial account and contribute to future educational work. This paper is therefore an examination of the project evaluation research originally undertaken between 2001 and 2003 including further consideration of projects in Phase Two in particular, some of which are referred to in detail. I occasionally quote directly from individual project coordinator reports to illustrate significant aspects of my argument, which evolved after the projects had finished and after my commissioned evaluation had been completed. Some general remarks on the possible future conduct of ESD practitioners are offered towards the end of the paper. See Figure 1 for details of the *Learning to Last* management structure.

Governmentality

Established in 2000, the Learning and Skills Council is the principal planning and funding body for the post-16 sector. It acts as a collaborative partner with further

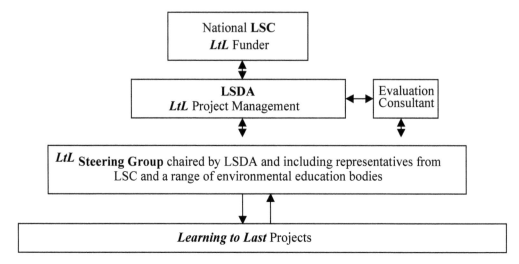

Figure 1. Management Structure for *Learning to Last* (Good Practice in Sustainable Development Education Phases One and Two)

education colleges and other learning providers with a government remit to be a model for transparent and efficient management. In 2002 the LSC's Bureaucratic Task Force published *Trust in the future*, encapsulating a series of actions, targets and times-cales through which a new model for post-16 educational governance would operate.

> The *culture* within which we operate and the *relationships, which derive from that culture,* determine the systems and processes of *planning, funding, audit and data.* At the same time these systems and processes underpin, reinforce and exemplify that culture.
>
> The culture modelled centrally by the LSC and replicated in its 47 local LSCs must be one which encourages local autonomy and responsiveness and accepts risk (and therefore, on occasion, failure) as unavoidable—even desirable—if progress is to be made. (Learning and Skills Council, 2002, emphasis in the original)

Learning to Last operated in this context. National and local LSC representatives attended steering group and network meetings and were in close touch with the *LtL* project managers at the LSDA. Consequently, the hegemony of routine procedures and protocols of project management, evidenced by a predilection for quantitative measures and regular monitoring, quickly became the norm. At its core *LtL* exhibited a tension between the rational, linear, engineered 'scientific' management approach common within the Learning and Skills sector and the more ecological, networked and synoptic methodology associated with and sympathetic to the values of ESD (Sterling, 2001; Capra, 2002).

Wals and Jickling (2002) argue that to 'grow' an understanding of sustainable devel-opment requires a learning culture that admits the merit of heuristic stratagems. Foster (2001) notes that education and sustainability is about creating a futures-orientated heuristic intelligence and Bonnett (1999) suggests ESD should look to develop an appropriate 'frame of mind'. This requires discursive activity with an emphasis on understanding and a sense that through learning, appropriate ideas and activities will emerge. Unfortunately, hard targets, characteristic of the new public management (NPM), limited the potential for transformative, creative and emancipatory learning by distinctly structuring the *LtL* in line with the ideological and instrumentalist assertions of efficiency, effectiveness, political neutrality, universality and 'value for money' (Hood, 1991). It also created significant tensions between the essentially qualitative and interpretative evaluation process I adopted and the LSDA's and LSC's demand for more legitimate, quantitative data. NPM's target-setting, checklists and 'box-ticking' is a way of thinking, of disciplining and of enabling controllable practices and preferred predispositions to characterise educational governance and ostensibly pioneering project work (Foucault, 1991; Dean, 1999; Selwyn *et al.*, 2001; Edwards, 2002). The technical fix, tight managerial control through regulative, accountability and monitoring mechanisms virtually define the rationale and form of governance, i.e. the governmentality, of the post-16 Learning and Skills sector in the UK.

The *Learning to Last* initiative

One early aim of *Learning to Last* was 'to develop a clearer definition of ESD', but the LSDA's and LSC's starting point was the UK Government's own definition and fourfold explication of sustainable development. Namely, as an early *LtL* briefing stated 'it is the simple idea of ensuring a better quality of life for everyone, now and for future generations to come' involving the meeting of four objectives:

- social progress which recognises the needs of everyone;
- effective protection of the environment;
- prudent use of natural resources;
- maintenance of high and stable levels of economic growth and employment. (Defra, 1999, chapter 1, paragraph 1.2)

The LSDA project managers curtailed a discussion at an early network meeting for project coordinators that was intended to focus on developing and furthering the deeper conceptual understanding of ESD, because they perceived the discussions to be inconclusive, unproductive and too time-consuming. The LSC representatives argued the need for a simple definition of ESD to 'operationalise targets' and 'deliverables'. These would include 'bite-size' learning, skills and competence development, pre-specification of learning outcomes, measurable targets and tightly prescribed performance indicators. Indeed, an online Toolkit became the major output of *Learning to Last*, implying that unsustainable education practices can be fixed. This offered policy-makers, funding managers and practitioners an easily identifiable and measurable target. On other occasions, bulleted *PowerPoint* presentations by steering group members—a college principal, a manager from a government agency and me—addressed issues of conceptual understanding and policy development in a more 'efficient' manner with clearly defined outputs recorded economically on a flip chart, enabling LSDA project managers to guide future development and monitoring. Consequently, the *LtL* initiative accepted, virtually without question, the authority of the National Panel's definition of ESD and despite *Trust in the future*, the audit culture continued.

This largely uncritical adoption of official definitions was supplemented by evaluation categories derived from a cultural repertoire provided by other education and training projects' further framing of the initiative under a tight managerialist agenda. As outlined in the original Phase Two bidding documentation, *LtL* aims therefore included:

- identification of common examples of existing good practice;
- identification of priority areas in which practice could be improved;
- provision of illustrative studies from a representative sample of colleges/partnerships which demonstrate elements of good practice;
- facilitation of the sharing of good practice between practitioners.

Areas of good practice would involve: the use of sustainability indicators; understanding of and commitment to sustainable development within a local environment; and evidence of partnership working to promote sustainability practices. The outcome-based indicators by which individual projects would be assessed and evaluated according to economic, environmental, social and curriculum criteria. Unfortunately, the short-term nature and limited funding (c.£25K each) offered to the projects militated against an effective, and perhaps more quantitative, evaluation of any longer-term impacts and/or achievements. There was also little in the 'technicist' orientation of the bidding document relating to the development of understanding, engaging creatively with issues, concepts and life experiences or even a facility to change targets or outputs once they had been agreed. The LSDA's and LSC's monitoring requirements tended to focus on compliance. However, contingent factors, such as a college restructuring or a failure to attract a sufficient number of business partners, sometimes made compliance difficult, occasionally requiring a project's targets or timelines to be renegotiated.

Phase Two started some months behind schedule in January 2003 owing to lengthy bureaucratic procedures focusing on financial, collaborative, contractual and partnership problems. Local LSCs were expected by the national organisation to take a leading role in coordinating and overseeing any *LtL* project in their geographical area. Project bidders were to be partnerships of private and public post-16 learning providers with interests in, or commitments to, sustainability. Each partnership was required to identify Specific, Measurable, Achievable, Realistic, Time-limited (SMART) objectives using as their guide the Government's 15 sustainable development headline indicators and five key themes identified by the LSC:

- Curriculum;
- Informal and Non Formal learning;
- Strategic Planning;
- Management;
- Social Inclusion.

I was required to produce regular interim reports clearly outlining how each individual project was meeting its stated aims and identified outcomes with my final report

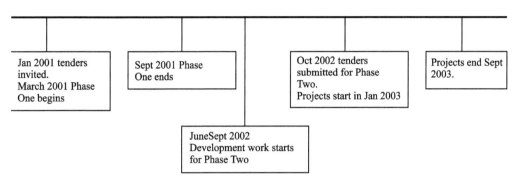

Figure 2.   *Learning to Last* timeline

including recommendations for the future development of ESD. See Figure 2 for details of the timescale of *Learning to Last*.

The *Learning to Last* experience

The *Learning to Last* projects varied in scope, ambition and perspective. They included the design of green transport plans, developing approaches to sustainable procurement, raising awareness of sustainability issues among 'hard to reach' learners, rural business diversification, informal learning through heritage and paper recycling, curriculum greening within further education, the creation of regional ESD networks and the fostering of groups of sustainability champions. The 'tangible' targets, distinguished in large part by their observable existence—CD-ROMs, learning materials, questionnaires, newsletters, websites, etc.—acted as the main drivers but were mediated somewhat by continuous lobbying by coordinators who argued that the pilot status of the ESD projects required a greater degree of latitude for their successful application than the LSC normally allowed. Too little was known and understood about ESD practice for there to be any certainty about what the precise outcomes should be. A compromise could have been to conceive targets not as fixed 'bull's eyes' but rather, in John Dewey's words, as 'ends in view' that would or could be modified or adapted to changing circumstances and unforeseen events as the projects(s) developed. A considerable amount of learning and critical reflection and what Mezirow (1991) terms transformation of meaning schemes and perspectives would necessarily occur. Pointedly, Mezirow writes:

> If a goal of education is to foster transformative learning, dogmatic insistence that learning outcomes be specified in advance of educational experience in terms of observable changes in behaviour or 'competencies' that are used as benchmarks against which to measure learning gains will result in a deductive distortion and serve merely as a device of indoctrination. (pp. 219–220)

The reluctance of the LSC and LSDA to be flexible and openly exploratory may be evidenced with three examples. First, many *LtL* partners exhibited little understanding of sustainability, sometimes having difficulty seeing its relevance to their core activities. For example, one project offered instruction on sustainability to local train-ing providers. Too few responded to enable the training days to occur within the pre-specified timescale. The project coordinator requested an extension to the agreed action plan but the LSC objected on the principle that changes would alter agreed targets and would therefore disrupt administrative and monitoring procedures. Even-tually, the LSDA and LSC agreed that necessity, i.e. learning from experience, might require greater flexibility. Indeed, actual outcomes may not necessarily be those orig-inally intended and unintended ones may conceivably be more important than those planned but future requests for change were carefully scrutinised with a view to potential effects on the pre-specified objectives, indicators and outcomes. Through-out the project lifetime some coordinators expressed the need 'not to be too specific about what or how people learn'.

A second illustration comes from the organisation of the network meetings, where representatives from the projects had opportunities to share information and experi-ence. Frequently, the LSDA insisted discussions focused on the Toolkit. This output remained non-negotiable even though internal DfES research presented to the LSDA noted that online toolkits or printed/web-based distributed materials ('down-loads') had been a relatively ineffective means of sharing good practice, of under-standing complex concepts, effecting institutional change or altering human behaviour in the health service. Toolkit discussions relentlessly centred on 'bite-size' materials, downloads, demonstrable institutional benefits, assumed transferability and relevance without critical reflection on how and in what context these online resources were to be used. A third illustration comes from the rather sporadic use of the *LtL* email group. A suggestion that projects might explore the visual articulation of sustainability through enlisting the interest of art departments in sixth forms, further education colleges and creative workers in the community met with no response, although the idea that *Learning to Last* should develop a corporate logo led to an active if short-lived debate. A logo of course, like the Toolkit, was a SMART objective.

Not surprisingly, the managerial constraints led to a conservative and institution-ally constrained articulation of ESD. The idea that networks of champions could be formed to promote learning around sustainability issues was greeted with a mixture of enthusiasm and caution. James, the Nottinghamshire Project Coordinator, noted in his final project report:

> The reality is that the 'Champion' within Further Education is often the person with the least amount of work, or someone who was unlucky (or honest?) enough to express an interest in Green issues. I would be prepared to break all academic convention and state that they are *never* identified through a proper process (such as the College Management Team discussing who would most fit the bill if they were seeking a facilitator, diplomat, senior enough staff member to command respect from Senior Management Team whilst not generating distrust from junior/support staff, orator, confidante, etc.). If an institution has such a person, they are invariably overworked because of the above abilities. Ideally, there needs to be a 'Champion' at a sub-regional level, so that interest in the Colleges can be stimulated and encouraged, and then any and all parties can benefit from a sub-regional presence to link projects to funding, policy makers and national priorities.

Those projects perceived by the *LtL* Steering Group to have the most potential for future development were those identifying possibilities for, and/or expressing the value of, technical or managerial solutions. The sustainable procurement project in Lancashire aimed to reduce institutional and sectoral impacts on the environment through waste minimisation and ethical trading strategies. A version of ecological footprint analysis informed the development of training opportunities on sustainable supply chains, intending to alter ways of working among local and national businesses. The West Yorkshire project focused on water and the development of learning experiences around the natural process of water purification for pre-university science and geography students. The project produced as its tangible output two interactive CD-ROMs offering information on course specifications, project work, site visits and assignments. As one of the project coordinators remarked, the underlying aim in West Yorkshire was to demonstrate how technology could fix the environment, securing its value as an economic asset and source of new job opportunities although there was space for legitimate, i.e. action-orientated, reflection.

Other projects offered less tangible short-term outcomes and identifiable products for the online Toolkit. For instance, the *LtL* project in Hereford and Worcester built on the Pershore Group of land-based colleges' attempt to fully integrate sustainable principles and practices throughout its educational, consultancy and partnership work. The colleges' stated rationale for curriculum development clearly stated that learning and development would need to be systemic and holistic 'and is viewed essentially as process rather than predetermined product, and as a learning experience rather than a teaching experience' (Baines & Sterling, 2001). Its *Project Carrot*, aiming at facilitating processes of rural business diversification, economic development, community regeneration and the conversion to organic farming practices, formed the background to the measurable *LtL* targets of establishing a network of sustainability advocates and provision of sustainability training to other providers. Sustainable farming practices in this context meant inviting farmers to transform the ways they understood their business, working practices and relationship to the land by moving away from industrialised agri-business. As one farmer told the *LtL* coordinator, 'going organic is about *being* a farmer again'. In other words, going organic entailed spiritual renewal and personal growth but such 'epiphanies' occurred despite the *LtL* initiative rather than because of it. At the final network meeting, when asked if the spiritual dimension should be a feature of future LSC support for ESD, members responded with a stunned silence. Spirituality did not figure in the public management culture or the governing mentality they were expected to reproduce. The idea was rejected by the LSDA as being simply bizarre.

Related issues emerged during steering group discussions of my draft evaluation reports, which aimed to present significant learning experiences, outcomes and impacts. My view was that policy-makers and managers should not predetermine what was considered valuable and significant with a practice still in an embryonic stage of development. To do so would be to close off possibilities and to view learning as a means rather than as an element of the sustainable development process (Scott & Gough, 2003). Modern evaluation methodology subscribes to the evaluator, acting democratically, as an educator brokering information, insights and data differentially to meet the needs of different groups. Thus one size fits all is not tenable to the multiple needs of different stakeholders and constituencies. This questioning of embedded practices of governmentality was not supported by the Steering Group either, who, at the behest of the LSC, agreed to adopt Forum for the Future's *Sustainability appraisal tool* as the preferred evaluation method for future ESD projects. This evaluation method, derived from the Forum's Higher Education Partnerships (www.heps.org.uk), is an example bureaucratic rationality consisting of three categories of sustainability, five capitals and 12 preset questions applicable to any sustainability project, irrespective of its focus in any institution, anywhere. Only one question directly relates to learning, itself conceived economistically.

Details of the 11 Phase Two projects may be found at: www.lsda.org.uk/ programmes/sustainable/LLtoolkit/intro.asp (accessed 20 May 2005).

Making space and needing time

Although the *LtL* initiative did not facilitate the questioning of the underlying premises and assumptions of the business and governance of the Learning and Skills sector, certain critical and reflective spaces did materialise. One coordinator remarked in his final project report:

> The network meetings allowed space and time to reflect on sustainable development, essential when faced with the busy environment normally found in Further Education. The chance to compare notes with others in similar situations and to be inspired by a range of activities/guest speakers have led me to a clear commitment to continue Sustainable Development activities in the future.

Unfortunately, there were only two formally constituted network meetings but informal meetings, visits and discussions between the projects occurred outside the formal parameters of *LtL* where informal learning and a nascent community of ESD practice began to emerge. Even within certain individual projects, particularly those concentrating on social inclusion, some person-centred activities generated valuable reflective activities and learning experiences for both project workers and participants.

Nat, a *LtL* project worker, worked closely with three 'hard to reach' young learners in Broxtowe. The latter were given a short questionnaire concerning issues relating to the environment, work and their personal aspirations and expectations. They were invited to reflect on their views in a learning diary and in conversation with the project worker. Such activity involved meetings, discussions and critical reflections. No easy answers appeared. Instead, more questions and more issues arose, indicating that critical reflection and transformative learning is a process requiring support, 'scaffolding', time and space—both cultural and physical. In his reflective evaluation, Nat inferred that learning for sustainability should not be reduced to immediate targeted skill or competence development. He wrote:

> I knew it would be hard work getting them interested, but perhaps I wasn't prepared for how little interest they would show. Although the progress hasn't been great, I believe I can take positive things from this project

...I know there weren't many well-educated answers, but I can remember being a teenager. I asked myself whether I would have done much better at that age, and the answer was 'No'. Ten years ago, I would have known less than these boys knew. What reasons are there for this lack of understanding? I've previously mentioned the lack of media interest; certainly the school syllabus does some good but is it enough? We must also help people look to the future. The students I worked with don't even look beyond the next week— with this in mind how can we expect them to care about future generations?

The student's diaries showed improvement over time. We spent some time discussing them and again the boys weren't fully grasping the implications of their lifestyles, but did engage in discussion regarding using resources and the consequences of their actions. ...What have I discovered? Sustainability is something that must be learnt over a long period. I do believe the three students I worked with are somewhat better prepared for adulthood, because of the advice I could share, and the discussions we had.

The most valuable and reflective learning consequently seemed to occur in the spaces between the target-setting, output monitoring and management of the projects and cried out for time *Learning to Last* did not provide.

ESD and the learning society

ESD is about making connections, understanding our experience of, and impact on, a world characterised by uncertainty, complexity and risk. *Learning to Last* sought to tackle this unsustainable world by seeking managerial and technical solutions— Senior Manager training, key skills development, curriculum audits, case studies, online toolkits—without seriously confronting those fundamental assumptions and practices governing the business of education and the 'learning society', which, as presently understood, are to support the needs of the economy (Coffield, 1999, 2000; Department for Education and Employment, 1999; Field, 2001) rather than the imperatives of sustainable development and the need for a less environmentally degraded and more equitable planet. Environmental awareness and public understanding have increased even if pro-environmental behaviour lags behind (Kollmuss & Agyeman, 2002; Barr, 2003). Many people do care about global warming, traffic congestion, food safety, risks of GM, endangered species, environmental pollution, poverty, conflict and famine. Unfortunately, this concern has not effectively transformed formal learning opportunities in school, college, university or the workplace. *Learning to Last* struggled to offer alternatives, to make a difference, but lacked the administrative flexibility, critical and creative capacity, imagination and courage to meaningfully do so. Learning, other than perhaps at its more functional levels, needs to move beyond the confines of pre-specified rules and outcomes if practices and perspectives are to change and sustainability is to become a defining educational aim. In circumstances allowing for reflexivity, ecologically informed learning may nurture the evolution of a wiser learning society where 'ends in view' are substituted for prespecified targets, and capabilities and capacity (Sen, 1999) are preferred to temporary skills development. For Edwards *et al.* (2002) reflexivity is central to developing a meaningful theory of lifelong learning:

It is the development of reflexivity, the capacity to develop critical awareness of the assumptions that underlie practices, especially the meta-cognitive, interpretive schemata that constitute worlds, which we see as central to an adequate theory of lifelong learning. By contrast, we would suggest that it is recognition and reflection that are the aspects of learning implied in policy. To develop a critical form of lifelong learning entails the capacity to develop and sustain reflexivity. Such learning should engender the potential for individuals and communities to (en) counter the trajectories of their lives and to enhance their capabilities; not simply to adapt to the (dis) locations of the contemporary condition, but also engage with them. (p. 533)

Unfortunately, the *Learning to Last* projects as a whole did not allow sufficient space to 'develop and sustain reflexivity' and the Secretary of State's foreword to the *Sustainable development action plan for learning and skills* (DfES, 2003, p. 3) reinforces such a position, clearly stating: 'we have theorised about sustainable development in education for long enough. That is why this is not a *strategy* but a plan for action.'

Few would object to the necessity for urgent action but this should not be at the expense of thoughtful reflection or the automatic maintenance of a managerialist governmentality, which is arguably a cause of, rather than a solution to, present problems (Ehrenfeld, 1997). The knowledge, understanding, skills and capabilities necessary to accommodate change, address complexity and fashion a more sustainable future are more likely to emerge from practice, reflection on experience and the sharing of significant insights within conceptual and managerial frameworks derived from systems thinking that enables creativity, cooperation and collaboration than in more rigid and linear processes. Models for such a practice already exist (Clayton & Radcliffe, 1996; Bell & Morse, 1999; Flood, 1999; Blewitt, 2002b). However, for the moment, the dominance of NPM and the lessons from *LtL* informal learning networks suggest that future support for cooperative and sustainable explorations will prove most educative. Edwards *et al.* (2002) continue:

Awareness of what is not known becomes more necessary as the range and potential impact of knowledge expands. Networks that emphasise open, dialogic inquiry would appear likely to make significant use of and develop reflexive practices. (pp. 533–534)

It will be in these sharing networks that perspective transformation and a fuller understanding of a sustainable education practice could be fashioned. Given the structural parameters within which ESD practitioners work, space will need to be crafted to construct alternative practices, communities, understandings, methods of evaluation and modes of operation that will foster these different conditions of possibility. The sociologist Michel de Certeau (1984) writes of how people in their everyday lives develop tactics to take advantage of opportunities, successions of moments, that cumulatively act to transform relationships of power-knowledge. These moments, spaces and tactics may therefore be the means by which ESD practitioners, in their professional work, negotiate our Foucauldian 'society of government' that so constricts the possibilities for articulating sustainability values and practices within formal education and lifelong learning.

Note

1. The *Learning to Last* strapline has been used from a number of related but separate ESD initiatives and publications

References

Baines, J. & Sterling, S. (2001) *A report for Project Carrot to inform the further development of a sustainable development curriculum for agriculture and land management at Holme Lacy and the Pershore Group of Colleges.* Available online at: www.projectcarrot.org/publications (accessed 6 June 2003).

Barr, S. (2003) Strategies for sustainability: citizens and responsible environmental behaviour, *Area*, 35, 227–240.

Bell, S. & Morse, S. (1999) *Sustainability indicators: measuring the unmeasurable* (London, Earthscan).

Blewitt, J. (2002a) Learning and sustainability, in: J. Cohen, S. James & J. Blewitt (Eds) *Learning to Last: skills, sustainability and strategy* (London, Learning and Skills Development Agency).

Blewitt, J. (2002b) Leadership for sustainable development education, in: G. Trorey & C. Cullingford (Eds) *Professional development and institutional needs* (Aldershot, Ashgate).

Bonnett, M. (1999) Education for Sustainable Development: a coherent philosophy for environmental education? *Cambridge Journal of Education*, 29, 313–324.

Capra, F. (2002) *The hidden connections: a science for sustainable living* (London, Harper Collins).

de Certeau, M. (1984) *The practice of everyday life* (Berkeley, CA, University of California Press).

Clayton, A. M. H. & Radcliffe, J. (Eds) (1996) *Sustainability: a systems approach* (London, Earthscan).

Coffield, F. (1999) Breaking the consensus: lifelong learning as social control, *British Education Research Journal*, 25, 479–499.

Coffield, F. (2000) Lifelong learning as a lever on structural change? Evaluation of white paper: Learning to Succeed: a new framework for post-16 learning, *Journal of Education Policy*, 15, 237–246.

Dean, M. (1999) *Governmentality: power and rule in modern society* (London, Sage).

Department for Education and Employment (1999) *Learning to succeed* (London, Her Majesty's Stationery Office [HMSO]).

Department for Education and Skills (2003) *Sustainable development action plan for education and skills.* Available online at: www.dfes.gov.uk/sd/docs/SDactionplan.pdf (accessed 20 May 2005).

Department of Environment, Food and Rural Affairs (1999) *A better quality of life: a strategy for sustainable development for the UK* (London, HMSO). Available at: http://www.sustainable-development.gov.uk/uk_strategy/quality/life/01.htm (accessed 3 February 2005).

Department of Environment, Food and Rural Affairs (2003) *Learning to last.* Available online at: www.defra.gov.uk/environment/sustainable/educpanel/pdf/sdeduc_draftstrat.pdf (accessed 20 May 2005)

Edwards, R. (2002) Mobilizing lifelong learning: governmentality in educational practices, *Journal of Education Policy*, 17, 353–365.

Edwards, R., Ranson, S. & Strain, M. (2002) Reflexivity: towards a theory of lifelong learning, *International Journal of Lifelong Education*, 21, 525–536.

Ehrenfeld, D. (1997) The management explosion and the next environmental crisis, in: H. Hannum (Ed.) *People, land, and community* (New Haven, CT, Yale University Press).

Environmental Audit Committee (2003) *Learning the sustainability lesson*. Available online at: www.parliament.uk/parliamentary_committees/environmental_audit_committee.cfm (accessed 20 May 2005).

Field, J. (2001) Lifelong education, *International Journal of Lifelong Learning*, 20, 3–15.

Flood, R. L. (1999) *Rethinking the fifth discipline: learning within the unknowable* (London, Routledge).

Foster, J. (2001) Education as sustainability, *Environmental Education Research*, 7, 153–167.

Foucault, M. (1991) Governmentality, in: G. Burchell, C. Gordon & P. Miller (Eds) *The Foucault effect: studies in governmentality* (Chicago, IL, University of Chicago Press).

Hood, C. (1991) A public management for all seasons? *Public Administration*, 69, 3–19.

Kollmuss, A. & Agyeman, J. (2002) Mind the gap: why do people act environmentally and what are the barriers to pro-environment behaviour? *Environmental Education Research*, 8, 239–260.

Learning and Skills Council (2002) *Trust in the future*. Available online at: www.lsc.gov.uk/ (accessed 20 May 2005).

Mezirow, J. (1991) *Transformative dimensions of adult learning* (San Francisco, CA, Jossey-Bass).

Scott, W. & Gough, S. (2003) *Sustainable development and learning: framing the issues* (London, RoutledgeFalmer).

Selwyn, N., Gorard, S. & Williams, S. (2001) The role of the 'technical fix' in UK lifelong education policy, *International Journal of Lifelong Learning*, 20, 255–271.

Sen, A. (1999) *Development as freedom* (Oxford, Oxford University Press).

Sterling, S. (2001) *Sustainable education: revisioning learning and change* (Totnes, Green Books).

Wals, A. E. J. & Jickling, B. (2002) Sustainability in higher education: from doublethink and newspeak to critical thinking and meaningful learning, *International Journal of Sustainability in Higher Education*, 3(3),

Wise, R. I. (1979) The need for retrospective accounts of curriculum development, *Journal of Curriculum Studies*, 11, 17–28.

Glossary

Department for Education and Skills: UK government department responsible for education

Environmental Audit Committee: scrutiny committee of the House of Commons investigating environmental and related matters

Learning Skills and Development Agency: a publicly funded quasi-autonomous non-governmental organisation acting as a strategic resource for the development of policy and practice in post-16 education and training

Learning and Skills Council: principal public funder and planning body for all post-16 education and training excluding higher education

Learning to Last: term applied to a range of ESD initiatives originally used by the LSDA as the title for a national series of seminars on ESD

Local Learning and Skills Council: 47 sub-regional LSC offices planning, overseeing and monitoring activities in the post-16 education and training sector in their particular locality

Sustainable Development Education Panel: a national advisory body on ESD operating between 1998 and 2003 and reporting to the Deputy Prime Minister

The action competence approach and the 'new' discourses of education for sustainable development, competence and quality criteria

Finn Mogensen and Karsten Schnack

Action competence has been a key concept in educational circles in Denmark since the 1980s. This paper explores the relationship between the action competence approach and recent discourses of education for sustainable development (ESD), competence and quality criteria. First we argue that action competence is an educational ideal, referring to the German notion of '*Bildung*' and that the very essence of action competence can be derived from the notion of 'action'. Second we emphasise that a particular focus must be put on education, when ESD is seen through the lens of the action competence approach. Next we suggest that the interpretation of 'competence' differs substantially in this approach from those connected to individualistic-oriented Human Resource Management theory, while some similarities and differences can be found in relation to subject-oriented notions of competence and the Organization for Economic Cooperation and Development-promoted DeSeCo (Definition and Selection of Competencies) perspective. Finally, we argue that quality criteria that are in concert with the action competence approach should: focus on enhancement of teaching and learning; reflect the democratic values that ESD seeks to promote; be co-elaborated by the relevant stakeholders; and foment institutional as well as individual learning and, thereby, instantiate the *Bildung* perspective embedded throughout this approach.

Introduction

In this paper, we examine the relationship between the action competence approach and some of the relatively new discourses that have dominated the educational agenda in Denmark in the past decade. In the first section we will argue that action competence should be seen as an educational ideal, and that a philosophical view on the action component of the notion reveals certain central characteristics of its interpretation in an educational context. We also explore the action competence approach in relation to education for sustainable development (ESD), focusing on the competence dimension of action competence. The language of competence has very rapidly become widespread and it would appear to be more than a fad. Prompted by this, we deal with questions regarding consistency, added value or pitfalls that can be identified, when different notions of competence are explored from the perspective of an action competence approach. In the final part of the paper, we apply this discussion to the increasing interest in evaluation of ESD. Much energy has been mobilised in the realm of quality criteria and indicators for 'green schools' and successful teaching and learning in ESD. Consequently, in line with the basic ideas of the action competence approach, we conclude our paper with a discussion of the central characteristics connected to a quality criteria set, as proposed by examples drawn from our involvement in the Environment and School Initiatives (ENSI) network.

The action competence approach and the 'new' interest in ESD

Since the 1980s and 1990s, 'action competence' has been a key concept in research and curriculum development in relation to environmental and health education at the Research Programme for Environmental and Health Education at the Danish School of Education in Denmark.[1]

In a broad sense, the notion refers to an educational approach that:

- is critical of moralistic tendencies in environmental education and health education;
- emphasises the educational aims of environmental education and health education, instead of reducing education to a technical means to solve certain political problems;
- works with democratic and participatory ideas in relation to teaching–learning;
- conceives of environmental education and health education as problem-oriented and cross-curricular, even holistic, without losing interest in academic knowledge and fundamental concepts;
- regards environmental problems as societal issues that involve conflicting interests;
- works with a positive and broad conception of health, including not only lifestyle, but also living conditions;
- looks for relationships between environmental education and health education.

More specifically, 'action competence' refers to an educational ideal. As such it is not a goal that can be reached, and even if it is a competence, it is not a specific competence among many others. As an educational ideal it is situated in a non-place, a utopia, where it maintains good company with such concepts as liberal education, democracy, human rights, sustainable development and equal (*herrschaftsfrei*) communication. All of these concepts live for, and indeed off, the fight against violence and oppression (Schnack 2000). In this perspective, action competence is closely linked to democratic, political education and to a radical version of the notion of '*Bildung*'.

The concept of *Bildung*, roughly translated as the formation of the personality through education and approximating to what is carried in the notion of 'being an educated man', can be traced back to German philosophers like Immanuel Kant, Wilhelm von Humbolt and the whole neo-humanist project of the early nineteenth century. Different approaches to a contemporary use of the concept have since then been identified (Giesecke 1978), but one of the most influential interpreters of the modern ideal of *Bildung* is the German scholar, Wolfgang Klafki (1991). Via his interpretation and responses to it, the concept and the ideas behind *Bildung* have had an enormous impact and influence on educational theory and thinking not only in Germany, but also in Scandinavian countries where the concept has been closely related to critical theory. Thus, *Bildung* cannot be reduced to mere education in the sense of cultivation, normalisation, or traditional socialisation. On the contrary and in concert with the utopian dimension of critical theory, it has as its aim the fulfillment of humanity: full development of the capacities and powers of each human individual to question preconceived opinions, prejudices, and 'given facts', and intentioned participation in the shaping of one's own and joint living conditions. Following this line, the Norwegian philosopher Jon Hellesnes (1976) characterises *Bildung* as a kind of socialisation that is different from pure adaptation to existing conditions, but instead '…emancipates people to become political subjects – and not just the objects of control and guidance exercised by other people' (Hellesnes 1976, 18).

Seen from a philosophical point of view, the main point of action competence is the idea of action. Inspired by analytic philosophy concerning explanation and understanding (Taylor 1966; von Wright 1971) and philosophical psychology (Kenny 1963; Peters 1958; White 1968) as well as pragmatist analyses (Bernstein 1971) and critical theory (Habermas 1968), the point can be made that human action differs from, or is a special kind of, mere behaviour and activity. Not only are actions intentional, the intentions, motives and reasons all have an intrinsic relation to the actions. So it will be a different action if the intention turns out to be different (Schnack 1977).

In this sense, it is our forte as human beings to be able to act, given the links to associated humanistic concepts such as personhood, experience, responsibility, democracy, and education – insofar as we take education to be more than schooling, training or manipulation.

In relation to problem-oriented environmental and health education, the notion of action is qualified by the criterion that actions should be addressed to solutions of the problem and should not just be activities as a counterweight to academic tuition. Not that activity is a bad thing or not good enough in certain situations, but the action competence approach emphasises the epistemological point that action-oriented teaching–learning has specific, important learning potentials. In this way, the notion of action in action competence is heavily loaded, philosophically and educationally. Actions are a special kind of behaviour: (a) qualified by the intentions of the agent, and in principle, not by someone else (which again challenges current discussions of participation in education discussed elsewhere in this collection; see Læssøe this issue); (b) qualified by being conscious and purposive, seen from the point of view of the agent, which also challenges the discussion of success criteria in education (see later). This latter perspective on the notion of action also means that the action must be addressed to solving the problem or changing the conditions or circumstances that created the problem in the first place. In adding this aspect to the action concept, this can be qualified in relation to the concept of activity. Hence, actions can be seen as specific activity.

The status of action competence as an educational ideal and its utopian goals means that it will never be possible to say: 'now it is not possible to be more action competent'. In this sense there is a parallel to the notion of sustainable development in that an objective reachable stage does not exist. In relation to sustainable development it is evident that you cannot satisfy the needs of people who live now without radically changing the conditions for the people to come for a number of reasons, not least that the satisfaction of human needs in specific (cultural) ways develops and changes the needs themselves. In the same way is it not possible to become the ultimate action competent individual because human actions will always produce intended and unintended changes and conditions that give rise to a quest for new capabilities. In this sense, the striving for qualifying one's action competence is a never-ending process.

The action competence approach seen in this *Bildung* perspective will be discussed further in a later section. However, a central element of the approach is to be critical of moralistic tendencies, preconceived ideas and hidden agendas when working with environmental education, health education, ESD or other teaching–learning sequences that deal with societal issues involving conflicting interests. Rather, the action competence approach points to democratic, participatory and action-oriented teaching–learning that can help students develop their ability, motivation and desire to play an active role in finding democratic solutions to problems and issues connected to sustainable development that may even consist of the aforementioned tendencies, ideas and agendas.

From the very beginning, the action competence approach has been critical towards any reductionistic tendency in what has been called the first generation of environmental education (Breiting 1993), where the goal of many of its campaigns and programmes is to change people's, including pupils', behaviour (Jensen and Schnack 1997). But the newcomer to the international agenda, 'education for sustainable development', must also be critically discussed when seen from the philosophical perspective of the action competence approach.

The notion of sustainable development, as introduced in the Brundtland Report, 'Our Common Future' (World Commission on Environment and Development 1987), and in ESD in particular, does not solve any questions. On the contrary, it leads to a lot of dilemmas. As the dilemmas are sound, this is a good thing, though you need to be on your guard: the more politically correct the rhetoric around sustainable development becomes, the more we may see a tendency to (mis)use ESD as a means to spread specific (political) viewpoints and interests. The point is then that in democratic education, as in taking an action competence approach, this should be analysed as part of the ideological criticism that continuously runs through the teaching–learning process.

Thus, we can start by observing that the whole idea behind ESD seems to be very much in line with the action competence approach. To treat environmental issues and health issues as not only interrelated, but also fundamentally connected to economic, social, cultural and political aspects (as happens in ESD) is in full harmony with the action competence approach, and aligns well with its broader insistence of understanding environmental problems as societal issues constituted by conflicting interests. At the same time, ESD without a democratic action competence perspective very easily becomes dogmatic and moralistic.

How, then, does the action competence approach developed within the field of environmental education fit into the pedagogy of ESD? This, of course, depends on the interpretation of the two concepts and the relationship between them. The research literature advocates highly different perspectives regarding the relationship between ESD and environmental education. Some claim that ESD is a different discipline to environmental education (Hopkins and McKeown 2003), some argue that ESD is replacing environmental education (Tilbury and Cooke 2005; Fien 2001), while others that ESD is considered a new paradigm on education (Sterling 2001). The different conceptualisations are in some situations, perhaps, used interchangeably to describe similar work, while in other situations they are expressions of more profound differences in focus and approach. Some commentators find this not only acceptable but actually stimulating (Scott and Oulton; in Summer, Corney, and Childs 2004) – and of course it is, even if it does complicate complex matters further.

In some studies in Sweden, for example, a democratic approach to environmental education is sometimes called 'pluralistic environmental education' and sometimes simply 'education for sustainable development' (Sandell, Öhman, and Östman 2004; Öhman 2004). This may, of course, be a terminological problem in some respects, but at the same time it illustrates, redolent of with Arjen Wals' (2006) arguments, among others, that the central point in the action competence approach is that it is the 'education' that matters the most. Environmental education, health education, and ESD are not the same, as they differ in their main substantive foci. More important, though, is the distinction between dogmatic, manipulative, and moralistic forms of these 'educations' on the one hand, and critical, open-ended, pluralistic and democratic forms on the other.

As mentioned previously, the action component is the most important part of the conception of action competence. However, not least because of the increasing international use of the word 'competence' in the past decade, the competence component of the notion has a new controversial status that must be explored in connection to the action competence approach.

The 'new' interest in competences

As stipulated earlier, the word competence was originally used to demonstrate that we were not only talking about action as different from behaviour, habit, activity and movement, but the educational ambition was, in a democratic perspective, enlightened and qualified action (Schnack 1994, 2003).

In this section we will explore different recent conceptualisations of 'competence' in order to discuss the added value that can be derived from them, and we will suggest dimensions of the notion that we can identify as not in concert with the original concept of competence in this approach.

The word competence was not overused at the time that 'action competence' was introduced, and it served the purpose of pointing to the need for relevant knowledge, will, skills and not least critical reflection, including values clarification. However, from the 1970s onwards, the notion of qualifications was dominant in official educational texts, and it was the keyword in studies of educational economics. 'Qualifications' referred most often to knowledge and skills necessary for the workplaces and/or were asked for in industrial development. You need 'qualifications' to do a good job, and both trade and industry, and society need people with specific qualifications. The educational system has a role to play here. This is, however, not the primary perspective for a democratic environmental and health education.

Talking about general education in the light of emancipation and democratic participation, a broader, softer and heavier concept was required. 'Competence' was usable, *in part* because it is a dispositional word, which can counterbalance the sometimes too here-and-now, violent, activity associations to 'action'. Action competence is, after all, located more between the ears than in the fists.

From the late 1990s, the competence discourse suddenly engulfed the international educational rhetoric. As with so many other buzzwords it comes up with several overlapping, and often very unspecific, meanings and connotations. Stefan Hermann, a Danish educationalist, stated in a jocular manner that:

...if you are waiting for a stable and simple definition of the concept, you are waiting on the wrong platform for a train that never comes. To get a good grip of the concept of competence seems to be like putting an armlock on a piece of toilet soap. (Hermann 2005)

A Human Resource Management-related use of 'competence'

From the beginning though, competence has also been intensely used in management cultures, especially in so-called Human Resource Management theory. Here, the focus on knowledge and skills has almost vanished without a trace in favour of an emphasis on personal virtues like creativity, flexibility, adaptability, and so on, treated in a rather technical and individualistic manner with effectiveness as the main value. Transfer to education has been heavily criticised and is of course problematic, not least because theories and concepts from academic disciplines are highly situated and primarily qualify the discipline's students' often naive and uncritical experiential kinds of knowledge; but also because general education at least should have higher ambitions than promoting efficiency or effectiveness. There are, however, uses of the notion that are more interesting from an educational point of view.

Parallel developments to – or perhaps better, as a consequence of – the emergence of postmodern ideas and ways of understanding societal conditions and characters of individuals have repositioned and recast our understandings of competence. As argued by theorists such as Anthony Giddens, Thomas Ziehe and Niklas Luhmann, in this paradigm focus is on individualisation and reflexivity in relation to individuals, who are embedded in a reality characterised by complexity, uncertainty and risk. In this context, individualisation refers to the transition from collective and social-cultural determinants of behaviour and identity towards more diversified understandings and choices of preferred lifestyles. Within such postmodern perspectives, the individual is called upon to be 'project manager' of their own life, to facilitate self-development and realise themselves in a society which they consider to be preference-regulated rather than norm-regulated (notes made by the author on a presentation by Ziehe on 14 March 2006). Criteria for choice of actions among postmodern individuals are first and foremost derived from and connected to the personal life world (Ziehe 2001).

The action competence approach is somewhat different from an individualistic perspective like this. Of course, the approach is focused on qualifying the virtues of individuals; competence is always linked to the individual. However, the notion of competence in the action competence approach is different from the aforementioned approach owing to the strong emphasis on scrutinising and developing criteria for action that are jointly communicated, discussed and accepted when dealing with issues that go beyond the immediate sphere of the individual person – for instance, sustainability issues. The rationale for the selection of criteria for action is thus not an *intra*subjective, but rather an *inter*subjective matter.

In an educational context, qualifying students' competence to take action is thus basically a matter of organising learning situations which make it possible for students to transform themselves into critical, democratic and political human beings. It is a question of helping the students become autonomous persons, who at the same time are not 'idiots', an allusion to Ancient Greece where people who lived 'privately' and took no part in the affairs in community were called 'idiots' (Schnack 2000). The point is that while the postmodern perspective seems to favour the forming of 'private' people who base their lives on individualistic decisions and choices, the action competence approach seeks to form a basis for decisions and choices that are connected to community and dialogue.

Among the many other contemporary uses of the word competence, two may be of special interest in relation to the conception of action competence. The first is linked to the discussion of school subjects, the other is of a more general character.

A subject-related use of 'competence'

Subject-oriented curriculum theorists have trouble with a common definition of the content of subjects. Normally, school subjects are defined by lists of syllabi, required reading, and examination requirements. This tradition has been criticised for two things in particular: (a) it represents a reductionistic view of the subject followed by a not very ambitious interpretation of the subject matter in the teaching–learning situation; (b) it makes it too difficult to compare the different forms of manifestation of a subject at different levels and in different parts of the educational system (Niss 1999).

A competence-based description of the subjects has been proposed as a way out of these difficulties by people working with the subject of mathematics (Niss 1999, 2003; Blomhøj and Jensen 2003). In Denmark, at least, this proposal was followed by similar proposals for the other main school subjects, stimulated by the Ministry of Education. In this movement towards competence descriptions, the politicians, who for a couple of years had talked about the need to improve the academic level in the school, obviously saw an opportunity to call it a 'new academic standard'. In this way it was easier for them to refute the accusation that the neo-liberal idea of quality in education was simply a reactionary step back to the traditional 'mechanical grind'.

The different subjects, of course, apply competence descriptions in quite different ways (Busch, Elf, and Horst 2004), even if mathematics was taken as a paradigmatic case. The main point, however, is a change in focus from an enumeration of knowledge and skills to a deeper answer to the question: What does it mean to master mathematics/language/science…? And the answers consist in pointing to the competencies that are characteristic for the subject; for example, posing and solving mathematical problems, modelling mathematically, and so forth.

Inspired by the Danish psychologist Per Schultz Jørgensen (1999), Blomhøj and Jensen (2003) express the perhaps most comprehensive definition of competence as: 'someone's insightful readiness to act in a way that meets the challenges of a given situation' (Blomhøj and Jensen 2003, 126). As the authors point out: (a) competence is headed for action; (b) all competencies have a sphere of exertion; and (c) competence is an analytical concept with a subjective side; i.e., it belongs to someone and has a social and cultural side: '…the degree to which some actions "meet the challenges" is always relative to the surroundings, adding meaning and legitimacy to the actions' (Blomhøj and Jensen 2003, 127).

These two perspectives correspond well with the interpretation of 'competence' related to the action competence approach. Here, the competence dimension not only points to the handling or mastering of qualified reflections that can facilitate conscious and purposive actions, addressing the solution to the problem at stake. It also underlines that a person in seeking legitimacy for an action must go beyond private, individualistic interests and wishes and must involve 'others' in the choice, if the 'challenges' presuppose collective decisions.

At the same time, the perspectives show that the rhetoric of competence does not need to be as ambiguous as it often is, and they shed light on some important aspects of the general notion of competence. In relation to environmental education, health education, ESD, peace education, and other fields of open, cross-curricular education, the action competence approach will warn against reduction into specific subjects. Nevertheless, this does not mean that academic knowledge from all kinds of subjects is irrelevant – quite the opposite. The learning accrued from the school subjects will probably appear more tempting and powerful in a problem-based and action-oriented education if they have been described and comprehended in this form of competence language.

A general use of 'competence'

The next example of contemporary use of the word 'competence' is the DeSeCo (Definition and Selection of Competencies) project under the auspices of the Organization for Economic Cooperation and Development (OECD), which is quite general and not related to specific subjects. From its inception in 1997 to the final report (Rychen and Salganik 2003), a large number of experts from many academic disciplines and countries contributed to answering whether it is possible to define, select and justify a finite number of 'key competencies for a successful life and a well-functioning society'.

The project not only looked for consensus, and synthesis, among the many viewpoints, but also for a consensus of the relationship between what is a good life for the individual and what is 'needed' by society. In spite of this, the results are not insipid or commonplace (though these are not what we are going to discuss here). Aside from the three times three sets of selected key competencies, the project comprises interesting analyses and discussions of the notion of (key) competence as used in the work. Inspired not least by the conceptual analysis of Franz E. Weinert (2001), the project decided to follow his five pieces of advice in his 'pragmatic conclusions' concerning the use of the concept of competence, in the hope of not finding 'themselves helplessly lost in Paul Valery's Dilemma: Everything that is simple is theoretically false, everything that is complicated is pragmatically useless' (Weinert 2001, 63).

The concept of competence used in the project is, thus, characterised by being functional or demand-oriented and contextualised. In summary, it says that:

> ...the underlying model of competence adopted by DeSeCo is holistic and dynamic in that it combines complex demands, psychosocial prerequisites (including cognitive, motivational, ethical, volitional, and social components), and context into a complex system that makes competent performance or effective action possible. Thus competencies do not exist independently of action and context. Instead, they are conceptualised in relation to demands and actualized by actions (which implies intentions, reasons, and goals) taken by individuals in a particular situation. (Rychen and Salganik 2003, 46–7)

This does not contradict the concept of competence in the subject-related project of, for example, mathematics, though neither the context nor situation nor the competence itself is defined in relation to subjects, even if some of the (particularly cognitive) prerequisites may very well have their roots in academic subjects. This more comprehensive idea about the contexts and the demands paves the way for what, in the action competence approach, has been called 'didactics, or curriculum, of challenge' (Schnack 1995b), where the demands are understood as challenges for the democratic processes in relation to, for example, health, environment, peace, equity, and sustainable development. Moreover, the conceptualisation of the psychosocial structure of a competence is in line with a model discussed in the action competence approach, where important components of action competence have been organised in cognitive, social, value-oriented, and personal dimensions (Mogensen 1995; Breiting et al. 2009).

However, one important difference between the concept of competence in DeSeCo and the action competence approach is that 'action competence' is not viewed as a countable word. Strictly speaking, you cannot speak of an action competence or action competencies. Action competence is an educational philosophical ideal, an overall perspective. From this viewpoint things will look different than from a behavioural change viewpoint, for example. Through the spectacles of action competence, you may look for and ask for and measure different (key) competencies, but action competence will not be one of them. Action competence will be the lens that makes some types of knowledge, skills, qualifications, competencies, abilities, and action readiness more educationally important and valuable than others.

Concluding this section of the 'new' interest in competences, we initially find that the interpretation of 'competence' differs from the one connected to individualistic-oriented Human Resource Management theories owing to their technical interests in effectiveness and focus on *intra*subjective criteria for action-taking. Next, we have acknowledged the value of a subject-oriented notion of competence in that it points to a shift in curriculum thinking from enumeration of isolated knowledge and skills to handling or mastering of knowledge, reflection, and action that meets the challenges of a given situation. Finally, the DeSeCo perspective gives value to a notion of competence that, among other things, paves the way for a 'didactic, or curriculum, of challenge' in pointing to the need for identifying, discussing and taking a stand on challenges in relation to sustainability issues in the teaching–learning process. The point is that competencies do not exist independently of the context to which a potential action will respond, but are co-determined by them. We find the two last perspectives on the notion of competence relevant and in harmony with the action competence approach as both of them help students to be *neither* solely 'objects of control and guidance exercised by other people' *nor* 'idiots' who take no part, but instead contribute to qualifying their own process of *Bildung*. At the same time it remains a category mistake (Schnack 1994) to talk about 'action competence' as one among other key competences.

The 'new' interest in evaluation, indicators and quality criteria

It would hardly be wrong to claim that since the introduction of modern information technology, nothing has been higher on the agenda in the educational system than the quest for evaluation. This development challenges the action competence approach, and we will argue that a certain perspective on evaluation and evaluation strategies is needed when considered in relation to the action competence approach. In the following sections, we will explore this issue, taking into account the close relationship between the action competence approach and the philosophy of *Bildung*.

To begin with, the strong focus on evaluation gives rise to at least two central questions: (1) will it make sense to 'evaluate' whether students have become more 'action competent' by taking part in an ESD project?; and (2) is it at all possible to operationalise the notion in order to 'measure' its constituting elements? Following the previous discussion on competences, the easiest (and perhaps wisest) answer to both questions is 'no'. This is evident because action competence is an educational ideal that, in principle, should be seen in relation to and evaluated against an unpre-dictable future, which by definition is impossible to measure here and now. Thus, it will make no sense to evaluate action competence *per se* and especially not when evaluation, in a summative perspective, asks 'has this and that been learned?' However, evaluation can also have a formative character in that it promotes further learning. Evaluation will, in this perspective, particularly focus on the *learning condi-tions* that, at the moment, are expected to develop and qualify action competence.

Indicators are becoming one of the most commonly applied and promoted evalua-tion strategies in sustainable development and ESD (Reid, Nikel, and Scott 2006). Tilbury and Janousek (2006) identify seven comprehensive indicator programmes for monitoring and evaluating ESD across Europe, North America and the Asia-Pacific region – for example, the United Nations Economic Commission for Europe project, the UK Strategy for Sustainable Development 'Securing the Future', and the United Nations Educational, Scientific and Cultural Organization/International Union for Conservation of Nature Asia-Pacific Decade of Education for Sustainable Develop-ment Indicators Project. Despite this global focus, it is argued that recent experiences in developing indicators have been limited in scope and many are still in their early stages (Tilbury and Janousek 2006, 5) reflecting the complexity of the mechanisms and processes in ESD, for example, whether the information is summarised by an outsider or by the participants themselves. This is evidently both because of the problematic, contested and discursive nature of sustainable development and ESD, and the difficulties in de-structuring or operationalising education itself into measur-able elements.

Different suggestions for the typology of indicators are put forward in the litera-ture. For instance, Sollart (2005) speaks of 'status', 'communicative', 'facilitative' and 'result' indicators; Tilbury and Janousek (2006) mentions 'status', 'facilitative' and 'effect' indicators, while Sterling (in Tilbury and Janousek 2006) distinguishes between 'mechanistic' and 'holistic' indicators. In the first place, this suggests the somewhat contested nature of indicators that makes it difficult to settle on a single approach that aligns with ESD. It also demonstrates that indicators can be relevant to more than one purpose in seeking to meet a number of needs in relation to a learner, an institutional and even a system level, by focusing on and guiding, for example, assessment, learning, reporting, planning, policies and intervention.

Indicators in a Bildung perspective

As mentioned previously, the action competence approach is essentially a matter of *Bildung* which makes the concomitant approach to ESD neither pure adaption to certain sustainable values, nor training in subject matters in the field of economics, environment and social science. Inherent in the *Bildung* perspective is that fixed knowledge, solutions and correct ways of behaviour within these areas are not speci-fied or given beforehand by experts, organisations or politicians who pursue certain interests. Essential to ESD from an action competence approach is to take guidance and advice from them seriously, but also to challenge critically such positions on sustainable development by learning in an open-ended rather than a prescriptive way the kinds of knowledge and values that lie behind them. In doing this, one key role for ESD in an action competence approach becomes that of developing the students' ability, motivation and desire to play an active role in finding democratic solutions to problems and issues connected to sustainable development. The challenge for ESD in this perspective is to identify what kind of learning can qualify the learners' sound choices in a reality that is often characterised by complexity and uncertainty, and which also motivates them to be active citizens who are able to set the agenda for changes if necessary. In this sense, sustainable development is more a matter of democratic citizenship than compliance and individual behaviour – and ESD is in a never-ending process of learning about how to qualify the participants to cope with this citizenship role in a sensible way.

The notion of indicators must reflect this *Bildung* approach. First by acknowledging that indicators cannot be seen as a mechanism that aims to prescribe and test the 'correct' content (knowledge, skills and values) in ESD, but rather must be formed in ways that stimulate and qualify students to become future citizens, who can make sound judgements, think critically and independently, and who can and will play an active role. To proxy adequately for such virtues, indicators must focus on both individual and institutional learning, i.e., teaching and learning processes as well as school policy and organisation, because the process of *Bildung* takes place in an educational context in which 'development' both refers to students as individuals and to the school as an organisation (staff development, school management, community cooperation, networking, etc.). Secondly, the process of working with indicators in this perspective is a dynamic and never-ending process, since the process of *Bildung* is a continuous process.

From an evaluation perspective, the action competence approach calls particular attention to self-evaluation, which provides an opportunity for the participants in the education process (teachers, students and other stakeholders) to assess their own strengths and weaknesses in contrast to the evaluation done from 'above' by outsiders with a summative purpose. Thus, indicators and the use of them within the action competence approach does not correspond with a position which merely considers teachers passive 'recipients' of external interpretations of what is or what is not supposed to be 'good' ESD. The focus is on indicator development that acknowledges the position that indicators should be co-generated together with the practitioners and, as such, should be dynamic and open for interpretation and change. This points to the epistemological value of working with ESD indicators, in that the participants in the education process themselves must be given the opportunity to discuss and contribute to the development of their own set of indicators that, according to them, promote good ESD. By doing this, they not only reflect on what to learn (or teach) and to what extent this learning seems to promote sustainable development or not, but also the epistemologically relevant idea that they learn something about what they learn when they learn (or teach). It is, for instance, valuable learning that takes place for both teachers and students when they, through an action research approach in the local community, realise that participation, involvement in critical investigations, and action-taking, can contribute to enhancement of sustainability within a specific area.

Summarising this section on indicators, we find that a desirable indicator typology that is in concert with the action competence approach should include quality criteria that enable and promote learning and innovation by focusing on enhancement rather than performance and control. The criteria should reflect the democratic values that ESD seeks to promote, rather than focus on 'correct' knowledge and behaviour. They should be co-elaborated by teachers and other stakeholders rather than directed 'from above', and they should reflect institutional as well as individual learning. Work on developing indicators should be in concert with a relevant question asked by Vare (2006) quoted in the stimulus material (Reid, Nikel, and Scott 2006) prior to a seminar on indicators for monitoring and evaluating ESD: 'Can we build an approach to "indicators" that promotes reflection on practice rather than simply hitting targets so that the shape of our ESD emerges, through practice, throughout the education system?'

The ENSI proposal on quality criteria

There is an indicator development project that follows the line of the action competence approach. It has been carried out within the frames of the ENSI network, and the publication *Quality Criteria for ESD-Schools* (Breiting, Mayer, and Mogensen 2005) proposes a non-exhaustive list of 'quality criteria' for schools that wish to work on developing ESD. The purpose of the quality criteria set, which is now translated into 17 different languages, is to provoke thinking and action regarding quality enhancement rather than quality control. The notion of 'quality criteria' can, in this context, be considered a 'translation' of a shared set of stakeholder values prepared in a transparent manner with a practical function. They are considered starting points for reflections, and are aimed at facilitating discussions within the educational context, to promote the view that developing quality criteria is a never-ending process involving ongoing criticism, evaluation and revision by the stakeholders.

To illustrate with an example from this publication how reflections on quality criteria/indicators can reflect the *Bildung* perspective in the action competence approach, we turn to students' work with 'conflicting interests'. The very notion of using conflicting interests as a starting point for the study of environmental problems has been central in many publications that deal with the development of an action competence approach in Denmark (Breiting et al. 2009; Jensen and Schnack 1997; Schnack 1995a, 1998; Mogensen 1997), in Nordic countries (Sætre, Kristensen, and Christensen 1997), and in the ENSI network (CERI-OECD 1991; OECD 1994; Elliott 1999). Many researchers also consider this approach to be highly relevant in the field of sustainable development (Breiting 2007; Lundegård and Wickman 2007; Robottom 2007; Schnack 2008) because issues within sustainability share common characteristics with environmental problems in that they are, by definition, essentially contested. Their meaning as issues belongs to differences of opinion among people with differing interests on development that reflect different values. Both environmental and sustainability issues are human constructs within a certain political, social and cultural context.

By working with conflicting interests in relation to sustainable development, the participants are encouraged to reflect on how much the following four quality criteria make sense for them, or whether they should be revised, and how they contribute to a combination of students' critical thinking with Giroux's (1988, 134) 'language of possibility':

- Students work with power relations and conflicting interests, e.g., in the local situation, between countries, between future generations.
- Students are encouraged to look at things from different perspectives and to develop empathy by identifying themselves with others.
- Students are encouraged to present arguments for different positions.
- Students are encouraged to look for examples that are useful and fruitful in other situations, in opportunities and alternative actions.

By dealing with conflicting interests as a means to combining critical thinking with the language of possibility, a central point within the action competence perspective is underlined, namely that for an individual to be a critical human being does not mean that the individual must be negative and sceptical of all and everything in a deterministic way. A critical thinker is not a 'no' man but a human being who strives to combine the critical process of reflection and inquiry with an empathetic and optimistic vision of potential, a search for solutions and a positive direction. The language of possibility underlines that the critical thinker does not look for limits and restrictions, but searches for and is inspired by ways that have been successful and fruitful for other cultures, in other periods of time, and in other situations, in a creative and open-minded way. Thus, by focusing not only on what may be 'wrong', but also on what might be 'right', critical thinking combined with a language of possibility gives human beings personal and collective capacities that can be transformative and point to new vision of the future, all of which is much needed for sustainable development to happen (Breiting, Mayer, and Mogensen 2005).

Perhaps by working with indicators in a way which focuses on quality enhancement rather than control, and by involving the stakeholders in reflections and revision of the criteria which constitute or define the indicators, a basis can be formed which contributes to reducing the gap between ideology and reality in relation to ESD. In 1987 (and reprinted in 2007) Stevenson claimed that there has been a pronounced discrepancy between the problem-solving and action-oriented goals associated with the philosophy of environmental education and an emphasis on the acquisition of environmental knowledge and awareness in school programmes (Stevenson 2007) – now referred to as Stevenson's gap (Barratt Hacking, Scott, and Barratt 2007). In connection to ESD, a similar gap may appear between the rhetoric and philosophy behind ESD and the reality of practice in schools, unless measures are taken against this, for instance by giving the stakeholders ownership in the development of indicators.

Conclusion

The action competence approach was developed in relation to environmental education and health education, but it fits radical and democratic interpretations of ESD as well. It is an educational ideal, and the key to the notion is the understanding of 'action'. This part has always been challenged from behaviouristic viewpoints, there is nothing new in that. However, the challenges from the expanding use of the notion of competence and the exploding interest in evaluation, indicators and quality criteria are relatively new. In both cases there are nuances and some of the less management-like and positivistic interpretations are more in line with and potentially useful to the critical-constructive educational conceptions of the action competence approach.

Note
1. The Danish School of Education in Copenhagen has gone through various incarnations: the Royal Danish School of Educational Studies, the Danish University of Education, and most recently, it has become the Danish School of Education, University of Aarhus.

References

Barratt Hacking, E., W. Scott, and R. Barratt. 2007. Children's research into their local environment: Stevenson's gap, and possibilities for the curriculum. *Environmental Education Research* 13, no. 2: 225–44.

Bernstein, R.J. 1971. *Praxis and action.* Philadelphia, PA: University of Pennsylvania Press.

Blomhøj, M., and T.H. Jensen. 2003. Developing mathematical modelling competence: Conceptual clarification and educational planning. *Teaching mathematics and its applications* 22, no. 3: 123–39.

Breiting, S. 1993. The new generation of environmental education focus on democracy as part of an alternative paradigm. In *Monographs in environmental education and environmental studies. VIII, Alternative paradigms in environmental education research,* ed. R. Mrazek, 199–202. Troy, OH: The North American Association of Environmental Education.

Breiting, S. 2007. Morphing EE into ESD with mental ownership and action competence. Paper presented at World Environmental Education Congress, July 2–6, in Durban.

Breiting, S., K. Hedegaard, F. Mogensen, K. Nielsen, and K. Schnack. 2009. Action competence, conflicting interests and environmental education – the MUVIN programme. Research Programme for Environmental and Health Education, DPU (Danish School of Education). http://www.dpu.dk/Everest/Publications/Forskning%5CMilj%C3%B8%20og %20sundhedsp%C3%A6dagogik/20090707140335/CurrentVersion/action-competence-muvin.pdf?RequestRepaired=true

Breiting, S., M. Mayer, and F. Mogensen. 2005. *Quality criteria for ESD-schools: Guidelines to enhance the quality of education for sustainable development.* Vienna, Austria: Austrian Federal Ministry of Education. http://seed.schule.at/uploads/QC_eng_2web.pdf.

Busch, H., N.F. Elf, and S. Horst. 2004. *Fremtidens uddannelser. Den ny faglighed og dens forudsætninger* [Education in the future. The new academic standard of the subjects and its basis]. København, Denmark: Undervisningsministeriet.

CERI-OECD 1991. *Environment, school and active learning.* Paris, France: OECD.

Elliott, J. ed. 1999. Environmental education: On the way to a sustainable future. Report of ENSI conference in Linz, Vienna, Austrian Federal Ministry of Education, Science and Culture.

Fien, J. 2001. Educating for sustainable future. In *Creating our common future: Education for unity in diversity,* ed. J. Cambell, 122–43. London: UNESCO & Berghanh Books.

Giesecke, H. 1978. *Einführung in die Pädagogik.* 8th ed. München, Germany: Juventa Verlag.

Giroux, H. 1988. *Teachers as intellectuals – toward a critical pedagogy of learning.* South Hadley, MA: Bergin & Garvey Publishers.

Habermas, J. 1968. Erkenntnis und Interesse [Knowledge and interests]. In *Technik und Wissenschaft als 'Ideologie',* ed. J. Habermas, 146–68. Frankfurt am Main, Germany: Suhrkamp Verlag.

Hellesnes, J. 1976. *Socialisering og teknokrati* [Socialisation and technocracy]. Oslo, Norway: Gyldendal.

Hermann, S. 2005. Kompetencebegrebets udviklingshistorie [The development of the notion of competence]. *Kvan* 71: 7–17.

Hopkins, C., and R. McKeown. 2003. EE ≠ ESD: Defusing the worry. *Environmental Education Research* 9, no. 1: 117–28.

Jensen, B.B., and K Schnack. 1997. The action competence approach in environmental education. *Environmental Education Research* 3, no. 2: 163–78.

Kenny, A. 1963. *Action, emotion and will.* London: Routledge & Kegan Paul.

Klafki, W. 1991. *Neue Studien zur Bildungstheorie und Didaktik.* Weinheim, Germany: Beltz Verlag.

Lundegård, I., and Wickman, P-O. 2007. Conflicts of interest: An indispensable element of education for sustainable development. *Environmental Education Research* 13, no. 1: 1–15.

Mogensen, F. 1995. Handlekompetence som didaktisk begreb i miljøundervisningen [Action competence as educational idea in environmental education]. PhD diss., Royal Danish School of Educational Studies.

Mogensen, F. 1997. Critical thinking – a central element in developing action competence in health and environmental education. *Health Education Research Journal: Theory and Practice* 12, no. 4: 429–36.

Niss, M. 1999. Kompetencer og uddannelsesbeskrivelse [Competencies and curriculum], *Uddannelse* 9: 21–9.

Niss, M. 2003. Mathematical competencies and the learning of mathematics: The Danish KOM project. www7.nationalacademies.org/mseb/Mathematical_Competencies_and_the_Learning_of_Mathematics.pdf.

OECD. 1994. *Evaluating innovation in environmental education.* Paris, France: OECD.

Öhman, J. 2004. Moral perspectives in selective traditions of environmental education – conditions for environmental moral meaning-making and students' constitution as democratic citizens. In *Learning to change our world? Swedish research on education & sustainable development,* ed. P. Wickenberg, H. Axelsson, L. Fritzén, G. Helldén, and J. Öhman, 33–59. Lund, Sweden: Studentlitteratur.

Peters, R.S. 1958. *The concept of motivation.* London: Routledge & Kegan Paul.

Reid, A., J. Nikel, and W. Scott. 2006. Background note. Paper presented at the 'Indicators for education for sustainable development: Engaging the debate' workshop, March 17, in Bath, UK.

Robottom, I. 2007. Some conceptual issues in education for sustainable development. In *Drivers and barriers for implementing learning for sustainable development in pre-school through upper secondary and teacher education,* ed. I. Björneloo and E. Nyberg, 25–30. Paris, France: UNESCO.

Rychen, D.S. and L.H. Salganik, eds. 2003. *Key competencies for a successful life and a well-functioning society.* Göttingen, Germany: Hogrefe & Huber Publishers.

Sandell, K., J. Öhman, and L. Östman. 2004. *Education for sustainable development: Nature, school and democracy.* Lund, Sweden: Studentlitteratur.

Sætre, P.J., T. Kristensen, and K.G. Christensen. 1997. 'Å arbeide med problem det ikkje finst løysing på': interessekonflikter i bruk av naturressurser som tema i miljøundervisningen. Report no. 2 of MUVIN 2 in Norway, Høgskolen i Vestfold, Tønsberg, Norway.

Schnack, K. 1977. Humanisme – livsanskuelse og menneskesyn [Humanism – philosophy of life and view of human nature]. In *Pædagogisk teori og praksis* [Educational theory and practice], ed. F. Nielsen, 107–28. Copenhagen, Denmark: Borgen.

Schnack, K. 1994. Some further comments on the action competence debate. In *Action and action competence as key concepts in critical pedagogy,* ed. B.B Jensen and K. Schnack, 185–90. Copenhagen, Denmark: Royal Danish School of Educational Studies.

Schnack, K. 1995a. Environmental education as political education in a democratic society. In *Research in environmental and health education,* ed. B.B. Jensen, 17–29. Copenhagen, Denmark: The Royal Danish School of Educational Studies.

Schnack, K. 1995b. The didactics of challenge. In *Didaktik and/or curriculum,* ed. S. Hopmann, and K. Riquarts, 407–16. Kiel, Germany: Institut für die Pädagogik der Naturwissenschaften an der Universität Kiel.

Schnack, K. 1998. Why focus on conflicting interests in environmental education? In *Environmental education for sustainability: Good environment, good life,* ed. Mauri Ahlberg and Walter Leal Filho, 83–96. Frankfurt am Main, Germany: Peter Lang, Europäischer Verlag der Wissenschaften.

Schnack, K. 2000. Action competence as a curriculum perspective. In *Critical environmental and health education – research issues and challenges,* ed. B.B Jensen, K. Schnack, and V. Simovska, 107–27. Copenhagen, Denmark: Danish University of Education.

Schnack, K. 2003. Action competence as an educational ideal. In *The internationalization of curriculum studies,* ed. D. Trueit, W.E. Doll, H. Wang, and W.F. Pinar, 271–91. New York: Peter Lang Publishing.

Schnack, K. 2008. ESD refers to human needs – what does that mean? In *Lifelong learning: Theory and practice of continuous education. Proceedings of international cooperation,* ed. N.A. Lobanov, and V.N. Skvortsov, 84–8. St.-Petersburg, Russia: Alter Ego.

Schultz Jørgensen, P. 1999. Hvad er competence – Og hvorfor er det nødvendigt med et nyt begreb? [What is competency – and why do we need a new concept?]. *Uddannelse* 9: 4–13.

Sollart, K. 2005. Framework on indicators for education for sustainable development: Some conceptual thoughts. Netherlands Environmental Assessment Agency (MNP). http://www.unece.org/env/esd/inf.meeting.docs/Framework%20onESD%20indic%20NL.doc.

Sterling, S. 2001. *Sustainable education – re-visioning learning and change. Schumacher Briefings* No. 6. Dartington, UK: Schumacher Society/Green Books.

Stevenson, R. 2007. Schooling and environmental education: Contradictions in purpose and practice. *Environmental Education Research* 13, no. 2, 139–55.

Summer, M., G. Corney, and A. Childs. 2004. Student teachers' conception of sustainable development: The starting-points of geographers and scientists. *Educational Research* 46, no. 2: 163–82.

Taylor, R. 1966. *Action and purpose.* Upper Saddle River, NJ: Prentice-Hall.

Tilbury, D., and K. Cooke, 2005. *A national review of environmental education and its contribution to sustainability in Australia: Frameworks for sustainability.* Canberra, ACT: Australian Government Department of the Environment, Water, Heritage and the Arts, and ARIES.

Tilbury, D., and S. Janousek, 2006. *Development of a national approach to monitoring, assessment and reporting on the Decade of Education for Sustainable Development: Summarising documented experiences on the development of ESD Indicators and networking with expert groups on ESD indicators.* Sydney, NSW: Australian Research Institute of Education for Sustainability and Australian Government Department of the Environment and Water Resources.

Vare, P. 2006. From region of nations to nation of regions: A report on the UNECE ESD indicator process and links to south west England. Presentation at 'Indicators for education for sustainable development: Engaging the debate', March 17, in Bath, UK.

Von Wright, G.H. 1971. *Explanation and understanding.* London: Routledge & Kegan Paul.

Wals, A. 2006. The end of ESD... the beginning of transformative learning – emphasizing the E in ESD. In *Seminar on education for sustainable development Helsinki,* ed. Mikko Cantell, 41–59. Helsinki, Finland: Finnish National Commission for UNESCO.

Weinert, F.E. 2001. Concept of competence: A conceptual clarification. In *Defining and selecting key competencies,* ed. D.S. Rychen and L.H. Salganik, 45–65. Göttingen, Germany: Hogrefe & Huber Publishers.

World Commission on Environment and Development. 1987. *Our common future.* Oxford: Oxford University Press.

White, A.R., ed. 1968. *The philosophy of action.* Oxford, UK: Oxford University Press.

Ziehe, T. 2001. De personlige livsverdeners dominans [The dominance of personal life worlds]. *Uddannelse* 10: 3–12.

Pluralism in practice – experiences from Swedish evaluation, school development and research

Karin Rudsberg and Johan Öhman

In the international policy debate, environmental education and education for sustainable development seem to be moving away from a focus on behavioural modifications to more pluralistic approaches. This article illuminates a Swedish example of a strategic interplay between evaluation, development and research that relates to this shift, involving actors from schools, governmental agencies and researchers. The specific purpose of the research was to analyse and describe teachers' attempts to stimulate a pluralistic meaning-making process among their students in the context of education for sustainable development. The empirical material consisted of video-recorded lessons in secondary and upper secondary schools. In the analysis we used a methodological approach based on John Dewey's pragmatic philosophy and Ludwig Wittgenstein's first-person perspective on language. A concept called 'epistemological moves' has been used to clarify the actions that teachers perform in order to guide students in procedures of meaning-making. The analysis shows that the teachers perform a number of actions that make pluralistic meaning-making possible: encouraging the students to compare, specify, generalise and test their arguments under different circumstances. The teachers also encouraged the students to examine and evaluate different alternatives and be critical of their own statements. Finally, the findings are related to a perspective of democracy as a form of life.

Introduction

There is a clear trend in the international policy debate suggesting that environmental education and education for sustainable development are moving away from a focus on behavioural modification to less openly normative approaches (Scott and Gough 2003). Commentators have repeatedly warned about the risk of environmental education and education for sustainable development becoming a political instrument that supports a specific ideology created by politicians and experts in power, thereby turning education into indoctrination (Jickling and Spork 1998; Wals and Jickling 2000; Jickling 2003; Jickling and Wals 2007). Accordingly, many authors have claimed that the democratic mission of an education that involves diverse interest groups, supports free opinion-making and critical thinking, and enhances students' competence to act, should be a significant feature of all environmental education and education for sustainable development (Jensen and Schnack 1997; Elliott 1999; Lijmbach et al. 2002; Rauch 2002; Stables and Scott 2002; Englund, Öhman, and Östman 2008; Huckle 2008).

This shift has also been a significant feature of the development of environmental education and education for sustainable development in Sweden. Indeed, the democratic dimension has become a key focus of evaluations, developmental projects and research. The overall purpose of this paper is to illuminate a Swedish example of a strategic interplay between evaluation, development and research with regard to this dimension, involving actors from schools, governmental agencies as well as researchers from different universities. The specific purpose of the paper relates to the fact that although participatory and pluralistic approaches are frequently promoted in policies and are often a significant feature of developmental projects, only a few studies relate to whether and how these kinds of approaches appear in the classroom (Winter and Firth 2007; Kyburz-Graber, Hofer, and Wolfensberger 2006; Jonsson 2008; Gustavsson and Warner 2008). We therefore present a study that investigates and describes a pluralistic practice of education for sustainable development through analyses of teaching actions and students' meaning-making processes. The study's empirical material consists of three video-recorded lessons, which in content and/or form relate to education for sustainable development. The analysis of this material rests on a pragmatic methodological approach and uses an analytical concept called 'epistemological moves'. The analysis identifies several kinds of moves in the actions that teachers perform in their interactions with their students in order to stimulate a pluralistic meaning-making process. In this way the teachers encourage the students to compare, specify, generalise and test their arguments under different conditions. Further, the teachers encourage the students to examine and evaluate different alternatives and to be critical of their own statements. Our conclusion is that the combination of the generative function of the generalising and specifying moves and the evaluative function of the comparative and testing moves makes it reasonable to characterise the studied educational practices as pluralistic.

National evaluation of environmental and sustainability education in Swedish schools

In 2000, the Swedish National Agency for Education delegated a commission to the universities of Uppsala and Örebro to evaluate environmental and sustainability education in Swedish schools.[1] The purpose of this evaluation was to describe the current situation and investigate the possibilities for a development of such activities. Twenty-four randomly selected schools, ranging from pre-school to upper secondary school and adult education, participated in the study. The basis of the evaluation was a questionnaire survey, which was completed by 568 teachers representing a variety of subjects. The survey was supplemented with interviews of a selection of teachers and principals from the majority of the schools.

One of the most important results of the evaluation was the identification of three selective traditions[2] of teaching about environmental and sustainability issues: a *fact-based*, a *normative* and a *pluralistic* tradition. These traditions were found to differ in their educational approach and interpretation of the role of education in democracy in the following ways.

In the *fact-based* tradition, teachers primarily treat environmental issues as knowledge problems. The tradition is based on the idea that environmental problems can be dealt with by more research and information supplied to the public. The position taken is that only science can provide a reliable foundation for our knowledge about environmental issues, and that scientific facts and models are of sole importance in an educational context. Thus, for students to be able to form opinions on a sound scientific and democratic basis, the primary function of education is to provide objective facts and model objectivity for decision-making processes.

The important task of education within the *normative* tradition is to support an environmentally friendly transformation of society. Answers to value-related issues are established deliberatively through discussions among experts and politicians on the basis of scientific facts about the current ecological state of the world, and are presented in policy documents and syllabuses. On the basis of such consensus and this process, schools are thus obliged to teach students the necessary environmentally friendly values and attitudes and, in this way, support changing students' behaviours in the desired direction.

The *pluralistic* tradition is characterised by a striving to acknowledge and engage different perspectives, views and values when dealing with various questions and problems concerning the sustainability and future of our world. The way of finding common answers to value-related issues, or recognising and accepting our different standpoints, is seen as being accomplished through deliberative conversations. Such conversations are an essential part of education in the pluralistic tradition, and the democratic process is accordingly situated *in* education itself. One could say that an aim of pluralistic education is to enhance the student's democratic action competence.[3]

The survey verified that all three traditions are well represented in teaching procedures at all levels in Swedish schools today. Among the teachers in the survey schools, the normative tradition dominated (52%). The fact-based tradition was least represented (14%), and about one third of the teachers reported that they taught according to the pluralistic tradition (complete results in Swedish National Agency for Education [2001a]).

In the follow-up interviews, many teachers said that they had got stuck in the normative tradition and found it harder to reach students nowadays using this approach. The teachers also reported that engagement in environmental issues on the part of teachers and students was less than it used to be. The evaluation therefore concluded that environmental education was on the decline in many schools. A considerable number of these teachers asked for new ways of approaching these issues in their teaching practice, although at the same time claimed that they needed more time, knowledge and support to be able to make these changes.

The HUS project

As a result of the national evaluation, the Swedish National Agency for School Improvement 2002–2003 supported a major school development project – the HUS project.[4] In order to establish a basis for its further implementation in Swedish schools, the project's purpose was to develop organisations, methods and models that would support the operationalisation of education for sustainable development. Around 40 teachers, organised in 9 teams and representing different subject areas, school types and geographical areas in Sweden, participated in the project. The project also involved two project leaders, four experienced supervisors from two teacher training departments and two PhD students documenting the process. One of the main ideas of the project was to avoid a top-down structure when it came to how this approach should be put into educational practice. Accordingly, the teachers in the project were assigned the task of finding ways to include education for sustainable development in their everyday encounters with their students. While carrying out these tasks the teachers received two years of the kind of support the teachers in the national evaluation had declared was missing. Their teaching hours were reduced too, so that they had time to study, discuss and plan together. Each of the teams received continuous supervision during the project work in their respective schools and all the teachers received further education in the form of a series of seminars with common literature and lectures given by leading researchers within the field. Time was also allocated so that teachers from different schools could exchange their own personal teaching experiences.[5]

Several authors have shown that there are many different understandings of sustainable development, and that these also have consequences for education for sustainable development (Bonnett 1999; Elliott 1999; Stables 2001; Jickling and Wals 2007; Sumner 2008). For example, in his conceptual analysis of the term sustainable development, Jabareen (2008) identifies seven distinct concepts, all of which contain ambiguities, contradictions and tensions. Moreover, Fergus and Rowney (2005) argue that the meaning of the term sustainable development has changed. It has, they maintain, become mainly a question of scientific facts in which success is measured by the ethics of finance, instead of 'a fully inclusive, integrated discourse based on an ethic of values and diversity' (Fergus and Rowney 2005, 26). According to Sumner (2008), these diverse understandings of sustainable development could result in different forms of education. Education for sustainable development could either be understood as a form of academic imperialism that supports the financial wealth of a privileged elite or as an education that prioritises co-operative forms of human engagement that develop the common wealth and well being of all. Thus, while some authors see education for sustainable development as a top-down concept in which education is treated as an instrumental and ideological tool proscribing a particular ideology of sustainable development with a specific end in view (cf. Jickling and Spork 1998; Jickling 2003; Jickling and Wals 2007), others claim that education for sustainable development can be viewed as a tool that strives for sustainability through a democratic educational practice, where the identification, development and critique of one's interpretation of sustainable development in the company of others is fundamental to its educational credentials (cf. Fien 1995; Gough 2002; Rauch 2002; McKeown and Hopkins 2003).

In response to this kind of debate, some important conclusions were drawn to form points of departure for the HUS project. The first conclusion was that if public education delivered *specific* answers to environmental and developmental questions it would not be in line with the democratic assignment of education, given that different, and sometimes conflicting, views on such issues, involving different ideological, ethical and knowledge perspectives, exist. Instead, education should illuminate the diversity of opinions and critically scrutinise different arguments. Thus, education for sustainable development should be aligned most strongly with a pluralistic tradition. Another conclusion was that education for sustainable development cannot simply be understood as an extension of the content of environmental education with the addition of more social and economic aspects to the ecological. It should also be regarded as providing a different view of the value dimension of environmental and developmental problems and the democratic role of education (Sund 2008; Öhman 2004, 2008).

As the project developed, a specific aim emerged to find ways of enhancing the students' ability to critically relate to environmental and developmental issues and participate in debates, discussions and decisions in these issues at both a private every-day level and at a comprehensive societal level. It became clear that this objective called for teaching methods that included participatory learning, learner-centred approaches, collaborative problem-solving, and so on.

In order to acquire knowledge about the development of these teaching methods systematically, scientific investigations were connected to the project. In this paper we will account for one of these studies. The purpose of this particular study was to anal-yse and describe the teachers' attempts to stimulate a pluralistic meaning-making process among their students in the context of education for sustainable development. In light of this, empirical material was collected in the form of video recordings of the teachers' actions in the classroom.

Epistemological moves

The analyses of the video-recorded material were undertaken using a methodological approach based on John Dewey's pragmatic philosophy (Dewey 1929/1958, 1929/1984; Bentley and Dewey 1949/1991) and Ludwig Wittgenstein's (1953/1997, 1969/1997) first-person perspective on language. A similar combination was used in earlier studies of the practice of environmental and science education by Wickman and Östman (2001a, 2001b, 2002a, 2002b), Lidar, Lundqvist and Östman (2006), Wickman (2006), Almqvist and Östman (2006), Öhman (2006), Öhman and Östman (2007, 2008). (See also Östman this issue.)

Among these studies, Lidar, Lundqvist and Östman (2006) have especially studied the role of the teacher in relation to the students' meaning-making in the classroom. In this study, a concept called *epistemological moves* has been used to clarify the actions that teachers perform in order to help students to identify what counts as knowledge, what they need to pay attention to, and the 'proper' way to create knowl-edge in science education. The present study is methodologically closely connected to that of Lidar, Lundqvist and Östman (2006), although in our case we are especially interested in the actions that teachers perform in order to guide the students in the *procedures* of meaning-making when trying to accomplish a pluralistic education for sustainable development.

When investigating teachers' actions it is often assumed that it is necessary to know the teachers' intentions with their actions. This means that the researcher either has to ask the teachers to recapitulate the situation and describe their intentions, or use a theory that makes it possible to translate observed actions in the classroom into mental entities that preceded the action (i.e., intentions).[6] Such methods often build on the idea that something (an intention, a thought, a will, an emotion and so on) is hidden behind the action, which is generally combined with the presumption that mind and reality are two separate spheres.

In this study we use a different solution to this methodological problem; one that is based on Dewey's pragmatism and Wittgenstein's perspective on language and the alternative these philosophers create to dualistic approaches. Both Dewey and Wittgenstein remind us that the separation of an inner mind and an outer reality is a theoretical image assumed from a third-person perspective, or, in other words, at a distance from real-life situations (see, for example, Dewey [1929/1958, 1929/1984] and Wittgenstein [1953/1997, §1 and §115]).

In order to dissolve this picture Dewey and Wittgenstein invite us to recall how we live through different events together with our fellow beings. When we are involved in the act of communicating things that are assumed to be part of an inner mind (meanings, thoughts, emotions, intentions, etc.) and an outer reality (language, action) they often appear as an entity, i.e., in a conversation we can often immediately understand what another person wants, thinks or feels.[7] This can be regarded as a first-person perspective on language (see Öhman and Östman 2007).

Wittgenstein uses the term language-game to underline that the meaning of words is not to be found in fixed connections to reality but in the role they play in different situations in life. In human practice, certain rules are created for how to express a specific meaning in a specific situation and by using these rules we can make ourselves understood. From this perspective a thought or an intention is not something that lies behind or is separate from speech, but rather: 'an intention is embedded in its situation, in human customs and institutions' (Wittgenstein 1953/1997, § 337; Almqvist and Östman 2006).

The first-person perspective has important methodological implications, namely, that it is possible to study intention as *action*. This is possible because the perspective doesn't pre-suppose an *a priori* separation of mind and reality. This also means that the observed data and the resulting conclusions can be kept at the same level, i.e., action, which in turn means that we do not need a 'translation theory' between action and mind.

In using this approach there is no need or reason to search for teachers' inner thoughts. Instead, the aim is to study the interaction between a specific teaching practice and students' meaning-making processes. We call teachers' actions that facilitate a certain meaning-making procedure 'epistemological moves'. With epistemological moves we mean the way in which the teacher interacts with the students by giving instructions, asking questions or making comments that indicate what counts as the right way of creating meaning. In this way the teachers' actions can be seen as guidelines that guide the students in a certain direction in the conversations that take place in the classroom. Here it is important to note that connected to a first-person perspective is the ambition to work with a strong empirical emphasis. This means that we categorise the teachers' actions in terms of the *function* the different actions have for the students' meaning-making processes. Events, therefore, have to be analysed in their entirety so that differences in the students' meaning-making before and after the teacher's intervention can be observed.

Research design

The empirical material collected in the HUS project consisted of video-recordings of 13 lessons. In the study presented here we focused our attention on the analysis of three of these lessons which showed clear examples of interactions between teachers and students in the classroom. The three lessons represent different subjects and different ages of the participating students. One lesson was in mathematics in a nine-year compulsory through school, and the second and third were from upper secondary schools in the subjects of religion and social science. All three lessons were related to education for sustainable development by their content and/or method.

The analytical work started with a repeated examination of the recordings of the chosen lessons in order to become acquainted with the conversations taking place and to search for sequences related to our specific interest. After this the video-recorded lessons were transcribed. The transcriptions were written down literally, the spoken language was expressed in a readable way, and gestures and facial expressions of significance were described in the transcript. Although the excerpts used in our article have been translated from Swedish, we have tried to reflect the original wording and intentions. Further, when coding the material we especially searched for changes in the participants' conversations and marked these changes in the transcript. The identified changes in the conversation were related to the teachers' utterances. The coding of the epistemological moves was made in relation to their function for the student's meaning-making. The next step was to compare the functions of the different epistemological moves made by the teachers and modify the coding accordingly. We then returned to the video-recordings in order to relate the moves to the content of the entire lesson and to check for any details that might have been overlooked during the transcription process. A comparison of the differences and similarities of the moves made during the different events and lessons was made, and here too the coding and descriptions of the moves were modified. This facilitated the identification of categories of epistemological moves with different functions for the students' meaning-making processes. The identified categories were accordingly judged by two criteria: internal homogeneity and external heterogeneity (Patton 2002). Finally, the categories were validated by other researchers through critical examination of the categories in relation to the empirical material, transcripts and video-recordings.

Results

The analysis resulted in a categorisation consisting of four different kinds of epistemological moves. The different functions of the moves concerning classroom interactions and meaning-making processes are described in Table 1, and discussed later.

In the following section we discuss the way in which we identified these different moves with the aid of an analysis of a sequence from one of the lessons. The lesson

Table 1. Descriptions of the identified moves.

Move	Function
	Generative:
Generalising	The teacher reformulates a student's earlier statement and brings it to a more general level, inviting the student to relate his/her statements to the introduced concepts and create generalisations.
Specifying	On the basis of a student's earlier utterance the teacher points to what the student ought to focus on, inviting the student to specify his/her statement.
	Evaluative:
Comparative	The teacher adds new positions and/or perspectives to the conversation to which the student is then urged to relate, inviting the student to compare and evaluate different alternatives.
Testing	The teacher asks for the validity of the student's standpoints and judgements in different circumstances, inviting the student to test the prerequisites of his/her statement.

was on environmental ethics in an upper secondary school class. The exercise in question was carried out as follows. The teacher and students sat together in a circle, leaving one chair empty. The teacher kick-started the exercise by reading out different value-related statements concerned with sustainable development. In the discussion that followed the students were expected to take a stand in relation to these statements and defend their individual points of view. The students indicated their stance by remaining seated if they agreed and changing seats if they did not. The students were also told that if they did not wish to express their particular standpoint they should remain seated. The sequence started with the teacher making a statement that involved two alternative ways of solving an environmental problem, namely, improving technology or changing lifestyle:

1	Teacher:	Improving technology is better than changing lifestyle if you want to solve environmental problems.
2	Student1:	Even if we get better technology we have to, if we still have the same attitude to the environment and so on we will still mis... [unsure which word to use] use it in the wrong way, we need to change our views about how we use things.
3	Teacher:	So it is people's attitudes that are the problem?
4	Student2:	I agree with you [referring to Student1]. If it is possible to solve all environmental problems with better technology then we should of course do that.
5	Teacher:	Do you think that this is more effective than a change of lifestyle? [*Comparative move*]
6	Student2:	I don't know. Put our trust in scientists will come up with better methods, no I don't know. But in any case it's better than just lowering our standards and having the same old crappy tools to... [doesn't end the sentence]
7	Student3:	Cars are well-known environmental villains. They've now invented cars that run on gas [natural or hydrogen] [inaudible]. Mexico City is going to buy 25,000 and use them as taxis and if in the future they succeed in making all cars run on gas or something else that's good, fuel cells or whatever they come up with, that would be a definite advantage. But I think it's difficult, sure people can stop using their cars so much, there could be a combination... [doesn't complete the sentence].
8	Teacher:	So you believe in technology? [*Generalising move*]
9	Student3:	Yes, quite a lot, a combination like that perhaps, but most of all technology.
10	Student4:	If we don't get as far as having completely environmentally friendly cars, but only almost environmentally friendly cars, then it will most likely be the case, I think, that we say, 'this is not very dangerous I can drive my car all the time because it is not so dangerous'. So there won't be any difference in any case, you think that you can use the thing more.
11	Teacher:	Aha, you mean that people will use it all the more? [*Generalising move*]
12	Student5:	For example if you sort your refuse, I don't think that it helps so much, if you, if you continue to do that, but if someone comes up with some really good technical solution, that we make something environmentally friendly out of it, then it would be much better, like Student3 said we use for example fuel cells in cars or whatever. But at the same time, if you, if you use a thing more, I don't think, we will still need to use cars, we'll still, that is nobody will then say 'I take the bus to work', there are terrible delays with SL [local bus company]... [inaudible] when it is

		much more fun [?] to take the car, I don't think that everybody will give that up. So we might just as well use cars with fuel cells instead of ordinary cars, therefore technology is still because nobody will, not everybody will change his or her lifestyle.
13	Teacher:	So you think that selfishness still in some way... [doesn't complete the sentence] [*Specifying move*]
14	Student5:	Absolutely, absolutely
15	Teacher:	...makes people... yes...
16	Student6:	One suggestion doesn't have to exclude the other as we just mentioned, it's not that. But then, we could be more precise and say that we have to, we have come so far now in the development, that we cannot go backwards we have to go forwards, and then this might be the only solution because we might not be able...
17	Teacher:	You mean technology? [*Specifying move*]
18	Student6:	Yes exactly, technology. We can't change our lifestyle to the extent that we exclude cars and that so many things have been developed today that we need, sort of, that we've lived with this technology, sort of.
19	Teacher:	But don't you think, if the situation was to become even more severe, don't you think that people would be prepared to change their lifestyles? Say that the environmental problems became really acute, don't you think that people would be prepared to change their lifestyles then? [*Testing move*]
20	Student6:	Yes, to some extent I think so. But I still think that we are so kind of intertwined in this net that we can't get out of it, sure we might be able to hitch ourselves up a few notches but we'll probably never get out of it completely. We will probably never be able to go back and live like in the Middle Ages.
21	Student7:	We've talked about new cars that were environmentally friendly and a lot of other things that were environmentally friendly. I was wondering what it was that makes us come up with technology that makes everything environmentally friendly. It cannot be directly connected to a change of lifestyle, but at least to a change in attitudes to the environment and how we treat it and this I think has something to do with lifestyle. So I think they are linked, so I would take up a middle position.
22	[Another student]	
23	Student8:	Yes, if we could improve the environmental situation just by changing lifestyle without lowering the standard of living then I think that people would already have done that and would do that. And that if you then change your lifestyle then the standard of living will go down and this is why it's better to try to improve the technology instead, because we are clearly not prepared to lower our standard of living in order to improve the environmental situation.
24	Teacher:	Are we too selfish, or? [*Specifying move*]
25	Student8:	Yes.
26	Student2:	Well, a thought just struck me, now I am not responding to any problem or any kind of argument, but... If you introduce new laws that say that you can only shower for ten minutes per day, that kind of in some way changes our lifestyle to, or so that these environmental problems are solved. How, how, I think, isn't this better than, you still work with technology and a change... [hesitates and doesn't complete the sentence].
27	Teacher:	You mean a third way, to use legislation to... [doesn't complete the sentence]. [*Specifying move*]
28	Student2:	I don't know, technology is progressing anyway and research is going on all the time. Now I was thinking that maybe we should

give more money to solve these problems, but yes if we made laws that would make everybody sort of … [doesn't complete the sentence].

29 [Another student]
30 Student1: Many of these changes in technology, like for example this with the cars going from petrol to gas means radical changes [pointing at Student3], but most changes are small changes that are a bit more environmentally friendly or a bit less so, and it is often the case that the less environmentally friendly are perhaps a bit cheaper and most people tend to kind of choose the cheaper alternative and so there would be no progress with technology alone. And then it's humans who have to change anyway.

In the analysis of the teacher's actions we have identified two different types of epistemological moves that both have a generative function. In both moves the teacher indicates what is important to notice in relation to what has been said earlier, which gives the students an opportunity to generate new meanings by creating new explanations and descriptions from things they have already noticed. The two moves with a generative function are *generalising* and *specifying*.

Within the *generalising* move the teacher's utterances have the function of raising the conversation to a higher level with the aid of more general terms. An example of this is when Student 3 [7] talks about cars and their use in relation to environmental issues: '…if in the future they succeed in making all cars run on gas or something else that's good, fuel cells or whatever they come up with, that would be a definite advantage. But I think it's difficult, sure people could stop using their cars so much, there could be a combination…' The teacher follows this up by asking 'So you believe in technology?' [8]. Here the teacher points to a more general aspect, which was not mentioned by Student 3. In her reply, Student 3 [9] also relates to the term 'technology'. In this way the teacher stimulates a development of meaning-making by creating opportunities for the students to make generalisations.

In what we have called a *specifying* move the teacher's actions have the function that the students develop their earlier utterances by specifying their opinions. A question that functions as a specifying move is asked by the teacher in line 27. The sequence starts with Student 2 [26] discussing an alternative that implies imposing restrictions 'that say that you can only shower for ten minutes per day, that kind of in some way changes our lifestyle to, or so that these environmental problems are solved'. The student then hesitates and stops in the middle of the sentence. It is noteworthy that Student 2 seems to be communicating thoughts that have suddenly struck him. The teacher then asks the student to continue and specify his contribution by saying 'You mean a third way, to use legislation to…' [27]. In this way the teacher shows the student that he has actually been talking and reasoning about a third option, namely legislation. The consequence of this move is that Student 2 continues and tries to explain and specify what has been said, albeit with some hesitation: '…but yes if we made laws that would make everybody…' [28]. In this way Student 2 specifies that legislation was indeed what he was thinking about.

In this lesson we also identified actions with an evaluative function, thus making the students evaluate and try out different alternatives. For example, the teacher adds new perspectives or prerequisites to the conversation to which the students are then encouraged to relate. In our analyses two categories of moves can be seen as having an evaluative function, namely, *comparative* and *testing* moves.

Comparative moves mean that new perspectives or statements are added to the discussion by the teacher, which the students are then expected to relate to in the conversation. This results in the different alternatives being compared and evaluated. This type of move follows on from Student 2 [4] saying that if it is 'possible to solve all environmental problems with better technology we should of course do that'. The positioning of Student 2 prompts the teacher to respond in a way that can be called a comparative move, by saying 'Do you think that this is more effective than a change of lifestyle?' [5]. Here the teacher gives the students an opportunity to develop their arguments by evaluating what has been said in relation to something else. At the same time the discussion is brought back to the perspective of conflict between different interests – of central focus in the statement that initiated this section of the lesson. The function of this move is that Student 2 [6] says that he does not know, although at the same time wonders whether to 'put our trust in scientists will come up with better methods'. Here it can be seen that the student has taken the teacher's question into account and considered it. Student 3 [7] also relates to the teacher's question by saying that 'there could be a combination'. The two students both discuss the comparison highlighted by the teacher, but take different stands.

The *testing* move is characterised by the teacher relating the students' statements to new circumstances. Here the teacher's utterance makes the students inquire whether earlier conclusions are still valid when circumstances change. A testing move section starts with Student 6 [18] saying that: 'We can't change our lifestyle...' [18]. The student motivates the statement by saying that today we depend on technology and that technology is part of everyday life. The teacher follows this up by saying, 'But don't you think, if the situation was to be become even more severe, don't you think that people would be prepared to change their lifestyles? Say that the environmental problems became really acute, don't you think that people would be prepared to change their lifestyles then?' In this way the teacher changes the prerequisites for the students' earlier statements. The utterance made by the teacher in line 19 has the function that Student 6 answers 'Yes, to some extent I think' [20]. Student 6 has now changed her statement from 'can't' to 'to some extent'. But Student 6 still holds on to the earlier conclusion that humans still are so '... intertwined in this net that we cannot get out of it' [20], although, the student also says that we admittedly '...might be able to hitch ourselves up a few notches but we'll probably never get out of it completely' [20]. The teacher's utterance [19] makes the student first of all test whether her earlier conclusion still holds when circumstances change and then modify his/her standpoint about possibilities of changing lifestyle.

Conclusions

The approach used in this study's analysis not only facilitates an analysis of teachers' manners of teaching, but also an investigation and description of the relation between teachers' manners of teaching and students' meaning-making processes. In the foregoing analysis we have identified four different categories of moves that appear with no hierarchical order – *generalising*, *specifying*, *comparative* and *testing* moves – comprising different properties and functions for interactions in the classroom (see Table 1). These same four moves were also identified in the other two lessons analysed in this part of the study.

The question is whether and in what way these moves can be said to constitute an educational practice that is in line with the ambitions of the pluralistic approach to environmental and sustainability education.

The *generalising* and *specifying* moves cannot be regarded as specific to a pluralistic practice. Similar moves have, for example, been found in fact-based science education (Lidar, Lundqvist, and Östman 2006). In that practice these moves mainly have the function of deepening the individual student's specific scientific knowledge. In the practice analysed here their function is somewhat different, as the generative function of the moves also supports a common conversation and an inter-subjective meaning-making process. By giving the students opportunities to create new explanations and descriptions from what they have already claimed or stated, the students are encouraged to clarify and develop their statements further. This facilitates the creation of new, more generalised or specified arguments for different standpoints, thereby contributing to a more nuanced discussion. These moves also help the discussion along by making the students' contributions clearer and more understandable, and give other participants a distinct statement to relate to when continuing the conversation.

What makes it possible to characterise this practice as pluralistic is that the generalising and specifying moves are combined with an evaluative function of the *comparative* and *testing* moves. When the teacher adds different perspectives and circumstances it provides the students with opportunities to develop their own points of view by comparing what has been said earlier with something new and, in the testing move, deciding whether earlier statements are still valid in the light of these changes. Likewise, a conflict perspective in which different interests are highlighted can also be introduced by the teacher. These moves support a pluralistic meaning-making process in that they make the students aware of the fact that there is more than one possibility, and they also allow them to examine and evaluate different alternatives and to be critical of their own statements. This connects to what Munby and Roberts (1998) describe as an education where the students are socialised towards intellectual independence, which means a focus on the students' ability to make statements and consciously evaluate different alternatives.

From the previous reasoning we can conclude that the teacher performs a number of actions that make a pluralistic meaning-making process possible: different arguments are encouraged and considered and no particular standpoint is privileged. The conversation can accordingly be said to be open-ended, even though it follows specific rules for the 'correct' way of creating meaning, or, in other words, how to participate in a pluralistic act of communication about value-related sustainable issues. One could, therefore, say that the *how* of learning is also the *what* of learning. By this we mean that the process is an essential part of the learning content. The examined educational practice can thus be seen as a way of learning to 'live democratically'.

From a theoretical perspective, the analysed educational practice relates to a view of democracy as *a form of life*. In recent years this democratic view has attracted a lot of attention in Swedish curriculum research (Englund 2006; Säfström and Biesta 2001; Gerrevall 2003; Larsson 2007; Tholander 2007). Of late the possibilities of applying this democratic perspective to education for sustainable development have also been explored by Swedish researchers (Englund, Öhman, and Östman 2008; Öhman 2008; Gustavsson and Warner 2008). Many of these authors talk about democracy in terms of a communicative activity. Founded in Dewey's (1916/1980) influential work, *Democracy and education*, and often referring to contemporary scholars like Habermas, Nussbaum and Gutman, these researchers have emphasised that the ideal of democracy is not a situation in which people relate to each other by declaring and defending their preconceived standpoints, but rather a situation where people create new possibilities by influencing each other. This means that democracy is 'not primarily a mode of management and control, but more an expression of a society imprinted by mutual communication, and consequently a pluralist life-form' (Englund 2006, 508). In this perspective pluralism can thus be seen as the very constituent of democracy and something that nourishes a democratic communicative process.

In relation to this view on democracy, education is understood as a forum where people can communicate different experiences and, accordingly, continuously reconstruct their experiences through common meaning-making processes. In this way education plays a significant role in the maintenance of a democratic form of life.[8] From a communicative understanding of democracy it is not only the content (the character of the standpoints) that is important, but also the form (the procedure that leads to the standpoint). The communicative understanding emphases the *inter-subjective* character of democratic competence. Communication is here seen as the means of reaching a deepened, nuanced standpoint where several different possibilities have been explored and valued. In order to be in a position to learn this democratic procedure the students have to have an opportunity to participate in such procedures, which implies that these procedures have to be an integral part of the teaching and learning processes.

Final remarks

The analyses presented in this paper can be seen as an example of a pragmatic research approach that has been developed within the Swedish research institute: Institute for Research in Education and Sustainable Development (IRESD) (www.did.uu.se/iresd; see also Östman, this issue). It is our hope that the pragmatic approach in general, and the 'epistemological move' method in particular, will inspire other scholars to further research focusing on a variety of procedures and aspects of environmental and sustainability education. The first reason for this is that the suggested approach can take both the process and the content into account, as both of these aspects and their relationships are essential when it comes to fulfilling educational purposes. The second reason is that the first-person perspective used in the analyses is similar to the way teachers use direct observation to understand their students' learning (in contrast to a theoretical perspective that tries to involve structures and mental entities that are assumed to lie behind what is observed). Hopefully this allows teachers to recognise and relate to the produced knowledge from their own experiences of teaching practice.

By using this method here we have been able to see what a pluralistic approach to education for sustainable development can mean in practice and how it works, that is, pluralism not only as a policy principle but as manifested in tools developed in teachers' own practice in order to stimulate a specific kind of meaning-making process. The inter-subjective communicative characteristics of this process relate this teaching and learning practice to a Swedish curriculum perspective on democracy as a form of life. In this way the findings of the study open a way to understanding education for sustainable development not only as a widening of the content of environmental education, but also as a form of *democratic education*. In this sense a pluralistic teaching practice appears to be one way of avoiding indoctrination in education for sustainable development and a narrowing of the scope of future possible responses to value-related environmental and sustainability issues.

We do, however, find it important to keep in mind that the idea of pluralism is in itself a specific norm, connected to the ideals of the enlightenment and the development of humanism and liberalism in western European philosophy. We must be open to education for sustainable development developing in many different ways and adjusting to the values and ideologies of other cultural and historical contexts. As Foucault (1982/1991, 343) reminds us: 'You can't find a solution of a problem in the solution of another problem raised at another moment by other people... My point is not that everything is bad, but that everything is dangerous'. In other words, it would be both dangerous and contradictory of us to determine a specific kind of pluralism as being the ultimate way of practising education for sustainable development, rather than one of many possible solutions.

Notes
1. The project was led by Johan Öhman, Örebro University and Leif Östman, Uppsala University.
2. The concept of selective tradition was originally developed by Williams (1973) to underline the fact that a certain approach to knowledge and a certain educational praxis is always selected within the frames of a specific culture. The regular patterns of selective processes that develop over time form a selective tradition. Within curriculum theory, the existence of such patterns in the praxis of different subjects has been highlighted in several historical studies of education (Englund 1986; Goodson 1987; Östman 1995; Fensham 1998). The implication of these studies is that the education pursued in a specific subject is historically variable and infrequently uniform at certain points in time. The selective traditions represent different answers as to what constitutes good teaching in a subject and include different practices with regard to the selection and organisation of the content, as well as the selection of forms and teaching methods.
3. For a more elaborated description of the three traditions see Sandell, Öhman and Östman (2005).
4. HUS is an acronym for Sustainable Development in School and also means 'house' in Swedish. The project was led by Johan Öhman, Örebro University and Leif Östman, Uppsala University.
5. The results of the project were published in the book *Hållbar utveckling i praktiken* [Education for Sustainable Development in Practice] (Öhman and Östman 2004). The book contains a number of examples of how education for sustainable development can be carried out in everyday educational practice. It was distributed to all schools in Sweden and is also available online at: http://www.skolutveckling.se/publikationer.
6. For a methodological discussion about a pragmatic alternative to cognitive approaches see Öhman and Östman (2007).
7. For example, we generally do not have any doubts about the feelings of a friend who says: 'I'm hungry'. In most cases the meaning is obvious to us because of the particular situation and circumstances. But this does not automatically mean that we always know the 'inner' state of other humans. The point is that the relation between mind and reality becomes an empirical question rather than a metaphysical one.
8. This communicative understanding of democracy has strong support in Swedish educational policy declarations. The National Agency for Education's official report on democracy in school declares that:

> Pre-schools and schools that use deliberative discussions that are characterised by respect, mutuality and a will to understand, to a great extent fulfils society's demands that the activity should be carried out with democratic working methods. Simultaneously, through deliberative discussions pre-schools and schools can develop children's and young people's communicative abilities, and with that, their democratic competence. Deliberative discussions make it possible for children and young people to develop the ability to form their own, well-founded standpoints as well as to develop functional relations to others based on democratic values. (Swedish National Agency for Education 2001b, 4, our translation)

References

Almqvist, J., and L. Östman. 2006. Privileging and artefacts: On the use of information technology in science education. *Interchange* 37, no. 3: 225–50.

Bentley, A.F., and J. Dewey. 1949/1991. *Knowing and the known.* Carbondale, IL: Southern Illinois University Press.

Bonnett, M. 1999. Education for sustainable development: A coherent philosophy for environmental education? *Cambridge Journal of Education* 29, no. 3: 313–24.

Dewey, J. 1916/1980. *The middle works, 1899–1924. Vol. 9, 1916: Democracy and education.* Ed. J.A. Boydston. Carbondale, IL: Southern Illinois University Press.

Dewey, J. 1929/1958. *Experience and nature.* New York: Dover publications.

Dewey, J. 1929/1984. *The quest for certainty: A study of the relation of knowledge and action.* Carbondale, IL: Southern Illinois University Press.

Elliott, J. 1999. Sustainable society and environmental education: Future perspectives and demands for the educational system. *Cambridge Journal of Education* 29, no. 3: 325–41.

Englund, T. 1986. *Curriculum as a political problem: Changing educational conceptions, with special reference to citizenship education.* Lund, Sweden: Studentlitteratur/Chartwell Bratt.

Englund, T. 2006. Deliberative communication: A pragmatist proposal. *Journal of Curriculum Studies* 38, no. 5: 503–20.

Englund, T, J. Öhman, and L. Östman. 2008. Deliberative communication for sustainability? A Habermas-inspired pluralistic approach. In *Sustainability and security within liberal societies: Learning to live with the future,* ed. S. Gough, and A. Stables, 29–48. London: Routledge.

Fensham, P. 1998. *Development and dilemmas in science education.* London: The Falmer Press.

Fergus, A.H.T., and J.I.A. Rowney. 2005. Sustainable development: Lost meaning and opportunity? *Journal of Business Ethics* 60, no. 1: 17–27.

Fien, J. 1995. Teaching for a sustainable world: The environmental and developmental education project for teacher education. *Environmental Education Research* 1, no.1: 21–34.

Foucault, M. 1982/1991. On the genealogy of ethics: An overview of works in progress. In *The Foucault reader,* ed. P. Rabinow, 340–72. London: Penguin Books.

Gerrevall, P. 2003. Bedömning av demokratisk kompetens: En pedagogisk utmaning [Judging democratic competence: A pedagogical challenge]. *Utbildning och Demokrati,* 12, no. 3: 41–66.

Goodson, I. 1987. *School subjects and curriculum change: Studies in curriculum history.* London: The Falmer Press.

Gough, S. 2002. Increasing the value of the environment: A 'real options' metaphor for learning. *Environmental Education Research* 8, no. 1: 61–72.

Gustavsson, B., and M. Warner. 2008. Participatory learning and deliberative discussion within education for sustainable development. In *Values and democracy in education for sustainable development: Contributions from Swedish research,* ed. J. Öhman, 75–92. Malmö, Sweden: Liber.

Huckle, J. 2008. An analysis of New Labour's policy on education for sustainable development with particular reference to socially critical approaches. *Environmental Education Research* 14, no. 1: 65–75.

Jabareen, Y. 2008. A new conceptual framework for sustainable development. *Environment, Development and Sustainability* 10, no. 2: 179–92.

Jensen, B.B., and C. Schnack. 1997. The action competence approach in environmental education. *Environmental Education Research* 3, no. 3: 163–79.

Jickling, B. 2003. Environmental education and environmental advocacy. Revisited. *Journal of Environmental Education* 34, no. 2: 20–27.

Jickling, B., and H. Spork. 1998. Education for the environment: A critique. *Environmental Education Research* 4, no. 3: 309–28.

Jickling, B., and A.E.J. Wals. 2007. Globalization and environmental education: Looking beyond sustainable development. *Journal of Curriculum Studies* 40, no. 1: 1–21.

Jonsson, G. 2008. An approach full of nuances: On student teachers' understanding of and teaching for sustainable development. In *Values and democracy in education for sustainable development: Contributions from Swedish research,* ed. J. Öhman, 93–108. Malmö, Sweden: Liber.

Kyburz-Graber, R., K. Hofer, and B. Wolfensberger. 2006. Studies on a socio-ecological approach to environmental education: A contribution to a critical position in the education for sustainable development discourse. *Environmental Education Research* 12, no. 1: 101–14.

Larsson, K. 2007. *Samtal, klassrumsklimat och elevers delaktighet: Överväganden kring en deliberativ didaktik* [Dialogue, classroom climate and students participation: Some aspects of deliberative didactics]. Örebro, Sweden: Örebro Universitet.

Lidar, M., E. Lundquist, and L. Östman. 2006. Teaching and learning in the science classroom. *Science Education* 90, no. 1: 148–63.

Lijmbach, S., M. Margadant-van Arcken, C.S.A. van Koppen, and A.E.J. Wals. 2002. 'Your view of nature is not mine': Learning about pluralism in the classroom. *Environmental Education Research* 8, no. 2: 121–35.

McKeown, R., and C. Hopkins. 2003. EE ≠ ESD: Defusing the worry. *Environmental Education Research* 9, no. 1: 117–28.

Munby, H., and D.A. Roberts. 1998. Intellectual independence: A potential link between science teaching and responsible citizenship. In *Problems of meaning in science curriculum,* ed. D.A. Roberts, and L. Östman, 101–14. New York: Teachers College Press.

Öhman, J. 2004. Moral perspectives in selective traditions of environmental education: Conditions for environmental moral meaning-making and students' constitution as democratic citizens. In *Learning to change our world? Swedish research on education & sustainable development,* ed. P. Wickenberg, H. Axelsson, L. Fritzén, G. Helldén, and J. Öhman, 33–57. Lund, Sweden: Studentlitteratur.

Öhman, J. 2006. Pluralism and criticism in environmental education and education for sustainable development: A practical understanding. *Environmental Education Research* 12, no. 2: 149–63.

Öhman, J. 2008. Environmental ethics and democratic responsibility: A pluralistic approach to ESD. In *Values and democracy in education for sustainable development: Contributions from Swedish research,* ed. J. Öhman, 17–32. Malmö, Sweden: Liber.

Öhman, J., and L. Östman, eds. 2004. *Hållbar utveckling i praktiken* [Teaching practice in education for sustainable development]. Stockholm, Sweden: The Swedish National Agency for School Improvement, Liber distribution.

Öhman, J., and L. Östman. 2007. Continuity and change in moral meaning-making: A transactional approach. *Journal of Moral Education* 36, no 2: 151–68.

Öhman, J., and L. Östman. 2008. Clarifying the ethical tendency in education for sustainable development practice: A Wittgenstein-inspired approach. *Canadian Journal of Environmental Education* 14: 24–40.

Östman, L. 1995. *Socialisation och mening: No-utbildning som politiskt och miljömoraliskt problem* [Meaning and socialization: Science education as a political and environmental-ethical problem]. Uppsala, Sweden: Acta Universitatis Upsaliensis.

Patton, M.Q. 2002. *Qualitative research & evaluation methods.* Thousand Oaks, CA: Sage Publications.

Rauch, F. 2002. The potential of education for sustainable development for reform in schools. *Environmental Education Research* 8, no. 1: 43–51.

Sandell, K., J. Öhman, and L. Östman. 2005. *Education for sustainable development: Nature, school and democracy.* Lund, Sweden: Studentlitteratur.

Scott, W., and S. Gough. 2003. *Sustainable development and learning: Framing the issues.* London: RoutledgeFalmer.

Stables, A. 2001. Who drew the sky? Conflicting assumptions in environmental education. *Educational Philosophy and Theory* 33, no. 2: 250–54. Repr. with comments by M. Peters, R. Soetaert, and A. Mottart in *Key issues in sustainable development and learning: A critical review,* ed. W. Scott and S. Gough, 41–44. London: RoutledgeFalmer, 2004.

Stables, A., and W. Scott. 2002. The quest for holism in education for sustainable development. *Environmental Education Research* 8, no. 1: 53–60.

Sumner, J. 2008. From academic imperialism to the civil commons: Institutional possibilities for responding to the United Nations Decade of Education for Sustainable Development. *Interchange* 39, no. 1: 77–94.

Sund, P. 2008. Discerning the extras in ESD teaching: A democratic issue. In *Values and democracy in education for sustainable development: Contributions from Swedish research,* ed. J. Öhman, 56–74. Malmö, Sweden: Liber.

Swedish National Agency for Education. 2001a. Miljöundervisning och utbildning för hållbar utveckling i svensk skola [Environmental education and education for sustainable development in the Swedish school system]. Report number 00:3041.

Swedish National Agency for Education. 2001b. Strategi för Skolverkets arbete med de demokratiska värdena – en sammanfattning. [Strategy for the National Agency of Education's work with democratic values – a summary]. http://www.skolverket.se/publikationer?id=753.

Säfström C.A., and G. Biesta. 2001. Learning democracy in a world of difference. *The School Field* 12, nos. 5–6: 61–72.

Tholander, M. 2007. Students' participation and non-participation as a situated accomplishment. *Childhood* 14, no. 4: 449–66.

Wals, A.E.J., and B. Jickling. 2000. Process-based environmental education seeking standards without standardizing. In: *Critical environmental and health education: Research issues and challenges,* ed. B.B. Jensen, K. Schnack, and V. Simovska, 127–49. Copenhagen, Denmark: Research Centre for Environmental and Health Education, Danish University of Education.

Wickman, P.-O. 2006. *Aesthetic experience in science education: Learning and meaning-making as situated talk and action.* London: Lawrence Erlbaum.

Wickman, P.-O., and L. Östman. 2001a. University students during practical work: Can we make the learning process intelligible? In *Research in science education: Past, present, and future,* ed. H. Behrendt, H. Dahncke, R. Duit, W. Gräber, M. Komorek, A. Kross and P. Reiska, 319–24. Dordrecht, The Netherlands: Kluwer Academic Publishers.

Wickman, P.-O., and L. Östman. 2001b. Students' practical epistemologies during laboratory work. Paper presented at the annual meeting of the American Educational Research Association, April 10–14, in Seattle, WA.

Wickman, P.-O., and L. Östman. 2002a. Induction as an empirical problem: How students generalize during practical work. *International Journal of Science Education* 24, 465–86.

Wickman, P.-O., and L. Östman. 2002b. Learning as discourse change: A sociocultural mechanism. *Science Education* 86, 601–23.

Williams, R. 1973. Base and superstructure in Marxist cultural theory. *New Left Review* 82: 3–16.

Winter, C., and R. Firth. 2007. Knowledge about education for sustainable development: Four case studies of student teachers in English secondary schools. *Journal of Education for Teaching* 33, no. 3: 341–58.

Wittgenstein, L. 1953/1997. *Philosophical investigations.* Oxford, UK: Blackwell.

Wittgenstein, L. 1969/1997. *On certainty.* Oxford, UK: Blackwell.

Environmental education policy research – challenges and ways research might cope with them

Jeppe Læssøe, Noah Weeth Feinstein and Nicole Blum

This essay examines the relationship between research and policy and, more specifically, how researchers might relate to policy work. Given the current international policy focus on climate change, green growth and sustainability in general, it argues for strengthening and widening policy research in the areas of Environmental Education (EE), Education for Sustainable Development and Climate Change Education. It especially makes a case for two kinds of research on EE policy: (1) a multi-sited approach to empirical documentation and theory development which explores the relationships between international policy agreements and local practice, and (2) an interactive policy-engaged approach to research.

Introduction

This essay is the concluding piece of a review symposium that elaborates on the themes of the IALEI-project on 'Climate Change and Sustainable Development: The Response of Education' (this volume). It examines the relationship between research and policy and, more specifically, how we, as scholars of Environmental Education (EE), Education for Sustainable Development (ESD) and Climate Change Education (CCE) might relate to the policy processes in the field. As such, it does not aim to present and document an empirical study, but rather to offer methodological reflections that, hopefully, might inspire future policy research on EE, ESD and CCE.

We do this by first outlining the ongoing gradual change in societal knowledge production and examining how this challenges the role of the researcher. We then suggest two ways forward for policy research related to EE/ESD/CCE. The first of these is a documentary type of policy research that emphasizes coordinated, explorative, sociocultural studies. These are not conducted independently from theory development, but provide an opportunity to link theory with historical–contextual or cross-contextual practices. The second way forward is an action-oriented and engaged type of policy research. Action research is not new in educational research, but it is more unusual as an approach to policy studies, particularly on the international level. Furthermore, action research is conducted in many different ways. What we propose is 'interactive research' – a version of action research that entails some risks but also has the potential to bring together empirical research, theory development and policy development. We do not claim that these two modes of research are the only 'right' ways to do policy research in those areas; instead, we argue that they are important ways to strengthen and extend the scope of such research.

Research in transition

The increasing market orientation of modern universities has raised a number of important questions about both the fundamental role of researchers and the aims of research in the contemporary world, and these questions deserve a great deal of reflection. Most academic researchers are committed to the standards, interests and rhythms of academic research, both because we positively identify with them and because we are measured according to those standards. Yet, researchers as a group are increasingly obliged, implicitly and explicitly, to adapt our work to the standards, interests and time frames of other agents, not least in the field of policy. This reflects a wider change in our societies and the ways they produce knowledge. For instance, universities and their research staff less frequently work as independent knowledge-producing units, and are increasingly linked up with governments, private sector entities and other stakeholders in networks that co-produce knowledge (Gibbons 1999; Nowotny, Scott, and Gibbons 2001; Hård and Jamison 2005).

We can respond to this change in many ways, but we should not ignore it. At present, the dominant scientific ideal about value-free knowledge production leads many scholars to abstain from deriving normative statements and policy prescriptions directly from their research results – though this is often expected, even demanded, by policy-makers. There is considerable political pressure on researchers to come up with useful answers, not least in relation to conflicts over environmental issues, sustainable development and climate change (Beck 1986; Lash et al. 1996; Nowotny et al. 2001). Even though the majority of this pressure is focused on techno-scientific innovations, the intertwined fields of ESD, EE and CCE are inseparable from this larger policy concern. As lack of progress in addressing climate change, especially due to sociocultural factors that oppose or counteract policy regulations, becomes more obvious over time, the role of education is likely to receive increased attention from policy-makers.

Requests for scholarly input into policy development take place at the international level as well as at national and local levels. Sustainability is a global issue as well as a local one; the challenge of climate change, in particular, will require a global policy response. In recent years, this has resulted in increased calls for scholars to participate in international empirical studies, evaluations and projects focused on the development of recommendations and guidance for many levels of policy development. The IALEI project, in which we took part, was just one example of this (Feinstein et al. this issue). A number of other, comparable studies have also focused on the Decade for ESD (Wals 2009; Gross and Nakayama 2010; Tilbury 2011; Wals 2012). A recent but important addition to the international picture is the global network of Regional Centres of Expertise (RCE), initiated by United Nations University with the purpose of establishing structures for cooperation between researchers and other stakeholders on ESD. The question that we now face is how such a mingling of UN-organizations with other international, as well as national, stakeholders may influence the development of EE/ESD research and policy.

In the coming years, activities associated with the end of the Decade for ESD, as well as new initiatives on CCE and greening of Technical, Vocational Education and Training might offer a unique opportunity to influence educational policy and practice in ways that extend far beyond climate change. As researchers, should we reject the invitation to participate in the construction of these (often narrow) policy agendas, or should we accept it and use it as an opportunity to try to expand the dialogue between researchers and policy-makers? Although we are sympathetic to those who defend the fundamental autonomy of academic research and criticize the often overly simplistic calls for 'evidence-based research', we believe that it is neither possible nor desirable to return to the classical model of autonomous university-based knowledge production. For us, it is rather a question of *how* to participate as scholars without compromising our own ideals for research and perhaps even to gain valuable theoretical insight from this interaction.

The key challenge relates to a methodological concern about how best to negotiate our relationships to the subject(s) of our research. How involved or detached should we be? In the social sciences more generally, detachment has often been emphasized in order to produce 'valid' results, yet we, as persons and researchers of human and social affairs, are already implicated in the subject we are studying (Østerberg 1971). Scholars in the field of EE are normally interested not only in creating descriptive accounts or theoretical contributions, but also, in many cases, fostering critical engagement and social change. We do not mean to suggest that there are partisan political agendas hidden in the ambitions of EE researchers, but it is hard to deny that many of us have a political orientation of some kind, and that this orientation can be difficult to separate from the scholarly discourse surrounding EE/ESD/CCE policy.

There are two traditional responses to the tension created by the demand for research-based policy, the need for objectivity and balance in research, and our own political orientations. One is to emphasize our independence by assuming a position on the sidelines of the policy process, from which current policy efforts can be described and criticized. The other is to plunge into the policy process, attempting to influence it using research-based knowledge and understandings. According to the Norwegian sociologist Thomas Mathiesen, however, both these strategies for social change are at risk of failure (Mathiesen 1982). The first strategy is at risk because radical criticism from the sideline can easily be excluded from the policy agenda if it is seen as invalid and of no relevance. The second strategy is at risk because direct involvement in the policy process can result in the distortion of research methods and perspectives to fit within the dominant policy discourses and structures.

As a potential way forward, Mathiesen suggests addressing these concerns by alternating between critical detachment and constructive involvement. Similarly, Jamison identifies the same exclusion and incorporation traps in relation to environmentalism and suggests coping with these by developing hybrid research strategies that transcend the affirmative position of green business as well as the residual opposing position of many environmental NGOs (Jamison 2001). Our discussion here aims to find ways forward for EE/ESD/CCE policy research that are neither (exclusively) critically detached nor naively involved. As will become clear, we also seek to dissolve the troubling dichotomy between an analytical approach towards theory development and an empirically-focused approach which meets the demands of policy stakeholders.

Roles of research and the need for documentation

Attempting to categorize research into particular types and roles will always, to some degree, discount the complexity of existing approaches and practices (Strokes 1997). However, such categories can still be useful as a way of highlighting differences within a field. They also enable researchers to evaluate their fields. Numerous authors have proposed taxonomies of education policy research. For example, Cibulka borrowed a venerable distinction from the natural sciences and argued that most policy research was either 'basic' or 'applied' (Cibulka 1994). The Danish sociologist Heine Andersen refined this dichotomy, dividing social research into the descriptive, explanatory, critical and change-oriented (Andersen 1994). In Andersen's system, these types of research are related in that descriptive research is a premise for explanatory research, which in turn feeds into critical research, and all three are necessary for change-oriented research. We argue that policy research in the intertwined fields of EE/ESD/CCE can potentially be described and conducted in all these ways. Yet, research is not simply influenced by a researcher's own knowledge, interests and methodological commitments: it is also shaped by wider societal expectations and the conditions in which the research takes place. The distinction between basic (descriptive and/or explanatory) or applied (critical and/or change oriented) research is therefore too simplistic and problematic a way to conceptualize the relationships between research and society.

Biesta has argued for a potentially more helpful distinction between the roles of research in society or, we might put it, ways of applying social research in society (Biesta 2009). The first is *the cultural role*, which is characterized by researchers' contributions to the formulation of concepts and theories that critically challenge existing discourses and practices and constructively open up discussions about more or less radical change. The other is *the technical role*, which is manifestly instrumental, with researchers describing what one should do in order to achieve a particular result or outcome. This distinction makes good sense in terms of EE/ESD/CCE research, which can contribute to societies by either delivering academically critical and innovative discussions (e.g. on the conceptualisations of ESD and CCE) or by making more direct contributions to policy and practice. Yet, we warn against making this dichotomy too rigid. Instead, we believe that it is important to support the development of a dialectic exchange between theoretical reflections and empirical insights.

To establish such a relationship, it is crucial to foster what we call the *documentary role* of policy research – to encourage research that documents what is actually going on in different contexts and on different levels, including international, national and regional policy, as well as local practice. This documentary role should not, as we will explain, be seen as something independent from the cultural role, but rather as something that complements and qualifies it. Before we explore this documentary role further, it is important to stress that we are not advancing an empiricist rejection of theoretical analyses related to EE/ESD/CCE. Such analyses remain important, especially in the early stages of a global programme like the UN Decade of ESD (2005–2014) (e.g. Blum et al. this volume). They enable researchers and policy-makers to use clearer and more specific language when discussing policy – in short, to understand what we are saying to each other. For example, Ferreira examined the use and meanings of the phrase 'education for' in both research and policy literature (Ferreira 2009). Furthermore, theoretical analyses can reveal hidden assumptions that may underlie policy discourse. For example, Sauvé (1999) examined how the language of 'sustainable development' perpetuates a capitalist ideology of education, in which people are treated as the accumulators of capital or as capital themselves. Expanding on this analysis, Barraza, Duque-Aristazábal, and Rebolledo (2003) argued that 'sustainable development' programmes can be used as a tool to impose the political will of wealthier countries in the global North on less economically prosperous countries in the global South. This type of analysis shows how policies may subtly reinforce certain institutions and ideational systems, and can help us anticipate (and perhaps avoid) the perverse, inequitable consequences of particular policy regimes.

Although valuable, analyses that focus only on the ideological roots or discourse properties of policy can be overly narrow in their scope and audience. According to Lall (2007) and Levinson and Sutton (2001), educational policy studies, as a field, has steadily moved from a singular focus on the role of the state towards exploration of more complex governance processes. At the same time, the field has shifted away from a narrow conception of policies as coherent power structures and towards the more generative idea of policies as complex social practices, constructed through discursive struggles and compromises that are open for multiple interpretations and transformations on their way to influencing practice (ibid). Bowe, Ball, and Gold (1992) emphasize that policy research needs to explore the histories and ideologies of policy actors – those who are both the targets and the interpreters of policies – as well as other sociocultural dynamics that influence how these actors cope with policy inputs. Bernstein identified the same phenomenon, which he framed in terms of *recontextualizations* taking place in the different steps from political ideas to practise (Bernstein 1996). Studies in this vein might well be inspired by Ball's identification of five contexts in which policy is made: the context of influence, the context of policy text production, the context of practice, the context of outcomes and the context of political strategy (Ball 1994).

The impression we got from our work as contributing authors on the IALEI cross-national study was that the intertwined fields of EE, ESD and CCE need more empirical research that explores the policy–practice interface by examining the struggles, negotiations, constructions and recontextualizations through which policy informs educational practices (Feinstein, Læssøe, Blum, and Chambers, this issue). It came as a surprise that researchers in the 10 countries had done relatively little to document and analyse how ESD and CCE policy is interpreted and transformed into practice. As the authors of the Canadian national report observed:

> There is a paucity of research on how ESD, CCE or EE policy is being implemented, and its impact on schools and classrooms. Reports that do exist come from government bodies and other organizations active in the area. These self-reports tend to be uncritical catalogues that focus on successes, and are silent about problems and failures. (Nazir, Pedretti, Wallace, Montemurro, and Inwood 2009)

In light of this, we feel there is an urgent need for more EE/ ESD/ CCE policy research that not only focuses on policy discourses but also engages with the full range of the policy cycle. Such research would lead to a broader awareness and deeper understanding of national and international decision-making processes, as well as the observable outcomes and effects of EE-related policies.

In the case of international EE/ESD/CCE policy development, there are only a few existing examples of empirical-based EE and ESD policy research which have contributed to our understanding of the policy-making process and of the influence of international agreements on practices in different contexts. In 1997, for instance, Annette Gough published a study exploring and analysing the policy processes and statements developed at UNESCO conferences and meetings (Gough 1997). Similarly, Bob Stevenson addressed the issue of a gap between political rhetoric around EE and educational practices. He noted this gap as early as 1987, and in 2007, he edited a special issue of EER where, with reference to a number of national analyses, he identified a number of factors that contribute to the persistence of this gap (Stevenson 2007a, 2007b).

Regarding ESD in particular, UNESCO has initiated a number of reports – in which researchers have taken part in the analysis of the collected data material – that aimed to describe progress and ongoing work during the decade for ESD (Wals 2009; Gross and Nakayama 2010; Tilbury 2011; Wals 2012). The IALEI project, conducted together with scholars from 10 countries, was an independent attempt to draw lessons from national studies of ESD policy and practice.[1] However, as in the UNESCO-initiated studies, we were forced to confront a lack of research on these processes at the national level. This might very well be due to a lack of funding for ESD research (Wals 2009, 60; Tilbury 2011, 106), but we also suspect that some researchers have reservations about cooperating with policy institutions on the empirical documentation of the implementation of ESD.

Our own experience suggests that working effectively within the technical–instrumental perspective of such policy institutions can be challenging but it also provides opportunities to encourage those institutions to support other types of empirical work. In studying ESD with an interest in contributing to the ongoing policy development, we believe it is particularly fruitful for policy-engaged researchers to focus on the stakeholders who influenced an ESD-related policy over time, and the manner in which the resulting policy affected a range of educational practices. Although less attentive to broad issues of discourse and ideology, this type of policy research is more attentive to the specific prescriptions and requirements in a policy document. It is also more likely to focus on the concrete processes of policy formulation and implementation, such as who attended particular meetings, supported particular platforms and implemented particular programmes. For example, Nomura and Abe (2009) described how the ESD movement in Japan emerged from a unique set of political relationships between government, private industry and prominent non-profit groups. Kwan and Lidstone (1998) took a similar approach to EE policy implementation in China, illustrating how centrally crafted policies were transformed by local and regional authorities. Like ideology-critical or discursive analytical research, this type of analysis reveals how the interests of different social groups remain embedded in the policies they produce. It goes further, though, illustrating how abstract theories of governance play out in a unique policy case, how policies succeed or fail in their explicit aims, and how one unique case may inform our perspective on others. In doing this, it might also relate to ongoing policy implementation by revealing a discrepancy between policy and practice or by highlighting the domains of educational practice ignored by a particular policy, thereby demonstrating the need for new policy action (Nolet 2009).

One interesting methodological approach that is compatible with these goals is George Marcus' multi-sited ethnography (Marcus 1998) in which researchers collect data by following a topic or problem through geographically or socially distinct field sites. The contrast between sites enables researchers to explore a variety of perspectives related to a specific idea, action or process. Multi-site ethnography can be used to explore transnational processes, groups of people in motion, and ideas that extend over multiple locations. It therefore has real potential to facilitate the study and documentation of the effects of international agreements on ESD and CCE around the world. It could also be applied at the national or regional level to investigate the movements of policy through different contexts and stages and into educational practice.

In our opinion, the most challenging aspect of a multi-sited approach is that it can easily become resource-intensive, bringing it into in conflict with the practical requirements of the policy processes which those who apply it might aim to influence. Although clearly related to practice, this approach is also often still thought of as being relatively detached from other agents involved in the area, including educational institutions, NGOs, private companies and policy-makers. In this way, it may not address the changing relationship between research and society that was our point of departure for this essay – an issue that we focus on in the next section.

Engaged and interactive policy research

The sociologists of science Maurice Gibbons and Helga Nowotny have described a gradual move away from the classical university and discipline-based knowledge production, called mode 1 research, towards a problem-oriented, interdisciplinary type of knowledge production, conducted in networks of agents, of which university researchers only are one type (Gibbons 1999; Nowotny et al. 2001). Although one of us (Feinstein) has, in another venue, criticized the work of Gibbons and Nowotny as lacking empirical substantiation (Kleinman, Feinstein, and Downey 2012), we all agree that the idea of mode 2 research poses important questions for the field of EE. In some respects, mode 2 research resembles an action research methodology, which is well known in the EE research community (Bradbury-Huang and Long 2012). However, action research in general is typically applied in studies of local practices, and is not typically used as an approach to policy research (Clausen 2011) or to international studies. Action research entails a number of risks and challenges – for instance, the potential for research agendas to be overwhelmed by the interests and perspectives of other agents than the researchers – which may also be a challenge within engaged and interactive policy research. However, we believe that it is worth considering what potential a perspective similar to that of action research offers for EE/ESD/CCE policy research.

We propose that more researchers should engage in what we call engaged and interactive policy research. The word 'engaged' signals the similarity of this approach to action research, while the word 'interactive' is drawn from the Nielsen and Svensson's taxonomy of action research (Nielsen and Svensson 2006). In interactive research, the research project is considered a joint venture where the researchers conduct research through interaction with the practitioners on issues that address both the knowledge and interests of everyone involved. As with action research, research into the full policy cycle requires involvement in a range of policy practices and close relationships between researchers and the different agents involved in the policy process; as such, it will inevitably reflect some of the messiness, awkwardness and imperfection of those relationships and practices. Yet, while action research is typically oriented towards local and concrete problems, we envision a form of policy-engaged research that could be applied to strategic EE/ESD/CCE policy issues at the national and international levels.

As with action research, finding the right balance between involvement and scholarly distance is critical for scholars practising engaged and interactive policy research. Nielsen and Svensson (ibid.) note that researchers conducting interactive research are not the practitioners themselves and neither are they responsible partners in the practitioners' practices. Certainly, it is important for researchers to take a 'critical stance' in their research, which might include being sceptical about the goals and projects of established political institutions. Yet, engaging with policy worlds may offer researchers the unique opportunity to develop transformational understandings that are needed to improve them. By taking this stance, engaged and interactive policy research violates the 'critical outsider' norm that permeates many areas of research. It becomes involved in the sense that it often takes particular institutions or agents as its starting point, and may implicitly, at least for a while, accept the nature and authority of the institutions or agency that it analyses. However, this engaged approach does not exclude the possibility of criticism. The position of the interactive researcher is the position of 'the critical friend' (Læssøe 2010). An EE policy researcher doing engaged and interactive policy research should be 'a friend' of relevant stakeholders by using research expertise to address particular situations and challenges, *but should also* reserve the right question the actions and discourses of the same stakeholders based on professional expertise and emerging evidence from the research project in question. As in private life, a true friend is not always the individual who uncritically agrees with you, but rather the one who is also able to challenge you in ways that are based on deep knowledge about you and your situation.

Engaged and interactive policy research is obviously not designed for development of theory at a universal level. First and foremost, it embraces more *situated* theory, relevant to a particular set of institutions or constrained by a particular problem frame (e.g. civic engagement, eco-regional conservation, etc.). Such theories are what the sociologist Robert Merton called middle-range theories, 'intermediate to the minor working hypotheses evolved in abundance during the day-by-day routine of research, and the all-inclusive speculations comprising a master conceptual scheme' (Merton 1957, 5). Compared to the very philosophical, abstract and principle-focused theoretical contributions which often characterize academic research, engaged and interactive policy research has the potential to provide theoretical contributions on this middle-range level by addressing issues in certain contexts and historical epochs. Engaged and interactive policy research may in this way be able to identify phenomena, dynamics and innovative trends of more general relevance to wider fields of research.

In the IALEI project, we found a number of examples of formalized as well as ad hoc collaborations between EE/ESD researchers and policy-makers. In Australia, researchers from the Australian Research Institute in Education for Sustainability are actively involved in both the design and implementation of nationwide EE policy. Korean and Danish researchers have also made direct contributions to the EE and ESD policies in their respective countries, while in the UK, researchers have worked alongside non-governmental organizations and policy-makers to explore the breadth and quality of ESD and EE policy and provision (Læssøe et al. 2009). At the global scale, the United Nations University network of RCE might, if sufficiently resourced and connected to influential policy networks, develop into an important organizational structure for periodic dialogues between ESD and CCE researchers, practitioners and policy-makers. As such, the RCE network could catalyze engaged, critical-innovative and documentary research of the sort that usefully informs both policy and practice.

Moving forward – engagement with research and policy

As researchers, we are also citizens and thus ourselves part of the field we study. Although normativity can be a sensitive issue, we would argue that most EE researchers in one way or another hope that their research will contribute to a better world. The repeated involvement of researchers in dialogue with policy stakeholders has the potential to enhance the relevance of research to policy, making it more difficult for policy-makers to exclude researchers as purely idealistic or ideological agents. We agree that this involvement in policy-making is risky. However, this risk can be somewhat mitigated if researchers are able to remain reflective about their relationships and positioning. In our own experience, for instance, it is possible for an engaged researcher to introduce historical and conceptual insights into dialogue with other agents about particular policy initiatives. By doing this, researchers can open the policy-making process to a wider set of reflections. This might, for example, prove useful in the emerging international discussions around CCE. The engaged policy researcher might also use his or her professional position to serve as mediator between agents from different sectors, institutions and/or levels. At its best, this kind of research has the potential to support a more democratic, less top-down approach to policy-making.

Establishing a new emphasis on engaged and interactive policy research does not eliminate the ongoing need for the more exclusively cultural and documentary types of policy research described earlier. On the contrary, these types of research may together act to prevent research from being restricted to the knowledge horizons and agendas of policy agents. Furthermore, engaged and interactive policy researchers themselves can offer more than simply support for concrete problem-solving. Contrary to many action researchers, who often regard their role as focused on facilitating local/context-bound knowledge production, engaged and interactive policy research also aims to contribute to the development of concepts and theories of a more general value to research. It is our hope that engaged and interactive policy researchers will be ideally positioned to support and energize other threads of policy research, bringing new insights back to the academic theoretical discussions (the cultural role), and catalyzing documentary research by providing researchers with insights into practice. In terms of EE, ESD and CCE, international research has primarily been focused on exploring and critiquing ideologies and principles. Engaged and interactive policy research could supplement this by researching questions such as: How are these principles transformed as they migrate from conceptual discussions into the development of concrete strategies, actions plans and initiatives? What can we learn from the similarities, differences and connections among different national policies? How does the construction of ESD policy vary from place to place? By researching such questions, engaged and inter-active policy research could offer important insights and theoretical contributions for those seeking to understand the interplay of local and national forces or the culturally contextualized framing.

Another potential advantage of engaged and interactive policy research might be to better catch up with the turning historical wheel and offer theoretical contributions that go beyond critical 'post festum' theories (Negt 1977) and abstract utopian speculation to become what the German philosopher Ernst Bloch has called *concrete utopian*, in that they identify 'the possible-but-not-yet-realised' (Bloch 1995). While a detached academic policy researcher is in a relatively weak position to do this, the potential to achieve it is much greater when policy researchers work in close interaction with other agents, take on a documentary role and apply their deep theoretical knowledge.

Note

1. See the introduction to this review symposium for more information on the IALEI project. The reports are available at http://www.edusud.dk.

References

Andersen, H. 1994. *Videnskabsteori og Metodelære* [Theory of Science and Methodology]. Copenhagen: Samfundslitteratur.
Ball, S. 1994. *Education Reform*. Buckingham: OUP.
Barraza, L., A. Duqué-Aristazábal, and G. Rebolledo. 2003. "Environmental Education: From Policy to Practice." *Environmental Education Research* 9 (3): 347–357.
Beck, U. 1986. *Risikogesellschaft – Auf dem Weg in eine andere Moderne* [Risk Society: Towards a New Modernity]. Suhrkamp Verlag: Frankfurt am Main.
Bernstein, B. 1996. *Pedagogy, Symbolic Control and Identity*. London: Taylor & Francis.

Biesta, G. 2009. Educational Research, Democracy and TLRP. Methodological Development, Future Challenges. London: TLRP.

Bloch, E. 1995. *The Principle of Hope*, Vol. 3. Cambridge, MA: MIT Press.

Bowe, R., S. Ball, and A. Gold. 1992. *Reforming Education and Changing Schools: Case Studies in Policy Sociology*. London: Routledge.

Bradbury-Huang, H., and K. Long (2012). "Action Research and Environmental Education: Conceptual Congruencies and the Imperatives of Context and Participation." In *International Handbook of Research on Environmental Education*, edited by R. B. Stevenson, M. Broady, J. Dillon and A.E.J. Wals, 459–468. New York, NY: Routledge.

Cibulka, J. 1994. "Policy Analysis and the Study of the Politics of Education." *Journal of Education Policy* 9:105–125.

Clausen, L. T. 2011. "At Gribe Muligheden for Forandring." PhD diss., Institut for Miljø, Samfund og Rumlig forandring, Roskilde University, Roskilde.

Ferreira, J.-A. 2009. "Unsettling Orthodoxies: Education for the Environment/for Sustainability." *Environmental Education Research* 15 (5): 607–620.

Gibbons, M. 1999. "Science's New Social Contract with Society." *Nature* 402 (C81): 11–17.

Gough, A. 1997. *Education and Environment: Policy, Trends and the Problems of Marginalization*. Melbourne: Australian Council for Educational Research.

Gross, D., and S. Nakayama. 2010. "Barriers and Deficits with Implementing ESD." 2000–2009. Report, 16. http://www.desd.sustain-future.org/Survey%20on%20UNESCO's %20Action%20Goals.pdf

Hård, M., and A. Jamison. 2005. *Hubris and Hybrids*. New York, NY: Routledge.

Hulme, M. 2009. *Why We Disagree about Climate Change*. Cambridge: Cambridge University Press.

Jamison, A. 2001. *The Making of Green Knowledge. Environmental Politics and Cultural Transformation*. New York, NY: Cambridge University Press.

Kleinman, D. L., N. W. Feinstein, and G. Downey. 2012. "Beyond Commercialization: Science, Higher Education, and the Culture of Neoliberalism." *Science and Education*. Published online. http://link.springer.com/article110.1007/s11191-012-9482-4.

Lash, S., and B. Szerszynski, et al., eds. 1996. *Risk, Environment & Modernity*. London: Sage.

Kwan, T., and J. Lidstone. 1998. "Understanding Environmental Education in the People's Republic of China: A National Policy, Locally Interpreted." *Environmental Education Research* 4 (1): 87–97.

Lall, M. 2007. *A Review of Concepts from Policy Studies Relevant for the Analysis of EFA in Developing Countries*. Brighton: Institute of Education – University of London.

Levinson, B., and M. Sutton. 2001. "Introduction: Policy as Practice." In *Policy as Practice: Towards a Comparative Sociocultural Analysis of Educational Policy*, edited by M. Sutton and B. Levinson. Santa Barbara, CA: Praeger.

Læssøe, J. 2010. "Education for Sustainable Development, Participation and Socio-cultural Change." *Environmental Education Research* 16 (1): 39–57.

Læssøe, J., and K. Schnack, et al., eds. 2009. *Climate Change and Sustainable Development: The Response from Education*. Copenhagen: Cross-National Report, International Alliance of Leading Education Institute.

Marcus, G. E. 1998. *Ethnography through Thick & Thin*. Princeton New Jersey: Princeton University Press.

Mathiesen, T. 1982. *Makt og motmakt* [Power and Counter Power]. Pax: Oslo.

Merton, R. 1957. *Social Theory and Social Structure*. New York, NY: Free Press.

Nielsen, K. A., and L. Svensson, eds. 2006. *Action and Interactive Research – beyond practice and theory*. Maastrict: Shaker Publishing.

Nazir, J., E. Pedretti, J. Wallace, D. Montemurro, and H. Inwood. 2009. *Climate Change and Sustainable Development: The Response from Education. The Canadian Perspective*. Centre for Science, Mathematics and Technology Education, Ontario Institute for Studies in Education, University of Toronto.

Negt, O. 1977. *Overvejelser til en kritisk læsning af Marx og Engels* [Reflections to a critical reading of Marx and Engels]. Kongerslev og Grenå, GMT.

Nolet, V. 2009. "Preparing Sustainably-Literate Teachers." *Teachers College Record* 111 (2): 409–442.

Nomura, K., and O. Abe. 2009. "The Education for Sustainable Development Movement in Japan: A Political Perspective." *Environmental Education Research* 15 (4): 483–496.

Nowotny, H., and P. Scott and M. Gibbons. 2001. Re-thinking Science. Knowledge and the Public in an Age of Uncertainty. Oxford: Polity Press.

Østerberg, D. 1971. *Meta-sosiologisk essay* [Meta-Sociological Essay]. Oslo: Universitetsforlaget.

Sauvé, L. 1999. "Environmental Education: Between Modernity and Postmodernity – Searching for an Integrating Educational Framework." *Canadian Journal of Environmental Education* 4: 9–35.

Stevenson, R. B. 2007a. "Editorial (Special issue: Revisiting Schooling and Environmental Education: Contradictions in Purpose and Practice)." *Environmental Education Research* 13 (2): 129–138.

Stevenson, R. B. 2007b. "Schooling and environmental/sustainability education: From discourses of policy and practice to discourses of professional learning." *Environmental Education Research* 13 (2): 265–285.

Strokes, D. 1997. *Pasteur's Quadrant: Basic Science and Technological Innovation.* Washinton, DC: The Brookings Institution.

Tilbury, D. 2011. *Education for Sustainable Development. An Expert Review of Processes and Learning.* Paris: UNESCO.

Wals, A. E .J. 2009. *Review of Contexts and Structures for Education for Sustainable Development.* Paris: UNESCO.

Wals, A. E. J. 2012. *Shaping the Education for Tomorrow – 2012 Full-length Report on the UN Decade of Education for Sustainable Development.* Paris: UNESCO.

Taking stock of the UN Decade of education for sustainable development: the policy-making process in Flanders

Katrien Van Poeck, Joke Vandenabeele and Hans Bruyninckx

In this paper, we address the implementation of the UN Decade of Education for Sustainable Development (ESD) in Flanders, a sub-national entity of Belgium. Our analysis shows how the policy-making process in Flanders is inextricably intertwined with three developments in environmental and educational policy: the increasing impact of ESD policy and discourse on environmental education, the framing of social and political problems as learning problems, and ecological modernisation. These trends give shape to a post-ecologist and post-political policy regime and, thus, affect what is possible and acceptable within Flemish ESD policy. However, this case study also revealed that these developments do not completely determine ESD policy-making in Flanders. Our examination thus allowed us to understand how the actual policy translation in a particular local setting brings about powers that legitimise and maintain as well as counteract the bounds of the policy regime that emerged in the context of the UN Decade.

The United Nations designated the period 2005–2014 as the Decade of Education for Sustainable Development (DESD). As this Decade comes to an end, the time has come to take stock of the actual policy translations and implementation processes it has brought about. In this paper, we aim to contribute to documenting the outcomes of the DESD with an empirical analysis of the policy-making process on education for sustainable development (ESD) in Flanders, a sub-national entity of the Belgian federal state. In academic literature, the concept of ESD and its desirability as a new leitmotiv for environmental education (EE) has been the subject of an extensive debate (see below). However, this lively discussion is characterised by a mainly 'non-empirical' approach 'dealing largely with theory or conceptual matters through literature review, discussion and/or commentary with no particular reference to the gathering or processing of empirical data' (Reid and Scott 2006, 582). Empirical studies analysing actual policy processes and outcomes (e.g. Huckle 2009; Nomura and Abe 2009) remain rare while political research on EE and ESD is vitally impor- tant so as to nourish this discussion by unsettling orthodoxies. Researchers, Ferreira (2009) argues, should therefore illustrate the battle between competing discourses and raise questions about taken-for-granted assumptions in ESD policy-making and about how these influence thoughts and practices in the field.

Hence, the aim of this article is to contribute to the empirical underpinning of the debate about EE and ESD with a case study of ESD policy-making in Flanders. In the next section, we analyse Flemish ESD policy so as to document the implementation of the DESD in this particular case. For this analysis, we have been inspired by the Policy Arrangements Approach (Arts, Leroy, and van Tatenhove 2006), an analytical framework that seeks a balance between examining strategic actions of the actors involved in a policy process on the one hand and taking into account overall social and political changes on the other. Thus, we document Flemish ESD policy-making in terms of the actors involved, the resources that are mobilised, the rules of the game as well as the discourses regulating policy practice on ESD and, subsequently, we relate this day-to-day policy-making process to three broader social and political developments that have been extensively described in literature: the aforementioned growing influence of ESD policy and discourse on EE, the tendency to frame social and political problems as learning problems, and ecological modernisation. The literature on these developments incited us to be attentive for the implications of these tendencies that have been addressed by several authors. As we will argue, these developments contribute to a post-ecologist and post-political policy regime with regard to ESD which governs to a certain extent that which is (im-) possible to think and to do in ESD policy and practice. By bringing this forward, drawing on the insights and considerations emerging from our case study, we want to illuminate orthodoxies in EE and ESD but also show how, at particular moments, something else does become possible and raise questions about some taken-for-granted assumptions within this regime. Thus, we aim at contributing to a more critical and in depth understanding of the DESD and to inspire researchers in other contexts to undertake similar inquiries.

ESD-policy in Flanders

Flanders is a sub-national entity of Belgium. The Belgian federal state (at the national level) consists of six sub-national entities: three communities (the Flemish Community, the French Community and German-speaking Community) and three regions (the Flemish Region, the Brussels-Capital Region and the Walloon Region). In Belgium, ESD is an authority distributed to the sub-national level. This article focuses on the sub-national entity of Flanders which consists of the Flemish Community and the Flemish Region. The Flemish authorities consist of the Flemish Parliament, the Government of Flanders and the Flemish administration. The last is subdivided into 13 policy areas, each composed of a department (responsible for the preparation and evaluation of the policy and regulations) and several agencies (implementing the policy). Flanders is a densely populated region with 6,300,000 inhabitants (466/km²) (Flemish Government 2012a). As to the available income, the region ranks among the top three of the best performing EU countries. The income of 10% of the Flemings does not exceed the poverty line. In 2007, the Global Footprint Network (2013) determined the footprint of an average Belgian at eight global hectares[1] which is significantly higher than that of an average world citizen (2.7) and also of the average inhabitants of neighbouring countries France (5.0), Germany (5.1), The Netherlands (6.2) and the UK (4.9). Several 'sustainability indicators' monitored by the Flemish government reveal a 'critical situation', particularly those with regard to energy, climate change, transport and biodiversity.

For this case study, we strived for triangulation of qualitative data sources (Patton 2002) and therefore gathered an empirical basis for our analysis by means of an in-depth interview, a postal survey, and an extensive document analysis. As interviewing all the relevant actors involved would have been unfeasible within the available time, we decided to interview a policy advisor responsible for the implementation of the DESD in Flanders who can be considered a key respondent with regard to Flemish ESD policy-making. It can reasonably be assumed that this policy advisor is the best qualified respondent so as to obtain up-to-date, first-hand information about the policy-making process and its output. We complemented the data derived from this interview by surveying the members of the 'ESD consultation platform' (see below). A postal survey with open questions has been answered by 15 respondents and the diversity of these respondents represents the variety of the actors involved. Further-more, we analysed 23 international and 36 Flemish policy documents. We imported the verbatim transcription of the audio-recorded interview, the answers to the survey questionnaire as well as the policy documents into the qualitative analysis software QSR NVivo. 'Sensitising concepts' (Patton 2002, 278) – built upon both the dimen-sions we aim to describe (actors, resources, rules of the game and discourses/policy programmes) and the three developments we want to take into account – guided our analysis and were the first nodes used for coding. As the analysis advanced, these sensitising concepts were complemented, refined, adjusted, etc. according to insights arising from the data.

A point of particular interest, methodologically, is the fact that the researcher who conducted the analysis had formerly been a civil servant involved in the imple-mentation of the DESD through facilitating networking within the ESD consultation platform as well as capacity building concerning ESD for EE practitioners. This position enabled an increased access to information as well as a thorough acquain-tanceship with the field. On the other hand, it should be acknowledged that, because of this 'double role', involvement with the subject of research can be regarded above average. We took these considerations seriously and made every effort to carefully consider and control the balance between distance and involvement with the subject of our analysis. We started the data collection in the field (the interview and survey – see below) as well as data analysis only after the researcher had quit being a civil servant and worked for the university with a PhD scholarship. Furthermore, we emphasised this independent position in the communication with the people under study and assured them that all the data would be treated anonymously.

The actors involved

As we will show, ESD policy in Flanders is a two-track policy strongly guided by international institutions and developments but also embedded in the Flemish overall sustainable development policy. At the high-level meeting of Environment and Edu-cation Ministries in Vilnius in 2005, Flanders committed itself to the implementation of the Strategy for ESD developed by the United Nations Economic Commission for Europe (UNECE). This Strategy stressed the importance of shared responsibili-ties, cooperation and participation of relevant stakeholders (UNECE 2005). UNESCO, designated by the UN General Assembly as the leading agency of the DESD, also emphasised in its International Implementation Scheme the importance of alliances and partnerships between relevant actors within governments (sub-national, national, regional and international) as well as in civil society and the private sector (UNESCO 2005).

As the in-depth interview, postal survey and policy documents show, this emphasis put on multi-level and multi-actor cooperation also characterised the Flemish ESD policy-making. The importance of cooperation and broad participation has repeatedly been underlined by all actors involved and was implemented by the establishment of an 'ESD consultation platform' (VLOR and Minaraad 2007; Verheyen 2009; Flemish Government 2009a). This platform was created in response to UNECE's appeal to install a coordination mechanism for the ESD Strategy in order to stimulate implementation, information exchange and partnerships. It was composed of representatives of diverse public administrations on different levels including ministers' political advisors and non-state actors such as NGOs, unions, institutes for higher education, school systems within compulsory education and strategic advisory councils. The platform was given a mandate by the Government of Flanders to coordinate the implementation of the DESD, to contribute to its implementation by formulating advisory opinions as well as to foster multi-actor, multi-level and multi-sector collaboration. In response to our survey, the actors involved described their contribution to ESD policy-making and the role they take in the platform on different domains. Public servants regularly mentioned their contribution to the preparation and implementation of ESD policy. Non-state actors often referred to the task of following up ESD policy, trying to influence it, representing their organisation or sector, and contributing to the implementation by applying ESD in concrete practices.

> I voice the stand of my organisation at the diverse consultative bodies. Within my organisation I transfer the information of the consultative bodies to those colleagues that coach the schools. Internally, I try to put ESD on the agenda of our coaching and training units. Up till now with limited results. Sometimes, I directly communicate with schools, e.g. so as to announce didactic tools, trainings. (a staff member of a school system)

Seven respondents explicitly expressed appreciation of the consultation and cooperation within this platform. They particularly valued the opportunities it brought about for a dialogue on how the different partners involved understand ESD, which was experienced as an inducement to applying the concept in practices.

> ESD policy in Flanders enabled me to further develop my perception of ESD. The administration paid a lot of attention to consultation and that allowed me to compare my own view with that of others. (a NGO staff member)

> The ESD consultation platform stimulated me and my organisation to take steps in translating ESD in our daily practices. Up till now, ESD is a very theoretical concept that is difficult to apply. Thanks to the exchange, we are able to further develop ESD in our own organisation as well as for other organisations. (a NGO staff member)

The document analysis as well as the survey revealed repeated and sometimes severe criticism as to the assumed lack of commitment to ESD on the part of the Government. Several participants particularly questioned the lack of resources provided for the implementation of ESD. We will go into this matter later on. Furthermore, they expressed scepticism concerning the commitment of all relevant administrations such as the departments of Education, of Culture and of Economy (e.g. Flemish Government 2008a, 2008b; Minaraad 2009). The interviewee explained that the Environment, Nature and Energy Department – specifically the EE Unit – was the driving force behind the Flemish ESD policy through establishing, financing and coordinating the ESD consultation platform and that, on the level of public administration, implementation always occurred in cooperation with the Department of Education and Training. The document analysis, interview and the answers to our survey questionnaire also showed a persistent concern about other actors that were not or insufficiently involved in the Flemish ESD policy. Discussions in the ESD platform, advices by strategic advisory councils, and remarks of the respondents reflected discontent regarding the limited involvement of ESD practitioners and the overrepresentation of actors in the field of formal education and people with an EE background. There has been insisted on enhancing the engagement of actors in the field of non-formal learning and on bringing in more stakeholders from outside the EE sector. Particularly the involvement of partners from business circles and industrial sector umbrella organisations has been under discussion.

> Seeking alliances with the business world has been debated in the platform. Maybe we should reinforce the attempts to get those actors involved. Yet, we never reached agreement about that. It remained unclear how to succeed in it. Moreover, some people in the platform were all for it while others were rather sceptical. (a civil servant)

In the course of the policy process, there has been an evolution in the participation of stakeholders. The interviewee explained that new actors, for instance from the field of higher education and the cultural sector, got involved appealed by concrete initiatives while others, such as the department of Economics, Science and Innovation as well as ministers' political advisors quit participation. The policy advisor assumed that ESD has never been more than a side issue for them and got more and more pushed into the background as they found that the initiatives taken by the platform did not fit within their overall assignment. All the same, he explained, the bonds between maintaining participants were strengthened: stable relationships of trust have arisen, actors 'genuinely committed' to ESD were distinguished, and the people involved learned to know each other better so that it became clear whose expertise can be applied for what ends, which collaborations are possible for which objectives, etc. The evolving participation of the actors involved in the platform went together with a more or less conscious strategy of the EE Unit to move beyond the formal procedures and channels in their attempts to implement the ESD policy objectives in Flanders as those formal structures have proven to be difficult, inert and resistant (see below).

> The rather formal endeavour to implement ESD through official channels has been abandoned early on. We chose to invest in those opportunities where we saw that people were committed to ESD and willing to contribute to its implementation instead of continuing to try to embed ESD in formal structures where it might have had little opportunities. (a civil servant)

As such, in the course of time, a coalition arose of diverse actors trying to enhance and accelerate ESD policy and practices in Flanders. This coalition, gathered in the ESD consultation platform, strived for political validation of the

ESD implementation plan (see below) as well as for providing the resources required to realise this plan. On the occasion of the election of the Flemish Parliament in 2009, for example, the president of the platform sent a memorandum to the relevant political actors in order to bring to their attention these concerns of the ESD consultation platform (Verheyen 2009). Members of the Strategic Advisory Council for Environment, Nature and Energy Policy who were also involved in the ESD consultation platform strengthened this coalition by writing advices for the Flemish Government and ministers that reflected concerns, opinions and proposals introduced in the consultation platform (Minaraad 2007, 2008, 2009).

The rules of the game

In our description of the rules of the game influencing ESD policy-making in Flanders, it is important to distinguish between formal rules, laid down in laws and documents, and informal or de facto rules connected with certain policy cultures. Furthermore, rules can be formulated very rigorously as well as more broadly and they vary strongly concerning their degree of formality and compelling nature (Arts, van Tatenhove, and Leroy 2000). ESD policy in Flanders was influenced by a number of rules of the game that were formally established though characterised by a low degree of authority. There was no imperative law forcing the Flemish Government or the other actors involved to implement ESD policy goals. Nevertheless, there were a few declarations and agreements with a powerful moral authority that influenced ESD policy and practice in Flanders.

At the international level, the roots of ESD policy-making were shaped by the Rio Declaration and Agenda 21 (UNCED 1992) that considered learning to be indispensable for reaching sustainable development. The importance of ESD was later confirmed by the Johannesburg Plan of Implementation (2002), bringing about the installation of the DESD through resolution 57/254 of the United Nations General Assembly. Resolutions 58/219 and 59/237 offered additional support for the Decade. UNESCO's International Implementation Scheme (2005) and the UNECE Strategy for ESD (2005) made these appeals more concrete. In Flanders, the foundations of overall sustainable development policy are captured in the Belgian constitution in which sustainable development was included in 2007.

> During the exercise of their respective competences the federal state, the communities and the regions will pursue the goals of a sustainable development in its social, economic and environmental aspects, taking into account the solidarity between generations. (Belgian Constitution, art. 7bis 2007)

This affected Flemish policy-making: the application of the basic principles of sustainable development is now a constitutional obligation for the Government of Flanders. As a result, this Government adopted a regional decree on sustainable development in 2008 by means of which sustainable development obtained structural legal grounds. The decree aimed at ensuring the continuation of the Flemish sustainable development policy by obliging every newly formed Government to develop and adopt a 'Flemish Strategy for Sustainable Development'. As neither in the constitution, nor in the decree on sustainable development ESD is mentioned, there is no statutory obligation for an ESD policy in Flanders. Nevertheless, in both the first (Leterme 2006) and the second (Peeters 2010) Flemish Strategy for

Sustainable Development ESD has been given a prominent place. The policy goals were formulated formalistically rather than addressing specific content with regard to ESD, e.g. organising an ESD consultation platform, providing process coaching, integrating ESD in policy-, planning- and regulatory frameworks, installing an ESD coordination unit encompassing diverse policy areas, promoting ESD with financial policy instruments, stimulating ESD in formal education through final objectives and competence profiles, installing learning networks, etc. In 2009, the Government adopted the Flemish Implementation Plan concerning ESD 'Learning for a viable future' (Flemish Government 2009a). The Plan was developed on a participatory basis via the ESD consultation platform and aimed at associating the UNECE Strategy for ESD with the specific Flemish context and the actions put forward in it were the same as these in the ESD-project of the first Flemish Strategy for Sustainable Development.

Several Flemish ministers stated in their policy documents for the term 2009–2014 that they intended to realise the ESD Implementation Plan (Schauvliege 2009; Smet 2009; Peeters 2009a, 2009b). Yet, numerous respondents were very critical and concluded that the political commitment to ESD is largely limited to paying lip service to the objectives formulated in the plan since those objectives were insufficiently translated in tangible measures or the provision of the necessary resources (see also below).

> ESD policy is extensively developed on paper. Yet, the realisation in real terms is less obvious. [...] It remains unclear to what extent the implementation is monitored, followed-up and if necessary adjusted. Nevertheless, this is a necessary condition for a successful implementation of the plan. (a staff member of a school system)

The only imperative rule of the game concerning ESD is the introduction of new 'cross curricular final objectives' in secondary education in 2010. In Flanders, final objectives (cross curricular as well as subject specific) adopted by the Parliament determine which key competences pupils have to achieve through compulsory education. Since all Flemish schools have the obligation to prove their efforts regarding the realisation of these final objectives, this legislative measure was regarded an important incentive for the implementation of ESD in formal education. Sustainable development was given a prominent place in these revised cross-curricular final objectives through which the Flemish Parliament aimed to create 'a sort of safety net for valuable and socially relevant content that is inadequately addressed within the subject specific final objectives' (Flemish Government 2009c – our translation). The key competences with regard to sustainable development were described as follows:

The pupils

- participate in environmental policy and environmental performance at school;
- recognise the interrelatedness of economic, social an ecological aspects of sustainability issues and the effects of technology and policymaking;
- try to use space, resources, goods, energy and transport in a sustainable way;
- try to find sustainable solutions for the improvement of their local and global environment;
- show interest in and appreciation for nature, landscape and cultural inheritance; and
- experience the value of nature and enjoy it. (Flemish Government 2009c, 18 – our translation)

Mobilisation, division and deployment of resources

UNESCO and UNECE both emphasised that the provision of the necessary resources largely influences the success of the DESD.

> The IIS [International Implementation Plan] urges governments and other potential funding sources to assess the existing resources and needs related to ESD in their juris- dictions and to reallocate existing resources and find ways to create new resources. Even with linking existing programmes to ESD, a need for new resources exists. Addi- tional human resources and funding will be necessary to augment current resources. (UNESCO 2005, 24)

Pointing to these international statements, the need for sufficient human and financial resources has been stressed repeatedly throughout the Flemish policy process (Flemish Government 2005a; VLOR and Minaraad 2007; Verheyen 2009; Flemish Government 2009b; Flemish Government 2010a). The conclusion that to date very little new resources have been provided brought about explicit criticism within the ESD consultation platform (Flemish Government 2010a). Participants that responded to our survey, too, voiced such criticism:

> Governmental support and resources for ESD are very limited, in my opinion too limited. The activities and reports of the ESD consultation platform show great enthusi- asm, a lot of creativity and devotion from the Environmental Education Unit [...] as well as other participating public services and NGOs. It is obvious that a more substantial funding and support by the Government would enhance Flemish ESD policy. (a university professor)

As our document analysis showed (e.g. Flemish Government 2010a) and the interviewee explained, since the Government of Flanders did not allocate resources specifically to ESD policy, the implementation of ESD in Flanders so far depended largely on the redistribution of funds within the existing budgets of several departments. Tangible policy measures were thus the result of the commitment of actors within public administration rather than the outcome of deliberate political decision-making. Initially, the actions put forward in the Flemish ESD Implementa- tion Plan were for the most part financed with funding for EE. Later on, however, other collaborating partners started to contribute, they too falling back on the reallocation of existing means.

When taking stock of the realisation of the ESD Implementation Plan and the Flemish Strategies on Sustainable Development, the consultation platform concluded that the lack of significant resources disabled the realisation of several actions such as an ESD project fund and process coaching for ESD organisations and profession- als (Flemish Government 2010a). On the other hand, the actors involved indicated that being on a budget also stimulated collaboration and creativity as a result of the search for co-funding and that it opened up a space for experimentation because of the absence of top-down steering and management.

> Restricted resources created the situation in which there were no indicators, evaluation tools, and expectancies embedded in hierarchic structures. This would have been the case if the minister would genuinely be interested in ESD and set targets that we have to reach. This could possibly have influenced the policy process negatively rather than positively because things get managed then and people feel obliged to do something. Whereas now, we are all in the same boat, with little support and funding from the

Government. This fostered collaboration instead of competition. [...] Yet, now time has come to help the matter along with the necessary funding. (a civil servant)

The situation with regard to the deployment and division of personnel was very similar (Flemish Government 2005b) in that new recruitment for ESD failed to occur while the DESD brought about changes in the tasks and responsibilities of existing personnel (Flemish Government 2010b). In the EE Unit, two policy advisors were deployed to coordinate the ESD consultation platform and to study and foster ESD as an important trend in EE policy and practice (Flemish Government 2010a). In other policy areas (e.g. the Department of Education and Training, the Tourism Flanders Brussels Agency, the Flemish Department of Foreign Affairs, the Department of Culture, Youth, Sport and Media and the Agency for Socio-Cultural Work for Young People and Adults), staff members were not full-time seconded but spent time on the promotion, coordination and implementation of ESD in their policy area.

Policy discourses and programmes

With our analysis of policy discourses, we both focus on the actors' views and narratives about sustainable development, education and ESD and on the specific content of policy documents and measures (Arts, Leroy, and van Tatenhove 2006).

Through cooperating with diverse actors for concrete realisations such as workshops or publications, the members of the ESD consultation platform experienced that ESD is a 'difficult' concept, a flag that covers a diverse cargo: it is applied in various and very different fields. Therefore, a task force was set up so as to create a common conception of ESD (Flemish Government 2009b) resulting in the brochure 'ESD: Flag and Cargo' (2010c) that described ESD as

> [...] learning to think about and work towards a liveable world, now and in the future, for ourselves here and others elsewhere on the planet. The aim is therefore to equip individuals and groups with the skills they need to make conscious choices for such a liveable world. (Flemish Government 2010c, 4–5)

In order to achieve these aims, according to the brochure, ESD has to pay attention to a number of key principles: transferring new knowledge, encouraging systems thinking, aiming at value development, taking into account emotional aspects and being action-oriented. The interviewed policy advisor argued how this brochure has influenced ESD practices in Flanders. It has been issued on 3.000 copies and diverse actors referred to it in their own publications, mission statements and educational materials. In our survey, seven respondents indeed explained that this brochure influenced their understanding of ESD. Furthermore, in the answers to our question about how they conceptualised ESD elements regularly occurring were the assumption that ESD is a matter of information, awareness-raising and participation that should contribute to a change in attitude, mind-set and behaviour; that it should foster support for sustainability measures; that it should prepare people for their role in a sustainable world by developing the necessary competences; and that it should enable people to make proper choices.

> [ESD is] showing students the need for a transition, preparing them for the things to come, and letting them participate in this transition. (a university college lecturer)

> [ESD is] the development of competences that contribute to making sustainable choices, taking into account the impact now and in the future, for ourselves and for others, here and elsewhere. (a NGO staff member)

Whereas some respondents understood sustainable development as a balance between people, planet and profit, others strongly contested this view.

> [Sustainable development is] the sustainable use of resources, thinking about the future (long term) while developing new processes in all areas, cradle to cradle, seeking balances between the economy and the environment ... (a civil servant)

> What should certainly be avoided, is taking for granted the image of a balance between people, planet, and profit. In contrast with assumptions from the managerial point of view, those three aspects are not of equal value. That is why I prefer the image [...] representing the economy (profit) as an embedded sphere within society (people) that is in its turn embedded in the environment (planet). This image is very useful to clarify what sustainable development is really about. (a university college lecturer)

A related discussion that regularly arose in the policy-making process regarded the relation between EE and ESD (Flemish Government 2005a; Minaraad 2007; Cherretté 2009). Most stakeholders considered EE as just one subset of ESD, alongside, for example, health-, peace-, citizenship-, development-, human rights education. This broad variety of educational efforts, it was argued by the strategic advisory councils for education and for environment, nature and energy policy, should contribute to ESD, which, then, serves as a 'compass' for all forms of education by interpreting various contents within the sustainable development framework (VLOR and Minaraad 2007). On the other hand, it was emphasised that not the entirety of EE practice should be reoriented towards ESD. Basic nature education remains valuable. This view was also reflected in the brochure 'ESD: flag and cargo' and has been expressed by three respondents that participated in our survey. Furthermore, 11 respondents explained that the DESD has been a trigger for reflection on current (EE) practices. Three of them particularly mentioned their participation in the task force that wrote 'ESD: flag and cargo'. The interviewee, too, stressed that the DESD has brought about a time for reflection about day-to-day practices, not only about EE but also about education in general. This also fostered discussions about how to understand education.

> A [...] tension with regard to the conception of education, is the difference between those who think instrumentally, based on a strong sense of urgency, and plea for direct behavioural change as opposed to others who support a pedagogical, emancipatory perspective putting the learning process and personal development first rather than direct results. (a civil servant)

Since 'green economy' was put forward by the UNECE Steering Committee for the DESD as an important topic, it was a core subject of discussion within the ESD consultation platform (Flemish Government 2011, 2012b, 2012c). In a UNECE discussion paper, ESD and green economy – understood here as 'an economy where economic prosperity can go hand-in-hand with ecological sustainability' (UNECE 2011, 3) – were considered to be 'two sides of the same coin' (ibid. 2), that is, ESD was assumed to master the greening of the economy from the bottom up 'because it has the ability to equip people with the values, competences, knowledge and skills that are necessary for them to put the green economy concept into practice'. Thus, the emphasis was on fostering 'green skills', raising awareness ('sustainable thinking'), and promoting sustainable consumption and production.

During the meeting of the ESD consultation platform in October 2012 (Flemish Government 2012c) the participants were asked to report on their intentions with regard to 'green economy' as well as on how they view the role of the platform in this respect. As to the latter, the response was somewhat ambiguous. On the one hand, the platform was urged to take concrete initiatives (e.g. curricular reform) and mobilise relevant stakeholders (e.g. the Minister of Education and business partners). On the other hand, however, several participants argued that the concept of green economy remains unclear and ambiguous and emphasised the need for further study, training and information exchange as well as the importance of 'remaining critical', particularly with respect to how the notion of green economy is framed on the international level.

Discussion: the interaction of Flemish ESD policy-making with broader societal developments

We analysed Flemish ESD policy-making as to the actors involved, the resources that are mobilised, and the rules of the game as well as the discourses regulating policy practice on ESD. In the remainder of this article, we discuss how this day-to-day policy-making process is inextricably intertwined with three overall developments in environmental and educational policy-making that influence ESD policy and practice: the increasing impact of ESD policy and discourse on EE, the framing of social and political problems as learning problems, and ecological modernisation. In this section, we address this interaction drawing on our empirical analysis and connecting it to the academic discussion on these developments. Next, in the conclusions, we critically synthesise the insights emerging from this analysis by bringing to the fore how these three developments contribute to a post-ecologist and post-political perspective on EE and ESD.

The influence of ESD policy and discourse on EE

With the Brundtland Report the concept of 'sustainable development' was launched as a 'development that meets the needs of the present without compromising the ability of future generations to meet their own needs.' (WCED 1987, 43). Since then this notion increasingly influences EE (Tilbury 1995; Postma 2004). This evolution is in essence policy-driven (Jickling and Wals 2007; Nomura and Abe 2009) as it has been furthered by a succession of decisions made by international institutions. Agenda 21, the global action plan that arose from the United Nations Conference on Environment and Development (Earth Summit) in Rio de Janeiro in 1992 considered EE as an essential instrument for the realisation of a sustainable future and devoted a chapter on 'Promoting Education, Public Awareness and Training'. The UN Summit in Johannesburg in 2002 (Rio + 10) endorsed the importance of education in the pursuit of sustainability and incited for the establishment of the UN Decade of ESD which, eventually, has been announced on 20 December 2002 by the UN General Assembly. Our case study indeed revealed how the growing influence of ESD policy and discourse did not only bring about a reallocation of resources (funds and personnel) from EE to ESD but also implied that policy-making within the EE unit was increasingly influenced by strategies that were put forward by international institutions.

Yet, the observation that ESD is becoming more and more established in EE does not imply that the relation between both concepts is clear for everybody. Several authors have argued that the distinction between EE and ESD remains insufficiently clarified and that a multitude of different perspectives exists simultaneously (Reid and Scott 2006; Chapman 2007; Gadotti 2008; Mogensen and Schnack 2010). The efforts made in Flanders so as to develop a shared understanding of ESD (cf. the brochure 'ESD: flag and cargo') can be seen as an attempt to clarify this notion that is perceived as a 'difficult concept' and to increase understanding as to how it relates to EE and other educational fields. The strategic advisory councils for environment, nature and energy policy and for education also engaged in such a discussion that resulted in an image of ESD as 'a compass' for all forms of education.

Furthermore, opinions concerning the desirability of ESD as a new leitmotiv for EE are also sharply divided. Whereas policy-makers worldwide pay lip service to sustainable development and ESD enthusiastically, in research literature a persistent debate is going on between advocates and opponents of the concept of sustainable development in general as well as of the idea to replace EE by ESD. Critics consider sustainable development an ambiguous catch all term. While the concept conjoins profoundly contradictory meanings, its vagueness allows a reconciliation of the most conflicting ideologies (e.g. Dobson 1996; Gunder 2006; Jickling and Wals 2007; Räthzel and Uzzell 2009). Sustainable development is thus the subject of a continuous, more or less explicit struggle over divergent interpretations which, critics argue, has been settled in favour of neoliberal economic thought and its concomitant political ideals which serve as an impediment for fundamental social change (Huckle 1999; Gunder 2006; Jickling and Wals 2007; Gadotti 2008). We observed how this struggle was also felt in Flemish ESD policy-making as it was reflected in the discussion about the conception of sustainability as a balance between people, planet and profit.

Thus, since this problematic notion of sustainable development turned up in the context of EE, it brought about contestation as to the desirability to complement or replace EE with ESD. We found how diverse actors in Flanders emphasised the value of 'basic nature education' and stressed that not the entire EE sector should be reoriented towards ESD. In the scholarly debate, advocates of ESD consider it an indispensable contribution to the pursuit of sustainable development (e.g. McKeown and Hopkins 2007; Paden and Chhokar 2007; Bajaj and Chiu 2009; Hopkins 2009), while opponents regard this stance as an undue instrumental approach to education, reducing it to merely an instrument to promote a specific, predetermined kind of 'sustainable' behaviour (e.g. Jickling 1994; Sauvé 1999; Scott 2002; Jickling and Wals 2007; Breiting 2009; Östman 2010; Lundegård and Wickman 2012). They argue that this brings about homogenising effects – all the more problematic because of the ambiguity that characterises the notion of sustainability – and reduces the space for autonomous decision-making. Therefore, they emphasise that EE and ESD demand a 'pluralistic' approach to education, one that acknowledges, stimulates and engages a variety of values, interests and knowledge claims. Although the plea for such a pluralistic approach is broadly supported by EE and ESD scholars, at the same time the concern is raised that pluralistic educational practices might be inadequate to address urgent sustainability problems (e.g. Læssøe 2007; Wals 2010;

Kopnina 2012). As the policy advisor we have interviewed indicated, a similar discussion between 'those who think instrumentally' and 'others who support a pedagogical, emancipatory perspective' emerged in Flanders as well.

Furthermore, the scholarly debate about EE and ESD elaborately addresses gaps between discourse and practice. Some authors argue that, because of the focus on ESD, the merits of EE's long tradition, that is, a body of literature and several (international) Declarations, is overlooked so that valuable ideas and experiences fall into oblivion and time is wasted on the 're-invention of the wheel' (Palmer 1998; Berryman 1999; Sauvé 1999; Chapman 2007; Gadotti 2008). ESD advocates acknowledge these merits, yet they raise objections to dominant practices of EE that are failing to realise the ambitious principles and purposes put forward in the discourse on it (González-Gaudiano 1999; Gough and Scott 1999; Smyth 1999). The DESD, it is argued, then provides the opportunity for a 'fresh start' (Huckle 1999). Opponents, however, doubt that the discourse on ESD will ensure 'desirable' practices. A similar gap between discourse and practice can emerge here as well (Sauvé 1999; Sauvé and Berryman 2005; Selby 2006; Mogensen and Schnack 2010). In Flanders, the interviewed policy advisor as well as several respondents to our survey indicated that the DESD served as 'a trigger for reflection' on current (EE) practices.

The framing of social and political problems as learning problems

An undeniable development within overall educational policy – but also educational theory and practice – is the tendency to frame social and political problems as 'learning problems' (Biesta 2004; Simons and Masschelein 2006, 2009). During the twentieth century, the role of education within society changed as national governments started to think of themselves as being responsible for governing the relation between education and society (Simons and Masschelein 2006). This relation has been conceived in different ways. For instance, education has been understood as a prerequisite in the pursuit of social transformation (e.g. reducing social inequality) but also as a necessary instrument for the conservation of particular social and cultural values and, thus, to secure the stability of society. Despite such ideological differences, Simons and Masschelein highlight the shared horizon for this governmental concern with the role of education in society: the assumption that governments have to intervene in education in view of social (and related cultural or economic) concerns. In other words, learning emerges as a solution for numerous problems and learning policy and experts in education are deployed to resolve social problems. Individual learners should acquire the 'proper' knowledge, insights, skills and attitudes. They have to 'learn' to adapt their behaviour to what is considered desirable and make themselves competent to deal with the given challenges. This tendency is part of a broader process of individualisation in contemporary society where the responsibility for social problems is increasingly reserved for individual people (Finger and Asùn 2001). Drawing on the insights of Michel Foucault, Simons and Masschelein (2006, 414) elaborate how the 'governmentalisation of learning' is closely linked to the individualisation and de-socialisation of problems as in the current governmental regime individuals are addressed as 'subjects that are situated in an environment which [they] have to adapt proactively and creatively in order to satisfy [their] needs – that is, a regime in which [they] are (interpellated to be) entrepreneurial selves'. Learning, thus, is increasingly understood as a condition for individual autonomy and people are addressed as being responsible for (regulating) their own learning.

This tendency to translate 'societal problems' into 'educational solutions' (Simons and Masschelein 2006, 395) pre-eminently applies to ecological issues and sustainable development. Ever since the relationship between people and their natural environment has been conceived as problematic, appeals have been made to education (Postma 2004). Since the beginning of the twentieth century, there is a field of educational theory and practice developing from nature education over conservation education and EE toward ESD (Tilbury 1995; Palmer 1998; Postma 2004). Within this historical development, at least one thing remained constant: education has predominantly been conceived as an instrument to tackle the evolving social and political challenges concerning the environment. In confrontation with changing ecological problems such as urban children's increased alienation of nature, problems of nature conservation, the environmental crisis and issues of (under)development educational policy and reform are designed to change people's behaviour, attitude and mentality in a particular, preconceived way.

In our case study, ecological and sustainability issues predominantly emerged as matters of individual learning, and the aims of EE and ESD were almost exclusively defined in terms of individual dispositions. This was strongly reflected in the only imperative rule of the game on ESD in Flanders, that is, the revised final objectives that translated sustainability in a set of 'key competences' individual pupils should achieve. Furthermore, the way ESD was defined in 'ESD: flag and cargo' as a process of 'equipping individuals and groups with the necessary skills to contribute to a liveable world', as well as the key principles put forward in this brochure and the conceptualisation of the relation between ESD and green economy also show how the social and political challenge of sustainability is easily translated in 'educational solutions' (e.g. the transfer of knowledge and values, green skills, competences such as systems thinking). The answers to our postal survey emphasising e.g. awareness-raising, behavioural adjustment and the need to prepare people for their role in a sustainable world by developing the necessary competences revealed the prevailing of a similar interpretation of ESD. An ecologically sound and sustainable society emerges thus as a challenge that can be met by applying the proper learning strategies and, thus, education becomes first and foremost a matter of socialisation, that is, the acquisition of particular knowledge, skills, competences or dispositions. EE and ESD are reduced to instruments to foster the values and principles of sustainable development, to promote corresponding behavioural changes, and to qualify people for the role of active participants that contribute to the democratic realisation of sustainable development (Ferreira 2009; Van Poeck and Vandenabeele 2012). As we already showed above, this tendency to frame sustainability as a learning problem is also addressed in the debate concerning the influence of ESD policy and discourse on EE as such an 'instrumental' approach to education is criticised by scholars as well as policy actors. A particular subject of discussion within the Flemish policy process was the taken-for-granted connection between a competence oriented understanding of ESD and the pursuit of a green economy.

Ecological modernisation

The framing of sustainable development as a learning problem is reinforced by a third development we want to address: the discourse of 'ecological modernisation' as the new dominant way of conceptualising environmental problems in the Western world that has emerged since the late 1970s as a result of a particular interplay between governments, environmental movements and key expert organisations (Hajer 1995). Here, too, the Brundtland Report is considered a milestone for the emergence of this discursive shift within different industrialised countries as well as in international organisations such as the UN, the OECD and the European Union (Hajer 1995; Mol and Spaargaren 2000). In line with Hajer (1995, 44), we understand 'discourse' as a 'specific ensemble of ideas, concepts and categorisations that are produced, reproduced and transformed in a particular set of practices and through which meaning is given to physical and social realities'. Acknowledging the consideration that (environmental) discourse is thus inevitably place and time specific as well as the need to differentiate between different sorts of ecological modernisation (Hajer 1995; Christoff 1996; Mol and Spaargaren 2000), we nevertheless want to depict the overall features of this discourse as these influence ESD policy-making in Flanders today.

Although within the discourse of ecological modernisation it is acknowledged that 'structural design faults' in the core institutions of modern society – i.e. the industrialised production system, the capitalist organisation of the economy and the centralised state – cause severe environmental destruction (Mol and Spaargaren 2000) it is all the same assumed that the existing political, economic and social institutions can *internalise* the care for the environment (Hajer 1995). Hence, a fundamental transformation of these societal structures does not appear here as a prerequisite for tackling this crisis. As such, ecological modernisation challenges the radical environmentalist critique of the 1970s that argued for a fundamental reorganisation of those institutions that are involved in the modern organisation of production and consumption. A key assumption is, thus, the possibility of reconciling economic growth, technological development and the solution of ecological problems. Within this discourse, the environmental challenge is regarded a management problem as well as a 'positive-sum-game': 'there would be no fundamental obstructions to an environmentally sound organisation of society, if only every individual, firm, or country, would participate' (Hajer 1995, 26). In Flanders, the influence of an ecological modernisation perspective can be found in the discourse about a green economy 'where economic prosperity can go hand-in-hand with ecological sustainability' as well as in the conception of sustainability as a balance between ecological, social and economic concerns. We also showed, however, that both discourses were the subject of discussion among the actors involved.

Hajer (1995) emphasises that although the political scientists who introduced the concept of ecological modernisation (Joseph Huber and Martin Jänicke) allocated a central role for technological innovation and economic development, the conceptual change actually stretches to many other domains (see also Mol and Spaargaren 2000) such as the techniques of environmental policy-making, the role of science and scientists, micro-economic and macro-economic strategies, the legislative discourse and finally, participatory practices. As to the last, ecological modernisation brought about a reconsideration of participation seeking to bring to an end the former sharp antagonistic debates between the state and the environmental movement by acknowledging new actors and creating new practices (e.g. active funding of NGOs, round table discussions). Læssøe (2007, 2010), too, highlights that ecological modernisation did not only put forward 'participation' as a new buzzword but also brought about a reconsideration, i.e. a narrowing of participatory practices.

His analysis of citizen participation in environmental issues in Denmark reveals an orientation towards consensus and the marginalisation of any conflicts or contestation concerning values, political ideology and the ever-present tension between private and collective interests. In our case study, such a reconsideration of participatory practices was reflected in the role of the ESD consultation platform (i.e. contributing to the implementation of policy), the way it was composed of a variety of actors collaborating as a coalition of ESD advocates, and the persistent criticism about the lack of involvement of 'all relevant stakeholders'. Yet, here too, contestation emerged as well, particularly as to the desirability to build alliances (and, thus, consensus) with partners from business circles.

Although this focus on consensus building is clearly a feature that sustainable development and ecological modernisation have in common, Langhelle (2000) highlights that both concepts should not be conflated. He argues that sustainable development attempts to address a number of issues about which ecological modernisation has nothing to say: global environmental problems, distributional problems, social justice (intragenerational as well as intergenerational), nature's carrying capacity, ecological limits and global ecological interdependence. As such, conceptualising 'education for ecological modernisation' might be very helpful to nurture the debate about EE and ESD that we addressed above. Theoretical as well as empirical research on how the discourse of ecological modernisation affects EE and ESD policy and practice could inform, for example, the discussions about whether or not ESD contributes to neoliberal globalisation and about the gap between discourse and practice of EE and ESD. It would move beyond the scope of the present article to go into this elaborately. Nevertheless, our case study revealed that although – as indicated above – the discourse of ecological modernisation influences Flemish ESD policy-making in some respects, the implementation of the DESD in Flanders cannot be reduced to the introduction or encouragements of education for ecological modernisation. We cannot maintain that all the aforementioned issues remain unaddressed. For instance, the emphasis put on the value of basic nature education – although the policy documents and respondents remain rather vague and superficial in this respect – reflects some kind of concern for ecological limits and the planet's carrying capacity. Furthermore, the issues of inter- and intragenerational justice is embedded in the brochure 'ESD: Flag and Cargo' that appeals for 'a liveable world, now and in the future, for ourselves here and others elsewhere on the planet'.

Conclusions

Our analysis of the Flemish policy practice shows how the increasing influence of ESD policy and discourse on EE, the framing of sustainability as a learning problem and ecological modernisation gave shape to the boundaries of a particular governmental regime. Drawing on Foucault's 'governmentality' perspective, Ferreira (2009, 612) argues that within such a regime 'a range of semi-normative prescriptions [...] work to include, exclude and govern what it is acceptable (possible) to think and what it is acceptable (possible) to do' (Ferreira 2009, 612). The policy-driven emphasis on ESD, for instance, tends to foster a consensual understanding of the ambiguous concept of sustainable development in favour of neoliberal economic and political thought thereby pushing into the background arguments for fundamental social change. The framing of sustainability as a learning problem reinforces individualisation and de-politicisation, whereby the responsibility for unsustainability is increasingly attributed to individuals. The discourse of ecological modernisation also marginalises appeals for fundamental transformations of societal institutions and reduces the space for conflict and contestation. Furthermore, its consensus orientation conceals genuine political issues regarding e.g. distributional problems, social justice or the question how to deal with non-negotiable ecological limits in an ecologically interdependent, globalised world. As such, that which is acceptable and possible to think and to do corresponds well both with what Blühdorn (2011, 2013) labels 'post-ecologism' and with the 'post-political' condition described by, among others, Swyngedouw (2007), Rancière (1999), and Mouffe (2005). Since the late 1980s, the post-ecologist turn that emerged in capitalist consumer democracies pushed the ecologist critique of 'the pathologies of modernity' into the background as well as the desire for and the vision of a funda-mentally different society in the economic, ecological, political, social and cultural sphere (Blühdorn 2013, 18–19). Within this context, the ecological issue has been thoroughly depoliticised (Blühdorn 2011). In this post-political era, the existing order is no longer disrupted and struggle and dissensus – indispensable ingredients in framing genuine political questions about ecological issues – are avoided.

The analysis we presented above shows how the three developments we addressed and the way they trickle-down in the international and Flemish ESD policy contribute to a governmental regime with post-ecologist and post-political boundaries. Nevertheless, our case study also shows that this regime does not com-pletely determine ESD policy-making in Flanders. We observed, for instance, that whereas stakeholders' role in the consultation platform has been set rather formalis-tically (representation, consultation and implementation of the DESD) participants themselves described it in terms of a valuable dialogue, where differences could sometimes be articulated and could work as a trigger for reflection on existing edu-cational practices and policy. The prevailing (competence-oriented) instrumental conception of education has been the subject of discussion as well as, for example, the connection between ESD and green economy and the need to build alliances with partners from business circles. Our analysis of the policy-making process with regard to ESD in Flanders within the context of those broader social and political developments allowed us to understand how policy settings bring about powers that legitimise and maintain as well as counteract the bounds of a particular governmental regime (Duyvendak and Uitermark 2005; Ferreira 2009).

Obviously, more empirical research is required so as to achieve a more comprehensive understanding of the DESD and the actual policy translations and implementation processes it has brought about. The need for further research can be situated at different levels of analysis: overall social and political developments (the three we addressed above can be further analysed and other significant tendencies might be identified), international policy-making, national and sub-national policy-making (in diverse geographical contexts), and practices in the field. Of particular importance so as to achieve a deeper understanding of the DESD are empirical case studies focusing on the *interaction* between social and political developments, pol-icy-making and educational practices. The present case study on ESD policy-making in Flanders is part of a broader doctoral research project in which we also studied very different educational practices: the Transition Towns movement, the project 'Environmental Performance at School' (Milieuzorg Op School), an EE centre, a Community Supported Agriculture initiative, a regional centre for action, culture and youth, a transition arena for a climate neutral city and an organisation that offers workshops to promote ecological behaviour change (Van Poeck 2013). These multiple case studies, too, show how social and political developments and the (international and Flemish) ESD policy-making contributes to the establishment of a particular regime which defines the contours of what is 'sayable', 'seeable', 'thinkable' and 'possible' (Simons and Masschelein, 2010, 512) in educational practices. It co-constructs what becomes (im)possible in concrete practices as well as how we can (or should) think and speak about these practices and here, too, this particular regime aligns well with the post-ecologist and post-political context described above. Our analysis revealed that the increased focus on ESD also influences the examined EE practices in that the consensual catch-all term 'sustainable development' reduces the space for contestation and controversy within these practices. Furthermore, we repeatedly observed how the prevailing discourse of ecological modernisation and its emphasis on 'collaboration' between 'allies' and on 'managing' ecological problems encourages practitioners to see the issues at stake and to think and speak about them in a post-ecologist and post-political way and to act accordingly. Finally, we found that the framing of sustainable development as a learning problem fostered an emphasis on socialisation and qualification within the examined EE practices. Yet, here too, the practices we studied were not fully determined by this regime and, at particular moments, something different emerged. For instance, we observed educators explicitly questioning the consensual account of sustainability implied in the Triple-P perspective (the balance between People, Planet and Profit). We witnessed practices where complex and contested sustainability issues and the often antagonistic values, interests and knowledge claims inherent in them were thoroughly explored and discussed. At such moments, educational practices did create a space for the enactment of controversy around the existing order, for the framing of political questions concerning how to understand and achieve sustainability, and for developing diverse visions about a fundamentally different society.

Masschelein and Simons (2003) emphasise that – although it might be tempting – a regime such as the one we described cannot be interpreted as a 'system' that can be changed (or, at least, that we can try to change) according to plan. Rather, it generates effects by *appealing* to people (i.c. ESD and EE policy-makers and practitioners but also participants) for a particular way of seeing, speaking, thinking and acting (i.c. in relation to sustainability issues and educational practices). With our research, we aim to describe and, thus, to show EE/ESD policy and practices sometimes legitimise and maintain but at particular moments also counteract the bounds of this regime. By bringing this forward in our descriptions we want to invite and inspire the reader to be attentive to different ways of seeing, speaking, thinking and acting. Such inquiries can contribute to what Ferreira (2009) calls 'unsettling the taken-for-granted' in EE and ESD, illuminating how certain orthodoxies have become 'normal' and 'obvious' all the same, how these orthodoxies assumes the possibility of infringement, and subversion (Duyvendak and Uitermark 2005; Ferreira 2009).

Acknowledgements

The authors thank the three anonymous reviewers of this paper for their valuable comments and very helpful suggestions.

Note

1. The world average bio-capacity, that is, the surface area of agricultural land, forest and fishing territory available, is 1.8 gha per capita.

References

Arts, B., P. Leroy, and J. P. M. van Tatenhove. 2006. "Political Modernisation and Policy Arrangements: A Framework for Understanding Environmental Policy Change." *Public Organization Review* 6 (2): 93–106.

Arts, B., J. P. M. van Tatenhove, and P. Leroy. 2000. "Policy Arrangements." In *Political Modernisation and the Environment. The Renewal of Environmental Policy Arrangements*, edited by J. P. M. van Tatenhove, B. Arts, and P. Leroy, 53–69. Dordrecht: Kluwer Academic.

Bajaj, M., and B. Chiu. 2009. "Education for Sustainable Development as Peace Education." *Peace & Change* 34 (4): 441–445.

Belgian Constitution. 2007. Amendments of April 25, art.7bis, Published in the Bulletin of Acts on April 26.

Berryman, T. 1999. "Relieving Modern Day Atlas of an Illusory Burden: Abandoning the Hypermodern Fantasy of an Education to Manage the Globe." *Canadian Journal of Environmental Education* 4 (1): 50–69.

Biesta, G. 2004. "Democracy – A Problem for Education or an Educational Problem?" In *Five Professors on Education and Democracy*, edited by T. Englund, 89–109. Örebro: Örebro University.

Blühdorn, I. 2011. "The Politics of Unsustainability: COP15." *Post-Ecologism, and the Ecological Paradox, Organization and Environment* 24 (1): 34–53.

Blühdorn, I. 2013. "The Governance of Unsustainability: Ecology and Democracy after the Post-democratic Turn." *Environmental Politics* 22 (1): 16–36.

Breiting, S. 2009. "Issues for Environmental Education and ESD Research Development: Looking Ahead from WEEC 2007 in Durban." *Environmental Education Research* 15 (2): 199–207.

Chapman, D. 2007. *Environmental Education/Education for Sustainability: What is the Difference?* [online] New Zealand Association for Environmental Education. Accessed 26 March, 2010. http://www.nzaee.org.nz/index.asp?pageID=2145880172.

Cherretté, M. 2009. *Visie – en beleidsnota Natuur – en Milieueducatie (2009–2014)* [Policy Plan and View on Environmental Education (2009–2014)], 1–9. Brussels: Flemish Government.

Christoff, P. 1996. "Ecological Modernisation. Ecological Modernities." *Environmental Politics* 5 (3): 476–500.

Dobson, A. 1996. "Environmental Sustainabilities: An Analysis and a Typology." *Environmental Politics* 5 (3): 401–428.

Duyvendak, J. W., and J. Uitermark. 2005. "De opbouwwerker als architect van de publieke sfeer [The Community Developer as an Architect of the Public Sphere]." *Beleid & Maatschappij* 32: 76–89.

Ferreira, J. 2009. "Unsettling Orthodoxies: Education for the Environment/for Sustainability." *Environmental Education Research* 15 (5): 607–620.

Finger, M., and J. M. Asún. 2001. *Adult Education at the Crossroads. Learning Our Way Out*. London: Zed Books.

Flemish Government. 2005a. *Verslag EDO-overlegplatform 9 juni 2005* [Report ESD Consultation Platform, June 9, 2005. Brussels: Flemish Government.

Flemish Government. 2005b. *Verslag EDO-overlegplatform 17 November 2005* [Report ESD Consultation Platform, November 17, 2005]. Brussels: Flemish Government.

Flemish Government. 2008a. *Verslag EDO-overlegplatform 17 April 2008* [Report ESD Consultation Platform, April 17, 2008]. Brussels: Flemish Government.

Flemish Government. 2008b. *Verslag EDO-overlegplatform 9 oktober 2008* [Report ESD Consultation Platform, October 9, 2008]. Brussels: Flemish Government.

Flemish Government. 2009a. *Leren voor een leefbare toekomst. Vlaams implementatieplan voor Educatie voor Duurzame Ontwikkeling* [Learning for a Viable Future. Flemish Implementation Plan for ESD]. Brussels: Flemish Government.

Flemish Government. 2009b. *Verslag EDO-overlegplatform 20 April 2009* [Report ESD Consultation Platform, April 20, 2009]. Brussels: Flemish Government.

Flemish Government. 2009c. *VOET@2010. Nieuwe vakoverschrijdende eindtermen voor het secundair onderwijs* [New Cross-curricular Final Objectives for Secundary Education]. Brussels: Flemish Government.

Flemish Government. 2010a. *Verslag EDO-overlegplatform 22 April 2010* [Report ESD Consultation Platform, April 22, 2010]. Brussels: Flemish Government.

Flemish Government. 2010b. *Rapport over de stand van zaken m.b.t. de implementatie van de UNECE Strategie voor Educatie voor Duurzame Ontwikkeling* [Report on the State of Affairs Concerning the Implementation of the UNECE Strategy for Education for Sustainable Development]. Brussels: Flemish Government.

Flemish Government. 2010c. *Education for Sustainable Development: Flag and Cargo*. Brussels: Flemish Government.

Flemish Government. 2011. *Verslag EDO-overlegplatform 22 juni 2011* [Report ESD Consultation Platform, June 22, 2011]. Brussels: Flemish Government.

Flemish Government. 2012a. *VRIND 2012 Vlaamse Regionale Indicatoren* [Flemish Regional Indicators 2012]. Brussels: Flemish Government.

Flemish Government. 2012b. *Verslag EDO-overlegplatform 16 April 2012* [Report ESD Consultation Platform, April 16, 2012]. Brussels: Flemish Government.

Flemish Government. 2012c. *Verslag EDO-overlegplatform 2 oktober 2012* [Report ESD Consultation Platform, October 2, 2012]. Brussels: Flemish Government.

Gadotti, M. 2008. "Education for Sustainability: A Critical Contribution to the Decade of Education for Sustainable Development." *Green Theory & Praxis: The Journal of Ecopedagogy* 4 (1): 15–64.

González-Gaudiano, É. 1999. "Environmental Education and Sustainable Consumption: The Case of Mexico." *Canadian Journal of Environmental Education* 4 (1): 176–192.

Gough, S., and W. Scott. 1999. "Education and Training for Sustainable Tourism: Problems, Possibilities and Cautious First Steps." *Canadian Journal of Environmental Education* 4 (1): 193–212.

Gunder, M. 2006. "Sustainability. Planning's Saving Grace or Road to Perdition?" *Journal of Planning Education and Research* 26 (2): 208–221.

Hajer, M. 1995. *The Politics of Environmental Discourse. Ecological Modernization and the Policy Process.* New York: Oxford University Press.

Hopkins, C. 2009. "Enough, for All, Forever: the Quest for a More Sustainable Future." *Education Canada* 49 (4): 42–46.

Huckle, J. 1999. "Locating Environmental Education Between Modern Capitalism and Postmodern Socialism: A Reply to Lucie Sauvé." *Canadian Journal of Environmental Education* 4 (1): 36–45.

Huckle, J. 2009. "Consulting the UK ESD Community on an ESD Indicator to Recommend to Government: An Insight into the Micro-politics of ESD." *Environmental Education Research* 15 (1): 1–15.

Jickling, B. 1994. "Why I Don't Want My Children to be Educated for Sustainable Development: Sustainable Belief." *Trumpeter* 11 (3): 2–8.

Jickling, B., and A. E. J. Wals. 2007. "Globalization and Environmental Education: Looking Beyond Sustainable Development." *Journal of Curriculum Studies* 40 (1): 1–21.

Kopnina, H. 2012. "Education for Sustainable Development (ESD): The Turnaway from 'Environment' in Environmental Education?" *Environmental Education Research* 18 (5): 699–717.

Læssøe, J. 2007. "Participation and Sustainable Development: The Post-ecologist Transformation of Citizen Involvement in Denmark." *Environmental Politics* 16 (2): 231–250.

Læssøe, J. 2010. "Education for Sustainable Development, Participation and Socio-cultural Change." *Environmental Education Research* 16 (2): 39–57.

Langhelle, O. 2000. "Why Ecological Modernisation and Sustainable Development Should not be Conflated." *Journal of Environmental Policy and Planning* 2 (4): 303–322.

Leterme, Y. 2006. *Samen grenzen ver-leggen. Vlaamse strategie duurzame ontwikkeling* [Backing Frontiers Together. Flemish Strategy for Sustainable Development]. Brussels: Flemish Government.

Lundegård, I., and P. O. Wickman. 2012. "It Takes Two to Tango: Studying How Students Constitute Political Subjects in Discourses on Sustainable Development." *Environmental Education Research* 18 (2): 153–169.

Masschelein, J., and M. Simons. 2003. *Globale immuniteit. Een kleine cartografie van de Europese ruimte voor onderwijs* [Global Immunity. A Small Cartography of the European Space for Education]. Leuven: Acco.

McKeown, R., and C. Hopkins. 2007. "Moving Beyond the EE and ESD Disciplinary Debate in Formal Education." *Journal of Education for Sustainable Development* 1 (1): 17–26.

Minaraad. 2007. *Advies van 22 maart 2007 over de organisatorische en beleidsmatige inschakeling en afstemming van natuur- en milieueducatie in de beleidsontwikkelingen rond EDO* [Advice of March 22, 2007 Concerning the Implementation of ESD in Environmental Education Policy]. Brussels: Minaraad.

Minaraad. 2008. *Advies van 8 April 2008 over het ontwerp van Vlaams implementatieplan voor Educatie voor Duurzame Ontwikkeling* [Advice of April 8, 2008 Concerning the Draft Flemish Implementation Plan on ESD]. Brussels: Minaraad.

Minaraad. 2009. *Advies van 10 september 2009 over de Vlaamse Strategie Duurzame Ontwikkeling: invulling operationele projecten* [Advice of September 10, 2009 Concerning the Flemish Strategy for Sustainable Development: organisation of the operational projects]. Brussels: Minaraad.

Mogensen, F., and K. Schnack. 2010. "The Action Competence Approach and the 'New' Discourses of Education for Sustainable Development, Competence and Quality Criteria." *Environmental Education Research* 16 (2): 59–74.

Mol, A. P. J., and G. Spaargaren. 2000. "Ecological Modernisation Theory in Debate: A Review." *Environmental Politics* 9 (1): 17–49.

Mouffe, C. 2005. *On the Political.* London: Routledge.

Nomura, K., and O. Abe. 2009. "The Education for Sustainable Development Movement in Japan: a Political Perspective." *Environmental Education Research* 15 (4): 483–496.

Östman, L. 2010. "Education for Sustainable Development and Normativity: A Transactional Analysis of Moral Meaning-making and Companion Meanings in Classroom Communication." *Environmental Education Research* 16 (1): 75–93.

Paden, M., and K. B. Chhokar. 2007. "Exploring Research Priorities for the DESD." *Journal of Education for Sustainable Development* 1 (1): 73–75.

Palmer, J. A. 1998. *Environmental Education in the 21st Century: Theory, Practice, Progress and Promise*. London: Routledge.

Patton, M. Q. 2002. *Qualitative Research & Evaluation Methods*. Thousand Oaks: Sage.

Peeters, K. 2009a. *Beleidsnota Algemeen Regeringsbeleid 2009–2014* [Policy Document General Government Policy 2009–2004]. Brussels: Flemish Government.

Peeters, K. 2009b. *Beleidsnota 2009–2014 Buitenlands beleid, Internationaal ondernemen en ontwikkelingssamenwerking* [Policy Document 2009–2014 Foreign Policy, International Enterprise and Development Cooperation]. Brussels: Flemish Government.

Peeters, K. 2010. *Samen grenzen ver-leggen. Vlaamse strategie duurzame ontwikkeling* [Backing Frontiers Together. Flemish Strategy for Sustainable Development]. Brussels: Flemish Government.

Postma, D. W. 2004. "Because We are Human. A Philosophical Inquiry into Discourses of Environmental Education from the Perspective of Sustainable Development and Man's Caring Responsibility." PhD diss., Katholieke Universiteit Leuven/Radboud Universiteit Nijmegen.

Rancière, J. 1999. *Dis-agreement. Politics and Philosophy*. Minneapolis, MN: University of Minnesota Press.

Räthzel, N., and D. Uzzell. 2009. "Transformative Environmental Education: A Collective Rehearsal for Reality." *Environmental Education Research* 15 (3): 263–277.

Reid, A., and W. Scott. 2006. "Researching Education and the Environment: Retrospect and Prospect." *Environmental Education Research* 12 (2/3): 571–587.

Sauvé, L. 1999. "Environmental Education Between Modernity an Postmodernity: Searching for an Integrating Educational Framework." *Canadian Journal of Environmental Education* 4 (1): 9–35.

Sauvé, L., and T. Berryman. 2005. "Challenging a 'Closing Circle': Alternative Research Agendas for the ESD Decade." *Applied Environmental Education and Communication* 4 (3): 229–232.

Schauvliege, J. 2009. *Beleidsnota Leefmilieu en Natuur 2009–2014* [Policy Document Environment and Nature 2009–2014]. Brussels: Flemish Government.

Scott, W. 2002. "Education and Sustainable Development: Challenges, Responsibilities, and Frames of Mind." *The Trumpeter* 18 (1): 1–12.

Selby, D. 2006. "The Firm and Shaky Ground of Education for Sustainable Development." *Journal of Geography in Higher Education* 30 (2): 351–365.

Simons, M., and J. Masschelein. 2006. "The Learning Society and Governmentality: An Introduction." *Educational Philosophy and Theory* 38 (4): 417–430.

Simons, M., and J. Masschelein. 2009. "The Public and Its University: Beyond Learning for Civic Employability." *European Educational Research Journal* 8 (2): 204–217.

Simons, M., and J. Masschelein. 2010. "Hatred of Democracy ... and of the Public Role of Education? Introduction to the Special Issue on Jacques Rancière." *Educational Philosophy and Theory* 42 (5–6): 509–522.

Smet, P. 2009. *Beleidsnota 2009–2014 Onderwijs: Samen grenzen verleggen voor elk talent* [Policy Document 2009–2014 Education: Backing Frontiers Together for Every Talent]. Brussels: Flemish Government.

Smyth, J. 1999. "Is There a Future for Education Consistent with Agenda 21?" *Canadian Journal of Environmental Education* 4 (1): 69–83.

Swyngedouw, E. 2007. "Impossible 'Sustainability' and the Post-political Condition." In *The Sustainable Development Paradox*, edited by R. Krueger and D. Gibbs, 13–40. New York: Guilford Press.

Tilbury, D. 1995. "Environmental Education for Sustainability: Defining the New Focus of Environmental Education in the 1990s." *Environmental Education Research* 1 (2): 195–212.

UNCED (United Nations Conference on Environment and Development). 1992. *Agenda 21, The United Nations Programme of Action from Rio*. New York: UN.

UNECE (United Nations Economic Commission for Europe). 2005. *UNECE Strategy for Education for Sustainable Development Adopted at the High-level Meeting of Environment and Education Ministries* (Vilnius, 17–18 March 2005). New York: UN.

UNECE (United Nations Economic Commission for Europe). 2011. *Discussion Paper on the Role of Education for Sustainable Development in Shifting to a Green Economy*. New York: UN.

UNESCO (United Nations Organization for Education, Science and Culture). 2005. *United Nations Decade of Education for Sustainable Development (2005–2014): International Implementation Scheme*. Paris: UNESCO.

Van Poeck, K. 2013. "Education as a Response to Sustainability Issues. Practices of Environmental Education in the Context of the United Nations Decade of Education for Sustainable Development." PhD diss., Katholieke Universiteit Leuven.

Van Poeck, K., and J. Vandenabeele. 2012. "Learning from Sustainable Development: Education in the Light of Public Issues." *Environmental Education Research* 18 (4): 541–552.

Verheyen, R. 2009. *Educatie als motor voor duurzame ontwikkeling in Vlaanderen. Memorandum van het EDO-overlegplatform naar aanleiding van de Vlaamse verkiezingen 2009* [Education as a Driving Force for Sustainable Development in Flanders. Memorandum of the ESD Consultation Platform on the Occasion of the Elections for the Flemish Parliament in 2009]. Brussels: ESD consultation platform.

VLOR and Minaraad. 2007. *Advies van 22 maart 2007 over educatie voor duurzame ontwikkeling in het leerplichtonderwijs* [Advice of March 22, 2007 Concerning Education for Sustainable Development in Compulsory Education]. Brussels: VLOR and Minaraad.

Wals, A. E. J. 2010. "Between Knowing What is Right and Knowing that it is Wrong to Tell Others What is Right: On Relativism, Uncertainty and Democracy in Environmental and Sustainability Education." *Environmental Education Research* 16 (1): 143–151.

WCED (World Commission on Environment and Development). 1987. *Our Common Future*. Oxford: Oxford University Press.

Globalisation and education for sustainable development: exploring the global in motion

Stefan L.Bengtsson and Leif O. Östman

The article explores education for sustainable development (ESD) as a policy concept in different spaces and how it is re-articulated as part of a process of globalisation. The objective is to explore empirically an alternative set of logics in order to conceive of this process of globalisation. With this objective in mind, the article investigates articulations of ESD and sustainable development in Vietnamese and Thai policy-making, and reflects upon how these articulations can be seen to relate to globalisation. In so doing, it addresses concerns about the globalising potential of ESD within the field of environmental education research, and aims to open up for an alternative understanding of the processes associated with the rearticulation of ESD in different national education policy settings. The alternative conception that is put forward promotes an understanding of these re-articulations of ESD as contingent, opening up a space for contestation and counter-hegemonic articulations.

Introduction

The overall ambition of this article is to explore a number of alternative conceptual logics for globalisation that place the phenomenon in the context of education for sustainable development (ESD) policy-making and research, and to see what alternate knowledge-producing capacities they entail.[1] With regard to the field of environmental education research, the article aims to explore empirically alternative means of conceiving of globalisation in the context of the discussion of ESD. Previous conceptions of the phenomenon of globalisation in environmental education research have in a number of instances appealed to logics of correspondence – in other words, a number of studies have aimed to uncover or implicitly appealed to a notion of essence of ESD. This logic of correspondence can be seen to be derived from critical social theory and to differentiate between different scales, spaces and hierarchies among them in order to provide universal reference points of historical development as an unfolding of a universal process of globalisation (Ferguson 2005; Giddens 1990; Hay 2005). According to this logic, the concrete articulation of ESD with its contextual specificity is corresponding to another overarching scale (the global) (e.g. Sauvé, Brunelle, and Berryman, 2005, 273f), where the determinate, universal aspects, that is to say the globalised aspects, of ESD are to be found. Especially with regard to issues of global power, studies within the field of environmental education research and beyond have drawn upon a notion of globalisation that feeds on a logic of determination in order to warn about the power of globalisation to homogenise the national and the local context (Jickling 2005; Jickling and Wals 2008; Sauvé, Brunelle, and Berryman 2005; Sumner 2005).

In order to empirically reflect on and feed into alternate conceptions of the relationship between ESD and globalisation, the exploration of the alternative conceptual logics in the fourth part of this article provides insights into globalisation as a process that is not a priori determined. These alternate logics have been provided by Buenfil-Burgos (2009) and are by the authors of this paper applied in the analysis of Vietnamese and Thai policy documents on ESD, education, socio-economic development and sustainable development (SD). The paper then reflects on which alternate understanding of globalisation these logics allow for by comparing these 'national' articulations in these documents with those in the 'global' United Nation's framework for the Decade of Education for Sustainable Development (DESD). These explorations aim to contribute to the field of environmental education research through empirically exploring logics that displace the logics of determination and correspondence with the logics of imbrication, displacement and apori in order to conceive of globalisation in the context of policy-making for ESD and SD. The aim is not to present any of the conceptual logics as best able to accurately capture the phenomenon of globalisation in the context of ESD policy development, but rather to empirically and conceptually develop further alternative entry points to the discussion of ESD as part of a global movement among different spaces, while incorporating its complexities and national variations (Gough 2009, 2013; González-Gaudiano 2005).

The alternative conceptual logics that are to be explored were provided by Buenfil-Burgos (2009) and have been earlier elaborated by the authors (Bengtsson and Östman 2013) in the context of ESD. However, before these logics are elaborated, the following section places them within the context of the ESD debate within environmental education research. The objective is to show that a specific set of logics, those of determination and correspondence, are by a number of scholars within environmental education research habitually appealed to in the conception of globalisation and how these habitual logics can be seen to share certain historical trajectories which frame how change, power and Being are conceived. The empirical section of this article explores the explanatory capacities of the alternate logics of globalisation as provided by Buenfil-Burgos (2009) by applying them to the context of Vietnamese and Thai policy-making as well as the DESD framework.

Conceptions of globalisation in the field of environmental education research

In the field of ESD and environmental education (EE), research dealing with the promotion of the DESD in various national contexts and criticism of the globalising potential of ESD has in a number of cases associated globalisation with the dispersion of neoliberalist ideologies (Jickling 2005; Jickling and Wals 2008; Sauvé, Brunelle, and Berryman 2005; Sumner 2005). These studies see ESD as contributing to globalisation as a form of homogenisation by providing prescriptive formulas that diminish the conceptual space for self-determination, alternative ways of thinking and autonomy. While the explication of the logics used to conceive of globalisation is often limited, arguments are often gathered from the broader globalisation debate. Sumner (2005, 2008) refers to 'corporate' globalisation, which incorporates structures and processes that increase the wealth of an elite group of people. Globalisation in these critiques of ESD is associated with ideology and economy (Jickling 2005; Jickling and Wals 2008; Sauvé, Brunelle, and Berryman 2005; Sumner 2008).

The logic of correspondence is by us interpreted to be constitutive for these conceptions of globalisation as the argument by which globalisation is conceived relies upon a logic that appeals to a point of correspondence and that this reference point is shared by a variety of national approaches to ESD. An example of this logic of correspondence can be found in the appeal to 'global trends' (Sauvé, Brunelle and Berryman 2005, 274) or 'ideological orientations' (Jickling 2005, 251). Correspondence translates in this conception into a form of universal reference points that guarantees comparability among different spaces or contexts. The logic of determination is by us seen to be constitutive for the conceptions and how they understand the changes that are associated with globalisation as process. The logic of determination is at work in two figures of reasoning in these conceptions. It is, on the one hand, involved in the relations of causality by which globalisation and exchanges between different spaces and scales are conceived. Appeals to causality are made in the form of appeals to 'influences', 'causes', 'consequences' (Sauvé, Brunelle and Berryman 2005, 273f), 'affects' (Jickling 2005, 251) and 'effects' (Sumner 2008, 91) in order to conceive of globalisation and its relation to environmental education. While some of these authors can be interpreted to soften these causal explanations of global exchanges by inserting the possibility of choice by different social actors at various levels and scales (Sauvé, Brunelle and Berryman 2005, 274), the logic of determination becomes especially prominent in appeals to 'power' (Jickling 2005, 251; Sumner 2008, 91). Sumner (2008, 91) exemplifies in her definition of power how causality and notions of power draw on a logic of determination where power is defined as: '"production of intended effects" (25). Institutional power, then is the production of intended effects by institutions'. Power is in this understanding associated with determinate effects, where the power of globalisation becomes a process of change that represents a realisation of a priori determined outcomes.

While the authors sympathise with the entailed warnings about neoliberalist capitalism's influences and effects on national education systems as put forward by these scholars and others (Hursh and Henderson 2011; Le Grange 2009; Lotz-Sisitka 2010; Payne 2010; Stevenson 2007), we believe it is important to complement the reasoning outlined above, since its constitution of globalisation limits the ability to highlight how the political moment, as appealed to by (Sauvé, Brunelle and Berryman 2005, 274), can emerge in the local and national context, as moments of decisions and conflicts of interest. This limit as we have argued elsewhere (Bengtsson and Östman 2013) can be seen to result out of an appeal to logics of determination and correspondence that see globalisation as an a priori determined phenomenon, that is to say that we already know that investment in or appeals to ESD will entail certain effects on education.

We see our efforts to compliment these warnings to be partially in line with conceptions of globalisation as they have been put forward by Gough (2009, 2013), as we are also drawing on Deleuze and Guattari's (1987) notion of rhizome in order to conceive on the complexities of the phenomenon and its contingency. In line with Gough (2013, 36), we (Bengtsson and Östman 2013; Bengtsson 2014) argue that globalisation can be associated with, both, homogenisation and heterogenisation. Hence, we interpret him to share our argument for not a priori confining the phenomenon to a necessary outcome, and to abandon appeals to causality and a logic of determination. Further, we readily share Gough's (2013, 40) commitment to Turnbull's (1997, 553) approach towards conceiving of global interactions as to referring to 'activities involved in producing knowledge in particular social spaces, that is on the contingent processes of making assemblages and linkages, of creating spaces in which knowledge is possible'. However, our approach can be seen to differ as it appeals to a notion of space as essentially overdetermined and fragmented (cf. Bengtsson 2014). As a result, we problematise the cohesiveness of spaces as product as well as the act of producing spaces. A conception of contested space that we belief to share with González-Gaudiano (2005). It is the impossibility of this cohesiveness, which we conceive of in terms of quasi-ontological antagonism (Laclau 1990; Laclau and Mouffe 1985), that we interpret to require practices of naming and knowledge production in the first places. For us, globalisation represents not an exchange *between* closed or cohesive systems – for example, knowledge systems (cf. Gough 2013) – but to be characterised by constant political struggle over meaning *within* and *among* particular spaces. Hence, it is with this outlook in mind that this article investigates how the articulation of ESD is characterised by differences in meaning-making, where we see these differences to not only characterise relations among spaces but see these constitutive differences to be characteristic for particular spaces.

In order to conceive of these differences and resulting social antagonisms within and among spaces, the article will engage in a comparison between actual policy-making on SD and ESD in Vietnam and Thailand. The focus of this empirical engagement and comparison will be on the political aspects of contestation of the meaning of SD and ESD within and among spaces.

Alternative logics of globalisation

As already mentioned, the authors (Bengtsson 2014; Bengtsson and Östman 2013) have already explored a constitutive perspective on globalisation by drawing on Laclau and Mouffe (1985) discourse analytical framework. In the following, the key characteristics of this constitutive perspective on globalisation are briefly summarised to highlight the logics drawn upon to frame globalisation. It is crucial to highlight that Laclau and Mouffe's discourse theoretical outlook does not try to look beyond the particular to identify regulating forces. They do not rely on a logic of correspondence, but instead focus on the particular practices by which order is established in meaning-making processes. For them, order is not a necessity caused by a singular-evolving process, that is to say they do not appeal to a notion of an unfolding of a universality. Instead, they see order, or 'hegemony', as a temporary result of action that builds upon the active exclusion of other possibilities. By depicting ESD as an empty signifier, González-Gaudiano (2005) was able to adumbrate how at the national space a certain policy concept, seemingly polysemic, can contribute to the establishment of hegemony. Buenfil-Burgos' (2000, 2009) conceptualisation of globalisation as connection, together with her formulation of the three logics of imbrication, displacement and aporia, provide conceptual and analytical entry points for conceiving of globalisation as a contingent and political process resulting out of a diversity of political practices in various spaces.

Buenfil-Burgos's logics of relationship and movement among spaces can be seen as informed by the conception of rhizomic globalisation. The rhizomic conception of territorial movement (cf. Deleuze and Guattari 1987) entails a mutual process of deterritorialisation – as imposition – and a process of reterritorialisation – as appropriation. For the purposes of the next section's exploration, this means that the introduction of the concept of ESD into a territoriality, as a process of deterritorialisation, is understood to be inseparable from the process of reterritorialisation as part of the articulation of the concept in the socio-historical context produced in a specific space. This conception of movement between different spaces entails a focus on the *changes in Being* that take place due to the processes of deterritorialisation and reterritorialisation.[2] Globalisation thereby becomes a contingent phenomenon.

The second part of the next section is aimed at empirically exploring this set of alternative logics of globalisation that have been provided by Buenfil-Burgos (2009) and to see how they allow us to conceive the political aspect of the articulation of ESD and SD in and among different spaces. These logics focus on the territorial movements that globalisation entails, where this movement is conceived through the logics of imbrication, displacement and aporia. In our exploration, these alternative logics are put into play to empirically engage with the circulation process of ESD in various contexts. According to Buenfil-Burgos (2009), the logic of imbrication denotes the territorial relationship of a systematic overlapping at the edges. This overlapping, e.g. of various national ESD policies, aims to portray how particularity and similarity can be conceived in the various national policies. It also aims to show how that which is compared is constituted by differences but at the same time seen as equivalent. As with hybridity, the logic of imbrication denotes something close to a status of indigenous foreigner (cf. Popkewitz 2005) and points towards a process of appropriation. This phenomenon of change as part of the movement between spaces is captured in the logic of displacement, which denotes a supplementarity (Derrida 1987) that is seen as a result of difference of Being in repetition or *re*-articulation in context. The authors interpret the logic of displacement, according to Buenfil-Burgos' definition, to suggest that every move of deterritorialisation or introduction of policy concepts such as ESD is inevitably repositioned, that is to say reterritorialised, in regard to the existent discursive formation of a particular signifying system, and that the policy concept thereby attains a hybrid character. The authors interpret Buenfil-Burgos' conception of aporia to underline the productive character of the tension and conflict that emerges in and among the articulations connecting different spaces. The incompatibility between the value systems that characterise different spaces can make a single meaning of, for example, ESD impossible, which in turn can create value conflicts. With regard to globalisation, therefore, aporia deals with the multiplicity and non-correspondence of Being as it is relative to a spaces and the potential-for-becoming in movements among spaces.

In the following section, the authors will be exploring these logics in order to conceive the global movement of ESD as policy concept in the context of how ESD is articulated in the DESD framework as well as in Vietnamese and Thai policies development for ESD and sustainable development.

Exploring the logics of globalisation

ESD as a process of becoming

In order to make the analyses of imbrication, displacement and aporia intelligible, it is important to specify how the authors analyse connections among different articulations. Connections can be seen to be remainders of territorial movements. They can be seen to exist, in both explicit and implicit forms in articulations within different spaces, that is to say articulations in different discursive formations. Explicit connections can take the shape of references to other articulations, e.g. references to other documents or oral statements within a particular articulation. However, implicit connections can also exist among articulations that do not reference to another. Such implicit connections can be seen to exist when a comparison between two and more articulations shows similarity of their patterns. Based on this conception of connection, it is possible to compare two instances of articulation of ESD as expressions of two different spaces.

In order to find an entry point for our exploration of the alternative logics of globalisation and to explore the implications of an understanding of globalisation as connection, we use a potential explicit connection in a Vietnamese ESD policy document with various other spaces. The Vietnamese *National Action Plan for ESD* (VNCDESD 2010, 3) states:

> As a member of the United Nations and UNESCO, Viet Nam has and will continue its active involvements in activities under the framework of the United Nations Decade of Education for Sustainable Development.

This statement articulates an explicit connection between the Vietnamese national action plan and the framework of the DESD as formulated in the forum of UNESCO. Key documents articulating this framework include the *Framework of the UNDESD International Implementation Scheme (FIIS)* (UNESCO 2006) and the *International Implementation Scheme* (IIS) (UNESCO 2005). If we interpret this reference to the framework as an explicit connection established through articulation in different spaces, it might be possible to reflect on the relation between the two spaces that has shaped these two articulations. This relation among spaces might be conceived in terms of powers of influence (logic of determination and correspondence), where the relation between two spaces might lead to homogenisation or heterogenisation depending on which spaces, or actors within that space, is associated with power. Indicators for one of these forms of influence might be established with regard to similarities and differences provided by a comparison between two chronologically divergent articulations of ESD. Chronologically divergent in this regard refers to two sequentially separated events, where event A might or might not have an impact on subsequent event B. As it is shown in this article the effects, or relationship, will differ depending on the focus of the comparison. A comparison shows that 12 of the 15 strategic themes (perspectives) stated in the strategic summary of the DESD framework (UNESCO 2006, 2) are also stated as central themes for ESD in the Vietnamese National Action Plan (VNCDESD 2010, 6), which articulates a total of 17 themes. Themes appearing in both include: rural development, sustainable urbanization, climate change, human rights, disaster prevention, gender equality and HIV/AIDS. Based on this comparison, it might be concluded that the DESD framework, articulated in the 'global space', to some extent determined the re-articulation of ESD in the Vietnamese National Action Plan. Additional significant equivalences are also found to exist between the articulation of objectives for the DESD in Vietnam (cf. UNESCO 2006, 26; VNCDESD 2010, 8ff) and in the DESD framework, e.g. awareness raising on SD-related issues, as well as means of implementation. Based on this equivalence, it might be concluded that the circulation of ESD within different national spaces as part of globalisation represents a universal phenomenon.

However, if the Vietnamese National Action Plan (VNCDESD 2010) as a whole is considered, not only with a focus on similarities or equivalences, the reader might become aware of significant differences in the articulation of the respective documents. These become especially apparent in the context of the role of ESD in a broader Vietnamese socio-economic development. For example, the Vietnamese National Action Plan (VNCDESD 2010, 5f) states that:

> In the first half of the Decade, education has increased the people's intelligence, trained manpower, and made active contributions to the cause of industrialization, modernization of the country, aiming at meeting the requirements of all-round growth of Viet Nam in the context of international integration and globalization. Besides, the first half of the Decade of Education for Sustainable Development has also seen major challenges to the role and quality of education. Although it has achieved lots of progresses, the education system is more of theoretical education, with slow renovation in educational contents and teaching methods being made.

While the FIIS of the DESD (UNESCO 2006) does not promote ESD as a means to international integration, industrialisation or modernisation, similarities between the above reference and the *Vietnamese 2001–2010 Education Development Strategic Plan* (EDSP) (MoET Vietnam 2001) become evident with regard to the guiding principles outlined for the education sector. The EDSP (MoET Vietnam 2001, 16f) states that:

> 3.1. Education is the foremost National Policy.

> Education is the foundation, the highly qualified human resources are one of the important driving forces that accelerate the industrialisation and modernization process, the basic factor for social development, rapid and sustainable economic growth.

> 3.2. Education should make one step in advance to improve mass knowledge, to train manpower and to nurture the talents in order to carry out successfully the socio-economic strategic goals.

> 3.3. The guiding idea of the Education Development Strategic Plan for period 2001–2010 is to overcome the shortages in many aspects; [...]; to create the basis for significant enhancement of quality and effectiveness of education; to serve actively industrialization, modernization and the prosperity of the country, to make our country develop rapidly in a sustainable manner, to keep pace with other developed countries in the region and on the world in a short time.

We argue how the observed differences between the global DESD framework and concrete national policies are conceived will depend on the logics that are appealed to in the analyses. An appeal to a logic of correspondence and determination will ultimately see the similarities as indicators of power and influence, that is the re-emergence of a global ESD within Vietnamese policy-making. According to such an understanding, differences will be perceived as degenerate or blurring side-effects in a complex yet a priori determined global process of dispersion, homogenisation or mere ornaments of an original ESD.

However, if we conceive of the portrayed differences in our alternative perspective the quoted articulations of ESD in Vietnamese policy to indicate that these articulation do add something different to ESD, we might conceive of the process of globalisation differently. We argue, based on our conceptual logics, that this difference can be interpreted as representing a process of aligning the concept of ESD to existing contextual formations or to the specificity of the space that it articulated against. This constitutive difference alongside similarity is then by us not seen to be an *essential* deviation, as a deviation or loss of purity from origin in the global, but is instead, based on our underlying theoretical perspective, seen as *supplementary, as adding something in order to replace.* The observed differences in the comparisons are then seen as a process of *becoming*, as the death of the ESD of the DESD and the emergence of a Vietnamese ESD not as an imperfect copy but as something else.

ESD and the logics of imbrication, displacement and aporia

In the following analyses, the authors elaborate in more detail how this becoming can be conceived through appeals to logics of imbrication, displacement and aporia.

Logic of imbrication

To continue our discussion above, a closer reading of Vietnamese policy shows that the meaning of ESD can be seen to be deferred to the signifier of sustainable development in the Vietnamese action plan for ESD. The Vietnamese *National Action Plan for ESD* (VNCDESD 2010, 3) initially states that:

> The implementation of Decade of Education for Sustainable Development requires us to change our perspectives on education, change and improve educational programs (i.e., objectives, contents and approaches, etc.), develop new ways of thinking towards sustainable development aspects so as to successfully implement basic elements in 3 pillars of sustainable development: culture-society, environment and economy.

The authors interpret the quote to underline that, in order to make statements of the meaning, or being, of ESD, it is necessary to acknowledge that its meaning is deferred to the articulation of the meaning of SD. This deferral of the role and also meaning of ESD can also be seen at work in the division between Vietnamese ESD policy and SD policy, since the national action plan for ESD holds that it aims basically to fulfil the Vietnamese SD objectives as defined in the *Vietnam Agenda* 21 (GoV 2004). The above-assumed process of reterritorialisation as part of the movement of ESD into the Vietnamese context can be seen to be initiated by the contextual alignment. In the case of the *Vietnamese National Action Plan for ESD* (VNCDESD 2010), the meaning of ESD is interpreted to be deferred to or *displaced by* the meaning of SD in the national context or with regard to the specificity of that space.

 The above comparison between the *Vietnamese National Action Plan for ESD* (VNCDESD 2010) and the global UNDESD framework (UNESCO 2005, 2006) is interpreted to exemplify how the logic of imbrication is able to capture how the first-glance meaning of ESD seems to have significant similarities, and how these similarities to a large extent dissolve into particularities, which become evident in the historical and cultural embedment of the concept of SD. To start with the case of Vietnamese policy-making for SD, the framing of SD in the *Vietnam Agenda* 21 (GoV 2004, 5) shows how the associated three dimensions of social, economic and environmental development are re-articulated:

> The views about sustainable development are reaffirmed in the documents of 9th National Communist Party Congress and the Strategy for Socio-economic Development in the period 2001–2010 stating that 'fast, effective and sustainable development, economic growth should occur in parallel with the implementation of social progress

and equality and environmental protection' and 'socio economic development is closely tied to environmental protection and improvement, ensuring harmony between the artificial and natural environment and preserving bio-diversity'.

What the above quote highlights is the active association of the concept of sustainability with broader Vietnamese socio-economic policy, that is to say the *Strategy for Socio-Economic Development in the period 2001–2010* (CCCPV 2001). This alignment is highlighted in the following passage from the *Vietnam Agenda* 21 (GoV 2004, 6), which shows that SD does not replace prior formations within policy discourse, but concretises, or 're-articulates' them.

> The Strategic Orientation for Sustainable Development in Vietnam cannot replace existing strategies, overall planning and plans, but serves as a basis to concretise the socio-economic development strategy in the period 2000–2010, the National Strategy for Environmental Protection Until 2010 and the visions towards 2020 and to develop the 5-year plan 2006–2010 and overall development strategies and plans for sectors and localities with a view to acquiring close, reasonable, harmonious combination of economic development, social progress and equality and environmental protection and ensuring the country's sustainable development.

The following comparison between the role of SD in broader policy formations in Vietnam and Thailand highlights how in both contexts SD is not articulated as a self-contained concept defining national policy. Instead, SD is ultimately described as a compatible end-state of development based on context-dependent and historically evolved formations in policy discourse. These policy formations can already be centred around other key policy concepts, such as 'harmonious development' or 'socialist-oriented market economy' in the Vietnamese context (cf. GoV 2004).

In Thailand, as the quote below shows, the concept of sustainable development is associated with the concept of sufficiency economy at the policy level as well as in other social sectors (Mongsawad 2009). Thailand's *10th National Economic and Social Development Plan* (2007–2011) (ONSEDB 2007, 2) states:

> A new development paradigm that focused on 'people-centered development' was therefore brought into use, and the economy was employed as a tool to enhance happiness and quality of life. At the same time, the segmented approach to development was replaced by a holistic approach to development, with more opportunities for all sectors to participate in every stage of development. The new paradigm is under the principles of 'Sufficiency Economy' to which His Majesty has adhered since his ascension to the throne. The philosophy is in accordance with the Thai way of life and will lead to sustainable development of the nation.

A comparison of the articulations of SD in Vietnamese and Thai policy show similarities; both articulate that the relationship between the economy and other aspects of national development are to be changed. The Thai policy uses 'holistic' to describe the new, desired relationship, and the Vietnamese policy uses the term 'harmonious'. At first glance, it appears that the Thai concept of a 'holistic' approach to development can be seen as in line with 'holistic' approaches to ESD, as frequently called for in the DESD framework (FIIS) (UNESCO 2006). However, the next quote makes it clear that this envisioned change deviates significantly from the formulation in the DESD framework (FIIS) (UNESCO 2006), or the *Agenda 21* (UNDESA 1992). In the *10th Thai National Economic and Social Development Plan*, 'sustainability' is interchangeable with, or attains meaning through, the concept of 'sufficiency':

The Ninth Plan (2002–2006) adopted the Sufficiency Economy philosophy to guide the development and administration of the country, at the same time as continuing the holistic approach to people-centered development from the Eighth Plan. The plan prioritized solutions to problems arising from the economic crisis in order to build an economy with strong internal foundations and resilience to external changes, while aiming for balanced development with respect to people, society, economy, and environment in order to achieve sustainable development and the well-being of the Thai people. (ONSEDB 2007, ii)

While sustainable development can be seen as a form of state, sufficiency economy is used to describe the end state strived for. Sufficiency economy is defined as follows:

(1.1) The principle of 'sufficiency', which consists of three qualities must be strictly adhered to. The first quality is 'reasonableness'. It must be used to analyze and make sense of the situation of the country with respect to strengths and weaknesses, threats and opportunities. This way, it is possible to select what is appropriate for national development and for coping with threats. Reasonableness leads to 'moderation' which must be used in decision-making to create a balance between self-reliance and competitive capability in the world market and between rural and urban society. A self-immunity system must be built into economic systems through risks management in order to handle the impact of changes both inside and outside the country. (ONSEDB 2007, 39)

It has to be stated that reasonableness, moderation and self-immunity are not mentioned in either the *DESD Framework for the International Implementation Scheme (FIIS)* (UNESCO 2006) or *Agenda* 21 (UNDESA 1992) as means of assuring sustainable development and that sufficiency is only used in the *Agenda* 21 to refer to 'self-sufficiency' in food production (UNDESA 1992, § 17.87), in low-energy technology (UNDESA 1992, § 32.5d), or waste management (UNDESA 1992, § 20.7, § 20.24). In the Thai context, however, the concepts of sufficiency or sufficiency economy attain a much more central position than SD with regard to holistic and 'people-centered' development.

The brief exploration of articulations of SD within two national contexts or spaces aimed to problematise the capacity of logics of correspondence and logics of universalism to explain and account for differences between those articulations. In the appeal to the existence of a global SD as corresponding reference point, the conceptions of sufficiency and harmonious development according to the logic of correspondence would exclude explanatory means of accounting for the constitutive characteristics of these conceptions of SD, but would retain useful explanatory capacities within a narrow focus on the similarities between sufficiency economy and harmonious development as *species* of a global SD. The logic of imbrication obviates this need for conceptual convergence. Instead, besides applying a constitutive focus on similarities, the logic of imbrications allows for simultaneous difference to become a constitutive aspect of globally travelling policy concepts. In other words, the logic of imbrication allows us to conceive how the concept of SD, shared among spaces, becomes associated with sufficiency, and becomes a placeholder for, that is to say imbricates with, sufficiency economy. The logic of imbrication does not a priori assume which of the national or global space has the capacity to define the articulation of SD in the other.

Logic of displacement

The logic of displacement suggests that every move of deterritorialisation, including the introduction of policy concepts such as ESD or SD into a national context or a specific space, is inevitably repositioned with regard to the existent discursive formation of a particular signifying system, and that the policy concept thereby attains a hybrid character in relation to this signifying system. The authors illustrate below the specific form that this hybridity takes in the context of policy formation in Thailand and Vietnam.

The concept of sufficiency economy, which promotes SD in the Thai context, was developed under the patronage of His Majesty King Bhumibol Adulyadej of Thailand and is strongly influenced by Buddhist philosophy (UNDP Thailand 2007). In Vietnam, on the other hand, SD is, as we have seen, closely associated with the concepts of economic growth, social progress and social equality. This partly reflects an established connection in both countries between economic development and sustainable development in SD policy. Certain conceptions of globalisation would see this focus on economic development as an indicator of the influence of global economic or capitalist forces. However, one needs to be careful before applying this to Vietnam, where policies also highlight 'social progress' and 'social equality', demands which are arguably more in line with a socialist discourse than a 'global' neoliberalist one. For example, one of the key principle for education in the *2001–2010 Education Development Strategic Plan* (EDSP) (MoET Vietnam 2001, 16) is: 'To build up a popular, national, scientific, modern, socialist oriented education, based on Marxism-Leninism and Ho Chi Minh's thoughts'. In a similar appeal to socialism, the *Vietnam Agenda* 21 (GoV 2004) and the *5-Year Socio-Economic Development Plan (2006–2010)* (MoPI Vietnam 2006) share the ambition of implementing a socialist-oriented market economy. In this context, the concept of harmony re-emerges. The *Vietnam Agenda* 21 (GoV 2004, 2) describes its role as to 'sustainably develop the country on the basis of close, reasonable and harmonious coordination of economic and social development and environmental protection'. The current analysis illustrates that the same concept attains different meanings due to specific circumstances, that is to say its meaning is displaced as part of the concept's movement from one space to be re-articulated in another.

The situatedness of the meaning of SD, that is the displacement of SD's meaning in relation to specific discourses and language games, becomes even more accentuated when the comparison turns towards how *un*sustainable development is given meaning. The documented divergence in the articulations of unsustainable development can be seen to be accounted for by the logic of displacement, which does not see the movement from the global to the national to be determined a priori, in contrast to a logic of determination. For example, in the Thai context, sufficiency economy, as a guarantor for SD, is contrasted with western modes of thinking and presented as a counter-globalising movement based on distinct national development in the *10th National Socio-Economic Development Plan* (ONSEDB 2007, 18):

> The 'Sufficiency Economy' philosophy, according to the group of thinkers who developed the theoretical framework of the philosophy, is a concept that goes beyond monist and dualist western ways of thinking. [...]

> For Thailand to a place of honor and dignity in the world community and achieve 'green and happiness society' under globalization, it is necessary to revise the country's 'dynamic equilibrium'. Thailand, then, needs to reorient its paradigm and approach to

national development towards the middle path so as to balance socio-economic differences between rural and urban societies.

A closer look at causes of unsustainable development articulated in Thai policy (ONSEDB 2007, 11) shows how the topic is clearly linked with economic liberalism:

> Unbalanced and unsustainable development was caused by strategic planning that adopted economic liberalism or capitalism which focused mainly on wealth and income flow into the country and used income per capita as a success indicator of development.

One can say that economic liberalism as associated with the global and Western world views is perceived as unsustainable, which gives SD a very space-specific meaning. A comparison of the Thai and Vietnamese articulations of sustainable and unsustainable development also shows that the logic of displacement allows for a paradoxical positioning of frontiers between sustainability and unsustainability, that is to say that the space-specificality of an imbricating concept of SD can lead to paradoxical meanings. For example, with regard to sustainable development in trade, the *Vietnamese Agenda* 21 (GoV 2004, 28) states:

> To successfully implement sustainable development, it is essential to carry out the following activities:
>
> [...]
>
> Perfect the legal foundation, state management mechanisms about commerce and markets in order to develop markets and expand commercial relations

And with regard to sustainable development of regions and localities (ibid. 33), it says:

> Areas and regions have to bring into full play their comparative advantages and create their own strengths in accordance with open economic structures which attach the domestic markets needs with those of foreign markets.

The comparison of the Thai articulation of *unsustainable* development and the Vietnamese articulation of *sustainable* development suggests a paradox between the ways they articulate the relationship between these types of development and economic liberalism. This paradox shows that the deterritorialising move of the introduction of a 'foreign' or 'global' SD in a particular space, according to our constitutive perspective on globalisation, cannot *determine* the reterritorialising move of SD in that space. Put differently, if 'foreign' SD equals economic liberalism, our Thai example leads to the conclusion that the re-articulation or appropriation of SD does not determine what it becomes, as SD is seen to be contrary to economic liberalism. Hence, it is impossible to see this movement from 'global' to national space as *determined,* that is to say as forms of reproduction and re-articulation of an original, since our two examples show that paradoxical articulations of SD are *possible* among national spaces.

However, from a theoretical perspective, the reterritorialising move, or the displacement, is not a move towards providing an elusive or obscure SD with a final, fully constituted being within a national space. Instead, as the exploration shows, SD remains ambiguous, that is to say undecidable. In the Vietnamese context, sustainable development is not solely equated with economic liberalism or an economist discourse, it is associated with more than just economic growth. The *Vietnam*

Agenda 21 (GoV 2004, 14) can be seen as articulating SD in the context of a socialist discourse:

> The objective of the sustainable development in social terms is to obtain high results in the implementation of social progress and equality, ensure ever improved nutrition in diets and quality of health care for the people, ensure opportunities of education and employment for all people, reduce hunger and the poverty ratio and lessen economic disparity among different social classes and groups, reduce social evils, improve equality in rights and duties of members and generations in a society, maintain and develop the diversity and identity of natural culture, constantly upgrade the civilisation levels in the material and spiritual life.

The exploration of the logic of displacement is able to show how SD attains a *contingent* position as a result of its articulation against the background of the discursive formation of a given space. This contingency stands opposed to the logic of correspondence where the Being of SD is ultimately a priori determined by the global concept. However, following the logic of imbrication, SD in its displacement does not *become detached,* but retains a connection to its meanings and Beings in other spaces. In relation to the logic of displacements, our conception of the movement of SD to the national space of Vietnam suggests that the articulation of SD within these spaces does not determine or redetermine its meaning, but highlights that imbricating articulations of SD exist *within* and *among* spaces. Hence, rather than understanding the process of movement, that is to say territorialisation of SD within and among spaces, as complete or concluded, the displacement should be understood as ongoing, or, as the authors call it, *becoming.* This becoming is shaped by the existing discursive formations within a space, but is not fully determined by it, as there is a moment of contingency in its articulation, as well as an increase in valence as connections among spaces are established and remain. Thus, in contrast to the logic of correspondence, the moment of reduction to an absolute singular meaning never arises, since SD, according to the logic of imbrication, always retains a trace to a meaning within another space or another discourse. Certainly, within a logic of correspondence one can evaluate certain similarities as more important than others and thereby create a uniformity. When doing so the number of particular purposes inherent in discourse practices will be reduced to one. If one instead takes the different meanings and values connected to SD in the different discursive practices, that is to say articulations, in Vietnam or Thailand seriously one can say that the global is there in a form of imbrication, but not as singular correspondence, but rather as a plurality of displacements that take many different forms.

Logic of aporia

The logic of aporia highlights the impossibility of an absolute and final singularity of meaning or identity of signifiers such as SD, and the futility of any attempt to determine such a meaning. Thus, the logic deals with diversity and particularity, and the necessary failure of attempts at universalization. As we have seen in our analysis of Thai and Vietnamese policy-making, the aporia can be seen to exist with regard to the plurality or incommensurability of articulations of ESD and resulting tensions among demands that are associated with SD and ESD – for example, the demands of economic growth and social equality.

Tensions among group-specific demands may pose a problem to politics that need to bring different groups of social actors together, and to highlight equivalences between those groups' specific demands. Holistic policy concepts can usefully create such equivalences while remaining, as names of an ultimate state of fullness beyond unsustainability, an empty signifier (Laclau 1996). By way of example, we might recall how socialist-oriented market economy and sufficiency economy can be seen to address the tensions in the Thai and Vietnamese discursive formations and make policy without alienating any groups. The incommensurability underlying these tensions cannot be articulated but only be shown through paradoxes and aporias in policy-making. For example, in the case of Vietnamese policy, this antagonism is apparent in an articulation of progress, which is on the one hand, equated with social equality, and on the other hand, with economic growth. The examples from Vietnamese policy-making suggest that the call for social equality can be associated with a socialist discourse, while economic growth can be associated with an economist discourse. Similarly, in the Thai context, sufficiency economy can be seen to face other antagonistic positions within the field of policy-making and within the national context or a space at large, but it has to remain empty in order not to become associated with a particular demand. If it does, the concept of sufficiency economy would loose its ability to denote equivalence among diverse demands, and hence become more likely to allow for the articulation of antagonisms among these demands. Due to such a function in politics, SD does have to remain obscure or ambiguous, only vaguely articulating something that has to be opposed: unsustainable development.

It is here in this need for the articulation of a shared enemy that we are dealing with an aporia, in that particularity and the universal reject each other and yet at the same time require each other. Laclau (2000, 56) formulates it in the following fashion: '[w]hat is inherent in the hegemonic relation, if the universal and the particular reject each other but require each other, is the representation of an impossibility'. It is here that SD can name a universal, as a place beyond particularity, but cannot represent it, since it relies on the articulation of a particular that is to be overcome.[3] The articulation of this vague enemy, however, can threaten the name of that universal with a possible collapse into a particularity, as our exploration of the position of liberal economics in Vietnamese and Thai policy-making shows.

The empty signifier adds key signifiers associated with a number of particular discursive positions into a chain of equivalences, as it was the case with the themes that ESD has been associated with in the DESD framework (UNESCO 2005, 2006) or the Vietnamese national action plan (VNCDESD 2010). An empty signifier can therefore be seen to be a premise for hegemonic articulations that try to elevate particular demands, yet maintain the equivalences created under the empty signifier, to which all kind of particulars are ascribed to represent the universal (Laclau 2000, 57).

Yet, while our earlier analyses have dealt with aporias *within* a space, the exploration and theoretical constitution of the movement among spaces reveals a second aporia. This second aporia can be analytically approached if we compare the

Sufficiency-as-Sustainable Development		Vietnam (Socialist-oriented Economy)
	DIFFERENCE	
Harmony-as-Sustainable Development		Thailand (Sufficiency Economy)
Sustainable Development-as-*X*	SIMILARITY	UNDESD Framework ('global')

particular metaphors associated with an internationally travelling empty signifier (SD) *among* different national scales.

The table above is to highlight the aporetic aspect of the articulation of sustainable development that emerges once we compare the meanings of the concept in Vietnam, Thailand and the UNDESD Framework. The aporetic aspect emerges as SD is to signify both, *different* notions of progress (Sufficiency and Harmony) as well as to signify that which is *shared* among these different notions of progress. To put it differently, the second aporia exists in the difference/similarity logic that is relied upon when ESD is articulated as a globally inclusive and uniform policy concept. This inclusive and uniform notion of ESD beyond a space and the aporia it entails, which cannot be articulated in standard rules of logic, can be observed within the *Framework for the UNDESD International Implementation Scheme* (FIIS) (UNESCO 2006, 24).

> [DESD] objectives may be *articulated* at each level, from community to the global *context*, but each level the Decade should offer *a framework* for enhanced action and a link to other *contexts* and other levels.

The permission to articulate DESD objectives at various levels logically entails variation (difference), since a total consistency between articulations at various levels would render those articulations redundant. However, the variation is limited by the framework of the articulation as the quote above highlights in its appeal to presenting a framework for action and for linking contexts. The question that arises is what relationship the articulations have to each other or how context relates to context? The UNDESD framework (FIIS) (UNESCO 2006, 24f) clarifies this as:

> The Decade provides an opportunity for developing countries to *define for themselves* the kind of path they wish to follow. From the perspective of sustainable development it is clear that models derived from the industrialised countries are neither appropriate nor desirable, given the pressing need for those countries themselves to adopt more sustainable lifestyles. Building on strong commitment to values of community and solidarity, the developing countries have a chance to develop – and to model – viable, alternative approaches to sustainable development.

The above passage clearly shows how sustainable development, in its singular form, becomes a signifier for differing and alternative approaches that share a common reference to sustainable development. In this articulation, SD is used *as a collective and inclusive name* as part of an abstract movement beyond context, where, however, the differential Beings of ESD as they relate to the national contexts are acknowledged. Yet at the same time, in the DESD framework (FIIS) (UNESCO 2006, 27), these different visions of SD are miraculously seen to fit into a development of *vision* for ESD, highlighting uniformity among difference in the plurality of visions:

> Progress towards sustainable development requires that the growing global awareness of social, environmental, cultural and economic issues is transformed into understanding of *root causes*; it also means that local, national and global *visions* of *what it means* to live and work sustainably are developed. Building *vision* enables *ESD* to take root in local *realities* and to build at the same time a global commitment and *unity across diverse contexts*. Future ESD vision building is related to the vision building that has gone on in developing local Agenda 21s in many countries.

While the prior example hints at an articulation of SD as a collective name for differences among spaces or contexts, these multiple processes (building vision in general) are paradoxically assumed to lead to a necessary unity across diverse contexts, the articulation of ESD in the second example requires the neglect of a logical inconsistency in order to *name a necessary process of conversion*.

The exploration of the logic of aporia aimed to conceptualise the logical paradoxes that are characteristic of the conception of ESD and SD as points of convergence, as places of uniformity, confronting apparent dissensus. While a logic of correspondence and associated logic of universality could conceive this paradox as a problem that could be solved through synthesis, as a movement towards greater or more accurate knowledge, the logic of aporia highlights that this universalism is out of reach and the field of knowledge will be characterised by dissensus and politics. It is in this context of an aporetic articulation that ESD and SD can appeal to policy-makers, since they allow for adumbrating an attainable global universality beyond particularities and potential antagonisms, as they emerge *among* and *within* context-dependent articulations. In these aporetic articulations of ESD that point towards a place beyond context and particularity, ESD becomes a central placeholder of an absent presence still to come, of still-absent unity *within* and *among* spaces. It is in this double aporetic form that SD and ESD allow for the hegemonic articulation of similarity among the different, *within* and *among* the discursive formations that present the horizons against which various national policies are written. These hegemonic articulations will aim to elevate particular demands and means as privileged and potent to achieving SD and ESD, yet, since they aim to realise an empty signifier as denoting a universalism, these group-specific attempts are always in danger as being contested.

Discussion

The authors' ambition in this article has been to empirically explore the movement of the policy concept of ESD and SD *between* spaces through comparing policy-making for SD in various contexts. Thus, the authors have attempted to give meaning to similarities and differences in the articulation of SD within different spaces. As such the article aims to exemplify on how the for us constitutive logics of globalisation allow us to conceive of these movements among spaces based on concrete cases of discursive practices that aim to give meaning to SD and ESD.

The exploration of alternative logics of globalisation conducted by us does not claim to have exhausted globalisation and the particular configurations of SD and ESD. The authors neither wished nor attempted to dismiss the warnings of colleagues within the field of environmental education research on the relationship between neoliberalism and globalisation (Hursh and Henderson 2011; Le Grange 2009; Lotz-Sisitka 2010; Payne 2010; Stevenson 2007) and ESDs globalising potential of ESD (Jickling and Wals 2008; Sumner 2008). Instead, the aim was to explore the explanatory limits of certain logics of globalisation, which would elevate these warnings to a universal status. The exploration in the contexts of Vietnamese and Thai policy-making did not exhaust the possible configurations of the movement of SD and ESD among various spaces, but problematised certain theoretical constitutions of this movement.

The alternative set of logics of globalisation also specifically addresses the notion of determination (logic of determination) and especially the appeal to power. Here, the logics of imbrication and displacement limit the power of the global movement, at a theoretical level. We might ask ourselves, if globalisation is a universal phenomenon of international change, what role do warnings about the globalising tendency or power of ESD have? If it is a truly universal process, what influence can a particular resistance have? The appeal to a logic of displacement in our conception of globalisation is aimed to mitigate, or rather replace, this power of the global movement, by highlighting how the movement and meaning of ESD as a concept among spaces and the potential homogenising tendencies depend on contingent practice, that is to say the realignment of ESD within the context of the national context or a specific space. It is in this way that the focus of the presented alternative conception of globalisation moves away from its focus on what the objective position (logic of correspondence) and the resulting Being of ESD is with regard to a universal space. Instead, the article aims to highlight the divergences and different trajectories that the articulation of ESD within different spaces produces. The question of what ESD ultimately is, is not so much of interest as what ESD can become in particular. Based on the underlying logic of contingency, this process of becoming will, from a theoretical perspective, remain for us non-predictable and emerge in practice against the socio-cultural contexts that diverse sub-spaces of the global represent. The logic of displacement does not rule out that the articulation of ESD might not prioritise economical aspects of development (Jickling 2005; Sauvé, Brunelle and Berryman 2005; Sumner 2008), but the articulation is not conceived to be determined by a deeper, global or transcendental Being of ESD or SD (logic of determination).

The authors want to point out a central problem with the logics of determination and logic of correspondence, namely that these logics eliminate any theoretical space for politics. The logic of determination and the logic of correspondence do away with any true chance for resistance, intervention or to govern a national or subnational context or space, since these logics subdue these spaces a priori to the remote influence of the global or international. The authors hold it to be of importance to evaluate the conceptual logics used to explain social change and social regulation – including globalisation – with regard to space for interference or ability to influence of nation states and local actors in relation to the global. It is here put forward that a reliance on appeals to the power of globalisation can become problematic for attempts to provide conceptual frameworks for resistance against certain patterns of social formation and change. If we conceive of the global in terms of power where for example institutions or particular groups are able to impose their will, to dominate and to possess the ability to a priori produce certain effects, we argue that it will be difficult to conceive of the ability to influence and resist and the global will become an omnipotent self-unfolding process. What the exploration is interpreted to highlight is the possibility to challenge power, that is to say to say the abandonment of an appeal to a logic of determination in our exploration opened up an analytical sensitivity for the political that we see to be at work in paradox articulations of ESD within different national spaces. To specify, the empirical engagement portrayed the paradoxical ways in which ESD and SD are articulated in different spaces. While we according to a logic of correspondence might argue that these paradoxes indicate the complexities of the phenomenon of globalisation, the authors would like make an argument for an alternate interpretation of the ontological condition that these paradoxes can be seen to give account for. Instead of seeing them as irrationalities or misinterpretations of an objective or original ideological position of ESD or SD within the global field of forces dominated by the economy, we see these paradoxes to highlight the impossibility of certain ideological positions to determine what education and sustainability is supposed to be. The portrayed paradoxes are by us interpreted to underline the blind spots of critical social theory that feeds upon the logics of determination and correspondence, as these paradoxes trouble understandings of globalisation that see it to lead to a seemingly shrinking world moulded around neoliberal economic principles. They are troublesome as they can only be explained in terms of irrationalities or historical peculiarities, that will over time be eradicated due the a priori ascribed power of an elite to produce global effects. For us, the in the paper portrayed paradoxes highlight the conditions that require the appeal to concepts such as SD and ESD, where the impossibility to impose a certain will and interpretation of the world forces different political actors to investigate in concepts that are supposed to denote that what is universally shared, yet, where there is no underlying common referent that provides a positive meaning that is fully inclusive and that all political actors can ascribe to.

For us, these paradoxes highlight a space of resistance, an opportunity to change the frontiers of the war of position and to denote neoliberal ideological demands as that which is equivalent to unsustainability.

Notes

1. Logics are not used to refer to the logical foundation of a language, but rather to the types of relationships between entities of a particular language, as a form of life, where these types render possible the operation of a language as a system. Logics thereby deal with the properties of entities within language games as part of a language as a system of rules (Laclau 2000, 284).
2. Being is here understood as discursively constituted, that is to say the temporary result of discursive practice. Its being is, by extension, interpreted to be relative to specific formations in the discursive, that is to say in relation to context.
3. Representation in the form of articulation requires that certain relational differences be articulated to give meaning to a signifier. In the case that a signifier is articulated without any differentiation it loses all meaning. Even empty signifiers bear the mark of such a need for differentiation. Sustainable development, for example, needs to distance itself from something, e.g. unsustainable development.

References

Bengtsson, Stefan L. 2014. *Beyond Education and Society: On the Political Life of Education for Sustainable Development*. Uppsala: Acta Universitatis Upsaliensis.

Bengtsson, Stefan L., and Leif O. Östman. 2013. "Globalisation and Education for Sustainable Development: Emancipation from Context and Meaning." *Environmental Education Research* 19 (4): 477–498.

Buenfil-Burgos, Rosa Nidia. 2000. "Globalization, Education and Discourse Political Analysis: Ambiguity and Accountability in Research." *International Journal of Qualitative Studies in Education* 13 (1): 1–24.

Buenfil-Burgos, Rosa Nidia. 2009. "Politics, Global Territories and Educational Spaces." *Yearbook of the National Society for the Study of Education* 108 (2): 67–88.

CCCPV (Central Committee of the Communist Party of Vietnam, 9th National Congress), Vietnam. 2001. *Strategy for Socio-Economic Development 2001–2010.* http://web.worldbank. org/WBSITE/EXTERNAL/COUNTRIES/EASTASIAPACIFICEXT/VIETNAMEXTN/.

Deleuze, Gilles, and Felix Guattari. 1987. *A Thousand Plateaus: Capitalism and Schizophrenia.* 11th ed. Minneapolis, MN: University of Minnesota Press.

Derrida, Jacques. 1987. *The Truth in Painting.* Chicago, IL: University of Chicago Press.

Ferguson, Niall. 2005. "Sinking Globalization." *Foreign Affairs* 84 (2): 64–77.

Giddens, Anthony. 1990. *The Consequences of Modernity.* Cambridge: Polity Press.

González-Gaudiano, Edgar. 2005. "Education for Sustainable Development: Configuration and Meaning." *Policy Futures in Education* 3 (3): 243–250.

Gough, Noel. 2009. "Becoming Transnational: Rhizosemiosis, Complicated Conversion, and Curriculum Inquiry." In *Fields of Green: Re-storying Culture, Environment, and Education,* edited by Marcia McKenzie, Heesoon Bai, Paul Hart, and Bob Jickling, 67–83. Creskil, NJ: Hampton Press.

Gough, Noel. 2013. "Thinking Globally in Environmental Education: A Critical History." In *International Handbook of Research on Environmental Education,* edited by Robert Stevenson, Michael Broady, Justin Dillon, and Arjen Wals, 33–44. Washington, DC: American Educational Research Association/Routledge.

GoV (Government of Vietnam). 2004. The Strategic Orientation for Sustainable Development in Vietnam (Vietnam Agenda 21). Decision No: 153/2004/QD-TTg. http://va21.gov.vn/ gioithieu/vanphong/anpham.html

Hay, Collin. 2005. "Globalization's Impact on the State." In *Global Political Economy.* 2nd ed, edited by John Ravenhill, 314–345. Oxford: Oxford University Press.

Hursh, David W., and Joseph A. Henderson. 2011. "Contesting Global Neoliberalism and Creating Alternative Futures." *Discourse: Studies in the Cultural Politics of Education* 32 (2): 171–185.

Jickling, Bob. 2005. "Sustainable Development in a Globalizing World: A Few Cautions." *Policy Futures in Education* 3 (3): 251–259.

Jickling, Bob, and Arjen E. J. Wals. 2008. "Globalization and Environmental Education: Looking beyond Sustainable Development." *Journal of Curriculum Studies* 40 (1): 1–21.

Laclau, Ernesto. 1990. *New Reflections on the Revolution of Our Time.* London: Verso.

Laclau, Ernesto. 1996. *Emancipation(s).* London: Verso.

Laclau, Ernesto. 2000. "Identity and Hegemony: The Role of Universality in the Constitution of Political Logics." In *Contingency, Hegemony, Universality: Contemporary Dialogues on the Left,* edited by Judith Butler, Ernesto Laclau, and Slavoj Zizek, 44–89. London: Verso.

Laclau, Ernesto, and Chantal Mouffe. 1985. *Hegemony and Socialist Strategy: Towards a Radical Political Politics.* 2nd ed. London: Verso.

Le Grange, Lesley. 2009. "Participation and Participatory Action Research (PAR) in Environmental Education Processes: For What Are People Empowered?" *Australian Journal of Environmental Education* 25: 3–15.

Lotz-Sisitka, Heila. 2010. "Changing Social Imaginaries, Multiplicities and 'One Sole World': Reading Scandinavian Environmental and Sustainability Education Research Papers with Badiou and Taylor at Hand." *Environmental Education Research* 16 (1): 133–142.

MoET Vietnam (Ministry of Education and Training, Vietnam). 2001. *Education Development Strategic Plan for 2001–2010.* Hanoi: Education Publishing House.

MoPI Vietnam (Ministry of Planning and Investment, Vietnam). 2006. *The Five-year Socioeconomic Development Plan 2006–2010.* http://siteresources.worldbank.org/INTPRS1/ Resources/Vietnam_PRSP(July-2006).pdf.

Mongsawad, Prasopchoke. 2009. "Sufficiency Economy: A Contribution to Economic Development." *International Journal of Human and Social Sciences* 4 (2): 144–151.

ONSEDB (Office of the National Social and Economic Development Board, Thailand). 2007. *10th National Economic and Social Development Plan (2007–2011).* http://eng.nes db.go.th/Default.aspx?tabid=402.

Payne, Phillip G. 2010. "The Globally Great Moral Challenge: Ecocentric Democracy, Values, Morals and Meaning." *Environmental Education Research* 16 (1): 153–171.

Popkewitz, Thomas S. 2005. "Inventing the Modern Self and John Dewey: Modernities and the Traveling of Pragmatism in Education – An Introduction." In *Inventing the Modern Self and John Dewey: Modernities and the Traveling of Pragmatism in Education*, edited by Thomas S. Popkewitz, 3–38. New York: Palgrave Macmillan.

Sauvé, Lucie, Renée Brunelle, and T. O. M. Berryman. 2005. "Influence of the Globalized and Globalizing Sustainable Development Framework on National." *Futures* 3 (3): 271–283.

Stevenson, Robert B. 2007. "Schooling and Environmental Education: Contradictions in Purpose and Practice." *Environmental Education Research* 13 (2): 139–153.

Sumner, Jennifer. 2005. *Sustainability and the Civil Commons: Rural Communities in the Age of Globalization*. Toronto: Toronto University Press.

Sumner, Jennifer. 2008. "From Academic Imperialism to the Civil Commons: Institutional Possibilities for Responding to the United Nations Decade of Education for Sustainable Development." *Interchange* 39 (1): 77–94.

Turnbull, David. 1997. "Reframing Science and Other Local Knowledge Traditions." *Futures* 29 (6): 551–562.

UNDESA, Division of Social Development. 1992. *Agenda 21: The United Nations Programme for Action from Rio*. New York: UNDESA.

UNDP Thailand. 2007. *Thailand Human Development Report 2007: Sufficiency Economy and Human Development*. Bangkok: UNDP Bangkok.

UNESCO. 2005. *United Nations Decade of Education for Sustainable Development (2005–2014): International Implementation Scheme*. Paris: UNESCO.

UNESCO. 2006. *Framework for the UN DESD International Implementation Scheme*. Paris: UNESCO.

VNCDESD (Vietnam National Committee for the Decade of Education for Sustainable Development). 2010. *National Action Plan for Education for Sustainable Development. Decision 850/QD-VHDN-UNESCO*. Hanoi: Education Publishing House.

Environmental and sustainability education policy research: a systematic review of methodological and thematic trends

Kathleen Aikens, Marcia McKenzie and Philip Vaughter

This paper reports on a systematic literature review of policy research in the area of environmental and sustainability education. We analyzed 215 research articles, spanning four decades and representing 71 countries, and which engaged a range of methodologies. Our analysis combines quantification of geographic and methodological trends with qualitative analysis of content-based themes. Significant findings included temporal spikes in published policy research occurring in the mid-1970s, late 1990s, and after 2005, as well as geographic under-representation of Africa, South and Central America, Eastern Europe, and North and West Asia. The majority of articles reviewed were non-empirical; empirical articles overwhelmingly focused on teaching and learning directives, rather than exploring the complexity of policy development or enactment. We conclude our analysis by describing key research gaps as high-lighted by the review and propose directions for moving forward policy research in environmental and sustainability education. In particular, we suggest greater research attention to critical policy theory and methodology, issues of intersectionality, and climate change education policy research. By outlining in greater detail the policy research that has been undertaken to date, the review provides a platform for a broadened diversity of policy studies in environmental and sustainability education.

Introduction

This paper responds to calls to strengthen policy research in sustainability education (Læssøe, Feinstein, and Blum 2013; Robottom and Stevenson 2013), by offering a systematic review of existing policy research in environmental and sustainability education, and particularly in the area of kindergarten to grade 12 (K-12) education. As Læssøe et al. (2013) write in a recent special issue with a focus on policy research and sustainability education, 'there is an urgent need for more EE/ESD/ CCE[1] policy research that not only focuses on policy discourses but also engages with the full range of the policy cycle' (Læssøe et al. 2013a, 235). Likewise, Nazir et al. (2009) suggest that there is a lack of research on the implementation of sustainability education[2] policy, and what documentation does exist tends to be self-reports from government or sustainability organizations that function as 'uncritical catalogues that focus on successes, and are silent about problems and failures' (27). By outlining in greater detail the policy research that has been undertaken to date, this review aims to provide a platform for a broadened diversity of policy studies in environmental and sustainability education.

Educational policy research is a relatively recent field of inquiry (Ball 1997). With an initial focus on a 'policy science' approach in which one works to determine 'the technically best course of action to adopt in order to implement a decision or achieve a goal' (Fay 1975, 14), research in education policy has since expanded and diversified. Education policy studies now often include a focus on policy origins or the influences on policy development, as well as considering policy implementation as a situated and interactional process in which policies may be shaped, resisted, or otherwise enacted in practice (e.g. Ball, Maguire, and Braun 2012; Heimans 2014; Webb and Gulson 2015). How policy is understood has important consequences for the approaches taken in policy research: from the questions that are asked, to the methodologies and methods engaged, to recommendations made. In this paper we undertake a literature review of how various studies in environmental and sustainability education have framed and engaged in policy research.

In the review we limit our discussion to K-12 education policy studies that self-define as sustainability or environment-related, recognizing that in doing so, we may have excluded research with important connections to sustainability, for example, education policy research in areas of multiculturalism, Indigenous knowledge and pedagogies, health and wellness education, or school food policies. Throughout the paper we use 'sustainability education' as an umbrella term encompassing environmental education, education for sustainable development (ESD), education for sustainability, and other forms of education concerned at least in part with land and environment. However, where contextually or historically appropriate in relation to the literature being discussed, we use the specific terms used in the research.

The review seeks to offer a descriptive analysis of trajectories, gaps, and scope of policy research in sustainability education. Key themes and findings of this systematic literature review include the following:

- We observed three apparent 'spikes' in policy research output: first, in the mid-1970s; second in the late 1990s; and third, from 2005-present. The last spike may indicate increased policy research activity resulting from the Decade of Education for Sustainable Development (DESD).
- Geographic categorization of research indicated under-representation of large geographical areas, including Africa, South and Central America, Eastern Europe, and most of North and West Asia.
- Most of the studies reviewed (70%) were 'non-empirical' in approach and focused on discussion or reporting of national and international policy contexts.
- While empirical approaches to policy research diversified over the last several decades, most studies focused on teaching and learning directives, leaving policy development and enactment relatively neglected area of research.
- Environmental degradation and international policy contexts were frequently described as drivers of sustainability uptake in education policy. Despite this, we noted a dearth of research that examined education policy in relation to climate change, particularly prior to 2005.

In what follows, we outline the methods of the literature review, and describe our findings in further detail. We conclude by describing key research gaps as highlighted by the review, and propose directions for moving forward policy research in sustainability education.

Methods

Data were collected for the literature review during the period of October to December 2013. We began by searching the Education Resources Information Center (ERIC) database using the search terms, 'environment*' OR 'sustainab*' combined with 'education' AND 'policy' and excluded all articles classified through ERIC as 'Higher Education.' We performed an additional search of all articles classified under the ERIC descriptor 'education policy' for environment* or sustainab*, again excluding all Higher Education articles. These complementary search techniques allowed us to capture relevant articles that may have been classified in different ways. After removing dozens of unrelated articles (e.g. 'sustainability of mathematics curriculum,' 'classroom learning environment'), we performed a crosscheck in the Scopus database using the same search terms. Finally, in order to ensure we had not excluded important policy research, we manually reviewed the following five journals, from their inception to 2013: *Environmental Education Research, Journal of Environmental Education, International Journal of Educational Development, Journal of Education for Sustainable Development,* and the *Canadian Journal of Environmental Education*. This last journal was included because of our positioning as researchers of Canadian education policy.

Despite attempts to provide a comprehensive survey of the policy literature to date, we recognize the limits of surveying only English language literature. Based on the database and English-language journals reviewed, this analysis of existing policy research includes mainly research on settings in the UK, US, Australia, Canada, and New Zealand, and relatively few studies focused on sites in Latin America, non-Anglophone Europe, and parts of Asia. In countries where English is widely spoken in post-secondary institutions and research centers (e.g. China, South Africa), exclusion effects due to review search methods may be weaker.

Hart and Nolan (1999) discuss the challenges of delimiting literature searches when reviewing a field of research, including acknowledgment that the material selected as representing a body of research represents only one of several legitimate choices. We chose to limit our review of policy research to literature published in peer-reviewed journals, so as to provide a comprehensive and systematic review of this particular body of research. While we do not define our work as meta-analysis, we consider it a systematic review within the noted delimitation for its specified inclusion/exclusion criteria and triangulation through multiple search methods, in line with search processes described for qualitative research syntheses (Major and Savin-Baden 2010). After a complete review of all papers and the exclusion of those that were not policy focused (i.e. contained only brief allusions to policy in the introductory or concluding sections, or focused on higher education or nonformal education, etc.), there were a total of 215 articles.

We completed several cycles of reading and analysis of the collected articles. The first round of reading involved an open reading of the articles and note taking, and then based on emergent themes, we determined several categories of analysis. These analysis methods were exploratory in nature, combining basic quantification of trends (regional and national counts and percentages) and research approaches (counts of research types), with deeper qualitative analysis of content-based themes discussed within the publications. In alignment with typologies used previously in analysis of environmental education research (e.g. Reid and Scott 2008), all publications were classified as either 'empirical' or 'non-empirical.' Empirical articles were defined as studies that used quantitative or qualitative research methods. We further subdivided this category into 'survey,' 'textual analysis,' 'case study,' 'mixed,' and 'other.' The category of non-empirical included all articles in which research methods were not defined by the authors, and included the following types: discussion of international policy discourse ('discussion-international'); discussion of national policy discourse ('discussion-national'); or descriptive reports of national or regional projects/programmes with little to no commentary ('report') (see Table 1). A small number of papers in this category also discussed proposals for alternative policy approaches to sustainability education and were identified as 'alternative policy proposals.' By using the terms empirical and non-empirical, we are not suggesting that one categorization is superior to the other, but that both are common and valid ways of engaging in policy research.

Findings

Temporal and geographical trends

The total of 215 research articles had publication years spanning from 1974 to 2013 and focused on education policy in 71 different countries. Dividing the literature into three periods of research, 1970–1989; 1990–2004; and 2005–2013, there was an overall increase in number of published policy related articles, with an average of 1 per year in 1970–1989 (20 total), 5.1 per year in 1990–2004 (77 total) and 13.2 per year in 2005–2013 (118 total). There appear to be three distinct 'spikes' in policy research output: first, in the mid-1970s; second in the late 1990s; and third, from 2005-present (Figure 1). The first small spike in the mid-1970s we attribute to a flurry of studies from the United States examining national and state-level policies for environmental education. This timing follows the official nascence of the field of environmental education, which is often dated in relation to the 1970 meeting of the IUCN (Palmer 1999), as well as the U.S. Environmental Education Act (Hepburn and Keach 1974). There is another spike in the number of policy studies in the late 1990s, in which many articles discuss the implications of Agenda 21 – the outcome of the 1992 United Nations Conference on Environment and Development held in Rio de Janeiro, Brazil. After a brief dip in research in the first half of the 2000s, there is another increase in policy research around the mid-2000's, in which a number of articles discuss the advent of the UN DESD (2005–2014).

Table 1. Categorization of research approach.

Empirical	Non-empirical
Survey	Discussion-international
Textual analysis	Discussion-national
Case study	Alternative policy proposal
Mixed	Report
Other	

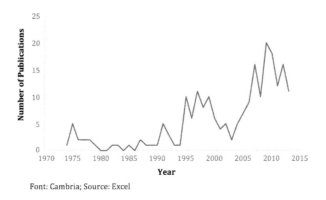

Font: Cambria; Source: Excel

Figure 1. Number of policy-related articles from 1974 to 2013. Note the spike in the late 1970s, late 1990s (post Agenda 21) and late 2000s-onwards (UN DESD).

Figure 2 provides a broad overview of the number of articles from countries in each of four regions: Africa, Americas, Asia-Pacific, and Europe. While this review encompassed research based in 24 African nations, Africa was the most under-represented region by total number of papers (21). There were a total of 52 publications on settings in Europe (20 countries), 47 publications on the Americas (15 countries), and 43 publications on the Asia Pacific region (12 countries). The remaining 59 papers[3] in this review were international in scope. Gaps in research-coverage are apparent (Figure 2): many countries in South America, Eastern Europe, North and West Asia, and North Africa are entirely unrepresented in the reviewed literature.

The review also indicates a high quantity of papers from particular countries (Figure 3). The majority of countries included in this review are represented by a single publication, with the most frequently researched countries – the United States,

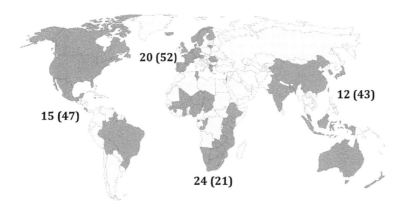

Font: Cambria; Source: freeworldmaps.net

Figure 2. Map of research on sustainability education policy included in this review. Shaded countries are represented by at least one publication. Regional totals for Africa, the Americas, Asia-Pacific and Europe are included with total number of countries represented, and in brackets, total number of studies based in those countries.

the United Kingdom, Australia, China/Hong Kong, and Australia – representing over half of the total publications in the review. This finding is aligned with previous discussions of the geographic distribution of published environmental education research (Reid and Scott 2008), and is particularly significant in the interpretation of major themes arising from the review. In other words, we suggest that the issues of policy concern as identified through this review are largely reflective of the most heavily researched national policy contexts.

In what follows, we discuss other review findings in relation to the terminology used in the articles, type of research papers, and key themes in the literature.

Terminology

The reviewed research suggests that sustainability has been included in K-12 formal education policy research over the past four decades mainly using the terminology of 'environmental education' and 'education for sustainable development.' Acknowledging roots in conservation ecology and rural studies, articles authored in the 1970s and 1980s referred to environmental education, or education for the environment (e.g. Schoenfeld 1975; Wheeler 1983). Though the concept of sustainable development began circulating in UN documents as early as 1980 (Sauvé, Berryman, and Brunelle 2007), it was the Brundtland Report (Brundtland 1987) that cemented use of the term. This review shows a corresponding emergence in 1990 of research focused on education for sustainability/sustainable development policy imperatives. Figure 4 tracks the terminology used in publication titles of all articles reviewed, sorting references into three categories: 'environment/environmental education,' 'sustainable development,' and 'sustainable/sustainability.' We found that titles referencing environmental education peaked in the late 1990s, while titles referencing sustainable development spiked sharply after 2005, the inauguration of the UN DESD. There has been a small, consistent increase in the number of titles using the terminology 'sustainable/sustainability' beginning around 2005.

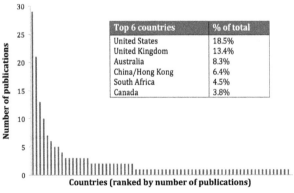

Font: Cambria; Source: Excel

Figure 3.   The relative distribution of articles by country, with each bar representing the total number of publications per country. Countries on the left were the focus of a large proportion of the publications (as included in inset table).

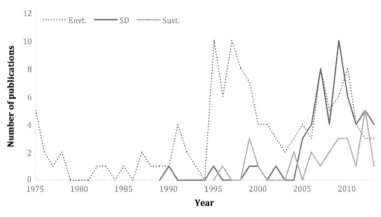

Font: Cambria; Source: Excel

Figure 4. Tracking use of terminology in titles of reviewed articles from 1975 to 2013. The upper dotted line represents publications which included 'environment' in the title; the solid line represents publications which included 'sustainable development' in the title; the dashed line represents all publications which included 'sustainable/sustainability' in the title.

Research approach

Of the total of 215 papers reviewed, the majority were non-empirical articles (150 or 70%), while 65 were empirical (see Table 2 for a breakdown of the number of papers per specific method type). Surveys made up the plurality of empirical articles, though textual analysis, case study, and mixed (multiple) methods were also identified. Most non-empirical articles focused on national level discussions, and most of the reports were of national policy developments.

Over time, empirical approaches to policy research have diversified (Figure 5). The 1970s and 1980s are characterized by the use of surveys to assess policy implementation and outcomes, while the 1990s through to 2004 saw the introduction of

Table 2. Categorization of literature review articles by research type.

Research approach	Categorization	Number
Empirical	Survey	26
	Textual analysis	18
	Case study	13
	Mixed	5
	Other	3
	Total	65
Non-empirical	Discussion-international	37
	Discussion-national	51
	Discussion-other	7
	Report	45
	Total	150

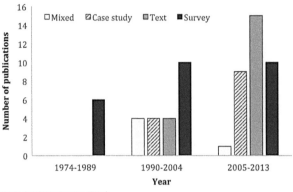

Font: Cambria; Source: Excel

Figure 5. Changes over three time periods in types of empirical policy research.

other research methods. In the final temporal period (2005–2013), most researchers chose either textual analysis or case study research to undertake policy research.

Thematic coding

The 215 publications were analyzed through a process of iterative thematic coding, inductively developing a set of themes and subthemes (Table 3). Our initial reading and subsequent coding coalesced around four main themes identified in the articles reviewed pertaining to education policy: (1) policy drivers; (2) competing paradigms; (3) teaching and learning directives; and (4) marginalizations. In the following sections, each of the sub-themes will be discussed. Our definition of policy includes a broad conception, which extends beyond considerations of policy texts, to influences on policy development as well as on the enactment or practice of policy (Braun, Maguire, and Ball 2010). The policies which constitute the focus of study, in their form, development, or enactment, include not only those texts labeled as policies at a national or regional level, but also international declarations and proposals.

Many of the papers included in the analysis were represented by multiple themes, addressing, for example, both policy drivers and teaching and learning directives (e.g. Iyengar and Bajaj 2011; Stimpson and Kwan 2001). Though themes were often overlapping, we can report on the overall 'extent of engagement' with

Table 3. Content analysis themes and subthemes from literature review.

(1) Policy drivers
Sustainability contexts as policy drivers
International contexts as policy drivers
(2) Competing paradigms
(3) Contexts of curriculum and pedagogy
Curriculum
Teaching and pedagogy
Competing policies
(4) Marginalizations

each thematic area. Within the four main thematic areas, two thirds of papers included discussion of teaching and learning directives (67%), one third of papers discussed policy drivers (33%), 22% competing paradigms, and 18% marginalizations.

Policy drivers

One of the main content themes identified in the policy research was a focus on policy drivers, or in other words, on factors that have contributed to the development of policy. Key drivers discussed were (i) environmental and social imperatives influencing policy development, as well as (ii) international policy initiatives and their impact on national and regional policy. In what follows we discuss each of these areas in turn.

Sustainability imperatives as policy drivers. The impetus for sustainability education policy was often described in instrumental terms, in terms of having particular political or environmental aims. Sustainability education was positioned in policy research as a solution to environmental degradation, and as well as socio-cultural degradation, (Adara 1996; Adedayo and Olawepo 1997; Breiting and Wickenberg 2010; Stimpson 1997). Adara (1996), for example, in discussing the social studies curriculum in Nigeria, suggested that the directives provided by policy did not 'adequately empower the citizen for responsible environmental action' (238); and thus adequate environmental education was deemed necessary to halt 'socio-cultural and environmental decay' (238).

The papers reviewed also included studies that examined how sustainability education policy was responding to specific environmental disasters, or inversely, research which found a lack of adequate response to disasters through policy. For example, papers discussed how education policy should better respond to tragedies such as the Bhopal chemical spill (Iyengar and Bajaj 2011), and the Walkerton, Ontario, water-contamination (Puk and Behm 2003). Based on their analysis of state and national syllabi in India, Iyengar and Bajaj (2011) wrote that '[o]ur findings indicate that the national and state syllabi have made little to no effort to contextualize EE by using the Bhopal gas tragedy as a learning experience' (425). In a state policy context in which there were distinct required EE courses, this study found a focus on decontextualized scientific knowledge versus sociocultural considerations across the syllabi. They concluded that this disciplinary bias and lack of local contextualization left human factors unaddressed, such as errors that led to the Bhopal disaster or the social injustices associated with its implications, which could assist in preventing such incidents in the future.

Climate change stood out as increasingly being invoked as an impetus for sustainability education policy (e.g. Clarke 2009; Hägglund and Samuelsson 2009; Viertel 2010), and in some cases, as having led to changes in education policy. Overall our review suggests that uptake of a focus on climate change in the education policy research literature has been slow, as is the case across the education literature more broadly (Feinstein et al. 2013). In the first five years post-Kyoto, only one of the reviewed articles (Palmer 1999) mentioned climate change. Beginning in 2006, however, there was a steady increase in climate change references in the policy literature, and 50% of all reviewed articles published since 2010 invoked climate change in some capacity (Figure 6). This may be related to the DESD (2005–2014) placing climate change education on the policy agenda (Feinstein, Jacobi, and Lotz-Sisitka 2013; Feinstein et al. 2013), or it may simply reflect increasing climate concerns globally, especially in light of recent extreme weather events. Several authors noted that the challenge of coping with such events might actually reduce participation in sustainability education initiatives, as available resources are channeled into disaster mitigation and prevention, without recognition of education's potential longer-term contribution to climate mitigation and adaptation (Bangay and Blum 2010).

Alongside papers examining social and environmental drivers of sustainability education, a handful of articles instead interrogated surrounding assumptions of environmental degradation as a pressing need requiring an urgent policy response (Bak 1995; Sauvé, Berryman, and Brunelle 2007). Bak (1995), for example, discussed a South African context with limited resources and a 'backlog' of basic need provision (348). Suggesting that immediate public policy concerns of housing, health, employment, and basic schooling take precedence over environmental education, Bak asked: 'What moral base is there for maintaining that we need to ensure the survival of future generations when the *present* generation is dying as a result of lack of housing, healthcare and food?' (348, emphasis in original). While recognizing the need to legitimize learning for sustainability, Sauvé, Berryman, and Brunelle (2007) also cautioned against imperatives for rapid educational re-orientation toward sustainability, wherein the need for action discourages reflexivity and critical thought.

International policy contexts as policy drivers. Prevalent across the reviewed articles were descriptions of the desire to align with international policy imperatives as an impetus for the development of sustainability education policy. Furthermore, international organizations, including United Nations affiliates, the International Union for the Conservation of Nature, and the World Bank, were cited as organizational actors spurring on the uptake of sustainability in education policy (Bernon 1978; Pace 1997; Smyth 1999; Vare 1998). According to Wheeler (1983), within a few years of the conceptualization of environmental education, there was a perception that it was

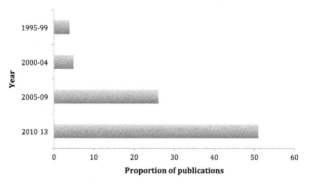

Font: Cambria; Source: Excel

Figure 6.   Proportion of articles referencing climate change across four time periods.

spreading 'world-wide through the agency of [the] IUCN and UNESCO' (10). The Tbilisi declaration (1977) continued to be cited as motivation for environment education policy in reviewed articles through the 1990s (e.g. Adara 1996; Adedayo and Olawepo 1997). In a recent case study of Flemish education policy, the authors noted the importance of the Rio Declaration and Agenda 21, followed by the Johannesburg Plan, in setting sustainable development as a national policy imperative to be addressed by lower levels of government (Van Poeck, Vandenabeele, and Bruyninckx 2013). Other authors discussed national and international non-governmental organizations (NGOs) as applying pressure to national governments to adopt policy for environmental education (e.g. Pace 1997; Stimpson 1997; Vare 1998). In exception to the above, González-Gaudiano (2007) noted that Latin American nations have rarely adopted sustainability education policy in response to international summits.

In Vare's (1998) survey of 15 African countries, bureaucrats responsible for the preparation of National Environmental Actions Plans (NEAPs) expressed concern that World Bank Funding was conditional on the completion of an externally acceptable NEAP. Vare suggested that any environmental education initiatives resulting from this process were likely to be externally motivated and lacking local support. As further evidence of the dominance of international influence relative to local participation, Vare cited comments from the Environmental Protection Agency of Ghana reporting that 'time constraints did not allow for a thorough grassroots participatory process in the preparation of the [environmental education] strategy' (13). Reporting on the views of diverse Latin American participants in an international seminar on environmental education policy, Barraza, Duque-Aristiza´bal, and Rebolledo (2003) noted the dominant perception of the inextricability of environmental issues and North-South politics. Thus, they suggested:

> globally 'agreed' environmental education perspectives (such as ideas around education for sustainable development) could be seen as providing the 'North' with yet another means to re-shape and re-define people's behaviours and thinking in the 'South', in what Escobar (1995) sees can become a subtle but effective control mechanism, and another expression of neo-colonialism. (349)

Competing paradigms

The second significant overall theme identified in the articles was that of 'competing paradigms,' or in other words, variations and tensions in the terminology and understandings mobilized through forms of sustainability education and research. Many articles referenced or contributed to discussions on the meaning of education for sustainability, (ESD)/sustainable development (SD), and their relationship to environmental education. Smyth described early detractors of ESD as policy-makers who 'suspect that it represents a "green" attempt to get away from development, or that it disguises what is to be sustained, namely a "northern" affluent lifestyle' (1995, 10–11). He noted that 'committing one's policy to a term the meaning of which is not clear to all, invites confusion by those who interpret it differently either by fault or intention' (11). Several authors suggested that that, by virtue of its openness to interpretation, ESD fails to challenge business as usual and supports economic primacy, allowing a neoliberal agenda to further dominant educational policy (González-Gaudiano 2006; Kopnina 2012; McKenzie 2012).

While a large number of articles reviewed presented critique and discussion of the competing paradigms of environmental education and education for sustainable development (e.g. Bonnett 1999; González-Gaudiano 2006; Kopnina 2012; Plant 1995; Smyth 1999; Tilbury 1995), only a handful presented systematic analyses of international level proposals and declarations (e.g. Sauvé and Berryman 2005; Sauvé, Berryman, and Brunelle 2007). Several more reported on analyses of national-level documents (Ferguson 2008; Locke 2009; Mannion et al. 2011; Van Poeck et al. 2013; Winter 2007) For example, through analysis of more than 30 declarations from international organizations, Sauvé, Berryman, and Brunelle (2007) described several key findings, including a consistent depiction of economic growth as the primary solution for development, accompanied by an inattention to the systemic causes of poverty. In a national-level analysis of UK curriculum policy for ESD, Winter (2007) suggests that the rhetoric deployed within policy allows ready assimilation of ESD into dominant economic discourse. She described how the main challenges to sustainability, described by the Brundtland report as poor management of the economy and physical environment, are reproduced within national curriculum policy in the UK due to lack of examination of fundamental assumptions. The pervasiveness of the Brundtland definition of sustainable development in policy documents was suggested by Winter to obscure the complexity and contestation of the concept of sustainable development, and the uncertainty of what is to be sustained, for whom, and for how long.

Another predominant theme regarding competing paradigms was the tension between conceptions of environment and nature, and the role of education. In the same analysis discussed above, Sauvé, Berryman, and Brunelle (2007) examined definitions of 'nature' and 'environment' within international documents, reporting that these have narrowed over decades, such that a 'resourcist' approach to the environment (i.e. managing resources for human survival) now dominates international declarations. The authors reported that although instrumentalist and resourcist views of education and environment are common across documents and decades, this focus intensified with increasing deployment of the terminology of sustainable development. Analyses of national level policies also evidenced resourcist and anthropocentric understandings of human-nature relationships (Ferguson 2008; Locke 2009; Winter 2007). Reporting on an analysis of primary curriculum guides in Costa Rica, Locke (2009) noted contradictory themes of human domination of nature, and promotion of harmonious interrelationship within nature. Ferguson (2008) described an anthropocentric orientation in curriculum guides in Jamaica, which she suggested was somewhat tempered by the parallel evocation of nature's 'divine dimensions.' In response to a perceived resourcist turn in sustainability education, Kopnina (2012) called for a return to the instrumentalist roots of environmental education, that is, toward developing an ethics of care and responsible environmental behavior.

Teaching and learning

The third major theme identified through the analysis was that of 'teaching and learning,' which we will discuss in terms of policy research articles with a focus on: curriculum, teaching and pedagogy, and competing policies in relation to teaching and learning. Empirical articles overwhelmingly focused (though not always exclusively) on teaching and learning, with all but 10 of the 65 empirical papers including this emphasis.

Curriculum. Across a wide variety of geographical contexts, reviewed articles focused on state-level policies designed to infuse sustainability education into the curriculum as interdisciplinary competencies (e.g. Adedayo and Olawepo 1997; de Haan 2006; Iyengar and Bajaj 2011; Lee 1997). Most analyses offered pessimistic findings on the success of cross-curricular integration: rather than infusion of sustainability, this approach was typically found to result in the marginalization of sustainability in the curriculum (Adedayo and Olawepo 1997; Gayford and Dillin 1995; Puk and Behm 2003; Scott and Reid 1998; Vare 1998). In an evaluation of ESD policy implementation, Bagoly-Simo (2013) documented heterogeneous implementation approaches across the different policy contexts of Germany (Bavaria), Mexico, and Romania. Using indicators to measure implementation success, Bagoly-Simó analyzed the extent of ESD incorporation into state-level curricula, noting that Mexico's top-down approach to sustainability resulted in greater curricular incorporation of ESD. Nevertheless, implementation approaches across all three contexts were found to treat ESD as 'a (hyper)specialized add-on knowledge in an overcrowded curriculum' (Jucker 2011, 109).

Through survey research with over 200 high school teachers in Ontario, Canada, Puk and Behm (2003) also documented a failure of the infusion model of sustainability education. In 2000, the provincial education ministry removed a stand-alone Environmental Science course, opting instead to infuse elements of ecological education throughout the sciences. In their analysis of data after this switch, Puk and Behm found that very little ecological education was being taught in secondary schools. The authors argued that this suggests a policy failure: teachers were teaching according to guidelines that mandated very little content or time for ecological education. Puk and Behm's resulting advocacy for the inclusion of environmental education as a separate course is echoed in a discussion paper from the UK (Scott and Reid 1998). In their evaluation of policy shifts in England and Wales, Scott and Reid reflected that 'it was, perhaps, a mistake for environmental education ever to have become so identified with, and dependent upon the success of, cross-curricular approaches' (1998, 216). Reporting on a more recent case study of Australian research, Kennelly, Taylor, and Serow (2011) noted that curricular content designated as sustainability-related often included no explicit reference to sustainability, across subjects such as English, Math, History, and Science.

As exception to the prior studies, an analysis of ESD policy implementation in the Icelandic curriculum demonstrated widespread incorporation of sustainability concepts across subjects (Jóhannesson et al. 2011). The authors used a holistic, seven-concept key to document how curricula responded to international policy mandates for ESD. Jóhannesson et al. (2011) suggested that the Icelandic approach to sustainability infusion effectively 'provide[d] a space for teachers and schools to deal with issues of sustainable development' (375).

In both the empirical and non-empirical studies reviewed, researchers noted the tendency of sustainability mandates to be associated primarily with science education. Several studies connected this to difficulties associated with interdisciplinary teaching, including teacher training approaches and subject-specific timetables (Bolscho and Hauenschild 2006; Gayford and Dillin 1995; Nixon et al. 1999). Reporting on results of a survey of 33 African countries, Vare noted that the majority of responding representatives (from both state and non-governmental organisations) equated environmental education with environmental science (1998,

13). Indeed, the early policy literature reviewed for the present study suggested a strong initial connection between science-based conservationism and environmental education. In a review of the first decade of the Council for Environmental Education in the UK, Wheeler reported that '[e]nvironmental education was thus conceived out of the aspirations of conservationists and educationalists to make people more aware of the natural environment' (1983, 10). In a paper discussing early contributors to environmental education, Gough (1997) contended that '[t]he roots of environmental education are in rational science' (10), citing the influence of environmental education founder Bill Stapp, who occupied a number of high-level policy positions, including first director of the UNESCO-UNEP International Environmental Education Program. Gough describes how, under Stapp's lead, the Program issued a number of science-based foundational statements on environmental education, which came to be broadly accepted and dispersed by an international community.

Despite overwhelming findings of environmental education implementation through science, a small numbers of policy studies reported on connections made between sustainability education mandates and social studies curriculum. In a report on implementation of the 1970 Environmental Education Act in the US, Hepburn and Keach (1974) evaluated uptake of environmental education in primary and secondary social studies curricula. They reported that environmental education mandates had little traction in this area, mainly due to traditional discipline-based teaching and inflexible timetables. Two decades later, Adara (1996) and Adedayo and Olawepo (1997) discussed incorporation of environmental education into social studies curriculum in Nigeria. The authors identified a faith in scientific progress and technocratic solutions to environmental problems among legislators and policymakers, which they suggested left little room for contributions to environmental education curriculum from the social sciences.

Several articles reported on approaches to sustainability policy that focused on the challenges of whole school implementation. The majority of these studies described policies of whole-school change attempted through a series of modest modifications, and operating at the margins because of lack of appetite for greater transformation (Elliott 1999; Lee 1997; Nixon et al. 1999; Scott and Reid 1998). One reason cited for implementation difficulties was low compliance due to policies being viewed as non-mandatory (Lee 1997; McNaughton 2007). For example, McNaughton (2007) described a mid-1990s Scottish policy approach to whole-school change, which envisioned this transition as progressing through stages to arrive at a whole-school cultural shift where 'pupils and staff are both empowered to take initiatives and able to make active, participative responses in local, national and global issues' (623). However, uptake of this policy initiative was not enthusiastic, in part related to an emphasis on standards and 'back to basics' education, in which sustainability was deemed a fringe subject. Lee (1997) reported a similar result in Hong Kong, also citing lack of resources and professional development opportunities for teachers as factors in the lack of uptake. In contrast, Barth et al. (2012) describe the modest success of a participatory, whole school approach in Germany in their empirical evaluation of student attitudes toward consumption. Students demonstrated higher self-reported sustainable consumption behaviors, as well as higher measures of perceived effectiveness of their own consumer choices, and perceived relevance of consumer knowledge gained while at school.

Teaching and pedagogy. Policy research on the teaching of sustainability education mainly focused on the extent to which policy mandates were successful in influencing teacher training, teacher knowledge and attitudes, or teacher decisions to incorporate sustainability-related content into their teaching. Conceptions of pedagogy, and questions of how sustainability ought to be taught, were largely absent from the policy literature reviewed until the 1990s, when these topics begin to be discussed in relation to discussions of educating for, in, and about the environment (Ferguson 2008; Jóhannesson et al. 2011; Lee 1997; Nam 1995; Pace 1997; Scott and Reid 1998). Learning as 'action research' or 'action competence' is increasingly discussed in relation to education curriculum and policy in the later 1990s through 2013 (e.g. Breiting and Wickenberg 2010; Elliott 1999; Fontes 2004). For example, in describing transitions in German educational policy, Scheunpflug and Asbrand (2006) compared two pedagogical strands associated with global education and sustainability education: action theory focusing on building solidarity, empathy, and a holistic world view; and systems theory focusing on complexity, abstract thinking, and self-organized learning for students. Other pedagogical approaches discussed in relation to policy texts or their enactment included inquiry-based (Clothey, Mills, and Baumgarten 2010), citizenship (Adara 1996; Iyengar and Bajaj 2011; Jickling et al. 2010), economic participation (González-Gaudiano 1999), and Indigenous (Mokuku et al. 2005) education.

Kennelly, Taylor, and Jenkins (2008) examined the relationship between policy and pedagogy in a qualitative, interview-based study of eight teachers. Their analysis investigated pedagogical responses to whole-school sustainability policy, with the majority of teachers expressing teaching philosophies aligned with education for the environment. Nearly all teachers interviewed described their role as encouraging collective action, as well as personal responsibility, and emphasized the importance of teachers supporting and acting on student ideas. Kennelly et al. found that the success of whole-school policies was deeply linked to the pedagogical practices and ideologies of coordinating teachers. They conclude that 'the fundamental ideas and practical procedures underpinning [whole school programs] should be incorporated into wider pre-service and in-service teacher professional learning' (62).

A subset of articles described teaching as a weak point in sustainability education policy (Bolscho and Hauenschild 2006; Nam 1995; Posch 1999; Puk and Behm 2003). This was variously articulated as: poor or absent policy in relation to teacher education (Bolscho and Hauenschild 2006), vague pedagogical and curriculum sustainability mandates (Huckle 2009), or low commitment on the part of teachers in policy implementation (Gayford and Dillin 1995). Stimpson (1997) suggested that instead of clear policy mandates, environmental education relies on the 'enthusiasm of teacher educators' (355) for its success. In some settings, low perceived status of teachers and low financial compensation combined with time constraints, were found to prevent a focus on sustainability education (González-Gaudiano 2007). Singh (1998) discussed the roles of teachers in reading and 'refracting' curriculum policies in order to enact a critical environmental approach to formal education. According to Singh, 'policies intended to effect educational innovation in Australia's school curriculum ... must be read as being in a dynamic and continuing relationship with them' (349). Singh identified a variety of policy readings undertaken by teachers, including resistance, adaptation, and re-making of policy meanings. He argued that educators must go beyond reading policy as critical engagement, and begin to re-write curriculum policy, through critique, strategic reappropriation, and creation of alternatives.

Competing policies. The reviewed literature suggests that sustainability education often exists within contexts where there are multiple policy discourses competing for primacy. Many authors described tensions between sustainability education and the perceived primary purpose of education: preparing students for examinations in core subjects (e.g. Gayford and Dillin 1995; Gruenewald and Manteaw 2007; Martina, Hursh, and Markowitz 2009; Nixon et al. 1999; Scott and Reid 1998). Huckle (2008) noted that when educational mandates focus on testing and performance this not only de-prioritizes sustainability education, but also, through a reliance on individual attainment and competition, discourages an ethic of environmental and social care.

Reviewed articles also noted increased pressure felt by educational bodies and institutions in keeping up with international competitors, particularly via student achievement in core subject areas such as math, science, and literacy (Kennelly, Taylor, and Serow 2011; Puk and Behm 2003). Two articles from the United States described how powerful standardized testing mandates, such as the federal 'No Child Left Behind Act' (NCLB) eclipsed other educational concerns, including a focus on sustainability (Gruenewald and Manteaw 2007; Martina, Hursh, and Markowitz 2009). Gruenewald and Manteaw (2007) suggested that teachers are thus left with two options in the face of heavy imposition of standards: resistance or accommodation. Martina, Hursh, and Markowitz (2009) described national-level implementation of a newly developed environmental health curriculum, which they contend was undermined by both state policies and the federal NCLB. In their survey of site-specific implementation, the majority of respondents indicated that standardized testing interfered with the implementation of sustainability education. Several projects also reported on accommodation tactics, such as incorporating the curriculum into Grades 2 and 5, the only grade-levels where state-level testing is not mandated.

Some studies put forward policy solutions for sustainability education to better compete within this policy environment, such as integration of sustainability into related policies (Renton and Butcher 2010), or the provision of dedicated sustainability-focused staff at ministries of education (Courtenay-Hall and Lott 1999). Renton and Butcher (2010), for example, evaluated the integration of sustainable development into child and youth-related policy frameworks in the UK. Other than offering general support, they found that many documents failed to integrate sustainable development principles, most conspicuously in policy frameworks with mutual-supporting goals, such as England's child health strategy (164). Renton and Butcher argue that not only should sustainability be embedded within all policies affecting children and youth, but sustainability education should include opportunities for youth participation in local and national government.

Marginalizations

A fourth and final focus identified in the reviewed articles was that of 'marginalizations,' or in other words, research which focused on which perspectives and knowledge are centered or marginalized, and by what mechanisms, in conceptualizations and enactments of sustainability education policy. Grounds for marginalization discussed across the research papers included a focus on cultural tensions; North-South divisions; and hierarchies of policy-makers, researchers, and practitioners in decision-making.

In terms of roles in the policy process, Stevenson (2007) noted that international meetings tend to privilege the voices of policy-makers and academics, at the expense of practitioners. Such exclusion is also noted in the development of state-level policies and resources (Courtenay-Hall and Lott 1999; Scott and Reid 1998). Stevenson contended that the products of international meetings (e.g. declarations, proceedings) obscure sites of struggle, not only of the discourses themselves, but also of different camps of environmental, development, and educational policy-makers. Multiple authors interrogated tensions between the claims to universality of sustainability declarations, and the exclusion of various voices and cultural groups (e.g. González-Gaudiano 2006; Mucunguzi 1995; Stevenson 2007). González-Gaudiano (2006) noted that at international conference venues where such statements are drafted, representatives are predominantly from industrialized nations. He cited as evidence the UNEP International Environmental Education Program, which spanned 20 years and 'only valued and, therefore gave voice to, the experiences and perspectives of representatives of developed countries' (293).

In relation to marginalizations enacted through globalizing processes, relatively few papers examined economic competitiveness or neoliberalism in the context of sustainability education policy (for exceptions see Mannion et al. 2011; McKenzie 2012; Sahlberg and Oldroyd 2010). McKenzie (2012) contends that critical examination of universal education mandates, such as the UN Millenium Development Goals must be understood within a neoliberalized global environment. Using a Saskatchewan-based critical policy case study, McKenzie documents how the 2009 UNESCO Bonn Declaration was interpreted in relation to local and regional contexts. She writes that 'slippage from an emphasis on "environment, conservation, and sustainability" to "education for sustainable development" at the level of provincial educational policy seems worryingly comfortable and easy' (173). Within a neoliberal framework, education for sustainable development can shift focus from the interdependent domains of environment, society, and economy, to simply being able to check off the 'ESD' box anytime educational activity pertaining to any one of these three areas is undertaken (McKenzie 2012).

Several articles included in our review examined the contexts of sustainability education policy in low-income countries, including those with histories of colonization. In high-income countries, the success of sustainability education was variously linked to policy uptake by government, teacher training and enthusiasm, presence and availability of resources, and participation in initiatives like the UN DESD. However, in many national contexts, under-resourcing of public education, and therefore access to basic schooling, are ongoing challenges (González-Gaudiano 1999; Vare 1998). Several authors noted that sustainability education cannot be assumed to be universally desirable; even as definitions and practices may be broadening, and wide space given to context-dependent interpretation, colonial histories are impossible to escape. Schooling, including for environment and sustainability, has displaced forms of traditional knowledge and its lines of transmission (Mucunguzi 1995; Vare 1998). In some contexts, policy for environmental education has been associated with forms of land conservation, in which Indigenous peoples and other citizens have been displaced and excluded from their land (Bak 1995; Mucunguzi 1995). Mucunguzi (1995) describes environmental education as representing a form of colonial education, which has effectively written over more holistic and situated traditional forms of environmental education.

Research gaps and implications

This review included policy research at a regional (e.g. Iyengar and Bajaj 2011; Puk and Behm 2003; Stimpson 1997), national (e.g. Adedayo and Olawepo 1997; Gough 2011; Nam 1995) and international scale (e.g. Chapman and Aspin 2013; Lotz-Sisitka 2009). More local-scale policy research (e.g. within a local school division or school) was absent from our review, which suggests that: (a) local-scale sustainability education policy is under-produced and/or under-studied; (b) this research is being reported in venues other than peer-reviewed journals; and/or (c) our search methods were biased against detection of local policy research (e.g. such research was not identified with the keywords searched). We suggest that all three may have contributed to a lack of local-scale policy research in this review.

As discussed in the findings, many regions were under-represented across this review, including South America and Northern Africa. We suspect that in some cases, policy research is being undertaken and communicated in venues other than English-speaking journals. In the interest of avoiding ethnocentrism and expanding the scope of the field of sustainability education research, it may be useful for the research field to discuss means of translating research articles.

The review spanned four decades of research into the policy contexts of sustainability education. The 215 articles represented 71 countries, in which policy was examined using increasingly diverse methodologies. Nevertheless, in concluding this review we echo Læssøe, Feinstein, and Blum (2013) in calling for increased engagement with policy research within the field of sustainability education. In particular, we propose greater research attention in the following three domains: critical policy theory and methodology; issues of intersectionality and sustainability education policy; and climate change and education policy. These recommendations arise from trends that we documented through thematic analyses (climate change and education policy), as well as from absences we noted during the process of coding and writing (critical policy research, intersectionality). A common thread across our recommendations is for increased empirical engagement within sustainability and environmental education policy research.

While methodological diversity in sustainability education has increased from an initial focus on survey-based research to a more recent encompassing of case study and multiple-methods, we observed a general inattention to developments in critical policy research more broadly. These developments include foremost a rejection of positivist frameworks that assume policy, and therefore policy research, to be a neutral process of problem identification and solution. Instead of objectively determining 'what works,' critical policy research understands policy processes as complex, with multiple actors intervening in ways that influence what issues are identified as policy problems, what solutions are available, and how these policy solutions are championed, borne out, resisted, or subverted in practice. Over the last three decades, strands within education policy research have responded to this messier understanding of policy, focusing not only on policy texts, but also on the locations of policy-making (e.g. Pinto 2012) and policy enactment (Ball, Maguire, and Braun 2012; Braun et al. 2011). Empirical research articles included in this review tended to focus on either textual analysis or policy enactment, neglecting systematic examination of policy origins or development, and of broader interactions among various aspects of the policy process.

Research into policy enactment suggests that the ways in which policy is practiced and examined can be interpreted in relation to contextual factors such as material resources, professional cultures, competing policies, and school history (Braun et al. 2011; Thrupp and Lupton 2006). Recent work on policy tensions, mobility, or networks and actors (Ball and Junemann 2012; Heimans 2012; Hursh and Henderson 2011; McKenzie, Bieler, and McNeil 2015) suggests directions for analyses that provide greater understanding into the situated contexts of policy development and enactment. As policy researchers, we are also intrigued by a theoretical re-orientation toward the material (e.g. Fenwick, Edwards, and Sawchuk 2011; Tuck and McKenzie 2015). 'New materialist' approaches advocate theoretical understandings that center on sociomaterial contexts and an attention to the effects of non-human actors. With histories of place and land-based pedagogical research, sustainability and environmental education research is well positioned to contribute to discussions of 'post-human' materialities and to disrupt the dominance of human-centric policy analysis.

In their call for 'reinvigoration' of critical policy research, Webb and Gulson (2015) note the challenges of using research to 'critique and change political structures and practices' (170). We note within the articles reviewed an inattention to how policy research itself might have greater political leverage. Despite ontological and methodological tensions, we believe that critical policy research must include engagement with research fields more oriented toward policy development and solutions and with generative political action (e.g. Davies and Nutley 2008; Rickinson, Sebba, and Edwards 2011; Sellar, Savage, and Radhika 2014). Research that effectively influences policy outcomes has been suggested to involve policymakers and practitioners from the outset (Edwards, Sebba, and Rickinson 2007; Stevenson 2013). According to Edwards, Sebba, and Rickinson (2007), this entails a shift in locus of control from university-driven project development to including policy 'users' as co-researchers, supported by the creation of 'sites of mutual learning' where knowledge flows are multi-directional (652).

In the final section of our thematic analysis, we discussed various forms of marginalization addressed in the policy literature, including elitism in policy development, neoliberalism, and colonization. Intersectional analyses, which explicitly address the interaction between categories of marginalization (e.g. among environment and race, gender, class, or other forms of oppression), were largely absent from the articles reviewed. Articles that did address intersecting marginalities tended to discuss the difficulties of universalized mandates for sustainability education, particularly in the context of education for sustainable development. Relatively few papers examined the tensions of racism and classism (Bak 1995) or colonialism (Gough 1997; Mucunguzi 1995) in relation to sustainability education policy. We noted a dearth of policy research that engaged with issues of gender or environmental justice, particularly within empirical articles. We emphasize the need for policy research that incorporates in-depth examination of policy contexts in relation to issues of justice and intersectionality. Intersectional and related approaches to policy research have been growing, with development of methodological tools by health policy researchers (Hankivsky 2012; Hankivsky et al. 2014). Using participatory, multi-sector stakeholder consultation, Hankivsky et al. (2014) developed an Intersectionality-Based Policy Analysis framework comprising core guiding principles and questions. According to the researchers, this framework 'captures the different dimensions of policy contexts including history, politics, everyday lived experiences, diverse knowledges and intersecting social locations; and ... generates transformative insights, knowledge, policy solutions and actions that cannot be gleaned from other equity-focused policy frameworks' (2). We propose that similar frameworks could be adapted for policy research into sustainability education. Recent work in place-based and land-based education (e.g. Tuck and McKenzie 2015; Tuck, McKenzie, and McCoy 2014) points toward more just, ethical, and decolonizing ways of practicing and researching sustainability education. A land and place-based framework for educational policy research has yet to be articulated; however, increased engagement with intersectional, Indigenous, and materialist methodologies suggests new ways of imagining policy research. Within the field of critical policy research, Ball (1994) noted that equity was an under-theorized area of policy research, and proposed extending an initial model of the policy cycle (Bowe, Ball, and Gold 1992) to include the contexts of political strategy and outcomes. Relatively little research to date has attempted to employ this model to empirical policy research (but see Gulson 2011), including in sustainability education policy research.

An additional finding of this review was the absence of a focus on climate change in articles published prior to 1995, and the relatively low engagement overall. Though the majority of recent articles invoked climate change in some capacity, it appears that sustainability education policy research is just beginning to respond to climate change concerns (e.g. Bangay and Blum 2010; Feinstein et al. 2013). As climate change and associated extreme weather events increasingly challenge human health, economic activity, and survival, it is expected that greater research efforts will be directed toward the development of more thorough approaches to climate change adaptation and prevention through education. The response and responsibility of education toward climate change goes beyond simple 'environmental and sustainability education as problem-solver' narratives (Van Poeck and Lysgaard forthcoming). Climate change effects are, and will continue to be, variegated and unpredictable, and responses from education policy will require innovation of both transversal and local approaches. Education systems will grapple not only with educating for climate change mitigation and adaption, but also with questions of how education policy should respond to climate inequities, such as differential historical responsibility for climate-modifying emissions. Educational directives must mandate more than knowledge of climate change issues if local and global adaptation is to be taken seriously. Climate change adaptation, including socio-economic and health crises, and loss of place with associated emotional implications for students and their communities, must be addressed in affective, tangible, and action-oriented ways. Such challenges will require engaged, political, practical, and imaginative forms of education policy research.

In closing, this review is concerned with the state of policy research in sustainability education and argues for increased empirical engagement with policy origins and enactment. We documented temporal, geographic, and thematic trends in policy research across nearly four decades. We described temporal spikes in published policy research occurring in the mid-1970s, late 1990s, and after 2005. We also documented geographic under-representation of regions and countries, including Africa, South and Central America, Eastern Europe, and most of North and West Asia. Through in-depth thematic analysis, we documented patterns in research foci, including enduring concerns related to the instrumentalism of policy drivers, to the larger contexts of competing research paradigms and competing (educational) policy paradigms, and the focus on teaching and learning directives. We have argued that policy research in sustainability education must attend to the challenges of theoretical and methodological rigor, incorporate intersectional and justice-based frameworks, and more fully address climate change. We have also argued for greater consideration of how policy research engages research 'users,' including policymakers, in order to function more effectively as forms of public scholarship (McKenzie 2009); informing, critiquing, and mobilizing policy development and enactment in sustainability education.

Disclosure statement

No potential conflict of interest was reported by the authors.

Funding

This work was supported by the Social Sciences and Humanities Research Council of Canada [grant number 895-2011-1025].

Notes

1. These acronyms stand for Environmental Education, Education for Sustainable Development, and Climate Change Education (Læssøe, Feinstein, and Blum 2013).
2. Nazir et al. (2009) use a range of terms, including climate change education, education for sustainable development, and environmental education.
3. The sum here (59 international + 163 regional = 223) yields more than the 215 total articles reviewed as several articles surveyed more than one region.

References

Adara, O. A. 1996. "Strategies of Environmental Education in Social Studies in Nigeria by the Year 2000." *Environmental Education Research* 2 (2): 237–246. doi:10.1080/1350462960020209.

Adedayo, A., and J. A. Olawepo. 1997. "Integration of Environmental Education in Social Science Curricula at the Secondary School Level in Nigeria: Problems and Prospects." *Environmental Education Research* 3 (1): 83–93. doi:10.1080/1350462970030107.

Bagoly-Simo, P. 2013. "Tracing Sustainability: An International Comparison of ESD Implementation into Lower Secondary Education." *Journal of Education for Sustainable Development* 7 (1): 95–112. doi:10.1177/0973408213495610.

Bak, N. 1995. "Green Doesn't Always Mean 'Go': Possible Tensions in the Desirability and Implementation of Environmental Education." *Environmental Education Research* 1 (3): 345–352. doi:10.1080/1350462950010309.

Ball, S. J. 1994. Education Reform: A Critical and Post-structural Approach. Philadelphia, PA: Open University Press.

Ball, S. J. 1997. "Policy Sociology and Critical Social Research: A Personal Review of Recent Education Policy and Policy Research." *British Educational Research Journal* 23 (3): 257–274. doi:10.1080/0141192970230302.

Ball, S. J., and C. Junemann. 2012. *Networks, New Governance and Education*. Bristol: Policy Press.

Ball, S. J., M. Maguire, and A. Braun. 2012. *How Schools Do Policy: Policy Enactments in Secondary Schools*. London: Routledge.

Bangay, C., and N. Blum. 2010. "Education Responses to Climate Change and Quality: Two Parts of the Same Agenda?" *International Journal of Educational Development* 30 (4): 359–368. doi:10.1016/j.ijedudev.2009.11.011.

Barraza, L., A. Duque-Aristiza'bal, and G. Rebolledo. 2003. "Environmental Education: From Policy to Practice." *Environmental Education Research* 9 (3): 347–357. doi:10.1080/13504620303462.

Barth, M., D. Fischer, G. Michelsen, C. Nemnich, and H. Rode. 2012. "Tackling the Knowledge-action Gap in Sustainable Consumption: Insights from a Participatory School Programme." *Journal of Education for Sustainable Development* 6 (2): 301–312. doi:10.1177/0973408212475266.

Bernon, G. 1978. "Environmental Education in FIJI." *The Journal of Environmental Education* 9 (3): 12–17. doi:10.1080/00958964.1978.9942018.

Bolscho, D., and K. Hauenschild. 2006. "From Environmental Education to Education for Sustainable Development in Germany." *Environmental Education Research* 12 (1): 7–18. doi:10.1080/13504620500526297.

Bonnett, M. 1999. "Education for Sustainable Development: A Coherent Philosophy for Environmental Education?" *Cambridge Journal of Education* 29 (3): 313–324. doi:10.1080/0305764990290302.

Bowe, R., S. J. Ball, and A. Gold. 1992. *Reforming Education and Changing Schools*. London: Routledge.

Braun, A., M. Maguire, and S. J. Ball. 2010. "Policy Enactments in the UK Secondary School: Examining Policy, Practice and School Positioning." *Journal of Education Policy* 25 (4): 547–560. doi:10.1080/02680931003698544.

Braun, A., S. J. Ball, M. Maguire, and K. Hoskins. 2011. "Taking Context Seriously: Towards Explaining Policy Enactments in the Secondary School." *Discourse: Studies in the Cultural Politics of Education* 32 (4): 585–596. doi:10.1080/01596306.2011.601555.

Breiting, S., and P. Wickenberg. 2010. "The Progressive Development of Environmental Education in Sweden and Denmark." *Environmental Education Research* 16 (1): 9–37. doi:10.1080/13504620903533221.

Brundtland, G. H. 1987. *Our Common Future: The World Commission on Environment and Development*. Oxford: Oxford University Press.

Chapman, J. D., and D. N. Aspin. 2013. "A Problem-solving Approach to Addressing Current Global Challenges in Education." *British Journal of Educational Studies* 61 (1): 49–62. doi:10.1080/00071005.2012.756166.

Clarke, P. 2009. "Sustainability and Improvement: A Problem of Education and for Education." *Improving Schools* 12 (1): 11–17.

Clothey, R., M. Mills, and J. Baumgarten. 2010. "A Closer Look at the Impact of Globalization on Science Education." *Cultural Studies of Science Education* 5 (2): 305–313. doi:10.1007/s11422-010-9258-6.

Courtenay-Hall, P., and S. Lott. 1999. "Issues of Inclusion in Developing Environmental Education Policy: Reflections on B.C. Experiences." *Canadian Journal of Environmental Education* 4: 83–103.

Davies, H. T. O., and S. M. Nutley. 2008. *Learning More about How Research-based Knowledge Gets Used: Guidance in the Development of New Empirical Research*. New York: William T. Grant Foundation.

Edwards, A., J. Sebba, and M. Rickinson. 2007. "Working with Users: Some Implications for Educational Research." *British Educational Research Journal* 33 (5): 647–661.

Elliott, J. 1999. "Sustainable Society and Environmental Education: Future Perspectives and Demands for the Educational System." *Cambridge Journal of Education* 29 (3): 325–340. doi:10.1080/0305764990290303.

Fay, B. 1975. *Social Theory and Political Practice*. London: Allen and Unwin.

Feinstein, N. W., J. Læssøe, N. Blum, and D. Chambers. 2013. "Challenging the Premises of International Policy Reviews: An Introduction to the Review Symposium." *Environmental Education Research* 19 (2): 198–205. doi:10.1080/13504622.2013.768603.

Feinstein, N. W., P. R. Jacobi, and H. Lotz-Sisitka. 2013. "When Does a Nation-level Analysis Make Sense? ESD and Educational Governance in Brazil, South Africa, and the USA." *Environmental Education Research* 19 (2): 218–230. doi:10.1080/13504622.2013.767321.

Fenwick, T., R. Edwards, and P. Sawchuk. 2011. *Emerging Approaches to Educational Research: Tracing the Socio-material*. New York: Routledge.

Ferguson, T. 2008. "'Nature' and the 'Environment' in Jamaica's Primary School Curriculum Guides." *Environmental Education Research* 14 (5): 559–577. doi:10.1080/13504620802345966.

Fontes, P. J. 2004. "Action Competence as an Integrating Objective for Environmental Education." *Canadian Journal of Environmental Education* 9: 149–162.

Gayford, C. G., and P. J. Dillin. 1995. "Policy and the Practice of Environmental Education in England: A Dilemma for Teachers." *Environmental Education Research* 1 (2): 173–183. doi:10.1080/1350462950010204.

González-Gaudiano, E. J. 1999. "Environmental Education and Consumption: The Case of Mexico." *Canadian Journal of Environmental Education* 4: 176–192.

González-Gaudiano, E. J. 2006. "Environmental Education: A Field in Tension or in Transition?" *Environmental Education Research* 12 (3–4): 291–300. doi:10.1080/13504620600799042.

González-Gaudiano, E. J. 2007. "Schooling and Environment in Latin America in the Third Millennium." *Environmental Education Research* 13 (2): 155–169. doi:10.1080/13504620701295684.

Gough, A. 1997. "Founders of Environmental Education: Narratives of the Australian Environmental Education Movement." *Environmental Education Research* 3 (1): 43–57. doi:10.1080/1350462970030104.

Gough, A. 2011. "The Australian-ness of Curriculum Jigsaws: Where Does Environmental Education Fit?" *Australian Journal of Environmental Education* 27 (1): 9–23. doi:10.1017/S0814062600000045.

Gruenewald, D. A., and B. O. Manteaw. 2007. "Oil and Water Still: How No Child Left behind Limits and Distorts Environmental Education in US Schools." *Environmental Education Research* 13 (2): 171–188. doi:10.1080/13504620701284944.

Gulson, K. N. 2011. *Education Policy, Space, and the City*. New York: Routledge.

de Haan, G. 2006. "The BLK '21' Programme in Germany: A 'Gestaltungskompetenz'-based Model for Education for Sustainable Development." *Environmental Education Research* 12 (1): 19–32. doi:10.1080/13504620500526362.

Hägglund, S., and I. P. Samuelsson. 2009. "Early Childhood Education and Learning for Sustainable Development and Citizenship." *International Journal of Early Childhood* 41 (2): 49–63. doi:10.1007/BF03168878.

Hankivsky, O., ed. 2012. *An Intersectionality-based Policy Analysis Framework*. Vancouver: Institute for Intersectionality Research and Policy. Simon Fraser University.

Hankivsky, O., D. Grace, G. Hunting, M. Giesbrecht, A. Fridkin, S. Rudrum, O. Ferlatte, and N. Clark. 2014. "An Intersectionality-based Policy Analysis Framework: Critical Reflections on a Methodology for Advancing Equity." *International Journal for Equity in Health.* 13: 119. doi:10.1186/s12939-014-0119-x.

Hart, P., and K. Nolan. 1999. "A Critical Analysis of Research in Environment Education." *Critical Studies in Science Education* 34 (1): 1–69. doi:10.1080/03057269908560148.

Heimans, S. 2012. "Coming to Matter in Practice: Enacting Education Policy." *Discourse: Studies in the Cultural Politics of Education* 33: 313–326. doi:10.1080/01596306.2012.666083.

Heimans, S. 2014. "Education Policy Enactment Research: Disrupting Continuities." *Discourse: Studies in the Cultural Politics of Education* 35 (2): 306–317. doi:10.1080/01596306.2013.832566.

Hepburn, M. A., and E. T. Keach, Jr. 1974. "The Impact of Environmentalism on the Social Studies Curriculum." *The Journal of Environmental Education* 5 (3): 15–18.

Huckle, J. 2008. "An Analysis of New Labour's Policy on Education for Sustainable Development with Particular Reference to Socially Critical Approaches." *Environmental Education Research* 14 (1): 65–75. doi:10.1080/13504620701843392.

Huckle, J. 2009. "Consulting the UK ESD Community on an ESD Indicator to Recommend to Government: An Insight into the Micro-politics of ESD." *Environmental Education Research* 15 (1): 1–15. doi:10.1080/13504620802578509.

Hursh, D., and J. Henderson. 2011. "Contesting Global Neoliberalism and Creating Alternative Futures." *Discourse: Studies in the Cultural Politics of Education* 32 (2): 171–185. doi:10.1080/01596306.2011.562665.

Iyengar, R., and M. Bajaj. 2011. "After the Smoke Clears: Toward Education for Sustainable Development in Bhopal, India." *Comparative Education Review* 55 (3): 424–456.

Jickling, B., L. Sauvé, L. Brière, B. Niblett, and E. Root. 2010. "The 5th World Environmental Education Congress, 2009: A Research Project." *Canadian Journal of Environmental Education* 15: 47–67.

Jóhannesson, I. Á., K. Norðdahl, G. Óskarsdóttir, A. Pálsdóttir, and B. Pétursdóttir. 2011. "Curriculum Analysis and Education for Sustainable Development in Iceland." *Environmental Education Research* 17 (3): 375–391. doi:10.1080/13504622.2010.545872.

Jucker, R. 2011. "ESD between Systemic Change and Bureaucratic Obfuscation: Some Reflections on Environmental Education and Education for Sustainable Development in Switzerland." *Journal of Education for Sustainable Development* 5: 39–60. doi:10.1177/097340821000500109.

Kennelly, J., N. Taylor, and K. Jenkins. 2008. "Listening to Teachers: Teacher and Student Roles in the New South Wales Sustainable Schools Programme." *Environmental Education Research* 14 (1): 53–64. doi:10.1080/13504620701843350.

Kennelly, J., N. Taylor, and P. Serow. 2011. "Education for Sustainability and the Australian Curriculum." *Australian Journal of Environmental Education* 27 (2): 209–218.

Kopnina, H. 2012. "Education for Sustainable Development (ESD): The Turn Away from 'Environment' in Environmental Education?" *Environmental Education Research* 18 (5): 699–717. doi:10.1080/13504622.2012.658028.

Læssøe, J., N. W. Feinstein, and N. Blum. 2013. "Environmental Education Policy Research – Challenges and Ways Research Might Cope with Them." *Environmental Education Research* 19 (2): 231–242. doi:10.1080/13504622.2013.778230.

Lee, J. C. K. 1997. "Environmental Education in Schools in Hong Kong." *Environmental Education Research* 3 (3): 359–371. doi:10.1080/1350462970030308.

Locke, S. 2009. "Environmental Education for Democracy and Social Justice in Costa Rica." *International Research in Geographical and Environmental Education* 18 (2): 97–110. doi:10.1080/10382040902861171.

Lotz-Sisitka, H. 2009. "How Many Declarations Do We Need? Inside the Drafting of the Bonn Declaration on Education for Sustainable Development." *Journal of Education for Sustainable Development* 3 (2): 205–210. doi:10.1177/097340820900300217.

Major, C. H., and M. Savin-Baden. 2010. "Qualitative Research Synthesis: The Scholarship of Integrated Practice." In *New Approaches to Qualitative Research: Wisdom and Uncertainty*, edited by M. Savin-Baden and C. H. Major, 108–118. New York: Routledge.

Mannion, G., G. Biesta, M. Priestley, and H. Ross. 2011. "The Global Dimension in Education and Education for Global Citizenship: Genealogy and Critique." *Globalisation, Societies and Education* 9 (3–4): 443–456. doi:10.1080/14767724.2011.605327.

Martina, C. A., D. Hursh, and D. Markowitz. 2009. "Contradictions in Educational Policy: Implementing Integrated Problem-based Environmental Health Curriculum in a High Stakes Environment." *Environmental Education Research* 15 (3): 279–297. doi:10.1080/13504620902770337.

McKenzie, M. 2009. "Scholarship as Intervention: Critique, Collaboration and the Research Imagination." *Environmental Education Research* 15 (2): 217–226. doi:10.1080/13504620802194208.

McKenzie, M. 2012. "Education for Y'all: Global Neoliberalism and the Case for a Politics of Scale in Sustainability Education Policy." *Policy Futures in Education* 10 (2): 165–177. doi:10.2304/pfie.2012.10.2.165.

McKenzie, M., A. Bieler, and R. McNeil. 2015. "Education Policy Mobility: Reimagining Sustainability in Neoliberal times." *Environmental Education Research* 21 (3): 319–337. doi:10.1080/13504622.2014.993934.

McNaughton, M. J. 2007. "Sustainable Development Education in Scottish Schools: The Sleeping Beauty Syndrome." *Environmental Education Research* 13 (5): 621–638. doi:10.1080/13504620701659087.

Mokuku, T., M. E. Jobo, M. Raselimo, T. Mathafeng, and K. Stark. 2005. "Encountering Paradigmatic Tensions and Shifts in Environmental Education." *Canadian Journal of Environmental Education* 10: 157–172.

Mucunguzi, P. 1995. "Environmental Education in the Formal Sector of Education in Uganda." *Environmental Education Research* 1 (2): 233–240. doi:10.1080/1350462950010208.

Nam, S.-J. 1995. "Environmental Education in Primary and Secondary Schools in Korea: Current Developments and Future Agendas." *Environmental Education Research* 1 (1): 109–122. doi:10.1080/1350462950010109.

Nazir, J., E. Pedretti, J. Wallace, D. Montemurro, and H. Inwood. 2009. *Climate Change and Sustainable Development: The Response from Education. The Canadian Perspective.* Centre for Science, Mathematics and Technology Education, Ontario Institute for Studies in Education, University of Toronto, Toronto, Ontario, Canada.

Nixon, J., K. Sankey, V. Furay, and M. Simmons. 1999. "Education for Sustainability in Scottish Secondary Schools: Boundary Maintenance or Professional Reorientation?" *Environmental Education Research* 5 (3): 305–318. doi:10.1080/1350462990050305.

Pace, P. 1997. "Environmental Education in Malta: Trends and Challenges." *Environmental Education Research* 3 (1): 69–82. doi:10.1080/1350462970030106.

Palmer, J. A. 1999. "Research Matters: A Call for the Application of Empirical Evidence to the Task of Improving the Quality and Impact of Environmental Education." *Cambridge Journal of Education* 29 (3): 379–395. doi:10.1080/0305764990290308.

Pinto, L. E. 2012. "Hidden Privatization in Education Policy as 'Quick Fixes' by 'Hired Guns': Contracting Curriculum Policy in Ontario." *Critical Policy Studies* 6 (3): 261–281. doi:10.1080/19460171.2012.717782.

Plant, M. 1995. "The Riddle of Sustainable Development and the Role of Environmental Education." *Environmental Education Research* 1 (3): 253–266. doi:10.1080/1350462950010301.

Posch, P. 1999. "The Ecologisation of Schools and Its Implications for Educational Policy." *Cambridge Journal of Education* 29 (3): 341–348. doi:10.1080/0305764990290304.

Puk, T., and D. Behm. 2003. "The Diluted Curriculum: The Role of Government in Developing Ecological Literacy as the First Imperative in Ontario Secondary Schools." *Canadian Journal of Environmental Education* 8: 217–232.

Reid, A., and W. Scott. 2008. "Researching Education and the Environment: Retrospect and Prospect." In *Researching Education and the Environment: Retrospect and Prospect*, edited by A. Reid and W. Scott, 325–341. Abingdon: Routledge.

Renton, Z., and J. Butcher. 2010. "Securing a Sustainable Future for Children and Young People." *Children Society* 24 (2): 160–166. doi:10.1111/j.1099-0860.2009.00280.x.

Rickinson, M., J. Sebba, and A. Edwards. 2011. *Improving Research through User Engagement*. London: Routledge.

Robottom, I., and R. B. Stevenson. 2013. "Analyses of Environmental Education Discourses and Policies." In *International Handbook of Research on Environmental Education*, edited by R. B. Stevenson, M. Brody, J. Dillon, and A. E. J. Wals, 123–125. New York: Routledge, American Educational Research Association.

Sahlberg, P., and D. Oldroyd. 2010. "Pedagogy for Economic Competitiveness and Sustainable Development." *European Journal of Education* 45 (2): 280–299. doi:10.1111/j.1465-3435.2010.01429.x.

Sauvé, L., and T. Berryman. 2005. "Challenging a 'Closing Circle': Alternative Research Agendas for the ESD Decade." *Applied Environmental Education & Communication* 4 (3): 229–232. doi:10.1080/15330150591004634.

Sauvé, L., T. Berryman, and R. Brunelle. 2007. "Three Decades of International Guidelines for Environment-related Education: A Critical Hermeneutic of the United Nations Discourse." *Canadian Journal of Environmental Education* 12: 33–54.

Scheunpflug, A., and B. Asbrand. 2006. "Global Education and Education for Sustainability." *Environmental Education Research* 12 (1): 33–46. doi:10.1080/13504620500526446.

Schoenfeld, C. 1975. "National Environmental Education Perspective." *The Journal of Environmental Education* 7 (2): 9–10.

Scott, W., and A. Reid. 1998. "The Revisioning of Environmental Education: A Critical Analysis of Recent Policy Shifts in England and Wales." *Educational Review* 50 (3): 213–223. doi:10.1080/0013191980500301.

Sellar, S., G. C. Savage, and G. Radhika. 2014. "The Politics of Disagreement in Critical Education Policy Studies: A Response to Morsey, Gulson and Clarke." *Discourse: Studies in the Cultural Politics of Education* 35 (3): 462–469.

Singh, M. 1998. "Critical Literacy Strategies for Environmental Educators." *Environmental Education Research* 4 (3): 341–354. doi:10.1080/1350462980040308.

Smyth, J. C. 1995. "Environment and Education: A View of a Changing Scene." *Environmental Education Research* 1 (1): 3–120. doi:10.1080/1350462950010101.

Smyth, J. C. 1999. "Is There a Future for Education Consistent with Agenda 21?" *Canadian Journal of Environmental Education* 4: 69–82.

Stevenson, R. B. 2007. "Schooling and Environmental Education: Contradictions in Purpose and Practice." *Environmental Education Research* 13 (2): 139–153. doi:10.1080/13504620701295726.

Stevenson, R. D. 2013. "Researching Tensions and Pretensions in Environmental/Sustainability Education Policies: From Critical to Civically Engaged Policy Scholarship." In *International Handbook of Research on Environmental Education*, edited by R. B. Stevenson, M. Brody, J. Dillon, and A. E. J. Wals, 147–155. New York: Routledge, American Educational Research Association.

Stimpson, P., and F. W. B. Kwan. 2001. "Environmental Education in Guangzhou in the People's Republic of China: Global Theme, Politically Determined." *Environmental Education Research* 7 (4): 397–412.

Stimpson, P. G. 1997. "Environmental Challenge and Curricular Responses in Hong Kong." *Environmental Education Research* 3 (3): 345–357. doi:10.1080/1350462970030307.

Thrupp, M., and R. Lupton. 2006. "Taking School Contexts More Seriously: The Social Justice Challenge." *British Journal of Educational Studies* 54 (3): 308–328.

Tilbury, D. 1995. "Environmental Education for Sustainability: Defining the New Focus of Environmental Education in the 1990s." *Environmental Education Research* 1 (2): 195–212. doi:10.1080/1350462950010206.

Tuck, E., and M. M. McKenzie. 2015. *Place in Research: Theory, Methodology, Methods.* New York: Routledge.

Tuck, E., M. M. McKenzie, and K. McCoy. 2014. "Land Education: Indigenous, Post-colonial, and Decolonizing Perspectives on Place and Environmental Education Research." *Environmental Education Research* 20 (1): 1–23.

Van Poeck, K., and J. Lysgaard. 2016. "Editorial. The Roots and Routes of Environmental and Sustainability Education Policy Research." *Environmental Education Research* 22 (3): 305–318.

Van Poeck, K., J. Vandenabeele, and H. Bruyninckx. 2013. "Taking Stock of the UN Decade of Education for Sustainable Development: The Policy-making Process in Flanders." *Environmental Education Research* 20 (5): 695–717. doi:10.1080/13504622.2013.836622.

Vare, P. 1998. "ECOSA: A Report on a Pan-African Environmental Education Survey." *Environmental Education Research* 4 (1): 5–24. doi:10.1080/1350462980040101.

Viertel, E. 2010. "Vocational Education for Sustainable Development: An Obligation for the European Training Foundation." *European Journal of Education* 45 (2): 217–235. doi:10.2307/40664662.

Webb, P. T., and K. N. Gulson. 2015. "Policy Scientificity 3.0: Theory and Policy Analysis in-and-for This World and Other-worlds." *Critical Studies in Education* 56 (1): 161–174. doi:10.1080/17508487.2014.949812.

Wheeler, K. 1983. "The End of the Beginning: The First Decade of the Council for Environmental Education 1968–78." *Review of Environmental Education Developments* 11 (3): 10–12.

Winter, C. 2007. "Education for Sustainable Development and the Secondary Curriculum in English Schools: Rhetoric or Reality?" *Cambridge Journal of Education* 37 (3): 337–354. doi:10.1080/03057640701546656.

Index

For Product Safety Concerns and Information please contact our EU
representative GPSR@taylorandfrancis.com
Taylor & Francis Verlag GmbH, Kaufingerstraße 24, 80331 München, Germany